Russia's American Colony

RUSSIA'S

AMERICAN COLONY

Edited by S. Frederick Starr

A Special Study of the Kennan Institute for Advanced Russian Studies
of the Woodrow Wilson International Center for Scholars

DUKE UNIVERSITY PRESS   DURHAM 1987

Library of Congress Cataloging-in-Publication Data
Russia's American colony.
(A Special study of the Kennan Institute for Advanced
Russian Studies of the Woodrow Wilson International
Center for Scholars)
Includes index.
1. Alaska —History–To 1867.   2. Russians—Alaska—
History.   I. Starr, S. Frederick.   II. Series: Special
study of the Kennan Institute for Advanced Russian
Studies, the Wilson Center.
F907.R976   979.8'02   86-19916
ISBN 0-8223-0688-3

Contents

Introduction

Tsarist Russia's outposts in the New World have long aroused the fascination of historians. The struggle against a merciless climate, the excitement of imperial expansion, the sometimes tragic impact of the Russian presence on indigenous Americans, and the combination of tense rivalry and fruitful cooperation between Russia and the United States—all provide drama on a scale commensurate with the Alaskan landscape. But the sheer romance of the story also contains the stuff of legend, history painted in black and white, and outright clichés.

A generation of scholars on two continents has labored to peel away the romantic accretions from the history of the Russian American Company and from the Russian presence on North America more generally. Such scholars, working in Canada, the Soviet Union, and the United States, have concentrated on three particular issues. First, they have replaced the earlier one-sided concentration on political and diplomatic history with a diversified study of the economy, society, and culture of Alaska during the Russian era. Second, they have attempted to reinterpret the political and diplomatic history of Russian America in light of what they have learned about the economic life of the Pacific Northwest. Third, they have brought to bear the insights of comparative history on both social and political developments in Russia's most remote colony. Finally, and perhaps most important, they have enormously expanded the number and range of primary documents upon which all such study must be based.

While all of the scholars participating in this exciting quest knew of one another's existence, the complexities of Soviet-American relations in the post–World War II era long hindered their actual meeting. Recognizing this, and sensing the value that might derive from more direct contact among the leading researchers in the United States, Canada, and the USSR, the Kennan Institute for Advanced Russian Studies of The Wilson Center in 1978 proposed a conference for scholars in various fields from the three countries. The American Historical Association and the Institute of History of the Academy of Sciences of the USSR responded enthusiastically to the idea, and a three day meeting was held at Sitka, Alaska, formerly the Russian colonial capital of Novo-Arkhangel'sk. The agenda called for each participant to present a paper on a designated topic, drawing on that primary material most readily accessible to him.

The conference proved to be a signal success. The historic setting and the equally historic meeting of persons who had long known and respected one another's work gave those brief days the mood of a lodge meeting: friendly, even exuberant, yet intense. Sharp differences of view were apparent, but they did not correspond to the nationalities of the participants. The discussions were reported by the present author in *Smithsonian Magazine* (December 1979), and on Radio Smithsonian, as well as by Professor N. N. Bolkhovitinov in *Novaia i noveishaia istoriia* (1981, no. 6). This volume now offers readers the various papers, revised in light of the critiques offered at Sitka. It also includes several significant reports on research that have appeared elsewhere but not received the scholarly attention they deserve.

What findings emerged from this tri-national scholarly collaboration? It is convenient to summarize the results in terms of the major sections in this volume: the opening of the Pacific Northwest; the tsarist government and its American colony; Russians and native Americans; cultural life in Russian America; Russian America and the United States; and documentation.

Professor B. P. Polevoi surveyed the complex process by which Russians gained acquaintance with the Pacific Northwest. He followed the course of discovery and the intricate steps by which the new lands were explored and mapped. Acknowledging the diversity of motives of the Russian participants over several centuries, Polevoi stresses particularly the tsarist treasury's need for new sources of revenue. Siberian trappers had long poured money into the Russian government's coffers, but their hunting grounds were gradually being depleted, thus prompting the state to encourage exploration further afield to the East. Paradoxically, it was also the government's financial plight that finally forced it, in 1743, to cut off further subsidies for exploration and turn the initiative over to private traders and entrepreneurs in eastern Siberia.

Professor James A. Gibson acknowledges in his paper various elements of continuity between Russian expansion in Siberia and in North America, but he points out several critical differences as well. Among these, the contrast between the demands of sable and sea otter hunting are especially noteworthy. The former, stalked in Siberia by single trappers during the winter months, permitted hunters to carry on inland agriculture as well. The latter, which required a group effort in spring and summer, kept hunters on or near the coastal areas and permitted little time for farming.

In her paper, Professor Mary E. Wheeler proposes a revision of the common notion that the Russian American Company was created to satisfy imperial ambitions for a state-run enterprise in the New World. Her research indicates instead that the government created the enterprise as a means of enlisting more private Siberian traders in the Alaskan market, not of driving them from it. This organizational solution was necessary, she suggests, because of the debilitating rivalries that grew up among leading traders in Irkutsk following the death of the pioneer Alaskan trader-developer, Grigorii Shelikhov, in 1795.

Dr. Alexander Martynov had originally prepared a paper for the conference on the interaction of the Russian American Company and the imperial Russian government. When professional duties prevented Dr. Martynov from revising that work, Dr. Raisa V. Makarova treated the same issue in a paper that has recently been issued in a Soviet anthology. Drawing on little-used materials in the Archive of the Foreign Policy of Russia (*Arkiv vneshnei politiki Rossii/AVPR*), Makarova's paper reveals the sanguine belief of the company's board that, as a result of reforms introduced in the wake of the disastrous Crimean War, the company would soon be on a sound financial footing and able even to pay dividends to its long-suffering stockholders. However, Makarova argues, the Treaty of Paris, by which a post-Crimean peace was established, so isolated the imperial Russian government that it had to take drastic measures, including the sale of Alaska to the United States, in order to forge new links abroad. This step became a necessity even

Bering
Strait

Seward Peninsula

Nulato

Unalaklit
Saint Michael Redoubt

Ikogmiut

Bering Sea

New Alexander Redoubt

Ninilch

Pribylov Island

Three
Saints
Harbor

Unimak Island

Illiuliuk (Unalaska)

Atkha Island

Unalaska Island

Amlia Island

Principal Russian
Establishments in Alaska

Yukon River

Kuskokwim River

Sushitna
River

New Russia (Yakutat)

Alexander Redoubt

Afognak Island

St. Paul Harbor (Kodiak)

Kodiak Island

Novo-Arkhangel'sk (Sitka)

St. Dionysius
Redoubt

Gulf of Alaska

Fort Ross Settlement (1812–1841)

before the effectiveness of reforms within the Russian American Company could be gauged.

The extent of Russian dependence upon the Alaskan native population is enumerated by Dr. James Gibson. Even though they had virtual powers of serfdom over the Aleuts and other peoples, the Russians became overwhelmingly dependent upon them for labor, provisioning in certain areas, and sex. But far from meliorating the Russians' behavior towards the native populace, however, this reliance led to a situation in which the Russians could neither fully control nor fully collaborate with the Aleuts and other peoples.

Dr. R. G. Liapunova exposes another side of the Russians' interaction with the native population. She provides ample evidence on the brutality of the Russians' behavior in many instances, but cites documents suggesting that when such cruelty by traders came to the attention of Russian authorities in Siberia and St. Petersburg they acted to put a stop to it. She also stresses positive consequences of the Russian presence, such as the end of internecine wars among tribal groups and the introduction of technical training. Yet in the end, she concludes, the cruelty had established memories and even a pattern for the future that were hard to erase from the minds of either Russians or native Americans.

A clear measure of the extent of Russian ambitions in the New World is provided by their efforts at town planning and architecture there, which are the subject of Professor Anatole Senkevitch's study. Senkevitch shows that at least during the late eighteenth century, when Grigorii Shelikhov dominated Russian America, there was hope of building a true colonial capital "in the style of the finer cities." Under his successors, however, this objective was scaled down, so that the grandeur Shelikhov sought was limited to a few classical facades on warehouses, pedimented gables on homes, and wooden churches in a modified Siberian style.

A central component of Russia's cultural presence in North America was the Orthodox Christian church. It might be expected that the tsarist government would have supported the church vigorously as an instrument of Russification. Antoinette Shalkop, in her study of heretofore unexamined church records, finds this not to have been the case. On the contrary, she reports a situation of widespread ecclesiastical poverty and hardship, of confusing lines of control over the church, and of inefficient centralization from diocesan offices in Irkutsk. Nonetheless, dedicated priests managed to foster the Christian faith and establish the rudiments of an educational system. Yet in the end the church could be no stronger than the creole clergy who constituted its backbone, and the Russians abandoned them to their fate with the sale of Alaska in 1867.

While the Russians in Alaska were almost obsessively concerned with the fur trade, they made impressive accomplishments in various scientific fields, including geography, ethnography, anthropology, linguistics, geology, biology, astronomy, and mineralogy. Dr. R. A. Okladnikova assesses these various discoveries. Many were accomplished by observant seamen and navigators, others by officials of the Russian American Company who were impelled by scientific curiosity. But the imperial Russian government itself fostered scientific research in America, both for the immediate benefits it could bring in such fields as mineralogy, and for less pragmatic purposes in such fields as astronomy and biology. Achievements in popular education were more limited, but training in basic crafts was pursued with some energy down to 1867.

No issue before the twentieth century brought Russia and America into closer contact than the Russian settlements in Alaska and California. Looking backward, it is tempting to find in this early contact the embryo of later relations between the superpowers. Until recently, the main thrust of scholarship has emphasized the competitive nature of the relationship, with emphasis on poaching activities of Boston merchant ships, on Tsar Alexander I's 1821 *ukaz* excluding United States citizens from Russia's American possessions, and on the Monroe Doctrine, issued in retaliation in 1825.

Professor N. N. Bolkhovitinov concedes that the Bostonians worked assiduously to break the monopoly of the Russian American Company in Alaskan waters. But he cites evidence of the practical benefits that such activity brought to both sides. Had the Russian American Company enjoyed a free hand, Bolkhovitinov argues, it might have developed its relations in America more extensively. But after the Napoleonic Wars, the tsarist government felt it best to rein in the company so as to minimize demands on its resources.

Professor James R. Gibson, in his essay on the sale of Russian America to the United States, joins both Martynov and Bolkhovitinov in acknowledging the financial constraints affecting the tsarist government's operations in the New World. But he sees these constraints in the context of a Russian American Company that had regained its profitability by the 1850s and, he implies, might have survived had it not been weakened by talk of sale in St. Petersburg. In the end, Gibson traces the Russians' decision to sell Alaska to pressures to consolidate Russia's position in East Asia and to a desire to gain American diplomatic support against Great Britain in the tsar's efforts to undo the humiliating provisions of the 1856 Treaty of Paris.

The Americans' motives in purchasing Alaska are examined by Professor Howard I. Kushner. Against those who would claim that Secretary of State Seward's imperial hopes alone were the decisive element, Kushner sees a pattern of highly competitive American economic expansionism in the area, extending over the half century before 1867. Even though the United States could have gained full access to Alaska's current produce without buying the colony, Kushner argues that the scales were tipped in favor of the purchase by dreams of even greater future gain to be achieved by exploiting the territory more thoroughly.

Many of the above points were hotly contested by the conferees, and their differing perspectives are fully reflected in the papers in this volume. However such issues are to be resolved in the future, the key element will surely be access to fuller documentation on Russian America. The two final papers are therefore devoted to the important problems of bibliography. Dr. Patricia Polansky offers an extremely useful survey of finding aids and of published sources, paying particular attention to the many recently issued items. Broken down by subject areas, Polansky's essay provides an essential starting point for future researchers.

Professor Richard A. Pierce has devoted many years to tracing down lost manuscripts on Russian America in the West, and has paused to review the state of the quest in his essay. In addition to enumerating new discoveries in collections in Scandinavia, Canada, and the United States, Pierce also presents interesting information on the compilers of existing collections, notably Ivan Petrov, the obscure and devious "translator" who worked with Bancroft in the nineteenth century.

These, then, are some of the main points touched upon in the fourteen papers that make up this volume. It would have been impossible for the conference to be held, or for this volume to have reached publication, without the generous help and cooperation of many persons. Among these, James R. Gibson played an especially important role, by helping to prepare the basic outline and to identify possible participants. Dr. Mack Thompson, then Executive Director of the American Historical Association, and Nikolai Bolkhovitinov of the Institute of History of the Academy of Sciences of the USSR were responsible for bringing the conference within the framework of the series of joint Soviet-American historical seminars held periodically in the two countries. Without their enthusiasm for the project it would have been impossible to proceed with the complex series of arrangements that were involved. Members of the Sitka Historical Society and numerous Alaskans who are devoted to the history of their state gave generously of their time in making local arrangements for the conference, and the entire population of Sitka seems to have exerted itself to provide warm hospitality for the international conferees.

Timely financial support for the conference came from the International Research and Exchanges Board (IREX), the U.S. Department of State, the American Historical Association, and the Kennan Institute for Advanced Russian Studies of the Wilson Center. Finally, Ms. Sabrina Palmer, then of the Wilson Center's staff, managed to arrange for several dozen persons to arrive at Sitka at one time from places as remote from one another as Siberia and Ontario, Moscow and Washington. Thanks to her good-natured presence and to the warm good will shown by all parties involved, the distances shrank to nothing.

S. Frederick Starr
Oberlin, April 1986

PART ONE
Opening the New World

The Discovery of Russian America

B. P. Polevoi

The vast majority of recent monographs devoted to the history of Russian America produced by both Soviet and American scholars begin only with Vitus Bering's celebrated voyages of 1728 and 1741. These works repeat the traditional view of the subject, which holds that in sending Bering to the Pacific, Peter I wanted above all to determine if a strait existed between Asia and America in the Chukotsk region.

This essay addresses this issue, but seeks to answer other questions as well: (1) when and how did Russian interest in the "unknown" shores of the American Northwest first appear? (2) what motives underlay V. Bering's two Kamchatkan expeditions? (3) why, despite the efforts of Peter I, was the founding of Russian America postponed for half a century? (4) what was the role of G. I. Shelikhov in the foundation of Russian America?

The Growth of Russian Interest in the Northwest of North America

The constant search for new lands and richer sources of furs caused an exodus of Russians eastward "to meet the sun." The Russians' appearance on the Northwest Coast of North America, a land which at the time was not claimed by any European power, was therefore the natural result of Russia's traditional policy in the East.

The settlement of the vast territory of Siberia by the cossacks, peasants, and commercial and trading peoples occurred with extraordinary

13

speed.[1] In August 1639, only fifty-seven years after Ermak first crossed the Urals, the first Russians reached the Sea of Okhotsk via the Ul'ia River.[2] Then, only nine years later—in 1648—the Iakutsk cossack Semen Dezhnev discovered the existence of a "great rocky nose" (the Chutotsk Peninsula) on the extreme northeastern extension of Asia near the northwestern region of America.[3] Dezhnev then learned of two more islands opposite the Chukotsk Peninsula on which lived "the toothed ones," Eskimos who wore pieces of bone in their cheeks.

Until recently, researchers were convinced that these two islands were the Diomedes in the Bering Strait.[4] In the early eighteenth century, however, the Anadyr cossacks had also reported the existence of two islands of "the toothed ones," and that they believed the second of these was a "Big Land": i.e., Alaska.[5] A recent scholar has suggested that Semen Dezhnev may also have had Alaska in mind when referring to this second island.[6] To be sure, information on Alaska and American Eskimos may have already reached the Russians on Anadyr via the Eskimos and the Chukchi. It is unlikely, however, that this theory can ever be proven by the documents. One point is clear: Russian explorers operating in Northeast Asia did not yet have any firsthand knowledge of America.

Other indirect sources of information were at hand. Blau's atlas, various west European cosmographies and even the first globes were all available in Moscow as early as the reign of Tsar Aleksei Mikhailovich (1645–76). Thanks to these, savants in Moscow could ponder the possibility of a close proximity between the "noses" (peninsulas) in the Russian Far East and the American coast. Nikolai Spafarii, chief of the Russian mission through Siberia to China in 1675, noted that a range of mountains extended from Baikal "to the Oceanic Sea, and once in the sea it continues on almost like a wall—no one knows where it ends—and it is impossible to explore it due to ice and bad weather. Many attempts were made to sail from the Lena, but the vessels were smashed up; it is said that this rock runs all the way to the West Indies, to the New World. . . ."[7] Some suspected that this range could even adjoin America.[8]

This version of a range extending into the sea was based upon information from a *rospis* (description) added to a 1673 map of Siberia that depicted a "rocky barrier extending far into the sea."[9] This text combines the reports referring to Chukotsk with those referring to the Kamchatka Peninsula.[10] As early as 1649 M. V. Stadukhin had sailed westward from the Kolyma estuary and had learned from residents of the Cape Shelagskii region that "there is a stone-cliff near the sea; the stone's termination point is unknown."[11] Later, a report on the settlements in the Lena region noted that "the Anadyr settlement is a six week trip across the range by sled from Kolyma, the lower settlement; there is no water because the range stretches into the sea."[12] Meanwhile, by the beginning of the 1660s Russians were already familiar with the northern sector of the Kamchatka Peninsula, including that point on the portage from the Lesnaia River to Karaga from which two seas—the Okhotsk and the Bering—were simultaneously visible in good weather.[13] A description of Siberia in 1673 speaks of the "rocky barrier" and explains that "the trip across this rock is one day in length, and once a man ascends it he can view both seas—the Lena and Amur [e.g., Okhotskoe]";[14] one could sail via this "Lena Sea" from the Lena River to the east bank of Kamchatka.[15]

Once local residents explained that the "rocky barrier" had a termination point, Russians began referring to it as a "nose" (peninsula) pointed "to the south."[16] They claimed, further, that the "nose" in the "Warm [teploe] Sea" was "500 poprishi" (versts) in length.[17] The name of the peninsula's principal river—the Kamchatka—appears by the 1660s. In the 1690s this was accepted as the name of the peninsula itself.[18]

In the second half of the seventeenth century, however, the best known of the Far Eastern "noses" was the Chukotsk Peninsula, with which the "rocky barrier" was identified.[19] As early as the second half of the seventeenth century, information on distant rivers to the northeast undoubtedly reached Moscow, giving rise to the notion that the "Northern Cape of America" was situated close to the Chukotsk Peninsula. This is corroborated by an account by F. Avril, a Jesuit who was in Moscow in 1687. During a conversation with Musin-Pushkin in the Siberian Department (prikaz), Avril learned of a "hippopotamus" industry on an island in the estuary of a far northern river.[20] This doubtless refers to the walrus industry on Anadyr. Citing promyshlenniki who were carried to sea on ice floes, Musin-Pushkin said: "I have no doubt that many hunters who have been thus trapped eventually are swept on the ice floes to the northern cape of America, a point not far from the part of Asia that borders the Tartary Sea. I am convinced of this by the fact that those dwelling on that part of America that extends farthest into the sea from that side have the same appearance as the islanders, who, out of an insatiable greed for profits, subject themselves to dangerous passage and even ruin."[21] It is significant that Musin-Pushkin spoke only of the proximity of the American shore and not of its union with Asia.

Thus, geographical information of some kind had reached Moscow by the mid-1680s, giving officials of the Siberian department reason to think that the Chukotsk peninsula was situated near the northern cape of North America. In the same years information originating in Moscow also reached the famous Dutch geographer Nikolaas C. Witsen. As a result, in his renowned 1690 map of North and East Tartary (Siberia), the "rocky barrier" shown as a peninsula with no termination point was located where the Chukotsk Peninsula is. Next to it is the notation, "Glacial Cape. Termination point unknown."[22] With this, Witsen expressed the theory that this glacial cape could adjoin America.[23]

Other European cartographers, including Karl Allard, Peter Shenk, and G. Delisle, copied this schema from Witsen's map. Delisle's 1706 map states that "It is not known where this mountain range ends, or whether it adjoins some other continent."[24]

It is interesting that while Peter I was in Holland in 1697 this question even became the topic of conversation in a discussion with Witsen. F. S. Saltykov, who had accompanied Peter I to Holland and had previously served in Tobolsk, denied that a junction between America and Asia existed. In 1697 he had proposed organizing a voyage from the Yenisei to the Amur estuary. Peter I modified Saltykov's plan so that the voyage would proceed from the Lena.[25] This indicates that even in 1697 Peter I was convinced that no isthmus existed between Asia and America. In that same year A. A. Vinius, one of the commanders of the Siberian Department, assigned the Yakutsk commander (*voevoda*), D. A. Trauer-nicht, the task of organizing a voyage from the Arctic Ocean to the Pacific.[26] Russian explorers familiar with northeastern Siberia had long believed such a voyage to be possible. After his return to Poland from Yakutsk, the Polish prisoner-of-war "Grishka" Kamienski (Adam Kamienski-Dluzik), a personal acquaintance of both Semen Dezhnev and Mikhail Stadukhin, claimed that he had participated in a special voyage that proceeded from the Lena estuary past Indigirka to the Amur.[27] That such a voyage was feasible had been demonstrated in several common Siberian maps issued in the second half of the seventeenth century, beginning in 1667.[28] By the end of the seventeenth century maps of Siberia portrayed only the "noses"—i.e., the peninsulas—which obviously had "termination points."

In conversations with Peter I, however, Witsen continued to maintain the existence of an isthmus in northeast Siberia uniting Asia and America. Two maps produced by Russian diplomats during negotiations in Nerchinsk in 1689 apparently supported this. Using their data, the Jesuit A. Thomas was able to render the peninsula in the far northeast of Asia as a "tongue" (Lingula) and note also its proximity to North America (Americae Septemtrionali).[29] Thomas used a report by another Jesuit, Father Gerbillon, a participant in the Nerchinsk negotiations. Regarding the presence of a "sacred" northern cape in Russian charts, Gerbillon wrote in his notes: "The Muscovites added that they had surveyed the coast of the Arctic and Northern Seas and found seas everywhere, except for one point in the northwest, where a mountain range extended very far out into sea. They have been unable to reach the end of these inaccessible mountains. If our continent does adjoin the American continent, then it is possible only at that point, but it is not known whether they link up or not."[30] Wishing to change Witsen's mind, Peter I promised to send him the latest Russian maps. Shortly thereafter Witsen received a map of Siberia that had been etched onto a wooden plank; it showed no junction between America and Asia. Describing this map in 1705, Witsen observed that: "This plank indicates that there is ice on the extreme northern sector of East Asia. Obviously, this indicates that there is water at the end of the cape and, consequently, that it does not adjoin America. [This contradicts] a certain commander who lived in these far eastern Siberian provinces for twenty years and who wanted to assure me that the cape stretches to America, but that nobody has traversed it simply because of the cold and barrenness of the region."[31]

The earliest Russian statement based on the words of the inhabitants of Anadyr themselves and relating beyond all doubt to Alaska remains the report on the islands' "poor quality sables" by V. V. Atlasov. This important report, which somehow escaped the notice of Dorothy Ray, author of *Eskimos of the Bering Strait, 1650–1898*,[32] is worth quoting at length:

Between the Kolyma and Anadyr rivers there is an impassable "nose" or peninsula that extends into the sea. Along the left side of this "nose" there is ice in the sea during summer, while in the winter this same sea is frozen over. On the other side of this "nose" there is ice during spring, while in the summer there is none. Volodimir never reached this impassable "nose." The local non-Russian Chukchi who live near this cape and in the region of the Anadyr estuary say that there is an island across from this impassable cape, and in the winter, just as soon as the sea freezes over, aliens arrive from this island, speaking their own language and carrying poor quality sables in packs of three. The tail on these sables was one quarter of an *arshin* in length, with horizontal black and red stripes.[33]

Researchers long ago established that the "poor quality sables with horizontal black and red stripes" were Alaskan raccoons.[34]

A copy of V. V. Atlasov's report was sent from Moscow to Witsen, who published a significant portion of it in Holland in 1705 in the second edition of *North and East Tartary* (pp. 670–76). The above report about the "island" that is quite recognizably Alaska was first cited in this same work (p. 671).

Witsen continued to be sent the most updated geographical charts, which finally prompted him to alter his conception of the far northeastern extension of Asia.[35] On February 8, 1714, N. Witsen wrote his friend G. Cuper, the Burgomeister of Denventer: "When I published my first map I made a notation thereupon that it was not known whether one cape adjoined America, but later I received supplementary information and I know now that they are, without a doubt, unconnected, and I have corrected this on my map."[36]

Several maps of Russia's far eastern lands appeared at the beginning of the eighteenth century. Without exception they all show the Chukotsk Peninsula without the slightest hint of its possible junction with another continent.[37] Abroad, however, Witsen was alone in this knowledge.[38] As a result, several people continued to advise Peter I to explore whether Asia and America were connected. Gottfried Leibnitz pursued this vigorously because he was familiar with Witsen's map of Tartary, 1690.[39] In 1697 he advised Peter to attempt immediately to settle the question.[40] Later, in 1711, Leibnitz asked I. V. Bruce, the friend of Peter I, to keep him informed of the results of the expedition that Peter had sent out to the "glacial cape." Leibnitz wrote Bruce: "A large strip of land extends far northward toward the so-called but as yet unknown glacial cape; it is necessary to determine if this cape exists and if this strip of land ends at the cape."[41] In 1716 Leibnitz again recommended to Peter I that he determine if it was possible to sail around Asia or if the "glacial cape" converged with America.[42]

There is a legend that it was these appeals by Leibnitz that engendered Peter I's interest in the problem of Asia's link with America;[43] even so distinguished a scholar as L. S. Berg believed this.[44] However, the evidence presented here indicates clearly that Peter I had long known that Asia was not linked to America. In the second decade of the eighteenth century, however, the Russian tsar used the suggestions of European scholars as a pretense for organizing a voyage to the Pacific Ocean aimed at solving the Russian Empire's more substantial problems.

Motives Underlying the Bering Expeditions

Complaints about the depletion of fur-bearing animals began to flow in from the far eastern regions of Siberia as early as the end of the seventeenth century.[45] As the treasury's profits plummeted a critical need arose to discover new territories where the fur trade could prosper. In 1709–10 the government gave orders to open up the wealth of the Far Eastern islands. The voyages to the Kurile Islands, begun in 1711, to the Shantar Islands (1713–19), and to Karaginsk Island did not, however, meet initial expectations. Frustrated in these efforts, Peter I began to consider the possibility of having Russian seafarers explore the "unknown" shores of the northwest of North America. He followed closely the progress of the War of the Spanish Succession, aware that a fierce struggle was underway between the European powers over the potentially lucrative eastern sector of North America. He was already convinced that the "unknown" America northwest would also yield significant fur wealths, much the way that the Russian absorption of the eastern lands had benefitted the treasury in the sixteenth and seventeenth centuries. Peter therefore supported a further advance eastward. Displaying a keen interest in globes and maps, he understood that the eastward advance would culminate on North America and that Russian maritime expeditions to America should be hastened lest the other powers preempt the opportunity. If Russia had made known her intentions in North America, however, it could have alarmed the rival powers and prompted them to advance more swiftly. For this reason Peter I decided that the expeditions organized for this purpose should be declared "secret."

In January 1719 Peter I sent the geodesists Ivan Evreinov and Fedor Luzhin eastward with the task of "travelling to Kamchatka and from there to where you are directed." They were charged with determining "if America and Asia meet, which must be done carefully, not only in the south and north but also in the east and west, and map all of this accurately."[46]

In 1721 the two explorers completed a voyage from Kamchatka south along the Kurile Islands. Some historians deny that this expedition had anything to do with the search for American shores situated near Kamchatka.[47] What they overlook is the fact that Peter I was well acquainted with the belief of certain Dutch sailors that the Urup Island ("The Company Land") was part of the western coast of North America.[48] Witsen at one time went so far as to propose that between the Kurile islands of Urup and Iturup there existed the legendary Anaian strait which supposedly separated America from the nearby Asian islands.[49] Naturally, Evreinov and Luzhin did not succeed in discovering the American coastline near the Kurile islands, but this was evidently their hope.

Peter I learned of Evreinov and Luzhin's failure in 1722. In that same year F. I. Soimonov discussed with the tsar the possibility of reaching North America from Kamchatka. Peter stated that he had long considered this, but the appropriate time for such a step had not yet arrived.[50] Only in December 1724 did Peter I decide to send out an expedition to search for a maritime route to America.[51] According to the tsar's plan, the "*shturman*" (Dutch *Stuurman*) or navigator of this expedition was to be a sailor who had already been to "North America."[52]

The choice for commander fell to Vitus Bering, who had previously travelled to the East Indies. On the day of his departure from Petersburg—February 5, 1725—Bering was issued the secret instructions of Peter I, who had just died.

They read:

(1) You are to build one or two boats with decks at Kamchatka or another place there.

(2) You are to [sail] on these boats along the land which goes to the

north* and it is expected (because its termination point is unknown) that that land will appear to be part of America.

(3) You are to search for where it adjoins America, and then proceed to some city under European control, or if you see some European vessel, find out from it what the coast is called, and record it; then go yourself and collect original information, record it on the map and return here.[53]

These instructions have been cited in the literature dozens of times. Nonetheless, their meaning can be perceived only when it is understood that they were drafted on the basis of the first printed "Kamchadalia map," (actually a map of the entire Russian Far East) commissioned by Peter I and I. V. Bruce in 1721 and printed by I. B. Homann in Nuremberg in 1722.[54] The use of this map accounts for the "obscurities" that specialists believe were present in Peter I's instructions.[55]

Peter I based his instructions on a map that indicates an enormous land lying next to the Kamchatka Peninsula. On the "Kamchadalia map," which Peter also used, this land had no name, but it was quite recognizably that mythical land which had been alternately named the "land of Juan De Gama," the "land of Ezonis," and the "Northern Land" ("Terra Borealis"). This land was sometimes portrayed as being linked to America, and at other times as separated from the continent by the Strait of Anaian, north of California.[56]

Speaking of the "Juan de Gama land" in 1741, A. I. Chirikov recalled that in the past "it was said to be part of America."[57] So when Peter I issued an order to sail "along the land which goes to the north and ... [which] will appear to be part of America" and "to search for where it adjoins America" and then proceed to "some town under European control," the tsar clearly intended an eastward voyage. It was then to proceed south of that particular non-Asian "northern land" to its south-

---

*The Russian for this phrase reads: "vozle zemli, kotoraia idiot na nord" (along the land which goes to the north). Apparently Peter wanted Bering to go to America and to do so by sailing along "the land which goes to the north" to the point where it joins America; that is, to sail east. This is confusing because although Peter used the Russian word *zemlia* (land), it has been translated as "coast" or "shore" thrice before ("coast which extends northward," W. H. Dall, 1890; "shore which bears northerly," F. A. Golder, 1922; and "coast which extends to the north," S. A. Thompkins, 1945), thereby implying that Peter had instructed Bering to sail along a coastline in a northerly direction, when in reality the instructions directed him to sail eastward (to where it adjoins America) along land which itself happened to "go to the north."

western region, where it either adjoined America or was separated from it by the Strait of Anaian. Then as Chirikov later noted, the voyagers were to proceed "to Spain's Mexican province,"[58] a step that was necessary so that Russia could lay claim to the entire Pacific coast north of the "Mexican province" by right of discovery.[59] Materials from the second Kamchatkan expedition confirm the correctness of this interpretation.

When it became known in St. Petersburg that Vitus Bering had sailed north in 1728 but failed to carry out Peter I's instructions,[60] it was decided that a second Kamchatkan expedition should be organized in order to rectify his mistake. In 1731–32 the government asked the Academy of Sciences to map the most suitable route for attaining the goal set by Peter I. Academician Joseph Delisle carried out this mission. Delisle's maps show the route just as our interpretation of Peter I's instructions would suggest: from the southern extremity of the Kamchatka Peninsula proceeding eastward and to the *south* of the mythical land of de Gama.[61] Bering had also chosen this route. Given this course, Delisle proceeded not from the Kamchatka River (Nizhnii Kamchatsk) but from the southern Avachinskii Gulf. At his point of departure was eventually established on "the harbour of the blessed apostles Peter and Paul," Petropavlovsk-Kamchatskii, the future capital of the Kamchatkan district.

Russia's new rulers made only one modification in Peter's original plan, namely, they rescinded Bering's order to sail "to a town under European control."[62] They reasoned that "if [the explorers] are required to travel from the region in which they are searching for America to European possessions as well, they will be unable to return to the Kamchatkan shores in the space of one summer."[63] Moreover, the sooner the Spaniards or other Europeans would learn that the Russians had reached the northwestern shores of America, the faster they would move to resist the Russians' advance down the Pacific coast. Indeed, when the Spaniards did learn of the Russians' appearance along the American coast, they attempted to preempt them.[64]

Bering and Chirikov had orders to collect tribute from the American aborigines during the second Kamchatkan expedition.[65] They were unable to do so on the 1741 expedition, however, for they had to speed the return trip. Even though certain objectives were not attained, M. V. Lomonosov was quite correct when, in his poem "Peter the Great," he had the tsar portentously declare that "our state shall stretch to America."[66]

N. P. Rezanov, a leader of the later Russian American Company, was among those who regretted that Peter's plan had not been pressed yet more vigorously. Referring in 1806 to the lands situated north of the Californian peninsula, he wrote N. P. Rumiantsev, the minister of commerce, that

> If [members of our] government had thought about this part of the world earlier; if they had respected it as they should have; if the government . . . had consistently followed Peter the Great's prescient vision to plan Bering's expedition, then it can be said with certainty that New California would never have become the property of Spain, for since 1760 the Spaniards have concentrated on permanently strengthening their hold on the best areas there through the enterprise of missionaries.[67]

Reasons for the Delay in the Founding of Russian America

Why was Peter I's plan unsuccessful and the foundations of Russian America not laid in the mid-eighteenth century? It is true that Peter's successors lacked his capabilities. Beyond this, they failed to understand that Russia's opportunity to take control of the northwestern shores of America would decrease with time. Above all, the second Kamchatkan expedition proved expensive for the Russian treasury and aroused great displeasure among Russians in Siberia. These considerations led St. Petersburg, willingly or unwillingly, to cut off funds for the expedition in 1743. Henceforth the government attempted to shift all the difficulties associated with tapping the fur wealth of the Pacific islands onto the shoulders of private traders (*promyshlenniki*). But the discovery of the commercial riches of the Aleutians diverted the attention of Russian entrepreneurs from America. Just when the government was hoping they would forge onto American shores, they asked themselves why they should expend great sums for that end when there was no shortage of valuable furs on the Aleutian islands near Kamchatka.

The Aleutian islands had been discovered during the Bering-Chirikov expedition of 1741. However, it was only in 1747 that they began to be called the "Aleutians." In that year a boy named Temnak, who had been taken to Kamchatka from the "Near Islands," told the Russians in Bolsheretsk that his kinsmen "call themselves Aleuts."[68] The question of the origin of this ethnonym has long troubled specialists. A. S. Polonskii

has suggested that it derives from the name for the local deity—
Aleutska-Agudakh."[69] I. Veniaminov believed that it came from the
words *Alik-uaia* (What is it?).[70] L. S. Berg supposed that "*Aleiut*" derived
from the Chukotsk word *aliat* (island) or *aliut* (islanders).[71] I. S. Vdovin
in turn demonstrated that Berg borrowed this explanation from William
Dall, who had relied too heavily on the work of geographer Engel.[72]
Vdovin pointed out that "the word for 'island' in the Chukotsk is '*ilir*',
and that an 'islander' is an '*ilitlen*'. Obviously, then, the Chukotsk word
'*ilir*' has nothing in common with '*aliat*'."[73]

Vdovin presented his own new interpretation, arguing that the word
Aleiut derives from the Chukot-Koriak roots *elev/aliavor*, e.g., "to tie or
wrap around a volumetrical object (the head, torso, a load on a sledge,
etc.) with something firm and resilient, for example fastening a load
on sledges with a walrus hide."[74] Vdovin concluded that the contemporary word *Aleiut* or *Aleiuty* is the Russian adaptation of the Chukot-
Koriak word in whose stem lies the root *elev/aliav*.[75]

Russian traders or *promyshlenniki* viewed the matter differently.
They held that the ethnonym *Aleiut* was the term by which Aleuts
referred to themselves.[76] More probable is the explanation of the term
Aleiut offered by the best Soviet expert on Eskimo-Aleut languages,
G. A. Menovshchikov. According to Menovshchikov, the ethnonym
Aleiut derived from the Aleut term *alitshukh*.[77] Among the Aleuts this
word meant "community," "detachment," "command," or "troops,"
depending on the situation.[78] In our opinion, this explanation corres-
ponds fully to all the data from historical sources. Hence, it is finally
possible to establish the origin of the ethnonym *Aleiut*, and hence the
name of the Aleutian Islands, which today comprise part of the state
of Alaska.

To tap the wealth of fur-bearing animals on the Aleutian Islands
required sustained effort by the Russian *promyshlenniki*. This task
diverted the Russians' attention from the Northwest Coast of North
America for two decades.

While thus engaged on the Aleutian Islands, Russians first learned
of the existence of the "forested Alakshak," from which the name Alaska
is derived.[79] The Russians first heard this name in 1759–60 on the
island of Umnak from an Eskimo prisoner of war named Kashmak,
when he created an original map "in a simple though quite understandable form" for the members of an expedition headed by the cossack
Stepan Glotov: "a map was drawn in level sand and the distances and

positions of islands were indicated with stones: large islands, big stones; small islands, little stones; etc."[80] To copy this map the Russian seafarers used an equally unusual method involving charred wood splinters and colored clays.[81] The renowned cartographer and former governor of Siberia, F. I. Soimonov, valued this unusual map very highly and expressed his wish "to preserve it for posterity in memory of such fearless and zealous people."[82] It was on this map, too, that the Russians first plotted the "forested island of Alakshak." A copy of it made such a strong impression on M. V. Lomonosov that in 1764 he drafted a new polar map.[83]

An early copy of M. V. Lomonosov's second polar map was discovered in 1976 in the Division of Rare Books and Manuscripts of the library of the USSR Academy of Sciences.[84] This map establishes that Lomonosov was the first Russian specialist to suggest that the "forested island of Alakshak" was in fact the "cape" of North America.[85] Using a loxodroma and other constructions on the map, he showed that the island lay on the hypothetical line of the Northwest Coast of North America. Consistent with this, he renders the cape as an elongated peninsula.

Dispatching Captain P. K. Krenitsyn to the Pacific, the Russian government obliged him to determine whether "Alakshak" was an island or part of the continent.[86] Earlier, Pyotr Shishkin, a member of Stepan Glotov's expedition, had reported that Russians had already managed to reach Alakshak in 1761. Shishkin's map of 1762 prominently shows Alakshak and identifies it with the notation: "Alakshak. A great many people. The merchant Bichevin's vessel wintered here."[87] The reference here is not to what we now call Alaska but to "Aliaksa" or "Alakshaka," the narrow peninsula on southwestern Alaska that points towards the Aleutians.

Since Kashmak, the Russians' principal informer, was from this Alaskan peninsula, he was able to describe his homeland in detail to the Russian sailors. Based on his account, Lomonosov noted on his map: "Many people, a standing forest. Many fox, bear and deer. Evidence of marten and wild boar."[88] Kashmak's report also convinced Lomonosov that Alakshak was most likely an American peninsula. It is likely that it was Kashmak's account that induced the merchant G. Pushkarev, I. Bechevin's subordinate, to sail here in 1761.[89]

Vague reports on other regions along the northwest coast of North America originated from this same Kashmak. Members of the expedition wrote: "Shugach Tani: there are animals; bear and deer, and a forest. The men wear skirts and loin-cloth shirts and they have broadswords, spears, mirrors and ink-wells."[90] Lomonosov reproduced this report in an abridged form on his polar map.[91] It obviously relates to the land of the Chugachi. In St. Petersburg it was correctly determined that several of the items enumerated had probably reached the Chugachi from the south via an intertribal exchange.

At Lomonosov's suggestion, the navigator P. K. Krenitsyn was assigned to explore the region inhabited by the Chugachi.[92] He never carried out his mission, however. Nonetheless, Krenitsyn, M. D. Levashov, and their fellow voyagers were able to gather sufficient information later in the 1760s to allow them to conclude that they had indeed reached the shores of the American continent. Thanks largely to the efforts of Lieutenant Ivan Kobelev,[93] by the early 1780s it was established that the "Big Land" situated opposite the Chukotsk Peninsula was also part of America.

It is helpful to recall once more how Alaska was discovered from the Chukotsk Peninsula. After the Russian government ordered an intensified campaign to gather information in the Far East relating to the populated islands in 1709–10, Chukchi accounts of islands across from the "Chukotsk Nose" (the Chukotsk Peninsula) reached the Anadyr Fort (*ostrog*). In 1711 the cossack Pytor Popov, the *promyshlennik* Egor Toldin, and the Iukagir Ivan Tereshkin were sent to the Chukotsk Peninsula. There Popov learned from the Chukchi that the "Big Land" (Alaska) had "sable, fox, martin, polar fox, wolf, wolverine, polar bear, sea beaver and large herds of deer" and that the "toothed ones" (Eskimos) living there had their own faith, customs, and language. These Eskimos occasionally made war on the Chukchi, and Popov saw ten of them who had been taken prisoner.[94]

The complex relations between the Russians and the Chukchi on the Chukotsk Peninsula did not allow for the immediate organization of a trip to the "Big Land." But Popov did gather information on the route there and made a map as well. Ivan L'vov later used data from this map on his chart.[95]

These two drawings show clearly that the route proceeds along the Diomedes islands. Alaska is depicted as a long island stretching out to the north. On this "island" it is noted that "The piece of land (*zemlitsa*) is large, and the people inhabiting it are called the '*kigin-eliat*' in the Chukotsk tongue. They have their own language and the wildlife includes sable, fox, and deer. Their yurts are in the ground and they fight with bow and arrow. The forest on this land includes pine, birch, and other deciduous trees, and they have a fort there.[96] Popov's drawing of the "Big Land" was reflected in several maps of the second decade of the eighteenth century[97] and also in the 1721 chart that was the basis for the 1722 Map of Kamchadalia by I. B. Homann mentioned above.[98]

As early as 1720 Prokopii Nagibin petitioned to be allowed to search for the Big Land, but was turned down.[99] In 1725 A. Mel'nikov, having just arrived in Anadyr, became interested in Nagibin's plan. In April of 1730 Mel'nikov visited the Chukotsk Peninsula and met Alaskan Eskimos, who told him that on the Big Land "there is every animal: sable, fox, beaver, wolverine, lynx, wild deer; there is also every variety of forest and a fair number of deer and aliens on foot."[100] Mel'nikov asked the Alaskan Eskimos to take him to the Big Land, but they adamantly refused. The Eskimos were obviously afraid of the appearance of Russians on Alaska, but their refusal was motivated also by a shortage of feed and dogs.[101]

The Russians' first appearance along Alaskan shores was related to the organization of Afanasii Shestakov's large-scale expedition. Shestakov was a Kolyma cossack.[102] As early as the end of the seventeenth century he participated in voyages to the land of the Koriaks in the Okhotsk Sea.[103] He was well acquainted with Anadyr and the Kamchatka Peninsula. While visiting St. Petersburg, he drew an interesting map of the Russian Far East that represented islands that were not yet under Russian control.

In 1726 Shestakov was ordered to organize expeditions to these islands in order to bring them under Russian authority. The navigator Iakov Gens was assigned to go to the Big Land (Alaska) but when Gens fell ill, I. Fedorov was appointed commander of the expedition. The experienced geodesist Mikhail Gvozdev was named to assist him.[104]

On August 21, 1732 (September 1 new style) Russian navigators reached Alaskan shores, but because of the inclement weather they decided not to disembark. The Big Land was subsequently plotted on maps in the form of a small strip of land based on M. Gvozdev's report.[105] In the 1730s the question of whether I. Fedorov and M. Gvozdev's Big Land discovery was part of America began to trouble many Russians. As early as 1733 A. I. Chirikov admitted that "there were sounds of America herself" in the reports of Fedorov and Gvozdev.[106]

A. Dev'ier, Commander of the Okhotsk port, suggested to Bering that he build *shitiki* (small boats) on Anadyr and go where Fedorov and Gvozdev had been. "There is no doubt," he said, "that the Big Land is the America for which we have been searching."[107]

These suggestions were not heeded, however. A. I. Chirikov allowed that the Big Land could be part of America but nonetheless recommended that they proceed along better known routes by sailing south from the Kamchatkan extremity towards the west bank of America "between fifty and sixty-five degrees, where the climate is mild for the residents and the land may not be uninhabited."[108]

As early as the seventeenth century, reports were being received in Europe that the Indians who had arrived in southern California from the north maintained that the northern Pacific coast of North America turned sharply westward. So in a few maps of North America published in Western Europe, the American coast is represented by a dotted line that extends in the direction of Kamchatka and Chukotsk. The "probable coast of North America" was depicted in the same way on M. V. Lomonosov's first circumpolar map of 1763.[109] Speaking of V. Bering's return trip in 1728, Lomonosov noted that: "It is unfortunate that in returning [they] ... did not proceed further west, where in the course of the journey the northwest shores of America would, of course, have been visible."[110] By April of 1764, however, Lomonosov had come to believe that at the point where many West European cartographers saw an extension of the northwestern region of North America an entire range of islands existed,[111] i.e., that the coast discovered by Fedorov and Gvozdev belonged to an island. Only the Alaskan voyages of Lt. Ivan Kobelev put an end to all doubts relating to the priority of Fedorov and Gvozdev in the discovery of the Northwest Coast of America.

The Delayed Foundation of Russian America

There has been a long-standing controversy among specialists as to when the first Russian settlements sprang up on the American continent. The version by the monk German telling of the Russians' appearance on Alaska from Novgorod during the era of Ivan the Terrible is doubtless beneath criticism. Equally dubious are the legends of settlements by the companions of Semen Dezhnev or Iurii Seliverstov. The account relating to the discovery of traces of an ancient Russian settlement on the Kenai Peninsula turned out to be groundless as well.[112] The mysterious story of the disappearance on the American coast of the group headed by the navigator Dement'ev—a group which never returned to A. I. Chirikov's packetboat in June 1741—undoubtedly warrants attention,[113] but it is unlikely that the fate of this group will ever be determined.

Russian *promyshlenniki* on several occasions established temporary settlements on the Aleutian islands, and some of these continued on for several years. The Russian settlement on Unalaska existed for a particularly long period of time.[114] It was only the permanent Russian settlement that G. I. Shelikhov established on the island of Kodiak in 1784, however, that became the starting point for new surveys of the Northwest Coast of America.

Shelikhov carried out his project on an extraordinarily large scale and with impressive commercial foresight. If other Russian *promyshlenniki* concerned themselves principally with immediate success, Shelikhov thought in terms of stable, long-term rewards. He was the first Russian merchant to advance the notion that trapping should be regulated in order to attain the natural reproduction of fur-bearing animals. In organizational matters Shelikhov was particularly bold. He clearly realized that his own efforts might not succeed in the presence of rival trading companies, each of which was striving for maximum profits from each new voyage. Instead of this, Shelikhov aspired to create a single monopolistic trading company.

As early as 1787 Shelikhov joined his Irkutsk friend I. I. Golikov in petitioning the government to grant them a monopoly on trade along the North American coast and the eastern Aleutian Islands. Catherine II, a believer in free competition, denied their request, declaring, "As Golikov and Shelikhov are good people, it is suggested that they be given an exclusive market, but one must not overlook the fact that, besides them, there may be other good people in the world."[115] And further: "As Golikov and Shelikhov alone would be engaged in commerce in newly-discovered regions, this request would create a monopoly and exclusive trade, which are against my principles."[116]

This setback did not disturb Shelikhov, for his company was already quite powerful. He therefore stepped up his activities along the American shores. Alarmed by the burgeoning rivalry between foreign powers, including the Spanish, English, and French, Shelikhov wanted to bring the greatest number of "new lands" on both the Pacific islands and the American continent itself under Russian control. He clearly realized that Russians would have less opportunity to achieve this with the passage of time.

On April 28, 1788, G. I. Shelikhov sent the navigators D. I. Bocharov and G. A. Izmailov to sea on the "Three Saints" *galiot* with orders to search for new islands and to chart the American shores so they could then be claimed for Russia. Thus began Russia's acquisition of new lands in North America. In 1794 Shelikhov wrote his assistant, A. A. Baranov: "I have found that it would be incomparably better to establish a permanent Russian settlement on continental land rather than on an island, which is too readily accessible to foreigners. If the need should arise, it would be easier to find refuge from these foreigners on the continent. On the other hand, for political reasons of which you are well aware, occupying the continental land would be a more difficult endeavor than [occupying] the islands."[117]

Shelikhov's words constituted Baranov's plan of action. By 1795 he had begun to devote special attention to the study of the shores of the American "continental land." Russians worked to produce maps of the various North American gulfs. By 1796 these efforts culminated in the drafting of a "comprehensive map" that used separate spliced inserts dealing with the North American gulfs of Iakutat and Ltua.[118] Over the following years Baranov continued to visit the shores of North America. Finally, in 1799, he founded the future capital of Russian America—Novo-Arkhangel'sk (Sitka)—on the island of Sitka. This event coincided with another important event: the founding of the Russian American Company. Hence, four years after his death in 1795, Shelikhov's grand plans were realized.[119] He had often predicted that only the creation of such a company would make it possible for Russia to acquire as quickly as possible a substantial sector of the Northwest Coast of North America. It was Shelikhov, too, who had dreamed of founding on the American continent a Russian capital for the area, which he wanted to name *Slavorossiia* or "The Glory of Russia."[120] Novo-Arkhangel'sk became that capital.

The founding of Russian America was thus the natural result of the Russians' long-term eastward drive "to meet the sun." To Grigorii Shelikhov should rightfully go the honor of being the founder of Russian America. The words which M. L. Lomonosov put in the mouth of his principal character in the poem "Peter the Great" had come true:

"Russian Columbuses, having defied a sullen fate, shall open in the ice a new route to the East, and our Empire will reach to America." Quite fittingly, the Russian poet, G. R. Derzhavin, christened Shelikhov the "Russian Columbus."

Russian Expansion in Siberia and America: Critical Contrasts

James R. Gibson

In 1812, as Emperor Napoleon Bonaparte's Grande Armée was nearing Moscow, Collegiate Councillor Ivan Kuskov's motley band was founding Fort Ross on the North American coast in New Albion. This outpost represented the farthest reach of a process of relentless eastward expansion that had been unleashed in 1582, when the renegade cossack Ermak had captured Isker, the capital of the Western Siberian Khanate and the last obstacle in the path of Muscovy's advance to the Pacific.[1] The next formidable obstacle was not encountered until two centuries later on the Northwest Coast of America, where the Russians finally came up against their westward-moving fellow imperialists from Great Britain, Spain, and the United States. Russia's open eastern frontier finally began to close, and with the rise of the United States and Japan as Pacific powers, Russia became as vulnerable to encircling alliances as the leading European states.

Meanwhile, the bulk of the Russian Empire had been won, thanks to the enterprise of a surprisingly small number of cossacks, *promyshlenniki* (trappers), *muzhiki* (peasants), and *meshchane* (townsmen). Largely on their own initiative—because their government was preoccupied with European affairs, and rightly so—these frontiersmen moved rapidly eastward in search of "soft gold."[2] Some sought adventure or solitude, many craved free farmland, others fled conscription or serfdom, and still others were exiled;[3] but initially, at least, the fur trade was the raison d'être of the Russian occupation of Siberia and

Alaska. In the process, the intruders altered the numbers and the mores of the aborigines by introducing their European diseases and spirits, Russian language, Orthodox faith, capitalistic exploitation, authoritarian bureaucracy, and inegalitarian society. And although the native cultures were changed less drastically and less bloodily than in New Spain, New France, or New England, they and their lands were nevertheless unmistakably Russified.

Thus, Russian expansion across Siberia and into America had certain features in common. But in a number of ways the two movements were significantly different. First of all, although both phases of expansion were spawned by the fur trade, in Siberia the sable was king, whereas in Alaska the sea otter reigned supreme.[4] Both were among the most valuable of furbearers. But the sable, a rather solitary and largely nocturnal creature, bears up to five young annually, whereas the "sea beaver," a daytime animal that congregates in large groups, drops only one offspring yearly, and the pelt of the female, moreover, was more valuable than that of her mate. So sea otters were depleted more rapidly than sables, and accordingly Russian occupancy in Alaska was less stable and less lengthy than in Siberia. Also, the sable is a land animal confined to the Siberian taiga. The sea otter, by contrast, is native to the coastal waters of the northern Pacific between Hokkaido and California. This contrast between continental and maritime fur trades—or between what Meinig has termed riverine and coastal empires[5]—was important. While the Russians were accustomed to, and competent in, the acquisition of pelts through tribute, barter, and hunting on land, they were ill-prepared for the maritime milieu of the far North Pacific. Partly for this reason, it took them only sixty-eight years after crossing the Urals to move across Asia and found a permanent port on the Pacific at Okhotsk in 1649, but up to 137 years—twice as long—after reaching the Pacific to move across the Bering Sea and establish a permanent post in America at Captain's Harbor on Unalaska Island in the middle 1770s and at Three Saints Harbor on Kodiak Island in 1784, despite the fact that the latter distance was far less than the former. The uncharted and stormy waters between Siberia and Alaska required ships and sailors and entailed far more risk and expense than land travel.

It was fortunate for the Russians that sea otter fur was even more prized than sable. In 1817, for example, a sea otter skin was worth ten times as much to the Russian American Company as a beaver pelt and forty times as much as a sable pelt.[6] In addition, sables were usually hunted in winter, when their tracks are more evident and their fur is thicker and longer, whereas sea otters were normally hunted in spring and summer, when the North Pacific weather is less inclement. Consequently, farming suffered more from temporal conflict with hunting in Alaska than in Siberia (where, however, there was some spatial clash). Also, the lack of winter hunting in America meant the absence therein of Siberia's *zimov'ia* or winter camps. These were replaced by Aleut hunting parties, which spent several weeks at sea during the warm season under a Russian foreman. *Ostrogi* (forts) were found in both regions but not *reduty* (redoubts, or ungarrisoned stockades) and *odinochki* (one-man posts); these were peculiar to Alaska, undoubtedly because of its shortage of manpower. Furthermore, the Russians had the sea otter trade all to themselves for half a century, and they controlled the habitats of the most valuable varieties of the animal. Great Britain and the United States did not enter the trade until the late 1780s, long after Bering's second voyage of the early 1740s had launched the Russian enterprise, and they concentrated their hunting on the Californian and Northwest Coast otters, which were less valuable than their better-furred but sorely depleted Aleutian, Kamchatkan, and Kurilian cousins.[7]

Fortunately, too, for the Russians, they controlled the Aleuts, whose skill in the use of kayak and harpoon made them unrivaled as hunters of sea otters.[8] "They are extremely expert in managing their canoes, and . . . are excellent marksmen with the rifle and spear," noted a Scottish seaman in 1807.[9] These "marine cossacks" managed even to learn European seamanship faster than their Russian conquerors. As a result, the Russians never mastered the chase, and indeed did not themselves do the hunting in America as they had in Siberia. Hence, the Aleuts were more ruthlessly exploited than any aboriginal group had been in Siberia, where the Russians equalled or surpassed the natives as trappers. The Aleuts were virtually enslaved; beginning in 1799 all males between eighteen and fifty years of age had to labor for the Russian American Company. The resultant toll in lives was appalling but not surprising. At least 80 percent of the Aleut population perished during the first and second generations of Russian contact.[10]

The markets for sable and sea otter also differed. Sable pelts were sold mostly in Europe, especially at Moscow and Leipzig as well as in Holland and England, where they were exchanged for a variety of hardware, metals, textiles, beverages, and foodstuffs. By contrast sea otter fur, not as warm as sable and therefore more suitable for trim, was marketed primarily in North China where it commanded higher prices than in European Russia. It became the royal fur of the Middle Kingdom, whose Manchu upper class exerted a strong demand. Although some sable was transacted, it was mainly the lustrous sea otter that enabled Russia to obtain such exotic Oriental commodities as tea, silk, and porcelain. In much the same way, the Americans' shortage of specie towards the end of the eighteenth century made it desirable for them to acquire the same goods by trade in furs.[11] In a very real sense the sea otter trade supported the Russians' tea habit. More important, it facilitated Russian-Chinese contact, commercial and otherwise. The China trade blossomed at a time when Canadian furs were taking the European market away from Siberian furs. The sea otter provided the Russians with a timely response to the Canadian beaver.

The fur trade dominated the economy of Russian America much more than that of Siberia. In 1719, for example, 60 percent of Siberia's Russian male population were peasants,[12] whereas at a roughly comparable stage of development in 1833 probably 90 percent of Alaska's Russian males were fur traders. Already by the eighteenth century agriculture was Siberia's principal economic activity.[13] Mining for gold, silver, copper, lead, and salt, plus smelting, were also important; and some brewing, milling, tanning, glass making, and cloth making were carried on, as were considerable fishing and hunting. But in America the fur trade remained the preeminent occupation. The local market was too small, and foreign markets too distant, to warrant much diversification; it was cheaper to import from European or Asiatic Russia or, better yet, from California or the Oregon Country.[14] Some farming and shipbuilding were attempted, but merely to serve the needs of the fur trade. And they did not prosper.

Little wonder that when the fur trade ended, so did Russian America. Its monolithic economy was simply too vulnerable. And because its maritime economy was less diversified and hence less autonomous than Siberia's, Alaska had to engage in more external commerce, so traffic with New England, the Californias, the Oregon Country, the Sandwich Islands, and occasionally even Chile and the Philippines loomed large. Alaska's trade was even responsible for some of Siberia's commerce, for Russian American sea otters dominated the traffic at Kiakhta.

The more specialized economy of Alaska also meant that it was dominated by one major town. This pattern was commonly exhibited by colonial territories. Novo-Arkhangel'sk (New Archangel), with half of the colony's Russian population and capital assets, was the primary center. The more varied economy of Siberia, however, gave rise to several towns of prominent rank—Tobol'sk, Tiumen', Eniseisk, Irkutsk, and Iakutsk.[15] Thus, in an economic sense Alaska was more "colonial" than Siberia, since its economy was more mercantile, that is, more directed to serving the needs of the mother country than its own.

The American entry into the maritime fur trade of the North Pacific reveals another contrast with the continental business of Siberia. In Siberia, following the defeat of Kuchum Khan, the Russians encountered no serious opposition from the mostly paleolithic natives, who were neither numerous nor united, particularly in the face of Russian firearms. And no foreign power challenged the Muscovite conquest. The two states that could have done so—China and Japan—became isolationistic with the advent of, respectively, the Manchu (Ching) Dynasty (1644–1912) and the Tokugawa Shogunate (1603–1867), just as Russia was advancing across Siberia. But America presented no such power vacuum. At first Russia was unopposed on the Northwest Coast, but soon Spain and then Great Britain and the United States became alarmed, especially when Cook's last voyage revealed that there was something worth competing for in the form of *Enhydra lutris*.[16] By 1800 American and British shipmasters had halted the Russian advance down the coast, undermining its basis by outtrading the tsar's men. Furthermore, the Yankees in particular were not above bartering firearms (including cannons) to the coastal Indians and inciting them against the Russians.[17] The Tlingits even managed to capture the Russian American Company's colonial capital of Novo-Arkhangel'sk in 1802. Indeed, thanks to their bountiful economy and cohesive society as well as to American military aid, the Tlingits resisted Russian encroachment more successfully than any other indigenous group in the course of tsarist eastward expansion, the sole possible exception being the Chukchi. By the middle of the nineteenth century Russia realized that she was overextended in America. In the climate of reform following the disastrous Crimean War she withdrew from the American Northwest and consolidated her position in Asia in the face of burgeoning American power. Alaska thus became the only part of the Russian Empire ever to be relinquished by the tsarist regime.

Nevertheless, expansion into America did—for a while, at least—make Russia more of a maritime power in the Pacific, whereas expansion across Siberia, an Asian land base, gave Russia about one-third of the Asian continent and thereby a vested interest in its affairs. It also brought Russia into contact with China much earlier than other European states. The Treaty of Nerchinsk of 1689, which delineated the Amurian frontier, was the first accord to be signed by the Celestial Empire with a European country. Siberia also brought Russia to the Pacific, albeit precariously, for until the acquisition of Amuria the Russian Far East was a tenuous oceanic foothold.[18] It was not until Russia crossed the Bering Sea to Alaska that she became a full-fledged Pacific power with designs on borderlands like California and archipelagos like Hawaii.[19]

Russia's fledgling navy was bolstered by round-the-world voyages to her American colonies, but it was no match either for the power of Great Britain's naval force or for the acumen of the United States merchant marine. Additional ships were bought and built and more sailors were trained in order to show the flag in the North Pacific arena, make voyages of exploration, trade with maritime nations, and supply the Russian Far East and Russian America.[20] Russian maritime strength in the North Pacific was restricted, however, by the closure of Chinese ports to the tsar's vessels until 1858. Consequently, Russian America marketed its sea otters by land at Kiakhta via the protracted Okhotsk-Iakutsk-Irkutsk route rather than by sea via the more expeditious route from Novo-Arkhangel'sk to Canton.

Russian America also made the Russian Empire more "colonial" to the extent that "colonialism" implies overseas or noncontiguous expansion. This situation did not, of course, apply to Siberia. With the acquisition of Alaska Russia joined the ranks of Great Britain, France, Spain, Holland, and other European colonial powers. But there was a difference. Alaska, unlike Canada, Mexico, or South Africa, was never the object of settlement by numerous colonists from the motherland. Many Russians, particularly serfs, migrated to land-rich and seigneur-free Siberia but few were willing to go as far as America.

Once in America, colonists found a situation that differed militarily from what prevailed in Siberia. In Siberia furs had for a long time been obtained not only by trapping and trading but also by tribute. As a result, cossacks and soldiers had to be stationed there to enforce collection, as well as to suppress the Western Siberian Tatars, repel the Kirgiz in the southern steppe, and guard the Amur frontier against

China. In Alaska after 1768 the exaction of tribute was officially banned. Notwithstanding the unruly Tlingits, no nomadic hordes or standing armies threatened the colony's borders, so the military was less prominent than in Siberia.

There were other important differences between Alaska and Siberia stemming from Alaska's more "colonial" nature. The Russian male population of Alaska was 563 in 1833; at a roughly comparable state of development in 1719 Siberia, with nine times as much territory, had 169,000, or 300 times as many.[21]

Females were scarce in Alaska, constituting only 10 percent of its Russian population in 1833.[22] This sexual imbalance prompted many Russian men to take native wives; their offspring, who were called creoles, came to form up to one-fifth of the colonial population, even outnumbering the Russians themselves. An important body of semi-skilled labor, this mixed-blood element was comparable to the métis of Canada and the mestizos of Latin America.[23] Far less intermarriage took place in Siberia than in Alaska. This greater degree of contact in Alaska likely meant a higher native toll from introduced diseases like syphilis, smallpox, and influenza. During the smallpox epidemic of the last half of the 1830s, for example, Alaska's natives suffered a fatality rate of 25 percent.[24]

Few, if any, exiles were sent to America. So many were banished to Siberia, by contrast, that they colored the very name of the region. The general dearth of Russian settlers was one of Russian America's basic weaknesses, for colonization was the surest way to substantiate territorial claims. With the sale of Alaska, Russia was able, in a sense, to escape charges of colonialism, although in fact her colonialism differed from that of other European countries mainly in that it was directed against contiguous territories, namely, Transcaucasia and Central Asia, rather than overseas. And no doubt partly because Alaska was not contiguous to the rest of Russia it was considered more expendable than Siberia.

The few Russians who did venture to America distributed themselves in a settlement pattern that differed markedly from Siberia's. The Siberian pattern was linear, with settlements being strung first along rivers, then along tracks, and finally along railway lines; the main sites for settlement were commonly native villages, arterial portages, and transportation junctions. In Alaska the pattern was likewise linear, but strictly coastal. The usual sites of posts were promontories (*kekury*) at the mouths of rivers or at the heads of bays. Such were the locational requirements of the sea otter and fur seal business and of marine transport. Few settlements were found inland, which was neglected by the Russians (with the exceptions of the lower reaches of the Yukon and Kuskokwim Rivers). This neglect further weakened their tenure, which remained marginal, literally and figuratively.

Missionary activity may have been greater in America than in Siberia. The church's missionary activity increased in post-Petrine Russia,[25] just as expansion to America occurred. The success of Catholic missionaries in the New World also provided a stimulus. The relative vigor of Orthodox mission work in Alaska was due particularly to the extraordinary work of one man, Ivan Veniaminov (1797–1879), whose untiring and versatile efforts earned him the unofficial title of "apostle of Alaska" and the official title of metropolitan of Moscow and Kolomna, the Russian Orthodox church's second highest office. Veniaminov's American mission still exists.

A further contrast is significant. In Siberia furs, tusks, gems, and other natural products were obtained by a host of individuals and companies competing against each other. Not so in Russian America, where no individual entrepreneur could afford the expense of acquiring, outfitting, and manning a ship for a voyage of several years. As the sea otters receded farther eastward and southward, voyages became longer and riskier, costs rose, and returns fell. Competition became viciously keen, occasionally erupting into warfare, which occurred mainly at the expense of the hapless Aleuts.[26] The government was eventually obliged to intervene in order to keep the peace and save the trade, particularly in the face of increasing international contact on the Northwest Coast. The result was the formation in 1799 of the Russian American Company, which the Russian government empowered to administer and exploit Alaska.[27] Despite a number of able governors, the joint-stock monopoly soon became stodgy and cautious, disabilities that weakened its capacity to compete with American and British traders. Another monopoly, the Hudson's Bay Company, fared much better against the Americans, so perhaps Russian entrepreneurial backwardness was more at fault than monopolistic privilege per se. In any event, these were shortcomings that the Russians in America could ill afford in view of their other difficulties.

Perhaps the most crucial of these additional problems was supply. Provisioning was relatively simple in Siberia for several reasons. First, more of the land was arable, especially in the steppe of western Siberia, with its virgin *chernozem*. Second, the warmer and drier climate of Siberia was better for crops and livestock. Third, some of the native groups (such as the Tatars, Buriats, and Iakuts) were at a relatively advanced technological level, high enough, at least, to practice farming and therefore enabling the Russians to use them as sources of provisions. Fourth, Siberia was, of course, much closer to European Russia and its pool of personnel and matériel. The situation was much worse in Alaska, with its rocky and hilly terrain, cool and damp climate year round, nonagricultural indigenes, and extreme remoteness from the Russian heartland. That the environment was rich in fish and, to a lesser extent, timber merely alleviated rather than resolved the supply problem. The Russians perforce turned to American skippers, Californian missionaries, and Hudson's Bay Company factors. These were able to meet the Russian demand, but they were also rivals of the Muscovites for control of the territory and resources of the Northwest Coast. In this way the search for provisions critically undermined Russia's presence in America.[28]

Indeed, most of the contrasts between Russian expansion in Siberia and Alaska underscore the flaws of the latter.[29] Ruthless exploitation of hunters and fur-bearing animals alike, stiff international opposition, monopolistic complacency, precarious logistics—these are some of the compelling factors that persuaded Russia to retreat to a more tenable position in Siberian Asia, with its promising imperial opportunities to the southeast in Amuria[30] and to the southwest in Turkestan.[31] These opportunities more than compensated for the loss of Russian America, where the tsarist imperial system, so successful in Siberia,[32] failed to withstand the extreme strain. To extend a Siberian proverb, Russian expansion in Alaska failed because God was too high above and the tsar was too far away.

PART TWO
The Tsars and Their American Colony

The Russian American Company and the Imperial Government: Early Phase

Mary E. Wheeler

In December 1799, one hundred years after Peter the Great urged Russian merchants to follow the example of foreign merchants and establish "East India-type companies,"[1] Tsar Paul I issued a charter to "The Russian-American Company under the Supreme Protection of His Imperial Majesty." This company was granted a monopoly, for a period of twenty years, to all the hunting, trading, and mining "on the north-east coast of America from 55° latitude north to Bering Strait and beyond, and also on the Aleutian, Kurile, and other islands situated in the North-Eastern Ocean."[2] The Russian American Company administered Russian America until it was sold to the United States in 1867.

The origins of the Russian American Company and its relationship to the imperial government need to be reassessed. Soviet scholars have maintained that the formation of the Russian American Company and its grant of a twenty-year monopoly was a conscious attempt by the government to create a mighty monopolistic company, under direct government control to strengthen and expand Russia's hold in the North Pacific, and to counter foreign expansion in this area. This view was first put forth in 1939 by Semen B. Okun in his study of the Russian American Company and is supported today by the Soviet historians Nikolai N. Bolkhovitinov and Raisa V. Makarova and the Soviet enthographer Svetlana G. Fedorova.[3] On the other hand, I have held that the Russian American Company grew naturally out of the practices of the

Russian merchants engaged in the Pacific fur trade and was the post-humous creation of the "astute and far-sighted" Grigorii Ivanovich Shelikhov.[4] I would like here to suggest that both these views may well be incorrect; that the company was established to establish order out of the chaos brought about by merchant rivalry in Irkutsk following the death of Shelikhov; and that the grant of privileges for twenty years was not the conscious creation of a strong monopoly for imperialistic purposes but an attempt to broaden — rather than limit — merchant participation in the North Pacific fur trade. These are only tentative conclusions based on a reexamination of the events leading to the formation of the Russian American Company, and they will require further investigation.

In each decade from the 1740s to the 1780s ever greater numbers of Russian fortune seekers risked capital, and often life itself, in the quest for furs in the North Pacific. During the 1770s thirty or more merchants participated in outfitting twenty-four voyages and shared in cargoes valued at 1,750,000 rubles. In the next decade the trend abruptly reversed; only sixteen merchants participated in the outfitting of nineteen voyages, and sixteen of these ships sailed from Okhotsk prior to 1785. There were several reasons the small merchants and even many of the wealthy merchants were no longer willing to invest in this trade. There was no dearth of furs — the total value of furs brought to Siberia by ships dispatched in the 1780s exceeded that of the previous decade by 250,000 rubles — but it was necessary to sail farther and stay longer to fill the ships' holds. This meant a larger initial investment and a longer wait for a return on that investment, factors that eliminated all but the wealthiest and most skilled of merchants.[5]

By 1795 only three merchants and their partners survived in the Pacific fur trade — Shelikhov, Pavel Sergevich Lebedev-Lastochkin, and the Kiselev brothers — and the competition between them had become increasingly intense. Shelikhov, who began his career in Siberia in 1773 as a merchant's clerk, was now one of the wealthiest and most influential merchants in Siberia. He had assiduously courted the favor of important men, ranging from the governors-general in Siberia to the empress's last favorite, Platon Zubov, and including the Tsarevich Paul and the industrialist Nikolai Demidov; and he dominated the Pacific fur trade by means of three companies.

Shelikhov apparently was the first merchant in Siberia to understand that if the Russian fur trade were to continue and to expand in the Pacific area, the financing of these activities must be organized in a new manner. He believed that it would no longer be profitable, or even possible, to finance the voyages through the customary temporary partnership (*kompaniia*) that lasted only for the length of one voyage. Therefore, he proposed to his former employer and current partner in two voyages, Ivan Larionovich Golikov, that they organize a permanent company (*postoiannaia kompaniia*) to build and outfit ships for fur-trading and hunting voyages which would operate for not less than ten years. By "permanent company" Shelikhov meant a company in a more modern sense, that is, the initial investment capital to be divided into shares (*aktsii*)* with each investor receiving shares in proportion to his investment. Furthermore, additional capital was to be obtained by selling shares.[6] The capital was to be divided into three funds: a reserve fund, a fund from which rewards would be paid to those who performed acts beneficial to the company (by discovering new islands, for example), and a working capital fund.[7]

Had Shelikhov's views of the Russian activity in the Pacific been limited to the purely commercial aspects, he would still stand out from the other Siberian merchants. His plans, as the Soviet historian Okun pointed out, "were distinguished by breadth of scope, revealing him as a man of great ability endowed with a spirit of enterprise, and far in advance of his contemporaries."[8] Shelikhov proposed that this new company establish permanent Russian settlements on the islands, that ships be sent each year to carry supplies to the colonists and to return with the year's accumulation of furs, and that these permanent settlements be officially annexed by the Russian Empire. This was a truly revolutionary proposal, for up to that time no merchant or *promyshlennik* had raised even a permanent hunting station on any of the islands. Furthermore, the new company's *promyshlenniki*, aside from

Pai was the term used to denote a share in a partnership or in a company that was organized for one trading venture and ceased to exist when that venture was completed. As far as can be ascertained, the first Russian proposal that spelled out the joint-stock form of a company; that is, a company with a permanent capital and open to all who wished to buy stock (*aktsii*) was made by Lorents Lange, a vice governor in Irkutsk, in 1739. Lange proposed to create a company that would take over the state monopoly of the China trade. For a discussion of Lange's proposal, see Clifford M. Foust, *Muscovite and Mandarin: Russia's Trade with China and Its Setting*, (Chapel Hill, 1969), 142–47.

hunting and bartering for furs, were to explore new lands, search for iron, copper, coal, and other useful minerals, and engage in agriculture and cattle raising. Shelikhov also considered it essential to establish peaceful and permanent trade relations with the natives. He believed that it would be possible to teach the natives reading, writing, and arithmetic and thus prepare them to become interpreters, navigators, sailors, and clerks. All of these measures, he pointed out to Golikov, would not only extend the Russian Empire into the Pacific and thereby increase its power and prestige—a point that Shelikov was to stress repeatedly in his petitions to Empress Catherine—but it would also vastly increase the opportunities for the hunting and trading of furs.[9]

This plan was as daring as it was novel. Shelikhov was apparently thoroughly persuasive. His former employer agreed to help organize and to be the principal investor in such a company. The ten-year company was formed on August 17, 1781, while Golikov and Shelikhov were in St. Petersburg. The initial capital of 70,000 rubles was divided into 120 shares. The original investors were Ivan Golikov (35,000 rubles), his nephew, Captain Mikhail Sergeevich Golikov (20,000 rubles), and Shelikhov (15,000 rubles).[10]

Golikov and Shelikhov agreed that for the company's initial venture they would have two ships constructed and outfitted in the vicinity of Okhotsk (three ships were actually built). These ships were then to sail together to collect furs and to establish permanent colonies on the islands and on the coast of Alaska. One of main stipulations of the agreement was that Shelikhov would personally supervise the construction and outfitting of the ships and then would sail with the expedition as well. He received additional shares in the company as compensation for his labors. If the 120 shares had been divided among the investors on the basis of their investment Ivan Golikov would have received sixty, Mikhail Golikov thirty-four, and Shelikhov twenty-six. It was agreed that each of the Golikovs would give Shelikhov one-third of his shares. In this way, Shelikhov owned fifty-seven shares or 47.5 percent of the company although he only invested 21.5 percent of the capital, while Ivan Golikov, who invested 50 percent of the capital owned only one-third of the company.[11] One can only conjecture as to whether this idea was Shelikhov's or Golikov's. The assumption can be made, however, based on the evidence of Shelikhov's personal direction of all of the company's activities from the time of its organization until his death, that the initial idea was his, and that he undertook this task with enthusiasm and with the accumulation of capital in mind.

By 1795, the year in which Shelikhov died, ships belonging to Golikov and Shelikhov had brought back furs that were valued at more than 1,500,000 rubles.[12] And they had made Shelikhov, if not Golikov, a wealthy man.[13]

Shelikhov was as persistent in petitioning the Crown for assistance as he was in accumulating capital. In this respect also he seems to have differed from his fellow merchants.[14] In 1787, when he returned from a three-year voyage to Kodiak, he began sending detailed, and no doubt exaggerated, reports of his activities to the Siberian governors-general as well as proposals that trade relations be established with Japan, coastal China, Korea, India, the Philippine and other islands, and with the Spaniards in America. He also petitioned the Crown for government assistance to carry out his plans and continued to do so until his death. His petitions included requests for a 500,000 ruble loan (later reduced to 200,000), a monopoly of the Pacific fur trade, a military detachment, a clerical mission to enlighten the natives in the Orthodox faith, and artisan and agricultural serf families, a few of whom would be sent to the Kurile Islands to establish a permanent colony there. His petitions were forwarded to Catherine II by the governors-general with their enthusiastic endorsements.[15]

After six years of writing detailed reports, proposals, and petitions with nothing to show for his efforts except a gold medal (bearing the likeness of Catherine) and a silver sword, Shelikhov's efforts were finally rewarded. In June 1793 the metropolitan of Novgorod and St. Petersburg was ordered to assist Shelikhov and Golikov in establishing an American mission. Of more importance to Shelikhov, however, was the *ukaz* Catherine issued in December, granting the company twenty artisan and ten agricultural serf families from among the Siberian exiles.[16] Shelikhov was greatly encouraged by her majesty's actions and by her statement to Governor-General Pil' that she found all of the enterprises of the Golikov-Shelikhov company "wholly useful to the state" and wished them all possible success.[17] He believed that this was an auspicious sign and decided to reorganize and consolidate all of his enterprises in order to be ready to take full advantage of any future royal favors.

In 1790 the ten-year Golikov-Shelikhov company had been reorganized to take into account the death of Ivan Golikov. The company was renamed the Northeastern American Company, and some of the merchants who no longer could engage in the North Pacific fur trade individually joined the company at this time.[18]

In 1793 while Shelikhov and Golikov were in St. Petersburg, they signed an agreement that extended the life of the company. They had also formed two temporary companies, one in 1790 and a second in 1791, each of which had sent a ship to the North Pacific. To consolidate these enterprises, the two merchants formed a second permanent company in 1794, named the North American Company, with the same rules and regulations as the Northeastern American Company.[19]

Shelikhov spent the summer of 1794 in Okhotsk supervising the loading and sailing of two new ships bound for Kodiak with the missionaries, the serf exiles, *promyshlenniki*, and provisions. He had also planned to send four of the agricultural serf exiles, twenty *promyshlenniki*, a foreman, agricultural tools, seed, cattle, and provisions to establish a permanent settlement on the Kurile Island of Urup. This enterprise would be financed by the newly formed Kurile Company. It was not until the spring of 1795, however, that the colonists were sent to Urup.[20] A large part of Shelikhov's success must be attributed to the fact that he traveled to Okhotsk every year to supervise personally the unloading of ships that arrived from the North Pacific and the division of furs as well as the outfitting and provisioning of ships leaving for the North Pacific. He realized that the continued success of his business required both his frequent absence from Irkutsk and the efficient management of his affairs there. He spent the winter in Irkutsk concentrating on this task. By the spring of 1795, he had his office reorganized and staffed with competent personnel who had been given detailed instructions for the conduct of affairs during his absences.[21]

Had Shelikhov lived, it is quite possible that he would have been able to dominate completely the Pacific fur trade, but he died unexpectedly in July 1795. His death gave new hope to those Siberian merchants who believed that, with Shelikhov out of the way, they could reestablish themselves in this lucrative trade. It was their attempts to do so that created such chaos that the imperial government intervened directly for the first time.

It had been the government's policy from the beginning to encourage the merchants in their activities in the North Pacific. As Raisa V. Makarova points out: "This is completely understandable in light of the fact that the fur trade not only brought the Crown a large income in the form of customs but it also increased the territory of the Russian Empire because it was the merchants together with the *promyshlenniki* (not the government) that brought the inhabitants of the areas where they hunted and traded under Russian subjection."[22] This policy was first enunciated by Empress Anna in 1733 when she ordered the Siberian governor to assist the merchants "because it was more convenient and without loss to the crown, for the merchants and *promyshlenniki* themselves to finance the voyages to distant places...."[23] Catherine II continued to carry out this policy. In April 1764 the Bol'sheretsk chancery was ordered to see that no obstacles were placed in the way of the merchants. Everything possible was to be done to assist the merchants in outfitting their ships, even to supplying them with state-owned materials that were in excess of the needs of the state and delaying payment until the return of the ships. That same year she initiated the policy of rewarding the merchants engaged in the Pacific fur trade by exempting them from service, from the quartering of troops on their property and by cancelling their debts to the treasury. She also ordered that a number of merchants be presented with gold medals with her portrait on one side and a suitable inscription on the other, and in 1766 she bestowed the rank of Siberian *dvorianin* (a nonhereditary gentry rank) on two men for the discovery of previously unknown islands.[24] But this was as far as Catherine II was prepared to go in encouraging this trade. She was as persistent in refusing to grant a monopoly of the fur trade as Shelikhov was in petitioning for one.[25]

It was during Catherine II's reign, however, that the imperial government sent two naval expeditions to the North Pacific and planned a third that was aborted by the outbreak of war with Turkey. In 1764, at the suggestion of Governor-General Chicherin and Mikhail Lomonosov, Catherine ordered the admiralty to make preparations to send an expedition to the Northwest Pacific to compile accurate information on the newly discovered islands and to formally annex them.[26] This expedition suffered many misfortunes but two ships, commanded by Captain Petr Krenitsyn and Lieutenant Mikhail Levashov, did sail in July 1768 to Umnak and Unalaska and returned to Kamchatka the summer of 1769. The only result of the expedition was a detailed description of Unalaska and its inhabitants. It is doubtful that the empress believed the expedition was worth the 100,000 rubles it had cost.[27]

Captain James Cook's voyage to the North Pacific and the publication of the account of this voyage in 1784 inspired the second Russian expedition. In the fall of that year Peter Simon Pallas, a member of the Russian Imperial Academy of Science long interested in Siberia and Russia's eastward expansion, proposed a government expedition "to complete the discoveries of Cook."[28] Early in August 1785 Catherine commanded the admiralty to draw up detailed instructions for this expedition under the command of a young English lieutenant, Joseph Billings, who had sailed on Cook's voyage as the astronomer's assistant. The primary purpose of the expedition was scientific, and Billings was instructed to survey accurately the Siberian Coast and then to chart the islands in the Pacific between Siberia and the coast of America. Islands and coasts discovered by Billings not claimed by a European country were to be annexed, but only with the consent of the native inhabitants.[29] The members of the expedition left St. Petersburg in 1786 for Siberia and returned to the capital in 1794, but the expedition spent less than two years (1790–92) surveying the Aleutian Islands and the Alaskan coast.[30]

If the main goals of the Krenitsyn and Billings expeditions had been scientific, the purpose of the proposed third expedition was to affirm the "first discovery" rights of the Russians in the North Pacific and to prevent other powers from encroaching on them. In December 1786 Catherine ordered the admiralty to prepare to send a naval squadron under the command of Captain Grigorii Ivanovich Mulovskii from the Baltic to the "Eastern Ocean."[31] By September 1787, the naval vessels chosen for the expedition had arrived at Kronstadt from Arkhangel'sk, but by the time they had been provisioned Russia was at war with Turkey. On October 28, 1787, Catherine ordered the admiralty to cancel the sailing orders and to send the ships to join the Mediterranean fleet.[32]

The Krenitsyn expedition had cost 100,000 rubles, Billings was still in eastern Siberia, and war had caused the cancellation of the Mulovskii expedition. It is not surprising that Catherine decided that it was not in the best interests of the state for the government to play a direct role in an area as remote as the North Pacific. She clearly expressed this opinion in 1788 when she wrote: "More expansion in the Pacific Sea will not bring sound advantages; to carry on trade is one affair, to take possession is another."[33] Catherine believed that "the natives of North America and the trade with them must be left to their own fate."[34]

Furthermore, the empress was convinced, unlike her successor, that the time for East India-type companies had passed. She asserted that the European trading companies were "all being ruined and soon the English and Dutch [companies] will be in the same decline that the French [company] now finds itself."[35]

There is no doubt that the imperial government was interested in the activities of the Russian merchants in the North Pacific. The evidence, however, does not support the contention that there was a consistent imperialist policy in regard to the North Pacific.

The two events that led directly to the formation of the Russian American Company occurred in Siberia in the summer of 1795: Shelikhov died in Irkutsk, and his ship, the *Phoenix*, arrived in Okhotsk with fifteen Japanese who had been shipwrecked on one of the Aleutian Islands. Immediately upon Shelikhov's death, the Irkutsk merchants, including Golikov, attempted to gain control of his companies. They made the mistake, however, of underestimating the ability and determination of Shelikhov's widow. Natal'ia Shelikhova was a most unusual woman—any woman who sailed the North Pacific Ocean, with her children, and spent two years on Kodiak Island as Shelikhova had would have had to be unusually strong in mind and body. After her husband's death, Shelikhova sent a written declaration to the proper authorities in Irkutsk stating that she had taken over her husband's affairs and was prepared to fulfill all of his commercial and Crown obligations. She was informed that she could not do this without a written will and that his capital would be disposed of in accordance with the law; that is, it would be divided among his children and his blood relations.[36] Shelikhova asserted that "this [decision] had been instigated by those who were jealous of my husband's vast establishments and who wished to make my children and me the victims of their cunning."[37] She then petitioned Catherine requesting that the property be disposed of as Shelikhov had outlined in a letter he had written his eldest daughter when he first became ill. Shelikhova noted, "it is as if he foresaw his death."[38] There is no direct evidence that her petition was granted, but later in 1795, in a letter to Platon Zubov, Shelikhova stated that she had inherited the Northeastern American Company; and, in 1796 in a letter to Governor Nagel, she wrote that she and her children were partners with Golikov in the American Company.[39] The fact that her eldest daughter, Anna Grigor'evna, was married to a member of the gentry and living in St. Petersburg probably facilitated her petition.

While Shelikhova handled the company's affairs at Irkutsk, her son-in-law, Nikolai Petrovich Rezanov, acted as her agent and lobbyist in St. Petersburg. Rezanov, born in St. Petersburg in 1764, was a member of the gentry—apparently "poor but proud." After serving in the military and then the civil service for a number of years, he rose to a position of some influence in the court toward the end of Catherine's reign. He probably was aided in this regard by his uncle, Ivan Gavriilovich Rezanov, chief procurator of the Senate's first department in 1778. Nikolai Petrovich traveled to Irkutsk early in 1790 to visit his father, Petr Gavriilovich, who was chairman of one of the Irkutsk courts. Here he became acquainted with Shelikhov and his family. In 1793 Catherine appointed Rezanov to accompany the ecclesiastical mission, which had been assigned to Russian America, to Irkutsk. On this visit Rezanov married Shelikhov's daughter, Anna Grigor'evna. He thus acquired a wife and shares in the Shelikhov enterprises. Shelikhov gained a son-in-law and a staunch and influential supporter in St. Petersburg.[40]

Rezanov was not only able to retain his influence at court after the accession of Paul I but was able to increase it. He rose very rapidly in the table of ranks, from the seventh rank (equivalent to captain, second class) to the fourth (equivalent to rear admiral) in 1799.[41] It was largely through his efforts and influence that the formation of the United American Company received official sanction in 1797 and was then transformed into the Russian American Company in 1799.

The merchants had failed to prevent Shelikhova from inheriting and taking over her husband's commercial interests in 1795, but a year later they took advantage of a second opportunity. In May 1796 news that the fifteen shipwrecked Japanese had been brought to Okhotsk reached the capital. Catherine, in July 1796, ordered Governor-General Ivan Osipovich Selifontov to arrange to return the Japanese to their homeland. They were to be transported on either a government or a merchant ship, and merchants were to be allowed to send goods. The return of the Japanese was to be used in an attempt to open trade with Japan.[42] This was the second group of Japanese who had been shipwrecked in the Aleutians and brought to Russia. The first group, at least those who wished to return, had been sent home with the same object in mind in 1792. Incidentally, Shelikhov and Golikov were the merchants chosen to supply the trade goods for this voyage.[43] Selifontov, who had not left St. Petersburg for his new post, wrote

Governor Ludwig Nagel in Irkutsk of Catherine's order and asked him to ascertain if any Crown ships were available for the voyage. Nagel, on October 16, 1796, notified the merchants in Irkutsk that Her Majesty wished to send the fifteen Japanese to their homeland on a Crown or merchant ship and that merchants would be allowed to send goods to trade with the Japanese.[44] This looked to the merchants, including Shelikhova, like a golden opportunity to expand their business, with the Crown bearing some of the expense. Shelikhova was the first to answer the call. On 5 November she wrote Nagel pointing out what her company had accomplished in the past and its financial success— shares in the American Company were now worth 2,000 rubles. She asserted that not only was she prepared to send the necessary goods to Japan on a Crown ship, which would be returned in the same condition in which it was received, but that she could have the goods in Okhotsk by March or April.[45]

A number of merchants saw this not only as an opportunity to gain government support but as a means of competing successfully with Shelikhova. Early in December 1796 Stepan Kiselev, a prosperous Irkutsk merchant, submitted an "Exemplary Endeavor to Establish a Commercial Company" to Governor Nagel.[46] He proposed forming a company to expand both domestic and foreign trade, and he noted that his proposal was in response to Her Majesty's wish to return the Japanese to their homeland. The company was to be composed of those who voluntarily contributed shares (*aktsii*) or portions (*chasti*) worth two hundred rubles each. Because of the difficulty and high cost of obtaining the necessary materials to build a new ship, Kiselev petitioned the governor to request Her Majesty to provide a Crown ship. In return for this, he graciously suggested that the company be named the Japanese Company. The company was to be in existence for a minimum of four years, during which time the original investors would not be allowed to withdraw their investment and no one new would be allowed to join the company. Furthermore, in order to protect the merchants who were willing to undertake the great expense and assume the risk of the uncertainty of being able to open trade with the Japanese, Kiselev requested that only merchants in this company be allowed to send goods. The original investors would be allowed to sell their shares at their value as of the most recent annual accounting, but only with the permission of the two duly elected directors and approval by them of the purchaser.

It would appear that Kiselev was not only asking for a four-year monopoly on any trade with Japan but was trying to assure that Shelikhova would not be able to buy into the company. This proposal, however, remained just that, despite the fact that on December 8, 1796, thirty-five merchants signed a formal statement that they were interested in participating in the proposed company. Thirty-three of the merchants were members of the second or third guilds (e.g. with total worth not exceeding 10,000 rubles), and it is doubtful that they could have raised the capital necessary for such a venture. Only five of them are known to have participated in the Pacific fur trade; three of the merchants had one share (pai) each in Lebedev-Lastochkin's 1790–97 voyage, and two had previously invested in one of Shelikhov's voyages.[47] It has not been possible to ascertain whether Stepan Kiselev himself had previously been involved in the Pacific fur trade; unfortunately, no patronymic is given. The Kiselevs who had a ship in the North Pacific in the 1790s were Fedor and Mikhail.

By February 9, 1797, Governor-General Selifontov, who was still in St. Petersburg, had received from Irkutsk Shelikhova's request to return the Japanese as well as the Kiselev proposal. On this date he forwarded them both to Prince Aleksei Kurakin, procurator-general of the Senate. In the covering letter Selifontov requested money to maintain the Japanese until they could be returned to Japan and for the expenses of the expedition. He stated that it was necessary for him to proceed to Irkutsk in order "to fulfill Her Majesty's Imperial order."[48]

In Irkutsk, one of the merchants who had indicated his interest in Kiselev's proposed company decided to take matters into his own hands. Nikolai Myl'nikov, a wealthy member of the first guild who had invested in a Shelikhov ship that sailed in 1780, wanted to reorganize the company. His plan was to send ships to a number of places, including the North Pacific, as well as to Japan. He petitioned Governor Nagel for permission to improve the company, for which purpose he needed government assistance (posobie), and for permission to send ships to the North Pacific, Canton, Batavia, and the Philippine Islands. Nagel wrote Kurakin and recommended that the emperor approve this undertaking. He expressed the opinion that in the past Myl'nikov's personal judgment on all such affairs had proven correct.[49] Nagel included a report to the emperor on the matter. The governor praised the activities of the Golikov-Shelikhov company but stated his belief that the establishment of a new commercial company would contribute to the expansion of trade and bring greater knowledge of the inhabitants of the islands already brought under Russian subjection. He also pointed out that such a company was needed because of the increase in the number of foreign ships that were sailing in the "northeastern" ocean.[50]

The emperor, on June 9, 1797, approved the formation of the Myl'nikov company providing that it did not harm the already established company of the first "acquisitor" Shelikhov.[51] But Myl'nikov had not waited for permission from St. Petersburg; he was already making the necessary preparations in Okhotsk in May.[52] According to Tikhmenev, Myl'nikov and his partners started operations with a capital of 120,000 rubles. They ordered construction of a ship and bought a quantity of goods and provisions on credit. Apparently Myl'nikov and his associates were faced with the very real possibility of bankruptcy.[53] Their solution to this problem was to merge their company, the Irkutsk Commercial Company of Myl'nikov and Associates (*Irkutskaia kommercheskaia Myl'nikov s tovarishchi kompaniia*), with the Golikov-Shelikhova enterprises now known as the American—North, Northeastern, Kurile—Company. According to Okun, Golikov extorted Shelikhova's consent by threatening to withdraw from the American Company and take all of his capital with him. For this "service" he received a fee from Myl'nikov.[54] Tikhmenev's version of this maneuvering differs from that of Okun. According to Tikhmenev, Myl'nikov asked Golikov to join his company and Golikov agreed on the condition that Shelikhova would not be allowed to enter the company, but Myl'nikov and his partners would not agree to this condition. Shelikhova merged with Myl'nikov in order to be rid of jealousy and envy and to put an end to her conflicts with Golikov.[55] Neither Tikhmenev nor Okun documents his statements, and I have found nothing in the archives to explain why the merger took place. Okun's version appears to be the more likely; Shelikhova, a strong-willed and astute businesswoman with a very successful and profitable business and with influential patrons in St. Petersburg, would probably not have united her share of the company with a newly organized and financially shaky company unless some kind of pressure were brought to bear. There is, however, the possibility that she thought it would be financially advantageous. And indeed it was; the 200,000 rubles she invested in the capital of the merged company in July 1797 increased to over 873,000 rubles in three years.[56]

Whatever the reason, on July 18, 1797, Golikov signed a merger agreement with Myl'nikov and his partners; the next day Shelikhova signed a similar agreement.[57] On July 22 Governor Nagel forwarded the two agreements with his recommendation to Prince Kurakin. He first explained that Myl'nikov's company had begun operating before it had received imperial consent. But he requested that they be pardoned because they had not wanted to waste time and such long distances were involved. Nagel then reported that Golikov and Shelikhova had now joined with Myl'nikov and his partners, and that the mutually agreed upon contracts had been confirmed in his presence. He requested Kurakin's assistance in obtaining the emperor's approval because the united company would benefit the state and be in the public interest.[58] What was to become known as the United American Company in 1798, renamed the Russian American Company in 1799, had come into existence in July 1797; and the imperial government had played no direct role in its creation.

On 5 August, 1797, Prince Kurakin delivered his report "On the Harmfulness of Many Companies in America and the Advantages of Uniting Them Into One, With an Explanation of the Means for [accomplishing] This" to the Emperor at Pavlovsk. This report was based on Nagel's reports, the 1796 proposals of Shelikhova and Kiselev in response to Catherine's order to return the shipwrecked Japanese, and Myl'nikov's proposal to form a new company to operate in the North Pacific.[59] Nagel's letter of 22 July and the two merger agreements had not yet reached the capital. Kurakin's report recommended that the emperor call for the "union of all those merchants [involved in the Pacific fur trade] following the example of the East and West India companies, which [company] would be administered by directors chosen from the participants and augmented by one [chosen by] the Crown, who would in no way meddle in commercial affairs. [He] would only see that the government regulations prescribed for the company were in fact being carried out and would report to the office or official appointed by Your Imperial Majesty."[60]

From the arguments that the procurator-general presented to support his recommendations, it would appear that he had been in contact with someone who represented the Shelikhov interests; the most likely person would have been Rezanov. Kurakin first pointed out that it was doubtful that the newly established company had more than 100,000 rubles of capital, not enough even to begin operations on a solid basis.

The results could bring irreparable damage rather than advantages. On the other hand, the Shelikhova-Golikov company had already strengthened its establishments in America. Furthermore, since Shelikhova and Golikov had a combined capital of approximately 1,500,000 rubles, they could continue to supply their settlements annually and bring glory and benefits to the state. Experience had proven this. In a short time this company had built a shipyard, started agriculture and cattle raising, and had transported and was supporting an ecclesiastical mission. This part of the report read as if it were written by Shelikhov himself. Kurakin pointed out that the new company had already received the emperor's approval, and that while it had many participants, "not one of them could be called a capitalist [*kapitalist*]."

This lack of capital had already brought jealousy and discord that threatened to destroy the trade. Shelikhova, however, was willing to take measures necessary to bring this to an end. In order to encourage Shelikhova's company to continue to advance the interests of the fatherland and to stimulate in the new participants the desire to end the rivalry, Kurakin recommended that the emperor place all companies under one office or person—to be called the "protector of the American companies." The "protector" would have two tasks: to assist the companies in obtaining from the government what was needed for their operations, such as navigators, master shipbuilders, and other necessities; and to receive the companies' reports and inform the emperor on the success and political advantage of their operations. He concluded his report with the recommendations that the existing companies and the new company be placed under the direction of the Commerce College (i.e., department) and that no similar companies be allowed to organize without the consent of the existing one and in accordance with a preliminary contract mutually agreed upon.[61]

The emperor immediately approved Kurakin's report. On the same day, August 5, 1797, Kurakin sent notification of Paul's decision to Petr Soimonov, president of the Commerce College, together with copies of all the papers he had on the subject.[62] Kurakin also wrote Nagel on this date informing him of the decision and pointing out that any one who wished to join the new company could do so only with the consent of the initial participants.[63]

It is clear that by calling for the formation of an East India-type company to be placed directly under the Commerce College, the imperial government now was directly involved in the Pacific fur trade.

What is not clear is why this action was taken. Was it to protect the interests of the Shelikhov family, a view that I have maintained; was it to further the imperialist goals, as Okun, Bolkhovitinov, and Fedorova believe; or was it, as Makarova asserts, to secure and increase an important source of income for the state?[64]

By September 7, the Commerce College had examined all the material sent to it and had found it "quite insufficient."[65] On that date the college requested the Irkutsk governor to gather and forward the following information: maps of the voyages to the northeastern sea; plans for new enterprises; information on the former and present participants and their mutual agreements; detailed descriptions of all the hunting and trading and of the settlements and forts on the mainland and the islands; information about the participants in the united company, similar information on the small traders; and an account of the Irkutsk merchants' attempts to open trade with Japan.[66]

One would assume that if the government planned to establish a strong company to carry out its imperialistic goals, it would not act without the requested information. But this was not the case. On 8 September the emperor issued an *ukaz* to Governor Nagel sanctioning the merger of the Golikov-Shelikhova and Myl'nikov companies and praising Nagel for his report.[67] The following day, the Commerce College reported to the emperor its recommendations concerning the merger. The college had found the merger "highly useful" and believed that "the union promises many advantages only if the act for the administration of this company and its offices will be made on a good and firm basis as mentioned by the widow Shelikhova in her agreement."[68] The members of the Commerce College, however, felt it necessary to point out officially to the emperor that the union of these two strong companies would mean that the largest part of the Pacific fur trade would be concentrated in a few hands, as would the trade with the Chinese at Kiakhta where most of the furs were sent. They noted that there were a number of small *promyshlenniki* who apparently were financially unable to join the company at the time of the merger. The college recommended that there should be no obstacles placed in the way of those who wished to join and that the Irkutsk governor summon all the small traders and invite them to enter the company on the basis of mutually agreeable contracts.[69]

The state council met on September 24, 1797, to consider the matter. After the council had heard both Kurakin's and the Commerce College's reports, it approved both the merger and the recommendation that the company be enlarged to include all those involved in the Pacific fur trade. The council urged that the Irkutsk governor help the small *promyshlenniki* to share in the advantages of the united company. In order to encourage participation in the Pacific fur trade, which, the council noted, "required great expense and no little courage," it recommended that the emperor grant the company privileges—similar to those enjoyed by foreign companies—for a period of twenty years. The state council asserted that such privileges could not be considered a monopoly because all who wished to participate in this trade could become participants in the company. The emperor approved all of the council's recommendations.[70]

The government's desire to bring order to the Pacific fur trade was not to be realized for several years. The merger of the companies of Shelikhova, Golikov, and Myl'nikov did nothing to lessen the rivalry. Each of the three major participants hoped to be able to dominate the United American Company, and they now transferred their efforts to St. Petersburg.[71] The attempts to discredit Shelikhova failed, and her influence in the capital grew. In November 1797 the emperor personally signed a decree that read:

> Our attention has been drawn to the services of the deceased Shelikhov who gave his life and property in subjecting to Our Scepter the peoples inhabiting North America. He laid the foundation there for the Greek-Orthodox Faith and a sound beginning for various trades useful to the State. We most graciously bestow on his widow Natal'ia Shelikhova, who shared with him the hardships of his travels, and to their children, the merit of *dvorianstvo* of Our Empire, and also grant them the continuance of their original right to trade.[72]

The Commerce College was frustrated in its attempts to obtain the information it requested in September 1797 or an official merger contract from the participants. In February and again in March 1798 Governor Nagel wrote that the original participants had asked for more time because of "the vastness and importance of their undertakings."[73] In July, however, his successor informed the college that the true reason was they were too busy with quarrels and disputes among themselves and between them and the small *promyshlenniki.* Soimonov renewed his demand and finally, on September 27, 1798, the Commerce College received the formal "Act of the United American Company."[74]

The act had been signed in Irkutsk on August 3, 1798, by Shelikhova, Golikov, Myl'nikov, and six second-guild and eleven third-guild merchants.[75] Of the 724 shares of stock (representing a capital of 742,000 rubles) Shelikhova and her children owned 240; Golikov and his son, 100; Myl'nikov and his sons, 132; the six second-guild merchants owned a total of 128; and the eleven third-guild merchants, 84.[76] Only four of the merchants had joined the company since it was first organized in July 1797. In addition to the stock capital of 724,000 rubles, the company had borrowed 400,000 rubles from Golikov and Shelikhova; article 4.2 provided that no profits would be distributed until this debt had been paid. In order to comply with the recommendation of the Commerce College, article 3.4 contained provisions for small *promyshlenniki* to join. The main office (*glavnaia kontora*) was to be located in Irkutsk* (article 7.1); and two directors (four if it were found necessary) would be elected by the stockholders, on the basis of one share–one vote, to manage the company's affairs (articles 8.1 and 8.2).[77]

The Commerce College studied the act carefully and on January 11, 1799, reported their findings to the emperor. The members of the college were concerned that the capital of 740,000 rubles was insufficient to accomplish all that the company proposed. Therefore, it recommended the issuance of an additional one thousand shares to be sold to all Russian subjects and foreigners who had registered as Russian subjects,** whatever their rank (*chin*) or station (*sostoianie*). Another important change the college recommended was that only stockholders who owned at least twenty-five shares could serve as directors, only those who owned at least ten shares could vote, and the votes were to be counted on the basis of the number of stockholders present—not the number of shares owned. The report also recommended that the company be renamed the Russian American Company, and that it report directly to the Commerce College.[78]

The state council met on the 4th and the 7th of July to consider the "act," the Commerce College's recommendations, the privileges to be granted the company for a twenty-year period, and a petition from Shelikhova asking that, until the majority of her son, one of the four

---

*The main office was moved to St. Petersburg in October 1800 (*P.S.Z.*., no. 19611, 26:348). This action had been taken at the request of Rezanov, and it signified the victory of the Shelikhov faction over that of Myl'nikov (TsGIA, f. 1374, op. 3, ed. khr. 2404, 11. 1-2, 40–46).
**The state council, on 4 July 1799, qualified this by adding "Provided that they own real property" (*A.G.S.*, 2:523).

directors be appointed to act as guardian or trustee of her interests.[79] At its first meeting, the council was informed that Paul had decided to place the company "under His protection" and to grant Shelikhova's petition.[80] The council accepted all the recommendations with only four changes: the changes noted above (p. 60); the stipulation that the stockholders would not withdraw any profits until the debt to Shelikhova and Golikov was paid would not apply to the purchasers of the additional one thousand shares; the company would be named "The Russian American Company under the Supreme protection of His Imperial Majesty"; and the directors would report not to the Commerce College but directly to the emperor.[81] These changes were incorporated in the emperor's *ukaz* commanding the Senate to prepare the necessary charter.[82]

This was done and on December 27, 1799, the emperor signed the "Charter Granted to the Russian-American Company under Our Supreme Protection—for the enjoyment of the privileges granted to it for twenty years."[83] The Russian American Company now had the exclusive right to hunt and trade in the North Pacific and on the coast of North America above 55° that was not occupied by or dependent upon any other nation; and the right to send ships to and conduct trade with all adjacent powers, with their consent and the emperor's affirmation.[84]

A comparison of the United American Company act and the rules and privileges of the Russian American Company with the charters of similar European companies indicates that the charters granted to the French West and East India Companies in 1664 served as models, although this is not explicit in any of the available sources.[85] There are a number of similarities, but there are two very significant differences. First, the French charters contained the stipulation that neither directors nor shareholders could be obligated to furnish any sum over and above their original investment. By contrast the stockholders in the Russian company had the right to share equally in the profits and the obligation to share equally in the losses.[86] Limited liability was not incorporated into the regulations of the Russian American Company until 1821, when the company received its second twenty-year charter.[87] Second, the French companies, unlike their Russian counterpart, received substantial financial assistance from the Crown; one-tenth of the capital of the West India and one-fifth of that of the East India company was contributed by the government. Is it not reasonable to assume that if the Russian government were attempting to establish a strong monopolistic company, under its direct control, that would expand its foothold on the coast of North America, it would have invested heavily in that company itself[88] and also have adopted the principle of limited liability in order to attract additional capital?

It is a pity that Grigorii Shelikhov did not live to see the Imperial Charter of 1799; it granted all the rights for which he so long petitioned the Crown. On the other hand, had he lived the Russian-American Company might never have come into existence because until his death in 1795, there was no need for the government to intervene directly in the Pacific fur trade.

Toward a History of the Liquidation of the Russian American Company

Raisa V. Makarova

The question of the cessation of activity of the Russian American Company and the liquidation of its affairs, which dragged on to the beginning of the 1880s, has not been specially studied either by Soviet or by foreign researchers. It is important, though, for us briefly to review what research exists.

The author of the first detailed research into the activity of the Russian American Company,[1] P. A. Tikhmenev,[2] followed its history through the beginning of the 1860s. Although at that time the question of the conditions of the further existence of the company was already being discussed, Tikhmenev could not even surmise that in several years the question of its liquidation would arise.

At the end of the 1930s, the Soviet historian S. B. Okun published a book[3] in which the history of the Russian American Company received a Marxist treatment for the first time. The author conducted his research up to the sale of the Russian territories to the United States, but did not consider the Russian-American treaty of March 18(30), 1867, and did not touch on the question of the transfer of the territory which the company administered for almost seventy years.

Academician A. L. Narochnitskii, in his fundamental work on the colonial policy of the capitalist powers in the Far East during the second half of the nineteenth century[4] and in the book *International Relations in the Far East*,[5] examined carefully the sale of Russia's territories in

America to the United States. A. I. Alekseev, in a recently published monograph, "The Fate of Russian America,"[6] and the author of the present article[7] also touch briefly on this problem.

S. G. Fedorova, in her historical-ethnographical work on the Russian population of Alaska and California[8] and in other works,[9] researched thoroughly the socioethnic processes taking place in Russian America until its sale in 1867.

Foreign, especially American, historians, have paid a fair amount of attention to the past of Russian America. In the 1920s the first work on the sale of Alaska was published in the United States by the famous scholar Frank A. Golder.[10] In connection with the centenary of the sale of the Russian American possessions, a whole series of new works appeared in the United States,[11] and Victor Ferrar's book on this problem was republished.[12]

Increased interest in the history of the Russian properties in America and the appearance of additional materials on the last period of activity of the Russian American Company give us a basis for examining the liquidation of this company, which had also fulfilled the function of a governing organ of the Russian state over the course of more than half a century.

Despite the company's external well-being, signs of decline can be detected from the middle of the nineteenth century. Not only did the fur trade decrease, but so did trade in fish, ice, timber, and coal. Toward the 1860s the trade in tea almost ceased; the company could not compete with English and French firms which exported tea from Chinese ports and flooded the European market with it. In addition, from the end of the 1840s, American expansion in the northern part of the Pacific was sharply strengthened: in 1848–49 the output of American whalers in Russian waters was valued at $17.4 million.[13] The Russian American Company was not in a position to contain foreign rivals without the help of its government.

The end of the third term of privileges of the Russian American Company on January 1, 1862, coincided with the abolition of serfdom in Russia.

In the revolutionary environment of 1859–60, when voices of protest were heard more and more often against the practices established in the Russian colonies, against the exploitation of the Aleuts,[14] and against the monopolistic character of the company's activity, the tsarist government was forced in 1860 to form a special committee on the organization of Russia's American colonies and to send two inspectors there: S. A. Kostlivtsev from the Ministry of Finances and 2d class Capt. P. N. Golovin from the Naval Ministry.

Golovin and Kostlivtsev, on returning from the colonies in 1861, presented the committee with an account of the inspection, as well as their own remarks and suggestions. In 1863 the committee completed discussion of these materials and presented for the government's examination a "Report on the organization of Russia's American colonies" along with a supplement.[15] The committee remarked that the Russian American Company by its activity promoted the spread of Russia's influence in the North Pacific and the development of trade in that part of the globe, but that in the past decade a depression in industry had begun to be observed, and that the natural resources of the region were being cultivated weakly.[16]

In its recommendations for the further organization of the colonies, the committee suggested freeing the Aleuts from mandatory labor for the company and liquidating its unlimited monopoly after limiting its privileges in the fur trade in its territories.[17] Despite sharply critical remarks, the committee considered that the preservation of the company was necessary for the further development of the area. The report indicated that "it is necessary only to direct the activity of the company so that it does not hinder the development of independent industry and merchant trade of the area; for this purpose it is proposed to limit its privileges, and together with that to define its administrative responsibilities so that they are under the supervision of the government of the colonies themselves."[18]

The governing board of the Russian American Company reacted quickly to the committee's resolution. In its "review" it objected to the reduction of the term of the company's privileges to twelve years (instead of twenty), since it considered this to be "tantamount to depriving the company of its credit, and consequently also the possibility of further existence, that in this reduction of the term is implied the near closing of its business in general."[19] The leaders of the company came out against the differentiation of Russia's American territories into "those subject to the *exceptional* right of trade and hunting for the company and those open to *free* trade."[20] They drew the attention of the committee members to the consequence of unimpeded access for foreigners to the Russian territories for pursuing the fur business and "any sort of illicit trade."[21]

The board also voiced objections in connection with inspector S. A. Kostlivtsev's remark concerning the weak settlement of the colonies by the company. It noted that even if the company should manage to settle the remote regions of the colonies, the situation of the settlers at a latitude of 60°, on rocky and swampy earth which thaws in summer to no more than one *arshin* (28 cm.), and among inhospitable tribes, would prove extremely difficult.

In conclusion, the board cited the fact that the Russian government, which had possessed the shores of the Sea of Okhotsk, Chukotskaia land, and Kamchatka already for over 200 years, had not concerned itself with their settlement and had done nothing to supply the area with provisions. "The reasons are the same: there is neither the land nor the means for the establishment of agriculture there."[22] At the same time the board expressed doubt that Russia needed settlements across the ocean, which at the smallest political upheaval "would be separated from her."[23]

By such means, the governing board of the Russian American Company countered all the inspectors' reproaches and committee's suggestions and insisted on the preservation of its former monopolistic privileges in the Russian territories in the Pacific. Defending the right of the Russian American Company for continued existence on its former basis, the board referred to the special position of the company, defined by a state council in 1841. In the council's opinion the government not only presented the company with an industrial and trade monopoly, but also gave it "part of its own power for administration of a distant and extensive region."[24] Therefore the company was not only a commercial enterprise, but in a certain sense also a political power. And if the government should abolish the company, then "the truest, the most reliable and conscientious agent," which is needed in those instances when the government finds it "inconvenient to act on its own behalf,"[25] would be lost. This is just what had occurred on the eve of the Crimean War, when the Russian American Company, having concluded a neutrality convention with the English Hudson's Bay Company, protected the Russian settlements in America from the attacks of a hostile Anglo-French squadron.[26]

The question of the possibility of the further existence of the Russian American Company was discussed throughout the following years. At the beginning of 1865, the Ministry of Finances gave a report in the state council about the revision of the regulations of the Russian American Company and the organization of Russia's American colonies. The report was examined in the Department of State Economy on February 17 and April 22, 1865. After extended discussion of the issue, the members of the department came to the conclusion of the usefulness of the preservation "of the company as a privileged institution" for the administration of Russia's colonies in America until January 1, 1882.[27]

Simultaneously, the department introduced a proposal for the organization of colonial administration and local residents. Referring to the successful abolition of serfdom in the Russian empire, the department recognized as "essential" the emancipation of the Aleuts and dependent "non-Russians . . . from mandatory labor for the Russian-American Company" and the granting to them of the right to settle wherever convenient.[28] Besides that, it was recognized as necessary for the ruler of the colonies to be appointed by the government and be subordinate only to it. The colonies and the management of the company's affairs were transferred from the Ministry of Finances to a department of the Naval Ministry.[29]

In its final form, the decision of the Department of State Economy was presented in the State Council for confirmation, after which it was published in the papers under the title "The Opinion of the State Council, Royally Ratified July 14, 1865."[30] In essence, these were the new regulations of the Russian American Company, by which its privileges were extended until January 1, 1882.

On September 15, 1865, a general meeting of the stockholders of the Russian American Company was held in St. Petersburg. At that time a new proposal for the regulations of the company, as set forth in the "Review" of the State Council, was presented. The meeting accepted the new regulations, albeit only partially, and at the same time introduced into them several changes and additions. In an instance of the government's disagreement with the opinion of the stockholders, the meeting resolved to ask "to commission whoever is appropriate to quickly take the place of the company in the administration of the colonies, with corresponding remuneration from the government."[31]

But after this meeting, discussion of the "Review" of the State Council by the stockholders of the company continued. On October 21, 1865, the governing board communicated to the Ministry of Finances that it accepted the greater part of the position of the "Review." But at the same time it petitioned to preserve several former exceptional rights for the Russian American Company, and, due to the extremely difficult financial situation, to have it granted an annual allowance of 200,000 rubles.[32]

An injunction by the director of the Department of Trade and Manufacturing to the board of the Russian American Company responded to this petition, as follows: (1) in the course of the term of privileges, confirmed by the State Council on April 2, 1866, that is, until January 1, 1882, an allowance of 200,000 rubles would be paid annually, as long as the company fulfills the responsibilities laid on it; (2) this allowance would be set by the estimate of the Naval Ministry; (3) the company's debt to the state of 750,000 rubles would be cancelled.[33]

Simultaneously with this, the company took several measures in order to emerge from the critical situation in which it found itself at the end of 1865: a "melting out" of tallow from the carcasses of sea bears was started, and its sale was organized in the Sandwich Islands (in 1866 up to 1,000 barrels of tallow were sold for a sum of around 15,000 rubles in silver);[34] in order to reduce transportation costs from 30 rubles per pud (36 lbs.) to only 80 kopecks, they started delivering furs to St. Petersburg by sea from port Ayan.[35] By the beginning of 1867, the board was convinced that, thanks to these measures, the company had emerged from the extremely difficult position which it was in at the end of 1865 and that since its further existence "for a newly extended 20 year term . . . [was] fully provided for, it could deliver to the stockholders satisfactory profits and even gradual compensation for previously incurred losses."[36]

However, such an optimistic conclusion contradicted the reality. The international situation taking shape in the second half of the 1850s was, for Russia, extremely complex. After the end of the Crimean War and the signing of the humiliating Treaty of Paris, the Russian government faced the problem of how to emerge as quickly as possible from its political isolation. In this context, any complications in the Far East were extremely undesirable. Meanwhile England, hostilely inclined toward Russia, laid claim to Russian America. But the northern United States developed no less an interest in it, and they certainly did not want to allow their rivals—the English—to successfully realize their intentions.

Around this time the conviction was arising among the ruling circles of Russia that it would be impossible to retain the territories in America because of the distance and the absence of a Russian fleet in the Pacific Ocean. Grand Duke Konstantin, head of the naval department, expressed these views. As early as 1857 he wrote to the Minister of Foreign Affairs, A. M. Gorchakov, that the company "cannot continue to follow its present system without involving our government in ever more awkward conflicts with the Americans."[37] Thus, the basis for negotiations on the sale of Russia's possessions to the United States was prepared, the latter having already begun preparing proposals on this.[38]

It is worth noting that the Russian government, finding itself in a difficult situation after its defeat in the Crimean War, considered it extremely important to maintain friendly relations with the United States, which was inclined to see in Russia a potential ally in connection with the growth of Anglo-American conflicts. Russian diplomacy bore this in mind. Therefore, when at the beginning of the 1860s the war between North and South began in the United States, the Russian Ministry of Foreign Affairs repeatedly expressed the opinion that the disintegration of the United States could not be permitted on account of its bearing on the international balance of power.[39]

In the summer of 1866 (shortly after D. Karakozov's unsuccessful attempt on the life of Alexander II) an American naval squadron arrived in Russia on a friendly visit. At its head was Gustavus Fox of the Department of the Navy, who congratulated the Russian tsar on his "miraculous deliverance" in the name of the American people and Congress.[40] A formal reception was presented for the American delegation in St. Petersburg, Moscow, Nizhni-Novgorod, and Kostroma. The significant union of two great peoples was spoken of at these splendid banquets.[41]

The presence of mutual interests between Russia and the United States found a reflection in the pro-government Russian press of the 1860s. Thus the *Moscow Gazette* wrote, "The rapprochement of two great peoples of the Old and New Worlds taking place before our eyes, this exchange of expressions of mutual national friendship between Russian and America, is a fact of the greatest importance, and moreover is nothing new, nothing sui generis. No kind of diplomatic agreement could be compared with an intimacy of this sort."[42]

Fox used the hospitality shown him in St. Petersburg to add a more definite character to the negotiations on the sale of the Russian possessions in America, which had been going on for several years.[43]

At this time, the Russian American Company was already in a rather difficult financial position and could no longer continue its activity without the aid of the government. Knowing this, the Russian minister of finance, M. Kh. Reitern, wrote in December 1866 to Prince A. M. Gorchakov, that the concession of the Russian colonies was desirable. He emphasized that the company was in a position close to insolvency, and could be maintained only by significant subsidies on the part of the government. Reitern indicated that if the company "doesn't stand firm," then they would have to take the colonies "under state administration, which without a doubt is linked with significant donations.... In such a situation of the matter it is impossible, in my opinion, not to recognize that our American colonies are of little use for us in a governmental-economic respect."[44]

Thus, the inclination of the Russian government to give up its possessions on the West Coast of the northern United States was becoming more and more evident.

In the course of negotiations, the American side proposed a sum of seven million dollars,[45] which immediately evoked a negative reaction in the Russian press. The newspaper *Voice*, which expressed the views of the liberal bourgeoisie, wrote in the beginning of 1867 that the designated sum was too paltry for Russia, and that if one took into account the necessary government compensation to the Russian American Company then only five to six million dollars would remain. And was that sum worth depriving Russia of its American territories right at the time when gold had been discovered there, "the working of which in two or three years will yield more than the Northern American States will give for them?"[46]

However, financial considerations did not play a definitive role in solving the issue of the sale of the Russian possessions in America. The Russian government was proceeding primarily from political considerations, before which it was impossible to stop for the sake of the rights of one company.

Reitern very openly pointed out that, apart from the impossibility of defending the colonies "from one of the naval powers" in case of war, the sale of the colonies to the United States would make them "neighbors of the English colonies not only in the south, but in the north-west," which, in his opinion, "could only have as a result the strengthening of our amicable relations with the United States, and the increase of the probability of disagreement of the States with England."[47]

On March 18 (30), 1867, an agreement was concluded with the United States by de Stoeckl, the extraordinary envoy and minister plenipotentiary of Russia, about the concession of the Russian territory in America with its adjoining islands for 7,200,000 dollars. Russia handed over to America Alaska, the Aleutians, the Pribilovs and other islands lying to the north of them. The border between the Russian and Northern American possessions thenceforth passed along the Bering Strait— along the 193rd meridian.[48]

Broad circles of Russian society condemned the sale of Alaska. While criticizing the activities of the Russian American Company and supporting the liquidation of its monopoly, the Russian public was against the liquidation of the colonies themselves.

Several English newspapers did not perceive in the Russo-American transaction the frustration of the interests of England, affirming instead that its influence in the Pacific remained stable.[49]

But Karl Marx very accurately noted the anti-English tendency of the agreement of March 18 (30), 1867, emphasizing that "from the economic side, this acquisition for the present is not worth a cent, but, thanks to this, the Yankees will cut England off from the sea from one side and hasten the annexation of all British North America to the United States. That's where the dog is buried."[50]

The American press noted that, as a result of the transactions, the United States would receive everything "that the earth produces from the tropical zones to the Arctic Ocean."[51]

The transfer of the Russian possessions to the United States had to be implemented in accordance with article IV of the treaty, which said that for this purpose both sides should send their representatives to Novo-Arkhangel'sk, the administrative center of Russian America.

On May 15, 1867, the Russian government appointed 2d class Capt. A. A. Peshchurov for the transfer to the U. S. representative of all the territory belonging to Russia and the Russian American Company. Together with the chief director of Russia's American colonies, 1st class Capt. D. P. Maksutov, Peshchurov was supposed to set about the transfer in accordance with the instructions given to him.[52] In the concluding part, they were instructed to finish all the affairs for handing over the colonies "without difficulties and in the spirit of the amicable relations existing between both governments."[53]

On October 18, 1867, an official ceremony was conducted in Novo-Arkhangel'sk to transfer Alaska to the United States. After lowering the Russian flag, the American one was raised.[54]

The ceding of Russian America to the United States created a whole series of unforeseen difficulties for the Russian American Company caused by the absence of an article providing for the protection of the company's interests in the agreement of March 18 (30), 1867. Indeed, it did not even mention the Russian American Company, putting the company officially "in a position deprived of rights, and consequently in dependence on the good will of the American authorities."[55] The matter reached the point at which the company's ships were deprived of the right to sail under a Russian flag "in certain cases," and therefore it was necessary "to acquire an American flag for them by various favors and compromises."[56]

The company suffered huge losses. According to the calculations of the commissioner of the Russian American Company, 2nd class Capt. F. F. Koskul', sent to the colonies especially for the realization of its properties, and the last chief director of the colonies, 1st class Capt. D. P. Maksutov, the sum total of the company's losses was 4,043,882 rubles 59 kopecks.[57]

The new governing board of the company was chosen by a general meeting of stockholders on April 21, 1867, "to take prepared measures for the execution of the treaty . . . and to conduct all negotiations for the transfer of the colonies and the realization of the company's properties."[58] It was composed of F. P. Wrangell, E. I. Tillo, N. I. Lyubabin, N. N. Antsiferov, and M. D. Teben'kov. Over the space of several years it repeatedly appealed to the committee "to take prepared measures for the execution of the treaty . . . for the concession . . . of our possessions on the north-west coast of America."[59] It also turned to the Ministry of Finances, to the Committee of Ministers, and to the emperor himself with a request to compensate the company for the losses borne by it. None of these appeals achieved its goal.[60] And in January 1869 the board's representative, F. P. Wrangell, received notification that the request earlier conveyed to the emperor had not been followed by "his most gracious pleasure."[61]

In November 1870 the representatives of the company and members of the auditing commission, "having considered all the circumstances, resolved" to appeal to the minister of finances with a request "on concluding accounts" with the Russian American Company.[62] But this appeal too went without result. The company's losses were compensated to a very insignificant extent. In all, 73,000 rubles of compensation were provided to the company for its sold property; the United States government paid the Russian government about 800,000 rubles.[63] There remained "a clean loss, not covered by anything, of 1,092,352 rubles 71 kopecks."[64]

The board had to emerge unaided from the difficult position in which the company and its stockholders found themselves. It paid out dividends (mostly in April 1867)[65] up to 1881, when the few remaining owners of stock received in all 3 rubles 95 kopecks in silver for each share.[66]

PART THREE
Russians and Native Americans

Russian Dependence upon the Natives of Alaska

James R. Gibson

In the literature on the early relations between the native occupants and the European colonizers of North America the former have commonly been seen as rather helpless dupes who were manipulated almost at will by the latter; many observers have held, moreover, that the natives soon became dependent upon European trade goods, particularly guns, liquor, tobacco, metalware, textiles, and even foodstuffs. Recently, however, this characterization of the contact period has been called increasingly into question.[1] This paper carries the revisionism further by trying to show that in the case of Russian America—or, more accurately, the insular and coastal margins to which the Russian presence was largely confined—the traditional characterization is not only oversimplified but downright erroneous, for in fact virtually the opposite situation obtained, with the Russians being dependent upon the Aleuts, Kodiaks, and Tlingits for such basics as furs, provisions, labor, and sex.

The fur trade was, of course, the raison d'être of Russian America, just as it had been of Siberia. Russian eastward expansion from the Urals was really a rush for "soft gold"—principally sables in Siberia and sea otters in America. The latter succeeded the former as the world's most valuable furbearers, and the resultant overhunting took the Russian *promyshlenniki* ever eastward—from the basin of the Ob' to those of the Enisei and Lena, then to the peninsula of Kamchatka, along the Aleutian archipelago to the Gulf of Alaska, and finally down the Northwest Coast. The depletion of sea otters was especially rapid because of the creature's low fertility (one offspring per year per dam) and high value (of the dam in particular). Thanks to the high luster, dark color, large size, and durability of sea otter pelts, they were the most prized of all furs, especially by the Chinese. In the 1810s a prime adult female pelt could bring the Russian American Company up to 1,000 rubles,[2] as much as the total annual salaries of three *promyshlenniki*. Other furbearers, particularly fur seals, were hunted in Russian America, but none approached sea otters in value.[3]

Although the Russians were primarily interested in sea otters, they themselves did not actually hunt them. In the continental fur trade of Siberia the *promyshlenniki* were able to bag sables as readily as the Samoeds, Buriats, Iakuts, Koriaks, and other natives, but the maritime fur trade was quite another matter. Pelagic hunting was foreign to the Russian landsmen. So they became abjectly dependent upon the native hunters' traditional expertise in the killing of sea animals, especially sea otters, which were the most elusive. As Governor Ferdinand von Wrangell (1830–35) noted, "of all hunts, the sea otter hunt requires the most experience, skill, and patience. Fur seals, sea lions, and walruses, despite their strength and size, are caught more easily and more quickly."[4] Moreover, the sea otter chase was "very toilsome, and sometimes dangerous," according to the Russian navy's Capt. Otto von Kotzebue, who twice visited the colony.[5] The inexperienced Russians were reluctant to exert their brawn and risk their lives, particularly when highly skilled and largely defenseless native hunters were readily available. Besides, the hunting of nimble sea otters in the open sea from flimsy kayaks with short harpoons was a formidable task that the natives practiced from childhood and took years to master. It was an integral component of Aleut and Kodiak culture. The German naturalist and physician Georg von Langsdorff, who accompanied the first Russian circumnavigation in 1803–6, found that "scarcely has a [Aleut] boy attained his eighth year, or even sometimes not more than his sixth, when he is instructed in the management of the canoes [kayaks], and in aiming at a mark with the water javelin."[6] In the same year Captain Iurii Lisianskii, one of the commanders of the circumnavigation, remarked that the Kodiaks (Koniaga Eskimos), "exercised from their childhood to this sort of hunting, are very expert at it."[7] And in 1820 on Unalaska Island Lt. Aleksei Lazarev of the Russian navy observed that "an Aleut is, so to speak, born in a kayak, skillful in all forms of hunting, and familiar from childhood with winds and currents."[8]

Furthermore, according to Father Ivan Veniaminov, who spent a decade (1824–34) among the Aleuts as a missionary, they were physically superior to the Russians as hunters. He pointed out that the Aleuts were solidly built and broad-shouldered and hence made strong, tireless workers.[9] Veniaminov concluded bluntly that "Russians . . . will never be sea otter hunters."[10]

The Aleuts were better sea otter hunters than the Kodiaks, too. They even liked to hunt sea otters, or so it was alleged by their Russian masters. One of them, Kiril Khlebnikov, who probably knew Russian America better than any other colonial official, having served fifteen years (1817–32) there, declared that the Aleuts were the only natives with an innate passion for hunting sea otters.[11] Similarly, Warrant Officer Friedrich Lütke of the Russian navy observed in 1818 that the Aleuts were as fond of catching sea otters as cats were of catching mice.[12] More importantly, the Aleuts were better kayakers than the Kodiaks (or any of the coastal natives of the Gulf of Alaska, for that matter), probably because they had better craft. Light, fast, and maneuverable, with a shallow draught, kayaks were admirably suited to the pursuit of sea otters in the kelp and shellfish beds of the rocky and shallow coastal waters. They weighed less than thirty-six pounds and could be carried by a seven-year-old boy, and in a "moderately smooth" sea they could easily do ten miles per hour.[13] Veniaminov asserted that "it seems to me that an Aleut kayak is so perfect in its type that not even a mathematician could add very much, if anything, to the perfection of its nautical qualities."[14]

So the Aleuts, as Governor von Wrangell acknowledged, were the most skillful hunters of sea otters.[15] In fact, their expertise with kayaks and harpoons was such that under Russian pressure it contributed to the rapid diminution of the sea otter population.[16] It was also such that the Russian *promyshlenniki* became totally dependent upon the Aleuts, not even bothering to learn how to hunt "sea beavers" themselves. Martin Sauer, secretary to the Billings expedition (1785–94), observed on Kodiak Island in 1790 that foxes and ground squirrels were the only animals that the Russians were capable of killing.[17] Lieutenant Lazarev noted on Unalaska Island in 1820 that the Russians were less competent kayakers than the Aleuts, so much so that if the latter were to refrain from hunting, the Russian American Company would be deprived of sea otters. He explained that "if the company should somehow lose the Aleuts, then it will completely forfeit the hunting of sea animals, for not one Russian knows how to hunt the animals, and none of our settlers has learned how in all the time that the company has had its possessions here."[18] And in 1830 the colonial administration admitted that the Aleuts' skill in sea otter hunting was irreplaceable.[19] Little wonder that Governor von Wrangell referred to the Aleuts as the "sole miners of the company's wealth."[20]

They also dominated the hunting of fur seals. The principal fur sealing grounds were the Pribilof Islands of St. George and St. Paul, where, from 1786 through 1830, 3,144,494 fur seals (an average of nearly 70,000 every fall) were killed.[21] In 1810, 200 Aleuts were sent from Unalaska to the Pribilofs; in 1814, 300 Aleut men with their wives and children worked on the islands under the supervision of several Russian *promyshlenniki* and clubbed 70,000 to 80,000 fur seals; and in 1820 the Pribilof fur seal hunt was carried out by 380 Aleuts and only 10 Russians.[22] Not surprisingly, the essential Aleuts constituted nearly one-third of company employees in 1832.[23]

Because their expertise was so necessary to the prosecution of the maritime fur trade, the Aleuts were severely exploited by the Russians. At first, sea otter pelts were exacted from the islanders as tribute, and hostages were taken to ensure payment. This practice was banned in 1788 but in fact lasted until 1794;[24] it was replaced by compulsory labor, with the Aleuts becoming, in effect, *corvée* serfs who were paid in kind (clothing, tobacco, food). All Aleut males between the ages of fifteen and fifty had to work for the Russian American Company,[25] which monopolized the administration and exploitation of the colony from 1799 to 1867. They were forcibly separated from their families, moved to new hunting grounds, subjected to arduous labor, and exposed to cold, hunger, accidents, disease, and Indian enemies.[26] By 1790, following fifty years of Russian contact, the Aleut population may have decreased by as much as two-thirds.[27] On the Fox Islands, the most densely populated of the Aleutians, the number of natives fell from 1,904 in 1806 to 1,046 in 1817[28]—a decline of almost 50 percent in a dozen years. Surely, the impact of the Russian maritime fur trade on the Aleuts belies the "enrichment" thesis, which contends that the fur trade was more beneficial than detrimental to native culture and caused minimal cultural change that the natives were able to control.

This decimation of the colony's best sea otter hunters prompted the Russians to use more and more Kodiaks or, as they were known to the Russians, *Koniaga*, whose ability with kayak and harpoon was second only to that of the Aleuts. Already by 1790, for instance, 600 two-hatched kayaks with 1,200 Kodiaks were hunting sea otters around Kodiak Island for the Golikov-Shelikhov company.[29] And in 1830, 880 Kodiak kayaks were hunting sea otters in the Gulf of Alaska for the Russian American Company; one group of 500 was supervised by fewer than 10 Russians.[30] Such exploitation quickly began to affect Kodiak numbers, too. Their population fell from 5,700 in 1792 to 1,500 in 1834[31]—a decline of 75 percent. From 1792 through 1805, 751 Kodiaks were killed in accidents alone, including 350 from drowning in 1805.[32] One-third of the Kodiak population succumbed to smallpox during the last half of the 1830s.[33] Fortunately, for the Russians, the rate of decrease of the Aleuts and Kodiaks was exceeded only by that of the sea otter, so a shortage of expert sea otter hunters did not arise.

The Russians even relied upon the Aleuts and Kodiaks to hunt land furbearers; otherwise they were bartered from independent natives. On Unalaska Island the Aleuts trapped foxes during the fall for the Russian American Company. In the Kodiak district in the last half of the 1790s an average of 250 natives and only 25 Russians hunted land furbearers.[34] "Very few" Kenais (Tanaina Indians) of Cook Inlet were employed by the company, probably because they were not considered good sailors,[35] but they hunted and traded land furs and skins (marten, lynx, bear, wolverine, river otter, beaver, muskrat, mink, caribou) for the company, whose Fort St. Nikolai derived most of its business from these natives.[36] And most of the land furs produced by the Novo-Arkhangel'sk district (especially mink, beaver, and river otter) were obtained for the company by the Tlingits. In 1821, for example, the company procured 150 river otters and 100 beavers, as well as 50 sea otters, from the Tlingits.[37]

The insular and coastal natives of Russian America were not only the providers of the Russians' peltry but also the suppliers of their very sustenance. The colony suffered from a chronic problem of supply, particularly food supply.[38] The shipment of provisions over land and sea from Siberia via Okhotsk and from European Russia via Kronstadt and the Cape or the Horn was prolonged and expensive, as well as subject to considerable loss. Importation from nearby foreign countries, colonies, and companies brought better provisions more rapidly and more cheaply but made the Russians precariously and embarrassingly dependent upon their American, British, and Hispanic rivals for control of the Northwest Coast. Farming in Russian America itself was unproductive, owing mainly to the raw climate and inexperienced manpower.[39] During a stopover at Novo-Arkhangel'sk in 1837, a young British midshipman exclaimed, "I should think there was not a single spot in the whole world where so much rain falls during the year as at Sitka; a fine day is really a perfect rarity."[40] Only certain vegetables, chiefly potatoes, succeeded. Aleuts worked the vegetable gardens at Novo-Arkhangel'sk, the colonial capital, but not with spectacular results. Nevertheless, potatoes fared better there than anywhere else in the colony. They were fertilized with kelp, and yields averaged seven and one-half-fold increases in the 1820s.[41] Six hundred 145-pound barrels of potatoes were produced at Sitka in 1821, one hundred fifty barrels in 1825; and in some years a hundred barrels were sold to visiting American and Russian ships.[42] The potatoes were tasty and nourishing and rivaled bread as a staple.

It was, however, the unruly Tlingits or *Kolosh*, as they were called by the Russians, not the placid Aleuts, who became the principal growers of potatoes. Relations between the Russians and the Tlingits contrasted sharply with those between the Russians and the Aleuts and Kodiaks. The *promyshlenniki* failed to subjugate and pacify the Tlingits, who consequently retained their culture longer than the islanders, and always remained suspect. The hapless Aleuts and Kodiaks were subdued quickly and easily, but the Tlingits, who were not encountered by the Russians until 1783, were able to resist them much more successfully. Described by Russian observers as strong, agile, hardy, brave, and clever, the Tlingits had a richer environment (more timber, fish, and land animals) and a larger territory (including a continental interior) to exploit, and they were less essential to the acquisition of sea otters than the Aleuts or Kodiaks. Without control of the Aleuts and Kodiaks the Russians would have had to either do their own hunting or, more likely, resort to barter, whereby the supply of pelts would undoubtedly have been less regular and more expensive. For example, the Russians had to pay the intransigent Tlingits three to five times as much as they did the enserfed Aleuts for the same furs.[43] The Tlingits were also more numerous, numbering 10,000 in 1805, including 2,000 Novo-Arkhangel'sk Tlingits.[44] In 1818 on Baranof (Sitka) Island alone there were 1,000 Tlingits, whose number doubled during the spring herring run.[45] The Tlingit population still totaled 10,000 in 1835, although by 1838 it had been reduced to 6,000 by smallpox.[46] Furthermore, the Tlingits were better organized than the Aleuts or Kodiaks, thanks partly, at least, to their more abundant food supply, which left them more time to create a more elaborate social system. They lived in large dispersed villages, each consisting socially of several independent clans whose intervillage allegiances overrode all intravillage ties; the Aleuts, by contrast, lived in more numerous and smaller villages closer to scarcer food sources, each village consisting socially of one autonomous extended family ruled by one man, with weak intervillage loyalties.[47] Among the Tlingits, clan identity and solidarity were accentuated by the restriction of inheritance to the female line and by the imposition of phratric exogamy.[48] This cohesiveness enabled the Tlingits much more effectively to resist Russian control. As von Langsdorff noted in 1805, "single families, as well as single tribes [clans], have contentions sometimes with each other ... but if attacked by a common enemy, suppose the Russians, they unite for their common defense."[49] Consequently, as Khlebnikov warned, "to kill several hundred of them would be to instill a tribal vengeance into several thousand men."[50] The Russian naval captain Vasilii Golovnin, who made a tour of inspection of Russian America in 1818, recognized the Tlingit problem at Novo-Arkhangel'sk.

> But because the local natives do not constitute one single tribe under one chief but are divided into various clans who live or roam as they please, quite independent of one another (often one of them even fights another), it is not possible to take revenge on them, for one cannot tell to which clan the guilty belong, unless one were to make it a rule to take revenge indiscriminately. But in that case they would all unite to attack the company's settlement.[51]

Golovnin added:

> The Aleuts and Kodiaks had permanent dwellings in villages and did not have firearms, so the company with a handful of *promyshlenniki* easily kept them in subjection; but the inhabitants of the Northwest Coast of America ... are strong, patient in their work, and extremely bold ...; they love independence so much that they would rather part with life than freedom, and to subjugate them is not only difficult but impossible, for they do not have

permanent dwellings but roam the channels from island to island and live in huts; they build their boats so well that no European rowed vessel, except a whale boat, is able to overtake them ... ; in battle they are so courageous that they are rarely captured alive, and they have learned quickly to use firearms, and they shoot very accurately.[52]

The Tlingits' adoption of firearms was yet another advantage. In this they were abetted by American traders, whereas the Aleuts and Kodiaks, being completely under Russian control, were unable to turn to foreign vessels. Yankee "coasters" plying the "straits" that fragmented the Alexander Archipelago supplied the Tlingits with powder, shot, and guns, including falconets, instructed them in their use, and incited them against the Russians.[53] In the process the Americans deprived the Russians of many furs; in 1805, for instance, Captain Lisianskii found that Novo-Arkhangel'sk could be getting 8,000 instead of 3,000 sea otter pelts annually but for American traders.[54] Lisianskii and von Langsdorff also found that the Tlingits had virtually abandoned their spears and bows and arrows in favor of the best English guns, which could be purchased more cheaply on the Northwest Coast than in England itself. The Sitkan Tlingits had muskets and small cannons, as well as iron breastplates, and Chief Kotlean owned no fewer than twenty of the "best" muskets and was an "excellent" marksman.[55] At this time Count Nikolai Rezanov, who was inspecting the colony, reported to the directors of the Russian American Company that "they [the Tlingits] are armed by the Bostonians [Americans] with the very best guns and pistols and have falconets too."[56] In 1825 Captain von Kotzebue observed that "no Kalush is without one musket at least, of which he perfectly understands the use."[57] And in 1860 another colonial inspector, Captain Pavel Golovin, found that "they [the Tlingits] always go armed with knives and often with revolvers and rifles, which are supplied to them nearby by the English and the Americans. They are very good shots and are bold ... and *Novo-Arkhangel'sk is constantly in a state of siege.*"[58] Golovin's fellow inspector, State Councillor Sergei Kostlivtsev, was likewise impressed by the military strength of the Tlingits. He reported that "when at our request the Kolosh living near the port were invited to show us how they warred against other savages ... we noted with no little surprise that the Kolosh [who] assembled on that occasion were all armed with rifles and pistols and fired rapid volleys, like the firing of regular infantry."[59]

No wonder that the Russians treated the Tlingits gingerly and respectfully, so much so that during the first fifty years of Russian contact, which reduced the Aleut population by two-thirds, the Tlingit population remained undiminished. And little wonder that the Tlingits impressed Captain von Kotzebue as a "warlike, courageous, and cruel race."[60] They hated the Russians for having seized their ancestral lands, occupied their best fishing and hunting grounds, desecrated their burial sites,[61] and seduced their women. Their hatred soon made itself felt. In 1802 about 600 Tlingits under Kotlean, all of them armed with guns, attacked and captured Novo-Arkhangel'sk three years after its founding; 20 Russians and 130 Aleuts were killed, 3,000 furs were lost, and a ship under construction was burned.[62] The settlement was rebuilt in 1804 amid some 2,000 Tlingits,[63] the Russians still being eager to tap the sea otter reserve of Norfolk (Sitka) Sound.[64] In 1805 the Indians struck again, destroying Yakutat and killing 27 Russian occupants.[65] As late as 1855 Novo-Arkhangel'sk was again attacked; it was not captured this time but two Russians were killed and nineteen wounded, while sixty to eighty Tlingits were killed or wounded.[66]

The colonial capital was precariously situated, for it was in fact a double settlement—a Russian fort with a Tlingit village just outside the walls. The former contained 1,230 souls in 1845 and 988 in 1860, when it comprised more than a hundred houses, three churches, two schools, two mills, two warehouses, and a two-storey governor's mansion.[67] The latter contained 500 to 600 Indians in the middle 1820s, 700 to 750 in 1837–38, and 600 to 700 in 1860.[68] Governor Nikolai Rosenberg (1850–53) reported in 1851 that "no fewer than 500 well-armed savage Kolosh, who are always ready to take advantage of our negligence, live right by our settlement."[69] Furthermore, every spring the two-to-three-week herring run brought even more Tlingits to Novo-Arkhangel'sk; in the early and middle 1820s up to 2,000, and in the early 1860s more than 1,000, assembled in Sitka Bay every March and April to obtain herring.[70] Inspectors Golovin and Kostlivtsev, who reconnoitered Russian America for six months in 1860–61, reported that Novo-Arkhangel'sk's fort contained 55 cannons mounted and 87 stored, as well as 1,170 other guns, and 147 soldiers and 39 sailors, most of whom, however, were "ailing" and "badly" trained in gunnery; they faced up to 1,000 Tlingit males in the spring and the fall and 500

Siberia

Russian Settlements and Points of Contact
in Siberia and North America

: Ocean

Bering
Strait
ni

Russian America

Norton
Sound
nce
and
thew
nd

Alognak Island

Pt. Bristol

Novo-Arkhaugel'sk

Kodiak Island

imak Island

Shumagin Island

id

Unalaska Island

nlia Island

Aleutian Islands

Vancouver Island

Fort Vancouver

Fort Ross

ic Ocean

Pt. San Francisco

Monterey

at other times—all "cunning and fearless" and "well-armed with pistols and rifles."[71] So many hostile and well-armed Indians so close to the capital endangered its residents and restricted their activities. Everything that company employees did outside the fort's walls—hunting, fishing, gathering, felling, watering, ballasting—was imperiled. As late as 1860, only half a dozen years before the sale of Russian America, Captain Golovin asserted that "no Russian dared to go 50 paces from the fort" for fear of the Tlingits. He added that the Tlingits, in their own words, "tolerate the Russians."[72]

Although the Tlingits had, according to Captain Golovin, an innate passion for petty trading,[73] at first they were understandably reluctant to trade with the Russian invaders. By 1805 the Tlingits of Novo-Arkhangel'sk had largely discarded their fur and hide garments for woolen clothes,[74] but American and British traders, not Russians, were undoubtedly responsible. At this time the Tlingits even refused Russian offers of liquor, fearing that it would render them easier prey.[75] In 1821 Lieutenant Lazarev found that trade between the Russian American Company and the Tlingits was "very insignificant" because American traders paid higher prices.[76] Thereafter, however, the Indians turned increasingly to the Russians for trade goods as their Yankee suppliers gradually disappeared from the coast with the decline of the maritime fur trade and as the Muscovites under the post-1818 breed of governors (naval officers) permitted closer but stricter contact. Mostly land furs and provisions, including potatoes, black-tailed deer, halibut, salmon, shellfish (especially crabs), wildfowl (grouse, ducks, and geese), birds' eggs, berries, roots, herbs, and even snails (or marine slugs), were provided by the Tlingits. By 1830 traffic had increased to the point where Governor von Wrangell was moved to complain that "we buy much of our food every year on the Kolosh market, in spite of the ever-increasing prices, which are now extremely high."[77]

That the Russians were willing to pay the mounting prices indicates that the Tlingit provisions played a vital role. In 1831 the company traded 29,100 rubles' worth of goods (mainly blankets, cloth, iron utensils, axes, tobacco, and paper) for Tlingit furs (chiefly beaver, mink, fox, and land otter), provisions, bark (for siding), clay (for bricks), and fat (for candles); the provisions accounted for 8,000 of these rubles, and they consisted mostly of black-tailed deer, halibut, salmon, birds' eggs, grouse, ducks, geese, and berries.[78] In 1832 the Russians introduced liquor into the "Kolosh trade,"[79] probably in order to meet increasing competition in the "straits" from the Hudson's Bay Company's new coastal posts. The explorer Lt. Lavrentii Zagoskin reported from Novo-Arkhangel'sk in the spring of 1840 that "the Kolosh . . . daily bring the food we eat in return for much tobacco and rum."[80] The trading was done every day at a special bazaar inside the fort. It was described in 1842 by Dr. Alexander Rowand, who visited the colonial capital with Governor George Simpson of the Hudson's Bay Company: "Their market, which is held within the Russian settlement, appeared to me quite extraordinary, presenting to view a goodly supply of deer carcasses, with salmon, cod, red-rock fish and herrings, together with abundance of wild fowl, partridge and wood-cock. The women are the sellers; their husbands considering them far more successful in driving a bargain than they could be."[81]

From 1841, Russian-Tlingit relations improved. By then the last of the Indians' American suppliers had withdrawn from the coastal trade, so the Russian American Company and the Hudson's Bay Company were the only sources of trade goods.[82] Tlingit resistance had been further weakened by smallpox in the last half of the 1830s; in 1836 alone, 400—almost one-half—of the Tlingits living at Novo-Arkhangel'sk had succumbed.[83] The smallpox epidemic broke the back of Tlingit resistance because: (1) it killed so many Tlingits (nearly half of their number perished in the first two months of 1836); (2) it particularly affected the elderly, who were the most hostile to the Russians and the most influential among the Tlingits; (3) it convinced the Tlingits of the efficacy of vaccination and consequently of the superior knowledge of the Russians; and (4) having changed their opinion of the Russians, the Tlingits lost faith in their shamans.[84] Perhaps the missionary zeal of the astute Ivan Veniaminov at Novo-Arkhangel'sk (1834–38 and 1841–50) also served to pacify the Tlingits, and perhaps, too, they were mollified by the abolition of the liquor traffic in 1842 by the two companies.

Whatever the reasons, from the early 1840s Russian-Tlingit contact increased and the "Kolosh trade" boomed, mainly on the strength of potatoes, black-tailed deer, and halibut. By 1860 the Tlingits were accustomed to flour, rice, molasses, tobacco, and vodka; they were obtaining more than 3,600 pounds of flour per month from the company at Novo-Arkhangel'sk.[85] The Kolosh bazaar was now held outside the fort and the trading was done with caution, as Captain Golovin found:

The Kolosh are not allowed inside the settlement, and trading at the bazaar is conducted in the following way: alongside the battery there has been erected a building, which contains all of the goods that are usually needed by the Kolosh; behind this building, towards the Kolosh village, there is a small parcel of land enclosed by a high palisade—this is the bazaar. The Kolosh are admitted through a portcullis, which, if necessary, can be lowered instantly. In the wall of the building or storehouse there is a window, which is closed from the inside with a thick shutter. When the Kolosh arrive at the market in the morning with provisions, consisting of deer [iamany], wildfowl, fish, and potatoes, the window in the shop is opened and the company agent accepts the provisions from each Indian in accordance with fixed prices and gives in return scrip or goods also at fixed prices.... When trading with the Kolosh has finished, the residents of New Archangel come to the shop and get the necessary amount of venison [iamanina], potatoes, and fish at fixed prices, paying in scrip.[86]

The Russians had shown the Tlingits how to plant and use potatoes, probably in the late 1810s or early 1820s.[87] This cultigen is well suited to the cool, damp summers and the light, well-drained soils of the Northwest Coast, and adoption was undoubtedly facilitated by the existence of a root-collecting tradition and of more or less permanent camps among the Tlingits. They were selling potatoes to the Russian American Company as early as 1841[88] (when an annual fair was inaugurated at the capital to facilitate the Indian trade),[89] and thereafter almost every year until at least 1861, but particularly during the 1840s (table 1). In 1843 the Kaigani Tlingits-Haidas of Prince of Wales Island accepted the offer of Governor Adolph Etholen (1840–45) to bring potatoes to Novo Arkhangel'sk every fall. In October 1845 more than 2,000 Tlingits in 160 to 250 boats, many of them from as far away as the Queen Charlotte Islands, assembled at Novo-Arkhangel'sk to sell potatoes.[90] This traffic allowed the company to ship 200 barrels of the tubers to Kodiak Island that year.[91] It also provided the Russian residents of Novo-Arkhangel'sk with their principal fresh vegetable.

More important to the sustenance of the Russians, however, than native farming were hunting, fishing, and gathering on the part of the Aleuts, Kodiaks, and Tlingits, and even the Kenais of Cook Inlet and the Chugach Eskimos of Prince William Sound. Native hunting, which

Table 1   Russian American Company Purchases of Potatoes from the Tlingits at Novo-Arkhangel'sk (Sitka), 1842–61

Year[a]	Barrels[b]	Year[a]	Barrels[b]
1842	550[c]	1852	0[e]
1843	490	1853	0[f]
1844	130[d]	1854	0
1845	1,060[c]	1855	0
1846	102	1856	?
1847	160	1857	?
1848	606	1858	?[g]
1849	500	1859	55[h]
1850	?	1860	?
1851	450	1861	260

Source: United States National Archives, File Microcopies of Records in the National Archives, no. 11, "Records of the Russian-American Company 1802–1867: Correspondence of Governors General," roll 47, p. 426; roll 48, p. 332; roll 50, p. 204; roll 51, p. 187; roll 52, p. 326; roll 54, p. 209v.; roll 55, p. 125; roll 58, p. 189v.; roll 59, p. 308v.; roll 60, p. 25; roll 61, pt. 1, p. 85; roll 62, pt. 3, p. 47; roll 64, pt. 1, p. 56v.
[a]These figures actually refer to the Russian American Company's accounting year of mid-May to mid-May rather than to the modern calendar year.
[b]These were probably 145-pound barrels.
[c]At four rubles per barrel.
[d]Out of 300 barrels brought for sale, and at three rubles per barrel.
[e]Seventy barrels were purchased from Kodiak settlers, and the company's own gardens at Sitka furnished thirty-three.
[f]One hundred thirteen barrels were purchased from Kodiak settlers.
[g]One hundred thirty-five barrels were purchased from Kodiak settlers.
[h]An additional 135 barrels were purchased from Kodiak settlers.

was dominated by the Tlingits,[92] provided virtually the only fresh meat in winter, since colonial stock raising did not thrive. The chief game were Sitka black-tailed deer, Dall or Bighorn sheep, and mountain goats, all found in the coastal mountains, including Baranof Island. The black-tailed deer and the mountain goats had "very tasty" flesh, and one of the species of sheep had thick, smooth wool.[93] The Kenais and Chugaches bagged some of these animals for the Russians, but the Tlingits were the main suppliers. They hunted mountain goats and deer with dogs and bows and arrows, usually from November into May, when the animals were driven to lower ground by deep snow.[94] Sometimes, when the black-tailed deer were driven right down to the coast by heavy snow (as in the winter of 1859–60), the Tlingits used clubs. From the "whitish, fine, and very long" goat hair or wool, which rivaled silk "in the delicacy and softness of its texture," the Tlingits wove their "very handsome" Chilkat dance blankets, which were "as soft and fine as the Spanish merino."[95] From the same fiber the Russians knitted stockings and hats, and from the skins they made leather; from the horns the Tlingits also carved spoons. It was as a source of *iamanina* (venison) that the black-tailed deer became important to the Russians at Novo-Arkhangel'sk. During the 1820s the company's Aleuts at the capital were bagging as many as 200 animals in a good

Table 2 Russian American Company Purchases of Black-tailed Deer from the Tlingits at Novo-Arkhangel'sk (Sitka), 1844–66

Year[a]	Head[b]	Year[a]	Head[b]
1844	400	1856	82
1845	324	1857	339
1846	899	1858	232
1847	1,118	1859	1,320
1848	290	1860	969
1849	329	1861	2,774
1850	100	1862	1,150
1851	25	1863	634
1852	19	1864	254
1853	70	1865	77
1854	7	1866	492
1855	15		

Sources: [Russian American Company, Head Office], *Otchët Rossiisko-Amerikanskoi Kompanii Glavnago Pravleniia za odin god . . . [Report of the Head Office of the Russian American Company for One Year . . .]* (St. Petersburg: divers, 1843–65), 1860, p. 44; 1861, p. 17; 1862, p. 28; 1863, p. 22; United States National Archives, File Microcopies of Records in the National Archives, no. 11, "Records of the Russian-American Company 1802–1867: Correspondence of Governors General," roll 50, p. 204v; roll 51, p. 188; roll 52, p. 326v.; roll 54, p. 209v.; roll 55, p. 126; roll 56, p. 125; roll 57, p. 251v.; roll 58, p. 189v.; roll 59, p. 309; roll 60, p. 25; roll 61, pt. 1, pp. 85–85v., pt. 2, p. 50; roll 61, pt. 1, p. 63v.; pt. 2, p. 71v.; roll 63, pt. 1, p. 76, pt. 2, p. 40; roll 64, pt. 1, p. 59v., pt. 2, p. 42, pt. 3, p. 15; roll 65, pt. 1, p. 57v., pt. 2, p. 33, pt. 3, p. 53v.

[a]These figures actually refer to the Russian American Company's accounting year of mid-May to mid-May rather than to the modern calendar year.

[b]The figures for 1844 through 1851 actually refer to *pudy* (1 *pud* = 36 pounds) of deer meat rather than head of black-tailed deer. But because a fat animal weighed 75 pounds ([Khlebnikov], *Colonial Russian America*, p. 99), and an average animal probably about 60 pounds, 60% (or 36 pounds) of which was likely edible, one *pud* of deer meat has been equated with one black-tailed deer.

year, but as early as 1824 the Tlingits were furnishing the settlement with a "sufficient number" of black-tailed deer, ducks, and geese.[96] From 1844 they supplied a remarkable average of more than 500 "wild chamois" annually (table 2). During the 1850s the capital consumed an average of up to 400 black-tailed deer (and up to 1,000 wildfowl) yearly,[97] thanks to the Tlingits. The *iamanina* was vital as inexpensive fresh meat for the colonial capital's officials and invalids; indeed, it was the only fresh meat available during the winter.[98] The limited supply and the large demand for fresh meat, however, drove the price of venison so high that the Russian authorities had to fix the price at the Novo-Arkhangel'sk bazaar at 6 rubles per *pud* (36 pounds) and to prohibit private transactions. This only led to illicit private trading of Russian liquor for Tlingit meat in the 1850s.[99]

Fishing was even more important than hunting as a source of food for the Russians. Owing to the difficulties of colonial agriculture and the irregularity of importation, as well as the "superfluity" of fish in colonial waters, the diet of the Russians and natives alike was dominated by fish. As Lieutenant Lazarov noted at Novo-Arkhangel'sk in 1821, "fish ... are to this place what bread is to Russia."[100] Even the opening of trade with California's missions in the late 1810s brought little relief. In 1824 Zavalishin found that there was barely enough beef and milk at Novo-Arkhangel'sk for the governor himself.[101] And in 1831 Governor von Wrangell reported that company employees at the capital were buying fish, wildfowl, and snails (or marine slugs) from the Tlingits at high prices for want of salted beef and cow's butter.[102]

Fish, supplemented by some flour and meat, remained the dietary staple. Officials and officers ate better than laborers, getting more and fresher food, as well as some luxuries like tea, wine, and sugar. For all, fish was the main source of protein and vitamin D. The most common food fish were salmon, halibut, herring, and cod, with halibut being preferred by the natives. Halibut and cod were abundant year round, although the former were caught mostly in winter; herring peaked in spring and salmon in summer. Shellfish, especially crabs, were also eaten. Most of the fish catch was salted, not dried, because of the dearth of sunshine. Captain Golovin found in 1818 on Kodiak Island that frequently 10,000 to 20,000 fish had to be discarded because they could not be cured in the "prolonged rains" (and probably also because there was a shortage of salt).[103] And at Sitka in the middle 1820s the "continuous dampness" impeded fish drying so much that more than half of the *iukola* (dried fish) was unfit for consumption.[104] Another problem had to do with fluctuations in the spring herring and summer salmon runs, which could range from "nil" through "moderate" to "very prolific." Nevertheless, fishing was much more productive than farming and from the late 1840s Novo-Arkhangel'sk was even able to export salted fish.

Natives did the fishing. On Unalaska Island the Aleut men fished all summer for the Russian American Company under the supervision of a Russian *promyshlennik*, and the women, girls, and *schopans* (homosexual boys) cleaned and dried the catch. On Kodiak Island the native men fished and whaled for the Russians in spring and summer; the catch was prepared by the women and children. Around 1800 more than half a million fish were dried annually on Kodiak Island.[105] The catch was smaller on Baranof Island, where Aleut employees did the company's fishing at Novo-Arkhangel'sk itself and nearby Ozërsk Redoubt. Most of the catch (including all of the herring and some of the salmon) was salted; from 1858 through 1862, for example, an annual average of 21,650 fresh and 90,350 salted fish (including 48,700 salted fish for export) were taken.[106] The company's catch of halibut, which was consumed fresh, was more modest, averaging 13,500 fish per winter from 1838–39 through 1847–48.[107] But even more halibut were purchased from the Tlingits (table 3), who again played a crucial role. Indeed, Tlingit provisions came to loom large in the capital's food supply, as Governor Mikhail Teben'kov (1845–50) reported in 1846:

> The harvest of vegetables and potatoes [at Sitka in 1845] was negligible because the gardens, which formerly extended along the entire shore towards the rocks, have been reduced by more than one-half by the construction of a bishop's house, a seminary, and a barracks for the married men. A major replenishment of potatoes was made by the Kolosh, from whom up to 1,060 barrels were bought. They brought them on request. . . . The Kolosh came to Sitka in October in about 250 boats. The industry, enterprise, and energy of this tribe warranted surprise; many of them were from the [Queen] Charlotte Islands! If we take into account all of the meanders of the straits that they travelled, their homes were probably no less than 300 miles from Sitka. In 1844 they supplied Sitka with 300 barrels [of potatoes], and it is likely that [my predecessor] Adolph Karlovich [Etholen] did not suspect that they would

expand this business when he said "Bring as many potatoes as you have, we shall buy all of them" and that they would bring 1,060 barrels. . . . During the winter [of 1845–46] 20,950 pounds of halibut were caught, and 11,700 pounds of deer meat were bought [from the Tlingits]. There was no herring catch at all in the spring; the herring passed us by, and only once were we able to fill over half of a six-oared seine boat. Fortunately, this shortage of fresh food at that time [spring] was not felt by us at all. Expecting the Kolosh in the spring [March], I intended to have a fair for them; about 1,500 of them gathered at Sitka. So as not to waste their time these active people veritably flooded our market with fresh provisions, so that this spring we feel no want of fresh food.[108]

The company's head office also acknowledged the contribution of the Tlingits, telling its stockholders in 1845 that "the Kolosh abundantly

Table 3   Russian American Company Purchases of Halibut from the Tlingits at Novo-Arkhangel'sk (Sitka), 1846–66

Year[a]	Pounds	Year[a]	Pounds
1846	56,986	1857	50,654
1847	43,299	1858	45,538
1848	27,482	1859	43,697
1849	76,812	1860	31,599
1850	74,032	1861	56,589
1851	138,096	1862	53,664
1852	125,745	1863	94,616
1853	107,075	1864	44,900
1854	91,342	1865	22,269
1855	34,223	1866	46,730
1856	83,493		

Sources: [Russian American Company, Head Office], Otchët Rossiisko-Amerikanskoi Kompanii Glavnago Pravleniia za odin god . . . (St. Petersburg: divers, 1843–65), 1860, p. 44; 1862, p. 28; 1863, p. 22; United States National Archives, File Microcopies of Records in the National Archives, no. 11, "Records of the Russian-American Company 1802–1867: Correspondence of Governors General," roll 52, p. 326v.; roll 54, p. 209v.; roll 55, p. 126; roll 56, p. 125; roll 57, p. 251v.; roll 58, p. 189; roll 59, p. 309; roll 60, p. 25; roll 61, pt. 1, pp. 85–85v., pt. 2, p. 50; roll 62, pt. 1, p. 63v, pt. 2, p. 71v.; roll 63, pt. 1, p. 76, pt. 2, p. 40; roll 64, pt. 1, p. 59v., pt. 2, p. 42, pt. 3, p. 15; roll 65, pt. 1, p. 57v., pt. 2, p. 33, pt. 3, p. 53v.
[a]These figures actually refer to the Russian American Company's accounting year of mid-May to mid-May rather than to the modern calendar year.

supply the Novo-Arkhangel'sk market with fresh provisions and firewood, giving the colonial authorities the means for rendering more
assistance to company employees and for making life in New Archangel
more economical."[109] And in 1860 Dmitrii Nedel'kovich, a young naval
officer in the company's service, recorded that:

> Every day from 8 in the morning until 4 in the afternoon they [the
> Tlingits] come to the bazaar to sell *iamany* (a combination of wild
> goats and deer), which replace meat here for want of livestock,
> and the Kolosh also bring fish, primarily halibut and various
> shellfish, wildfowl, other products, and berries. In this respect the
> Kolosh are essential to the Russians, since employees in the colony
> for want of free time cannot procure their own food; moreover,
> all of the Kolosh are excellent hunters and are used to the climate
> and the country.[110]

This dependency was confirmed that same year by Captain Golovin:
"Fearing the Kolosh, [the Russians of Novo-Arkhangel'sk] have long
contemplated driving them from the settlement, but they are afraid
that then there will be no fresh provisions because *the Russians do
not go into the woods to hunt, there are few gardens, and there are no
livestock except pigs. On the entire island there are five or six cows
and four horses.*"[111] Noting that the Tlingits supplied the capital with
more than 1,000 black-tailed deer annually, Golovin's colleague, State
Councillor Kostlivtsev, added that: "All of the inhabitants of Novo-
Arkhangel'sk, for the want of cattle there, are provisioned with the
fresh meat of deer and fresh fish by the Kolosh, and that is why every
time that the Kolosh quarrel among themselves or for some reason
are displeased with the Russians, the entire fort is left with old salted
meat and salted and dried fish."[112] Kostlivtsev concluded that:

> Although in the company's current charter, as well as in the one
> being re-drafted, these natives are considered to be completely
> dependent on the colonial authorities and to be residing in the
> colonial territory, I for my part would deem them more correctly
> to be completely independent. In no respect whatever can the
> Kolosh be considered dependent on the company; rather, it can
> be said that the company's very settlements on the American coast
> depend on them. The latter have only to make a noise, as is said
> here, and the port of Novo-Arkhangel'sk and its entire population

is deprived of all fresh food and even the opportunity of showing itself a few yards outside the palisade.[113]

This is not to say that the "Kolosh trade" did not fluctuate. It slumped especially during the 1850s as a result of renewed Tlingit unruliness. Because of "incorrect administration" on the part of the Russian authorities (apparently Governor Rosenberg), hostilities among the Tlingits, particularly between the Novo-Arkhangel'sk and Stikine groups, erupted in 1851 and 1852 and continued until 1859.[114] Consequently, the supply of black-tailed deer fell sharply in the first half of the decade (table 2), and Governor Aleksandr Rudakov (1853–54) complained in the spring of 1854 that traffic was "so poor that very often it is not possible to obtain any fresh provisions even for the sick," partly because the Indians were earning "a lot" (1 ruble daily) by cutting ice and firewood, a less onerous and more lucrative task than hunting or fishing.[115] In the fall of 1859 Governor Ivan Furguhelm (1859–63) even reported that the Tlingits were obtaining liquor from foreign ships "in such abundance that they not infrequently supply rum to our workers"—a complete reversal of the stereotype of shrewd white whiskey traders supplying firewater to gullible natives.[116] Generally, however, the Tlingits were a substantial and indispensable source of fresh food for the colonial capital during the period of the company's last charter (1842–61). Their role was especially important in view of the fact that during the 1850s provisions, after salaries, were the chief item of colonial expenditure by the company.[117]

Native gathering was a final and important source of food for the Russians, for berries and roots took the place of fresh fruits and vegetables. They at least served as anticorbutics. Kodiak Island abounded in bilberries (cowberries), cloudberries, crowberries, blueberries, and cranberries, which were generally large and juicy, if somewhat watery, as well as mushrooms and roots, particularly the Kamchatka or yellow lily, whose dried bulb was savored as *sarana*. The Kodiak women and children picked berries and dug and washed roots for the Russians in spring, summer, and fall; so did the Kenais and Chugaches. Bilberries and *sarana* were occasionally even shipped from Kodiak Island to Novo-Arkhangel'sk, although berries, at least, also proliferated on Baranof Island. Some berries, roots, and herbs were supplied by the Tlingits. The Tlingits even came to sell timber to the Russians. The under-manned Russians had difficulty meeting their own demand for wood, which rotted after ten years in the dank climate.[118]

Finally, the Russians were dependent upon the natives of the Russian-American colony—again primarily the Aleuts, Kodiaks, and Tlingits—for labor and sex. One of the main reasons the Russians relied so heavily upon the natives for so many goods and services was the shortage of Russians themselves. The legal bonds of serfdom immobilized most of the inhabitants of Russia,[119] and for those not tied to a landlord (or for those who simply fled) Siberia was a more attractive alternative than Russian America because it was less distant and more tamed. So few Russians went to "barbarous, desolate Sitka," as it was described by Governor Semën Ianovskii (1818–21); during his stay at the colonial capital in 1861 Captain Golovin found that "here it is just as if we were in a kind of wasteland where the voice of cultured people is rarely heard . . . if it were not for the isolation from the rest of the world and such a foul climate, it would be possible to live here . . . thank God that I do not."[120] Those who did reach the colony tended not to stay long (unless they had to stay in order to work off debts to the Russian American Company). Of 35 families of settlers sent to Alaska in 1784, only 4 individuals remained in 1818, whereas they should have multiplied to at least 175 souls by then (assuming that every family had stayed and had grown to 5 persons).[121] In 1838 Governor Ivan Kuprianov (1835–40) bemoaned the "utter shortage at present of workers in the colony."[122] The company was often simply unable to replace employees who died or quit. From 1838 through 1842, 101 laborers left Russian America for Russia proper, and 80 died in the colony, but only 67 recruits arrived from the motherland, for a net loss of 114.[123] In 1839 the colonial administration reported that the colony lost about 40 laborers annually, and the company's head office in St. Petersburg resolved to send 40 replacements every year; in fact, 70 were needed yearly, but instead 40 arrived in 1825, 81 in 1827, 50 in 1828, 30 in 1829, 33 in 1830, 40 in 1833, 55 in 1837, 31 in 1838, and 42 in 1839.[124] In 1846 Governor Teben'kov complained that "there is much work but no men."[125] In 1849, when the colony was short 100 men, he declared that "the shortage of laborers in the colony greatly influences everything and, incidentally, is very unfavorable."[126] In the spring of 1851 Governor Rosenberg reported that there were 426 adult male employees of the company at the colonial capital but that there should be 638.[127] From 1854 through 1858, 131 laborers (plus 202 soldiers) reached Russian America, but 176 departed for a net loss of 45.[128] And in early 1865 Governor Dmitrii Maksutov (1863–67)

bewailed the "extreme shortage of workers in the colony" and requested a reinforcement of 100 men, but instead their number was
allowed to decrease from 381 at that time to 299 in early 1867,[129]
leaving a shortfall of nearly 200 men.

Such labor deficits obviously weakened Russian occupancy, particularly in the face of Tlingit hostility and American rivalry. For example,
until the arrival of the Russian navy's 83-man *Loyal* and 74-man *Discovery* in the fall of 1820, Governor Murav'ev's force of some 200 Russians at Novo-Arkhangel'sk was insufficient to allow the sending of any
men outside the palisade to cut timber for a new fort (the old structure
being so dilapidated that it had begun to collapse), for this would have
left the post without enough defenders.[130]

Russian America's image was tarnished not only by its remoteness
and savagery. The foul climate, heavy work, low pay, and spare diet
further sullied the colony's reputation; hence a deacon's remark that
"it is better to go into the army than to go to [Russian] America."[131]
Moreover, these punitive conditions—plus negligence (there was no
doctor or infirmary at Novo-Arkhangel'sk, for instance, before 1820)—
debilitated the few Russians who did go there. Sickness and death
rates were high.[132] In the spring of 1819 Governor Ianovskii reported
that one out of every six men in the capital was sick on account of
the unhealthfulness of the climate and the scarcity of fresh food, and
in 1829 Governor Petr Chistiakov (1825–30) asserted that one-third of
the laborers in Novo-Arkhangel'sk were usually incapacitated by illness.[133] Captain Edward Belcher put in to the colonial capital in the
fall of 1837 and found that "the total number [population] is about
eight hundred, but of these many, if not the greater part, are invalids;
but few able-bodied men were visible."[134] The smallpox epidemic of
the last half of the 1830s especially reduced colonial manpower, native
in particular. But the most common afflictions, according to Alexander
Rowand, the Scottish physician who visited Novo-Arkhangel'sk in 1842,
were hemoptysis, typhus, pulmonary disorders, and venereal diseases.[135] During the 1850s a Russian doctor found that rheumatism
and catarrh predominated, owing to the changeable weather and the
excessive drinking.[136] It took Russian newcomers two years to become
"creolized," that is, acclimated to the colonial seat; in the meantime
they were "constantly" ailing.[137] No wonder that the number of deaths
not infrequently exceeded the number of births at the colonial capital
(table 4).

Table 4   Number of Births and Deaths at Novo-Arkhangel'sk (Sitka) for
Various Years between 1831 and 1846

Year[a]	Births	Deaths
1831	28	19
1832	29	26
1833	38	19
1834	29	33
1838	30	54
1839	32	34
1840	52	33
1842	39	37
1844	44	25
1845	47	51
1846	41	40

Source: United States National Archives, File Microcopies of Records in the National Archives, no. 11, "Records of the Russian-American Company 1802–1867: Correspondence of Governors General," roll 34, p. 204v.; roll 35, p. 87; roll 36, p. 215; roll 37, p. 196v.; roll 42, p. 306v.; roll 43, p. 221; roll 45, p. 275; roll 47, pp. 427–27v.; roll 50, p. 205; roll 51, p. 188v.; roll 52, p. 326v.
[a]These figures actually refer to the Russian American Company's accounting year of mid-May to mid-May rather than to the modern calendar year.

The disease-ridden labor force was further handicapped by drunkenness and incompetence, both of which were chronic problems in Russia proper. In 1805 Count Rezanov reported to the directors of the Russian American Company from the colonial capital that "most of the men who come here are depraved, drunk, violent and corrupted to such an extent that any society should consider it a great relief to get rid of them." He added that "they drink two or three bottles of vodka every day" in this "drunken republic," and "the depravity and wildness of the hunter threaten this country with ruin."[138] In 1815 the commandant of Okhotsk, where the company had an agency, complained that most of the company's laborers were drunkards and ruffians.[139] In 1842 Simpson rated Novo-Arkhangel'sk the most drunken and dirtiest place that he had ever visited.[140] His companion, Dr. Rowand, agreed, stating that the company's employees were a "drunken and dissolute set."[141] Little wonder that 150 of the company's laborers on Baranof Island in 1846 were considered "useless."[142] In 1860 Captain Golovin found that drunkenness, carousing, violence, idleness, and insubordination were "extremely common," especially among soldiers and laborers.[143] He added that "in general rum and vodka play an important role here . . . the creoles [halfbreeds] and common people are all generally given to drunkenness . . . all work here is valued in vodka."[144] Nedel'kovich concurred, declaring that "the creoles and Kolosh are extremely attached to intoxicating beverages."[145] Apparently healthy, sober, skilled men simply tended to spurn service in the company's territories. The head office admitted in 1818 that it was unable to hire "good men who know skills and trades, for . . . there are always very few such men, not even enough to replace those who are leaving, since good men and craftsmen can find work and make a living at home without seeking them in a distant land and without exposing themselves to dangerous seas and other risks."[146]

The problem still existed in 1860, when Captain Golovin concluded that the company could not be choosy in hiring lower and middle-ranking personnel because it paid a "relatively low salary" that "sensible and ethical" men could easily earn in Russia without having to go to such a "remote and largely quite unknown" region as Russian America, which they reached after going through "thick and thin" and where they "do not do their best."[147] Governor von Wrangell in 1832 decried the "downright shortage of healthy and competent men, especially sailors," and ex-governor Teben'kov admitted in 1852 that "a *good* worker not only will not go to the colony but a good man can get there only accidentally."[148] So desperate did the company become for Russian manpower that it even tried to use the so-called "colonial citizens"—retired and landed employees who married native women and were too ashamed, old, or sick to return to Russia. But they were too few (94 in 1860) and too feeble to be of much use. To Captain Golovin they were "immoral parasites, useless and burdensome."[149]

Not surprisingly, then, the Russian American Company hired many native workers. The use of Aleut and Kodiak hunters has already been detailed. Eventually even Tlingits were employed, mainly from the early 1840s, when the company was particularly desperate for recruits and the Tlingits were seeking new trading partners in the aftermath of the departure of American vessels from the Northwest Coast.[150] In 1842 for the first time the company hired some Tlingits at Novo-Arkhangel'sk (at one-half of the cost of Russian laborers, incidentally).[151] Every summer from 1842 through 1846 fifty Tlingits, and from

1847 twenty, were employed as sailors, woodcutters, stevedores, and fishermen.[152] According to Father Veniaminov, who ministered to the Tlingits in the 1840s, they were by nature "energetic and industrious," particularly the women, "who learned Russian very quickly."[153] By contrast, the Aleuts (whom the Tlingits regarded as cowards and slaves of the Russians) were characterized by Veniaminov as being lazy, gentle, peaceable, and patient. To him the Tlingits were the most capable of all of the natives of Russian America. In the 1850s a number of Kenais and Kodiaks were employed in, respectively, coal mining and ice cutting but they soon became exhausted or sick and were deemed "hopeless."[154]

Not only was there a want of Russians in general but also a lack of Russian women in particular. The colony had even less attraction for Russian females than males, and females were less mobile anyway, apart from the loyal and daring wives of some officials. For example, Russian males outnumbered females twenty-nine to one in 1819, fourteen to one in 1820, nine to one in 1833, and eight to one in 1836 and 1860.[155] So the Russian men turned to native women—mostly Aleuts and Kodiaks but also Pomos and eventually Tlingits—for sex.[156] The offspring of these liaisons were termed creoles, the counterparts of New France's métis and New Spain's mestizos and mulattos. Most creoles were illegitimate, their fathers not wanting to legalize the alliances because they already had wives in Russia proper. Considered to be "handsome and intelligent" by Lieutenant Zagoskin and generally capable, especially in mechanics, by Captain Golovin,[157] creoles were educated at company expense as prospective employees. In 1817 there were up to eighty creole pupils on Kodiak and at Novo-Arkhangel'sk.[158] And about the same time a dozen creoles were sent to St. Petersburg to be taught technical skills, especially navigation and shipbuilding; they learned quickly, but only two returned to the colony, the rest dying in Russia of consumption and melancholy.[159] Upon graduation most creoles became artisans or laborers for the company; under the company's second twenty-year monopoly charter (1821) creoles educated at the firm's expense became, in effect, temporary serfs, having to serve the company for ten years (with compensation).

As employees the creoles helped to offset the shortage of Russian manpower, particularly skilled manpower. But they were not without disadvantages. Captain Golovin found that they led a dissipated life, being inclined to debauchery, wildness, irresponsibility, and idleness;

drunkenness in particular was their undoing.[160] Also, by the age of thirty or thirty-five nearly all creoles suffered from chest ailments, especially tuberculosis, so that few of them reached old age.[161] Moreover, many shunned company service, preferring to live like their maternal relatives. Generally they were poor substitutes for Russians, Governor Teben'kov asserting in 1846 that one Russian was worth three creoles.[162] By 1818 there were already one-half as many creoles (280) in Russian America as there were Russians (450), and at the colonial capital there were just as many creoles (206) as Russians (204).[163] In 1832 152 of the company's 1,025 colonial employees, or 15 percent, were creoles.[164] Creoles outnumbered Russians 2 to 1 by 1843 and 3 to 1 by 1860.[165]

Clearly, then, the Russians became very dependent upon the coastal natives of Russian America for essential goods and services, just as they likewise became dependent upon American, British, and Hispanic rivals for such necessities as grain, beef, salt, and manufactures. This dependency, which reflected the cultural versatility and resilience and commercial acumen of the natives, as well as the small numbers and limited skills of the Russians, was both a serious economic drain and a major geopolitical weakness. Lieutenant Lazarev noted in the early 1820s that the "upkeep of this colony costs the Company very dearly."[166] It was to cost even more. Annual upkeep rose from between 150,000 and 175,000 rubles during the first half of the 1820s to between 250,000 and 300,000 rubles during the last half of the 1830s, thanks to the construction of new posts inland, the depletion of furbearers near old posts, the raising of the salaries of employees, and the expansion of various services (churches, schools, hospitals, charities).[167] Between 1824–25 and 1838–39, when the Russians were becoming increasingly reliant upon the natives for food and labor (and when furbearers were becoming increasingly scarce), colonial expenses rose 91 percent, from 337,000 to 645,000 rubles, while colonial revenues rose only 13 percent, from 1,189,000 to 1,341,000 rubles.[168]

The dependency made Russia's imperial position in the North Pacific tenuous, and it suggests that in the New World, at least, Russia's imperial system, traditionally continental in disposition, was simply no match for those of the maritime European colonial powers. The only reason Alaska remained in Russian hands as long as it did was the absence of any serious foreign competition for the land; there was such competition for the maritime resources, but the mainland was not a necessary adjunct to the acquisition of those resources. So the Russians were able to persevere, just as they had in Siberia in the face of minimal aboriginal resistance and virtually no foreign rivalry; being largely unopposed, Russia had been able to move eastward successfully with limited manpower. No other great powers really coveted the forbidding spaces of Siberia and Alaska. If they had, Russia probably would not have been able to acquire, let alone hold, the two territories, for her eastward drive was too undermanned and too overextended, especially in Russian America, where native support was consequently crucial.[169]

Relations with the Natives of Russian America

R. G. Liapunova

Documentary materials on the history of the Russians' discovery and assimilation of the Aleutian Islands and the North American Northwest provide extensive information on relations with the natives of Russian America—the Aleuts, Eskimos, and Indians. These relations posed one of the most difficult problems associated with the Russians' effort to absorb these new regions from the time of their discovery in the 1640s onward. The problem persisted throughout the existence of the Russian American Company and finally provided grounds for charging the company with incompetence in its governance of the territories prior to the sale of Alaska and the Aleutian Islands to the United States in 1867. Such circumstances, as well as the genuinely humanitarian interest in the fate of the natives on the part of progressive members of the intelligentsia (in this case certain sailors, explorers, various company officials, and others), gave rise to valuable publications and documents on the subject.

It should be stressed that the most damaging aspects of the Russian colonization of Alaska and the Aleutian Islands in the eighteenth and nineteenth centuries were the result of the reactionary system of feudal serfdom that prevailed in tsarist Russia. As is clear from the existing literature and will become evident from the following account, the natives of Russian America were cast into an extremely difficult position similar to that of the serfs of prereform Russia, to Russian traders of the Russian American Company, and to other cruelly exploited working peoples.

The problems associated with the natives of Russian America have been illuminated repeatedly by Soviet scholars. S. B. Okun thoroughly analyzed the position of the natives, together with that of the Russian traders working for the Russian American Company, on the basis of a large quantity of archival material.[1] But in his concentration on exposing the colonialist policies of tsarist Russia, Okun ignored all positive elements in the Russians' relations with the natives: the steps taken to eliminate the rapacious methods of the first Russian traders and trappers; efforts to limit the use of Aleut and Eskimo forced labor during the period of the company's existence; attempts to improve the natives' lives by improving material conditions and by introducing education and fostering literacy. V. F. Shirokoi in his work adopts a position similar to that of Okun.[2]

G. A. Agranat correctly points out the progressive nature of the Russian colonization of Alaska as a whole. He cites evidence that the process of Russian colonialization was ameliorated by attempts to encourage good relations with the natives; by efforts to draw together and even merge the arriving Russian population with the native communities; and by attempts to educate the aborigines and train some of them as artisans, explorers for the company ships, craftsmen, company officials, and clergymen.[3] In examining the history of Russian America in terms of the array of internal problems, government policies, and international relations, N. N. Bolkhovitinov also illuminates several positive aspects of relations with the natives.[4] Meanwhile, S. G. Fedorova has carried out a detailed study of issues involving the formulation of a Russian ethnic community and of social and ethnic problems in Russian America generally.[5] A volume by several Soviet specialists (U. P. Averkieva, L. A. Feinberg, R. G. Liapunova, G. I. Dzheniskevich, and others),[6] deals with the ethnography of the natives of Russian America. Also covered in this work is the question of cultural change among aborigines under Russian influence.

Yet the question of relations between Russians and the natives of Russian America has not been addressed specifically. In the present work we shall dwell primarily on the history of relations with the Aleuts and Kodiaks, basing our study on the Russian sources of that era, both literary and archival that are available to us. These two peoples, of course, were the first to be drawn into the sphere of the Russian communities and had the closest contact with the Russian populace.

As is generally known, the discovery, exploration, and initial economic exploitation of the entire Aleutian Island chain, the Alaskan peninsula, Kodiak and Afognak islands, the shores of Kenai (Cook) and Chugach (Prince William) bays, and the Northwest coastline to the south took place during the voyages of trading companies that sprang up spontaneously. During the eighteenth century there were upwards of one hundred such companies. By following the route established by the voyage of Bering and Chirikov, voyagers set forth in search of the new lands in the "Eastern Ocean," territories teeming with valuable furbearing animals, including sea beaver, sea bear, and fox.[7] The Bol'sheretsk and Okhotsk port offices assigned one or two cossacks to each departing ship with instructions to naturalize the natives and collect tribute from them and to forward information on the regions to the Russian authorities. The first reports on contacts with the natives of the newly discovered lands appeared in the "accounts," "reports," and "memos" that the voyagers sent back to the Kamchatka and Okhotsk port offices.[8]

These early private voyages were quite spontaneous, a manifestation of the continuing eastward migration of the Russian merchantry and traders following the discovery and conquest of Siberia. Yet the government did encourage the "animal trade," since it had already yielded the treasury significant assets from taxes.[9] At the same time the merchants and traders were expanding the borders of the Russian Empire and providing for the collection of tribute (similarly profitable to the treasury) from the inhabitants of the newly acquired regions. As early as the *ukaz* of *tsarevna* Anna Ioanovna, issued on September 20, 1733, to Pleshcheev, the governor of Siberia, the government committed itself to assisting the traders "as it is more advantageous and it brings a saving to the treasury, for the merchants and *promyshlenniki* themselves to explore remote Kamchatka and other regions; merchants and *promyshlenniki* have already discovered formerly unknown places."[10] During the reign of Catherine II, explorers and even *promyshlenniki* obtained loans, received compensation and medals, and were even elevated to the rank of nobility for discovering new lands. Merchants from towns across Russia founded trading companies in order, as official documents usually put it, "to search out unknown islands, bestow Russian citizenship upon the peoples living there, to found a trading industry for every variety of land and sea animal, and to establish pleasant and friendly trade with these peoples."[11] However, the traders themselves rarely traveled on the voyages, nor did their partners.

The expeditions were manned instead by free peasants who had signed on in various towns of Kamchatka and Siberia; by fugitive serfs, peasants on quitrent, or people who had been sent into penal servitude or deported; by déclassé sons of clergy and clerks (*raznochintsy*); by adventurers in search of their fates at the far corners of the earth; by outright vagrants; and by Kamchadals. Such a crew was commanded by a seaman and a director (*peredovshchik*) who was responsible for outfitting the craft, managing its finances, organizing its trade, and supervising the crew's behavior.

The contradictory nature of this era of private trading should be noted. No doubt, it was the hope of profit that provided the impetus for organizing such expeditions. Yet among the seamen, directors, and *promyshlenniki* many were honest and selfless, motivated by a genuine desire to discover unknown lands and thus glorify their fatherland. Such figures as M. Nevodchikov, A. Tolstykh, S. Cherepanov and many others are known today in Russian history as courageous and talented explorers. Their relations with the natives were similarly diverse and derived from complex motives—both antagonistic and friendly.

In the eyes of the Aleuts (who were themselves constantly carrying on internecine wars), the *promyshlenniki* who arrived on the islands were enemy invaders of their territory. Hence virtually every Russian landing party was met by armed Aleuts. The Aleuts had strictly demarcated their entire coastline into hunting grounds for specific groups. The *promyshlenniki* disrupted this system. Disembarking from their vessels, they divided into hunting groups and set up fur traps throughout the islands. They also had to provide for themselves from local resources that were often quite limited (fish, sea animals, or less). In other words, they invaded foreign lands and took foreign resources for themselves. But at the same time the Aleuts, particularly those inhabiting the western half of the island chain, were rather hospitable and maintained peaceful relations once the Russians presented them with gifts and demonstrations of friendship. Yet, the goods available to the *promyshlenniki* for gift-giving and trade were few, and friendship often ended in misunderstandings that led to conflicts, attacks, and plunder. The first contacts occurred in these conditions. The historical literature places great emphasis on the "*promyshlenniki*'s brutalities" but fails to consider the problem in all its complexity.

The Near Islands of the Aleutian chain were discovered during the 1745–46 voyage of the *Evdokim*, under seaman M. Nevodchikov and director Y. Chuprov. V. K. Berkh describes the first encounter with the islanders as follows: "He [Chuprov] met savages inhabiting this island in various places; he presented them with presents and received in return a mace, whose extremity bore a seal's head. Having given him this weapon, the savages began to ask for the gun he had in his hands [whose purpose the Aleuts did not yet know—author]. When Chuprov denied them the gun and headed for the rowboat, they followed him and seized the rope used to anchor the ship to shore. The unexpected brazenness of this move prompted Chuprov to fire."[12] Subsequently, relations between the *promyshlenniki* and the Aleuts improved until a confrontation occurred over women; it was then that the Russians "exterminated" the islanders. Upon their return to Okhotsk, the *promyshlenniki* were keelhauled after a cossack who had been on the voyage to collect tribute told the authorities of the crew's cruel treatment of the islanders.

During the 1758–63 voyage of the *Nikolai* under the command of the merchant Trapeznikov and the seaman L. Nasedkin a trader named Mukhachev was sent ashore and was attacked by Aleuts. "But when the Russians displayed their spears and guns and then threw them to the ground, the islanders' hostile attack ceased. They, too, lay down their arrows and some elders approached the *promyshlenniki* unarmed, while the latter gave them gifts of needles and wool."[13] But again, attempts to maintain friendly relations were unsuccessful.

During the 1758–63 voyage of the *Vladimir* commanded by the merchant S. Krasil'nikov and the seaman D. Pankov, the islanders, having at first encountered hostile *promyshlenniki*, "later took up with the *promyshlenniki* and helped them with their trapping harvest and other tasks."[14] Later, however, each side began killing the other.

On the voyage of the *Ioann Predtecha* (1758–63, under the merchant A. Chebaevskii and director R. Durnev) a "Cossack named Durnev was assigned to collect tribute on account of the fact that he had been to the islands, knew the Aleutian language and was liked by the Aleuts. The Bol'sheretsk Office thereupon issued him a document to be passed on to the *toen* [chief] of Attu Island, confirming the latter in that rank, making him a subject of Russia and asking of his parents' origin, a question the *toen* had asked Durnev during his previous stay on Attu Island."[15] During the voyage of the *Gavriil* from 1760 to 1762 under the merchant I. Bechevin and seaman G. Pushkarev, the traders' excesses in their treatment of the Aleuts were particularly numerous. Pushkarev "put ashore on the island of Attu and took Aleuts with him to point out the route to the outer Aleutian Islands. He took the Aleut Cherepanov from the Rubinskii vessel along as an interpreter." Subsequently Pushkarev set out in search of unknown islands and: "took with him from Atkhi and Amli Islands four Aleuts and two of their wives for help in fishing along with twenty-five women from neighboring islands to dig sarana for food and one young boy for training in the Russian language. Soon afterwards, the actions taken by the *promyshlenniki* altered their former relationship . . . in Protasov Bay [on the island of Umnak, in a village that has since been called Pogromnii] the *promyshlenniki* encountered resistance and practically had to run for their lives."[16] When the ship returned, forty *promyshlenniki* were condemned on the testimony of a certain Gorelin from the town of Suzdal and Popov from Totma. They were all sentenced to agricultural work in a Kamchatkan village.

During the voyage of the *Zakharii i Elizaveta* (1759–62, under the Volga merchants Fedor and Vasilii Kul'kov and seaman S. Cherepanov) the crew's arrival on the Near Islands met with a thoroughly peaceful reception by the Aleuts, as reported in the "account" of S. Cherepanov and the "news" of F. A. Kul'kov.[17] In his "account" Cherepanov writes: "These people are quite fond of, and have a taste for, provisions, as well as for any Russian clothing, a quantity of which was given to them as gifts from our company. We could not always give them provisions owing to a lack of a sufficient supply; whenever we began eating we would distribute [some food] to the Aleuts, never passing them over, which placed us in a special position of friendship."[18]

During the voyage of the *Prokopii i Ioann* (1760–63), the director, Shoshin, used armed force to extract beavers and fodder from the Aleuts. Shoshin wreaked such panic among the natives that when he approached, they carried the beavers, fish, and other prey to the shore and then hid.[19]

The Andreianov Islands were discovered and thoroughly explored during the voyage of the merchant-seaman Adreian Tolstykh on the *Andreian i Natalia* between 1760 and 1764. Tolstykh's reputation as a successful explorer can be attributed in part to the peaceful and friendly relations with the islanders that were always characteristic of his voyages. Tolstykh gave the Aleuts *lakhtaki* (seal hide used in the construction of canoes and kayaks), beaver nets, clothing, games and other curios, along with two canoes.

From their earliest voyages, the *promyshlenniki* attempted to draw in capable Aleut boys, to teach them Russian and reading, to baptize them and give them Russian names, to raise them as Russians, and even to take them away for a time to Kamchatka and Okhotsk to show them Russia itself. Some of these boys became capable interpreters.

The first such youth was a Temnak taken to Kamchatka by M. Nevodchikov from his voyage to the Near Islands. A boy named Khaliunasen was taken from Attu Island for training during the voyage of the *Petr* from 1750 to 1752. On the 1756–58 voyage of the *Petr i Pavel*, a young boy taken to Kamchatka and baptized later became a cossack known as Ivan Cherepanov. While the crew of the *Andreian i Natalia* was ashore on the Andreianov Islands, a fifteen-year-old Aleut orphan named Foma lived with the *promyshlenniki*, as did a twelve-year-old Aleut boy named Stefan who had devoted himself to the "defense" of the Russians, having fled from the Aleuts where he and his sister were being held prisoner. Both boys were taken to Kamchatka. As time went on, this practice spread. Through this process people trained in the Russian language and in the basics of the Christian faith and Russian cultural traditions began to appear in the Aleut communities. Many of these students of Russian later became Russia's designated chiefs, or *toens*.

The honor of discovering the Lise Islands belongs to the seaman S. Glotov, the director I. Solov'ev, and the tribute collector S. Ponomarev from the voyage of the *Iulian* (1758–62). This voyage of Glotov's (as opposed to the subsequent one) was characterized by peaceful relations with the Aleuts. As described in the "reports" of Glotov and Ponomarev, the islanders at first received them with armed hostility. But "observing no reply to their attack other than kindness, they approached the ship for a second time without any prejudice or aggression, and greeted [the Russians] in the normal manner, bearing dried meat and codfish for their consumption. In turn we, Ponomarev, Glotov and our companions, searched for gifts to give as best we could from such trifles as needles and cloth."[20] Glotov began christening Aleuts, including Ivan Glotov, the future chief *toen* of the Aleutian Islands, who was taken to Kamchatka and taught to read.

Overall, the larger and more belligerent group of eastern (Lise) Aleuts offered more active armed resistance to the Russian *promyshlenniki* than did the Aleuts of the western half of the island chain. On Glotov's 1762–66 voyage on the *Andreian i Natalia*, during which he discovered Kodiak Island, Glotov decided to spend the winter on Umnak Island due to the hostility of the Kodiak natives—Eskimos, Koniags, and Koniagmuts. Glotov found the Kodiak islanders already in a state of war with the *promyshlenniki*.

The Aleuts had killed the crews of three Russian vessels (four vessels according to some reports) and burned their ships. Later, Glotov participated in the "suppression" of the Aleuts, a process whose principal "hero" was I. Solov'ev, a man of exceptional cruelty who had exterminated entire Aleut villages. The conflicts between the Russian *promyshlenniki* and the Aleuts, including armed clashes and the destruction of Russian ships, are treated in detail in a number of publications.[21] The reflections of K. T. Khlebnikov, "the chronicler of Russian America," on this first page in the history of relations between the Russians and "Americans" are of particular interest:

Having pondered what has been written and said, I found the events connected with the occupation of the Aleutian Islands by trading peoples spurred by lust for profit and lacking any government assistance to be extraordinary. I was struck by [the *promyshlenniki*'s] unusual courage. How can one consider without wonder the courage of novices and amateurs who sailed unknown seas on poorly equipped vessels staffed by persons possessing no navigational skills? Striving for discoveries, they did not know the numbers, strengths or character of the peoples inhabiting the unknown islands. Cortez, a man who conquered a significant part of Mexico suddenly and by surprise, became famous as a courageous conqueror [but he] went ashore with experienced, well-armed soldiers who were outfitted by the government and were supplied with every necessity, hungering only for gold. In judging the progress of Nevodchikov, the first to occupy the Aleutian Islands in 1746, and later of Andreianovskii-Tolstov, it will become evident that their greatness, while not on a par with that of the Spanish conquistador, was not far behind in terms of the boundless territory conquered. Nor can it be denied . . . that Nevodchikov had only forty people, hastily selected in Kamchatka, unruly, half-starved men, who were unfamiliar with weapons and under no command system. Besides meeting primitive peoples who were virtually unknown to them and whom they were instructed to subjugate and naturalize, they had a still more urgent requirement when first coming ashore: to search for food for their crew. They had been unable to stockpile anything in Kamchatka, and they set off on their voyage with only a few bags of rye flour, dried fish and wild garlic. When the hungry men would put ashore on new islands, they would cross the tundra in search of edible roots; they would seek out edible marine life, whales, and other sea animals that had washed ashore. Such were the living conditions of our *promyshlenniki*, made worse by the thick fog, rains, and the cold. They merit more credit than the Spanish conquerors, who discovered one spectacular region after another, all of them yielding excellent produce.

The government assigned one or two Cossacks to the crews of the private trading companies to collect tribute from newly discovered peoples, but the crews' tasks had also to include subduing and naturalizing the natives and fending off their attacks. Hence, it is very likely that in occupying the islands, the Russians did not attract the natives to themselves but succeeded only in terrifying them. The natives, having no understanding of [colonial] dependence, were suddenly forced into servitude by their guests. The crude Cossacks who had been sent to collect tribute and were incapable of explaining to the islanders their new duties, were intractable, although peaceful, in their demands.

Either the trading ships brought no trade goods at all or they carried entirely insignificant items and used them to trade for valuable furs. Such an exchange, having no relation to the true value of items (a ratio of 1:100, for example) did not serve to elevate the new settlers in the eyes of the natives. In this history, we will encounter several incidents that gave rise to quarrels and conflicts. Yet they are hardly notable and are insignificant overall. Indeed, in the occupation of the Aleutian Islands and the northwest coast of America as a whole, we see no examples of the bitterness and predatoriness that history unfortunately associated with the Spanish conquerors in the New World.

Perhaps only on the Aleutian Islands and the coastline of the Russian continent do we observe the primitive inhabitants of America as they actually lived of old. This is the more so since no traces of [the primitive Americans exist] on the Antilles Islands or in the towns and villages of Spanish America. There only a mixture of interbred aborigines survives. If any aborigines themselves still remain, they are hiding in the inaccessible mountain highlands. This small observation reveals the characteristics of the conquerors. Gallant yet cruel Spaniards exterminated the idolatrous natives with a cross in their hands and God on their lips. Crude and powerful Russians bearing crosses on their chests made it a sin to kill off the natives unjustly. They beat them only when it was necessary in self-defense.[22]

Perhaps Khlebnikov was indeed right; that it was the nature of Russian colonization (when compared to other forms) that made it possible for the natives of Russian America to preserve their history and continue their ethnic development throughout this critical period, despite the continuous exploitation they had to bear under the new conditions. But without detracting from the role of the trading voyages in the discovery and exploration of the Aleutian Islands and the islands and coasts of North America, it should be noted that they also lay the foundation for this exploitation of the Aleuts, the Pacific Eskimos, and, to an extent, the Indians, a practice that continued throughout the period of the Russian American Company's existence.

Judging from much evidence, including that introduced here, the arriving *promyshlenniki* at first did the hunting by themselves. T. I. Shmalev, a Kamchatka worker, wrote of the *promyshlenniki* on the Aleutian Islands in the 1760s:

> Before the arrival of the *promyshlenniki* the locals hunted beavers with harpoons, but without using a bow—the arrows were hurled with a throwing stick. At fifteen *sazhens* these arrows could barely penetrate or wound a beaver. Hence, their take was very small. However, by following the Russian *promyshlenniki*'s practice of using a rifle and firing when the beaver climbed onto a rock, the yield was increased significantly. This is even more the case now, as threaded nets are used and placed near rocks, and when a beaver dives into its entrance it becomes caught in these nets and quickly dies.[23]

However, the hunting of beavers with nets and particularly with rifles soon frightened off the beavers, as it had also in Kamchatka. Consequently, the only successful method for obtaining valuable pelts that remained was the traditional Aleut harpoon hunting by sea. Moreover, increasingly hostile relations with the native population made the *promyshlenniki* wary of going out in small hunting groups. As time went on the *promyshlenniki* made a greater effort to exploit the remarkable methods used by the Aleuts (and later the Pacific Eskimos) in their traditional sea beaver hunting. This forced them to increase their efforts and to expand the sizes of their hunting parties by using Aleuts.

The methods used to get Aleut labor were openly coercive. In the journal of M. D. Levashev, a member of the governmental expedition of 1764–69 to verify information on the islands discovered by the *promyshlenniki* and to bring the newly discovered lands under Russian control, we find a description of such methods used by the *promyshlenniki* on the Lise Islands, where a great deal of energy was expended in the hunting of bountiful quantities of fox found there. Levashev writes that the ships that set out for these islands spent the winter at Commander (Bering) or Mednyi Island, where seal hides were stockpiled for use in canoe and kayak coverings and for boots, along with sea bear hides that were sewn into blankets, parkas, and boots. Putting ashore on the Aleutian Islands, the *promyshlenniki*

> made attempts to take the resident's children to Amanat, and if they were unsuccessful in doing it peacefully, then they used force . . . and they also gave these residents weapons they used to hunt fox, along with the noted sea bear and seal pelts that were called laftaki and were used to form a seal over kayaks; they also gave beads and regulus, goat skin, and small copper cauldrons; in such a manner they drove these natives into debt.

In return, the Aleuts

> during their time on this island tried to provide fish and roots; whatever animal they had caught along the coast or in the water was given to the *promyshlenniki* . . . these *promyshlenniki* had also tried to hunt these animals themselves, [but] it was dangerous for them to set out in small groups on such a hunt, since in a report sent the previous year [October 3, 1768] to the commander from the navigator Afanasii Ocheredin, fifteen people on his hunting vessels had been killed in various places, while in 1763 four ships were completely burned and people were killed on Alaska and Umnak and Unalaska Islands, and so it is impossible for these

promyshlenniki to increase their take through their own efforts without the help of these natives.[24]

When the stock was exhausted or lacking in one area, the *promyshlenniki* would set off together with the Aleuts or dispatch them to hunt alone on the other islands, as has been noted in the materials already cited. As time went on, the number of displaced Aleuts grew and the area widened, so that by the time of the voyage of the *Nikolai* from 1778 to 1785, Aleuts had already been taken to Kodiak Island.[25]

News of the "violence" and "crimes" perpetrated by the private trading companies found its way to the Okhotsk and Kamchatka offices, then to the Irkutsk governor, and finally to St. Petersburg. But it was only on June 15, 1787, that the Okhotsk commander, G. Kozlov-Ugrenin, took measures to suppress the *promyshlenniki* excesses and sent the islanders a "Document to the *Toens* and Peoples Inhabiting the North-East Ocean and Aleutian Islands that are Subjects of the Russian State." Kozlov-Ugrenin declared:

> Following my arrival in the Okhotsk and Kamchatkan regions, whose charge I have been entrusted with, your petitions reached me: (1) Via Sergeant Aleksei Builov, (2) From Izosim Poutov, a *Toen*'s son from Andreianovskii Island, and (3) From the Aleut Tukulan Aiugnana of Lise Island. From these petitions I have discovered to my heartfelt regret that inhumane acts have been perpetrated upon you by *promyshlenniki* on Russian vessels. The government had heretofore received no specific information on these acts, and had it known, of course, such illegal acts and brazenness would have ceased. As of now all your petitions have been forwarded by me to higher authorities, and I wish to assure you that everything will be [cleared up] to your satisfaction. Meanwhile I ask that you remain calm and not despair of the imperial grace of the Empress, who, of course, defends you from all, confident in your faithful unwavering loyalty. Display this document, which you are to keep, to all arriving Russian vessels; this stipulates that any resident native to his own island stay within his abode and not be taken against his will to other islands foreign to him.

Later the Aleuts did indeed show these documents when ships carrying *promyshlenniki* arrived. And on the document from which this copy was made there appeared these signatures: "read by Vice-Navigator

Gavrilo Pribylov, . . . read by Navigator Potap Zaikov, . . . read by Director Leontii Nagaev."

Concurrently, Kozlov-Ugrenin issued "A Document to the Leaders and Workers at Sea on Various Company Trading Ships" in which he announced that

> higher authorities are aware of all your violent practices with regard to the native islanders; henceforth all this shall cease, and [you shall] endeavor to follow the beliefs of Her Grace, who looks after the dissemination and preservation of the people of every nation. Do not count on getting away with what you have already done; you may be assured that both divine and monarchial laws shall place guidelines for rewarding good and for eliminating evil.[26]

In this regard K. T. Khlebnikov remarks that "the Aleuts had hardly obliged Ugrenin's attention, and he pointed out the severity of the laws and averted their final extermination with these measures."[27]

At this point a personal directive addressed to the Siberian military governor, Lt. Gen. I. V. Iakobi, entitled "On Prohibiting the *Promyshlen-niki* on the Eastern Ocean Islands From Perpetrating Cruelty and Robbery on the Natural Inhabitants" followed on August 13, 1787. It reads:

> Having seen your report to the Senate on the evidence against maritime *promyshlenniki* regarding various inhumane acts, savagery, and plunder purportedly committed against the islanders, we approve of your ordering an investigation and find it necessary to instruct you to (1) Direct Lt. Captain Billings [who by that time had already set off from Petersburg] to collect detailed, reliable information on said brutalities when he is on an island during his voyage; we instructed Captain Mulovskii to deliver this same directive when he set forth on his renowned expedition; (2) That at the conclusion of this investigation those guilty of such serious deeds and acts of plunder not escape the requisite punishment.[28]

Having set forth from St. Petersburg in 1785, the Northeast Geographical and Astronomical Expedition under the command of I. I. Billings and G. A. Sarychev received in the "Directive" from the admiralty such simple instructions as to avoid skirmishes with the islanders, establish friendly relations with them, and "lay a solid foundation for collecting tribute."[29] Supplemental instructions relating to the investigation of the *promyshlenniki* behavior were received in Irkutsk. In addition to pursuing scientific objectives, this expedition's purpose was to consolidate Russia's rights to those territories in the "Eastern Ocean" discovered by Russian explorers and *promyshlenniki*. Hence, issues involving the local populace received a great deal of attention from the expedition and found expression in the extensive efforts to collect tribute from the population, in the investigations of the *promyshlenniki*'s "atrocities," and, as is well known, in the collection of the most extensive and valuable ethnographic materials.

A committee was formed from among the expedition's members for the collection of tribute. This committee included Captain Kh. Bering, Staff Physician Robek, and Skipper [Captain] M. Sauer. The committee drafted extensive lists of the islands and settlements indicating which Aleuts had paid tribute and made copies of the receipts that had been issued to the Aleuts by previous tribute collectors. The expedition was outfitted with an enormous variety of items to be given as gifts of "kindness" to the Aleuts who were to be naturalized: "74 gold medallions; 292 silver medallions; 612 copper medallions; mirrors; knives; scissors; regulus; beads; ribbons; earrings; needles; pins; copper; brass and steel plates; sugar, tobacco; etc." Gold medallions (and medallion plates on Alexandrian paper) were given to the most influential Russian *toens* and to those that had distinguished service. The *toen* of Atkha Island, Sergei Pan'kov, was given a gold medallion, together with silver and copper medallions and a variety of gifts to be given to his subordinate *toens*. Also honored was the *toen* of Umnak Island, Ivan Glotov, of the village of Chalenakh (*Recheshnoe* in Russian), "since he had been with Captain Krenitsyn on his previous expedition on these islands and was later in Kamchatka where he was trained both to read and write Russian; apart from the others he should be given a gold medallion so he may more fully experience the generosity of the Empress."[30]

Regarding the investigation of "improper actions against the islanders," G. A. Sarychev writes in his report that the residents of the village of Illiuliuk on Unalaska island, about which Sergeant Builov wrote, affirmed their fair treatment and received assurances that the guilty would be punished. Sarychev attributed these abuses to the *promyshlenniki*: "As a result of either their own unbridled behavior or encounters with misfortune, they have become disillusioned and hence have concluded that they are compelled to depart for distant countries to seek fortune there in the face of great trials and danger. . . . These people," Sarychev wrote, "in poor, battered condition, many of whom have debased themselves by their vices, dare occasionally to engage in reprehensible excesses and self-indulgences on these distant and, apart from the islanders themselves, uninhabited islands."[31]

More substantive remarks on the *promyshlenniki* by expedition members can be found in the archives. In a letter to M. I. Antonovskii dated January 14, 1786, Sarychev writes from Iakutsk:

> I shall also inform you of local voyages launched by merchants from Okhotsk who call themselves *promyshlenniki*. They have no interest in trade; as soon as the first reach the Aleutian Islands they attempt to capture the local residents, take their wives and children from them, torment them, and send them [off to work in trading enterprises]. Every Aleut is compelled to bring a beaver or another animal to buy back his wife or son; otherwise, the children are taken away to the islands and are not released until they are ransomed.[32]

Billings's report from Okhotsk to the Admiralty, dated August 3, 1786, contained the following:

> According to the information I have received here, merchant ships that are putting out to sea for six or seven year periods have on board bread supplies of 10 *puds* per man and a few *puds* of tobacco, but no other goods that could be used for trading. They don't catch beavers themselves, but force the poor Aleuts [to do so]. Stated simply, they display all they have to the poor island inhabitants who are overjoyed that they can obtain one pack of tobacco for a certain quantity of beavers, food supplies, etc.[33]

During the process of collecting tribute from the populace on the Aleutian Islands, expedition members encountered *promyshlenniki* who were using Aleuts for their trading enterprises. The report of the Admiralty indicated that as a result of such practice:

> Not only does the treasury lose what belongs to it, but these Aleuts must endure the heavy yoke of serfdom, since the Company vessels, in order to draw Aleuts into their service, need do no more than: (1) ask permission of their *toens*, (2) guarantee a payment

for the entire period agreed to by both parties, (3) most important, the company . . . must without fail pay that tribute for him each year.[34]

In discussing the *promyshlenniki*'s exploitation of the Aleuts, the expedition's naturalist, K. G. Merk, also noted that the fruits of these same Aleuts' labor were used for payment, a practice subsequently employed by the Russian American Company as well. "In the Aleutian villages on Unalaska, Illiuliuk, Agamgik and Uchuiug," he writes:

> aside from women, I encountered only old, sickly men, and a few younger ones. The latter, however, were employed as rowers by the local Russian *promyshlenniki* on their kayaks made from sea lion hides. Some of the remaining able-bodied men have been taken by various *promyshlenniki* companies to uninhabited islands, often together with their wives, as the Aleuts maintained that they needed them. Others were sent to different islands to catch *chistiki*. The Russians would then distribute the parkas made from *chistiki* pelts as if they were their own property.[35]

The genuinely humane treatment of the Aleuts on the part of members of the Billings expedition, coupled with their efforts to help the Aleuts improve their lot, are evident. But the consequences are clearly apparent in a report by Aleksandr Baranov in 1791: "Apparently Billings promised the Aleuts a great deal; but the Aleuts grew corrupt, and in supplying food and necessities they would demand payment for their slightest effort; from the beginning I had to correct their prejudices. I didn't offend them in the slightest, yet brought about their obedience."[36]

It was characteristic of the voyages of the various trading company vessels to the islands and coastlines of the "Eastern Ocean" that no company stayed for long. As a result, they laid no solid foundations for the settlement of the region. Each company's goal was simply to obtain and export as many pelts as possible. Russian hunting parties would work in tandem and live on the islands and the coast of Northwest America for four to six years, housing themselves either alongside or a distance from the aboriginal settlements. Often they would live in the Aleuts' yurts, adopt their food, clothing, and kayaks, marry Aleut women, and generally assimilate to the Aleut way of life. Despite uncertain relations, the process of Russian cultural and educational penetration of the aboriginal community continued.

It should also be noted, however, that the bases for all future relations were established during this period and had only to be reinforced in the future. They included: (1) the exploitation of the locals' traditional methods in agriculture; (2) the exercising of influence and control via the institution of the *toens*, who were appointed from among those Aleuts who were already marginally Russified; (3) close contacts between the majority of *promyshlenniki* and the local populace. There were positive elements in these strategies: instances where young boys in the service of a *toen* were saved from sacrifice at his death as Aleut custom demanded; examples of mutual assistance; and close coexistence with the local populace unimpeded by racial prejudices and with regard for the traditional life and culture. Marriages, while not yet legal, laid the foundation for a creole populace and provided a blood link that unified the Russians and the Aleuts. The suppression, and later the elimination, of internecine warfare between various Aleut groups that had resulted from the Russians' arrival should also be noted. Such strife included wars between the Aleuts and Alegmutes (Eskimos of the Bristol Bay coast) and the particularly cruel wars between the Aleuts and Koniags (Eskimos of Kodiak Island and the coast of the Alaskan Peninsula in Shelikhov Bay) which resulted in the extermination of entire villages in some cases and in other cases the starvation of survivors who found themselves without providers following the siege.[37]

The second stage in the Russian advance in Northwest America dates from the activities of the enterprising Rylsk merchant and "Russian Columbus," G. I. Shelikhov. It was characterized by a fundamentally new approach, namely one aimed at establishing major settlements in the region for the first time.[38] In 1784, Shelikhov set off for Kodiak Island in command of an expedition of three ships built in Okhotsk (the *Three Saints, Simeon and Anna* and the *St. Michael*). His goal was to establish a permanent Russian settlement there and other settlements further along the northwest coast of North America. In the first year, residential structures, a fort, and fences were erected in Three Saints Harbor (named after Shelikhov's ship) on Kodiak Island. In 1786 a fort was built on Afognak Island as well. Shelikhov also founded a permanent Russian settlement on Unalaska in 1791 and in 1794 established the town of Slavorossiia at Cape St. Ilia.

A fundamentally new policy regarding the natives was announced, one that at first was actually observed. Shelikhov writes in his report that he "was warned of the belligerence of the Koniag people and of the reasons they were so successful in driving away all the visiting *promyshlenniki*."[39] Although only 130 men arrived with Shelikhov, he managed to establish a settlement on Kodiak Island. Shelikhov's principal consideration was to "impart peace to them [the Kodiaks] through gentleness, generosity, gifts and favors, and demonstrate that because of their savage killing of each other they lack true peace, as well as to show them a life they have not seen and thus . . . to avoid as much bloodshed as possible. . . . I showed that I wished to live with them in friendship, and not wage war. These and many examples of kindness and small gifts pacified them completely."[40] Shelikhov demonstrated to the Kodiaks the advantages of, among other things, using Russian iron tools, raising garden vegetables, and the need for literacy. He also immediately founded a school for children on Kodiak Island, where twenty-five Amanat boys learned reading and writing as well as trades. Shelikhov's own workers remained contentious, but he finally calmed them as well.[41]

In subsequent years, Shelikhov also managed to repeal the tribute laws for the natives of Russian America (which, admittedly, was a gesture made more in the interests of his company than in the interests of the aborigines). In his letters and reports to Irkutsk Governor General P. A. Soimonov, Shelikhov wrote of the danger the tribute posed for relations with the natives,[42] after which Soimonov testified before the government for its repeal. Soimonov's report, entitled "Trade and Trapping in the Eastern Ocean," was sent in 1787 to Count A. R. Voronets, head of the Commerce College, and reads: "The practice of collecting a tax tribute is an obstacle to close relations between the residents and the *promyshlenniki* . . . to say nothing of the abuses of the tribute collectors, whom the government cannot supervise or rebuke because of the distance involved. Hence the tax seems to be of no real advantage."[43] The Senate in a directive "On the Prohibition on Merchants' Collecting Tributes Not Set Forth by Government Order" dated September 12, 1788, stated that "above all it is requested by her Majesty to have information on what directive it was that imposed a tribute on the Aleutian Islands. If there was none, the merchants are forbidden from collecting tribute that had not been endorsed by the government."[44] And in a letter to Delarov, Shelikhov writes on August 3, 1789: "The Empress had deigned to forbid the collection of her tribute from all the islanders for last year, and you shall not collect tribute, lest you be subject to governmental fine."[45]

Evidence of Shelikhov's success in his endeavors is that in May 1785 he was able to organize an expedition in concert with a large number of Kodiaks: "In four canoes there were 52 Russian workers, 11 Lise Aleuts and 110 Koniags in other canoes, to the Chugach and Kenai Bays, from which 20 Amanats were returned to Kodiak Island in August."[46] In March of 1786, "to clarify further accounts" and to build a fort near the St. Ilia Cape, "5 Russians, one thousand Koniags from Kodiak and other islands and 70 Lise Aleuts set forth of their own free will, paid as workers."[47]

Leaving Kodiak Island for Russia, Shelikhov left his assistant, K. A. Samoilov, in charge. Shelikhov's instructions to Samoilov lay out a detailed plan of action, including references to the native populace. It contains, among other items, the following:

> [This is] so all the naturalized residents will not have need of food and clothing because of their inactivity or their neglect of the local produce; it shall not be like the poor life they led before our arrival because of inactivity or weak will. They will soon perceive the difference between their harmful free ways and the rule under which they now witness the building of homes and the establishment of order; their taste for a better life will bit by bit impart to them attention and ambition, and many will thereby become attracted to any type of work similar to the work of educated people.[48]

These and other orders of Shelikhov's cannot be taken as anything other than just, necessary, and humane with respect to the native populace. But unfortunately they were never enacted.

It is well known that G. I. Shelikhov and the Irkutsk Governor General I. V. Iakobi proposed a plan to create a powerful monopoly for colonizing Russian-discovered lands in Northwest America. Catherine II rejected it and Iakobi obtained approval only in 1798, with the ascension of Emperor Peter I to the throne. Shelikhov meanwhile had died in 1795.

The battle for a monopoly was also waged by the Shelikhov-Golikhov company on the islands and coastlines of North America. In this instance, the battle was waged not so much for control of the territories as for the opportunity to exploit the labor of the natives of these territories. These encounters occurred in particular on the Aleutians from 1792 to 1796 between representatives of the Golikhov-Shelikhov company and the Irkutsk merchant S. F. Kiselev. The Kiselev company evidently had control of a large contingent of Aleuts and defended them from the "workers" of the Golikhov-Shelikhov company. Aleut complaints housed in the Senate and synod archives testify to this.[49] The Kiselev company helped the Aleuts (and their defender and member of the Kodiak Ecclesiastical Mission, Archbishop Makarii) to leave the islands and travel to St. Petersburg to complain directly to the tsar on the activities of the workers of the Golikhov-Shelikhov company.

The first complaint, dated May 30, 1796, was written in the Aleutian Islands by the Aleut interpreter Nikolai Lukanin. It bore the seals (and signatures) of twenty-two *toens* of the Lise Islands and was sealed by his signature and that of the chief *toen*, Ivan Glotov. The next two complaints were from two Aleuts who had arrived in St. Petersburg (of the six who had left the islands). One complaint was from the Aleut Nikifor Svin'in and covered generally the same events that were covered in the first complaint dated July 10, 1798. A third complaint, dated May 30, 1798, from an Aleut interpreter and native of the Andreianov Islands, Nikolai Lukanin, tells of the *promyshlenniki*'s oppression of the Aleuts on the Andreianov Islands.

The Aleuts' complaints related that after the visit of the Billings-Sarychev expedition ships in 1791, the Aleuts "were at peace." However, in 1792, Russians from Shelikhov's company arrived under the direction of the *meshchanin* Ivan Kochvitin from Vologda and announced that they were the masters of the entire island chain. Arriving with them were the Aleut interpreters Aleksei Grigorii Shelikhov and Petr Filip'ev Mukhoplev who were presented as the chief *toens*. The chief *toen*, however, was generally considered to be Ivan Glotov, appointed by the Billings-Sarychev expedition. In 1794, sixty more people arrived from the Golikhov-Shelikhov company under the command of Danil' Shirokii.

The "calamities" that the natives endured from all these *promyshlenniki* included the following: from March to late autumn, Aleuts were sent off in beaver-hunting parties on the orders of the *toens* A. G. Shelikhov and P. F. Mukhoplev "against their will" to distant locations approximately 500 *versts* away, while their families remained behind and starved. When the Aleut hunters returned it was impossible for them to stockpile produce for the winter, since the migratory fish had already gone and they could not lay in a supply of bird hides for parkas. Women and children were forced at no pay to prepare roots for the *promyshlenniki* and to do other work for them. Women were forcibly taken as concubines. Even the furs that were to go to pay the government tribute were not given to the *toen* I. Glotov for sealing, but were taken for their own company. Only the intercession of Archbishop Makarii and persons from the Kiselev company saved the Aleuts from reprisals.[50]

The Aleuts were received by the tsar, but their hopes (and those of Kiselev) for measures against the Golikhov-Shelikhov company proved to be futile. Both Lukanin and Svin'in died in Irkutsk. Hopes for tsarist help were not realized, although the Aleuts were received "kindly" in the capital.

From 1790, the director of the Northeast Golikhov-Shelikhov Company (after 1799, the United American Company and the Russian American Company) was the Polish merchant A. A. Baranov, who served in this position for twenty-eight years. Baranov was the legendary first governor general of Russian America, whose efforts resulted in the creation of the colonies and the company's prosperity. But Baranov was in an extraordinarily difficult position with regard to a number of unpleasant circumstances: the severe shortage of Russian traders and reliable workers and a shortage of goods and produce (even to the degree that there was a constant threat of starvation in the colonies), which was aggravated by strained relations with the Aleuts and Eskimos and extremely hostile relations with the Indians of the Northwest Coast.

This is not the place to discuss reasons behind the colonies' complex economic situation.[51] But the result was that the burden of labor in the trapping industry and of supplying food for the colonies lay entirely on the shoulders of the Aleuts and the Eskimo-Koniagmuts (principally from Kodiak Island), whose position was essentially that of company serfs.

One of the circumstances behind the enslavement of the Aleuts and Eskimo-Koniags (outwardly the same and culturally similar to the Aleuts and who in company documents and the literature of the period were also called "Aleuts") was their extraordinary centuries-old art of otter hunting. If the hunting of polar fox, fox, and sea bear could be carried on by Russian *promyshlenniki*, the otter for the company was hunted exclusively by Aleuts and Koniags. Sea otter pelts were the principal and most valuable export up to the 1830s. In order to hunt otters at sea one needed a mastery at handling the small skin-covered kayaks for which the Aleuts and Koniags (whom I. Veniaminov first accurately called the "Sea Cossacks") were renowned. Veniaminov has written of the Aleuts' exceptional skill in hunting sea otters from kayaks.[52] By contrast, the complete inability of Russians, as well as other Europeans, to hunt at sea is corroborated by much evidence.

As V. N. Berkh has pointed out, it was the preserve of sea otters in areas to the east that had yet to be hunted intensively which prompted the movement of the *promyshlenniki* further toward the American continent. By 1760, sea otters had migrated from the Near Islands and Andreianov Islands to the Lise Islands and soon afterwards began to be encountered only in the Kenai and Chugach bays. Baranov began dispatching large Aleut and Koniag canoe hunting parties along the Northwest Coast of America. The first such party, commanded by E. Purtov, made it to Yakutat (Bering) Bay in 1794. A settlement was founded in Yakutat in 1796, and hunting parties reached out as far as the Khutsnovskii (Chatham) Strait. In July 1799 Baranov, on the *Olga*, put ashore on the island of Sitka and founded Fort St. Michael. In the summer of 1802, Tlingit Indians attacked the fort, destroying it and killing its inhabitants. Finally, in 1804, with assistance from the *Neva*, commanded by Iu. F. Lisianskii, Baronov again put ashore at Sitka, where on the site of an abandoned Indian settlement he founded another fort called Novo-Arkhangel'sk, which by 1808 had become the center of Russian America. Up to 1810, otters were being hunted in the bays of the Alexander Archipelago up to the Queen Charlotte Islands, with the hunting parties facing constant attacks by Tlingit Indians, who were supported and armed by American traders. Berkh writes: "In 1810, the honorable Baranov saw that the sea otter industry was shrinking annually, so he turned his attention to the shores of California, where he knew otters were plentiful."[53] And the Koniags and Aleuts hunted everywhere, often taking up arms, which helped in fending off attacks by hostile Tlingits. A large number of Koniags and Aleuts perished during this period.

During the period of Baranov's leadership, a large number of documents appeared which revealed the company's efforts to improve the position of the natives in some manner. Some of these documents were connected with the ecclesiastical mission that arrived on Kodiak Island in 1794 following Shelikhov and Golikhov's petition to the synod. The head of this mission was the Archimandrite Iosaf (Bolotov), and its members included the arch-monks Iuvenalii, Makarii, and Afanasii, the archdeacons Stepan and Nektarii, and the monks German and Iosaf.

The Aleuts' first exposure to Christianity began in the late 1750s. The first Russian *promyshlenniki* began baptizing the Aleuts, primarily for personal gain: baptized Aleuts were "devoted" to their godfathers and "gave their pelts to them exclusively."[54] It is widely known that Christianity played a crucial role in the tsarist policy toward the "foreigners" and was called upon to bring about more successful colonization and Russification of the native populace; it also served the goal of drawing the natives closer to the Russian population.

However, the activities of the ecclesiastical mission on Kodiak Island at the turn of the century and the early 1800s brought about a confrontation with the leadership of the colonies of this period, which included Baranov and his assistants. In short, relations with the church did not progress at all along the lines the company leadership would have liked.

During this period Baranov lived in the face of a constant threat of native rebellions, conspiracies against the natives organized by Russian *promyshlenniki*, Indian attacks on trapping parties and Russian settlements along the coast of northwest America, and piracy by foreign vessels there. The activities of the clergy, who were to draw the natives into the church's fold "kindly, peacefully and gently," ran counter to the methods the company employed to get the Eskimos' and Aleuts' forced labor.

Following the recall of Archimandrite Iosaf to Irkutsk for elevation to the episcopate and after reports of the loss of the ship returning him and his retinue along the coast of Northwest America, relations between Baranov and the remaining four clergymen turned into open warfare.

In a letter dated July 31, 1802, to the synod the mission members informed the synod of their difficult position:

Each of us has endeavored to the best of our ability to teach the peoples here; this required of us complete gentleness in our relations with the people. However, the Polish merchant Alexander Baranov, the Director of the Company, has burdened all the people, both male and female, with immeasurable difficulties by assigning Company labors to them; moreover, because of his jealousy of the peoples' love for us, he considers [our activities] to be detrimental to his significant power and authority over us, and he has allowed

a primitive anger to be vented upon us and ordered everyone to
run away from us.

When the monks attempted to have the natives take an oath of allegiance
to the tsarist manifesto of 1796, Baranov threatened to have the monks
shackled and their homes boarded up, to have any *toens* who showed
up to take the oath seized and thrown into a dungeon, and to use
armed force to chase away those Kodiaks who had already arrived.
"At various times, serious threats were voiced, and we were not capable
of redressing them in our church services ... services and baptisms
ceased completely ... we are always at great distances from Baranov
and the *promyshlenniki* and in mortal danger ..." the missionaries
wrote. The synod, "having heard the report ... orders for a note be
presented ... to the Oberprocurator ... Prince Golitsyn, to call this
case to the attention of the Empress."[55]

In 1804, Archmonk Gedeon arrived on Kodiak Island on the *Neva* to
conduct an investigation of the activities of the ecclesiastical mission.
Gedeon made attempts to reconcile the local leadership and clergy in
accordance with the instructions of N. P. Rezanov and to subordinate
the activities of the church to the interests of the company. Although
Gedeon did indeed try to do this, his letters to Metropolitan Amvrosii
revealed anger and indignation at the treatment of the aborigines at
the hands of the company leadership. Gedeon was also the author of
an essay describing the conditions of bondage which the company
imposed on the islanders. Above all, he enumerates the responsibilities
of the *kaiuri*, slaves whom the company had taken from among the
natives and claimed as its property. The *kaiuri* fished with nets and
by other means; they trapped fox and delivered firewood, timber, and
produce to the harbor; and they were used to prepare salt, make bricks,
and gather pitch. As reward they received food and occasionally
clothing from the company. Later, Gedeon states that the remaining
natives were used by the company for organizing hunting parties for
sea otters and birds. According to Gedeon, the take, i.e., the trapped
animals and birds, the berries and saranas gathered, and the parkas
hand sewn by the women, were all quitrent. Gedeon describes the
colonial system as allowing the company to "compensate" the Aleuts
for their work with the fruits of their own labor: the bird parkas sewn
by their wives and the produce they themselves had gathered.

As Gedeon wrote in one of his letters to Metropolitan Amvrosii, "the success of the ecclesiastical mission does not meet expectations, since our fellow countrymen who are serving in the Company in large part display corrupted morals themselves . . . , while the Americans are aggravated by endless labors."[56]

Gedeon founded a school on Kodiak Island for aborigines, who since the time of Shelikhov had fallen into idleness. He also founded an agricultural school, even though before his arrival, gardening and cattle raising had been developed successfully on the initiative of the missionaries.[57]

A highly educated man (previously he had been a seminary instructor), Gedeon devoted himself to studying the native language, and he translated into the Kodiak (Eskimo) language the Lord's Prayer, which in his time was sung in churches and studied in schools. During his tenure on Kodiak Island (until June 1807) Gedeon prepared several young creole students from the academy for instruction at the hands of the archdeacon Nektarii, while he directed the work in assembling a dictionary and a grammar of the Kodiak language. However, after his departure, all these useful initiatives gradually died.

Even more indignant than the clergy in their reactions to the existing relations between the company and the natives in the territories under company control were the naval officers visiting the colonies. The first officers to enter company service in 1802, Lieutenants N. A. Khvostov and G. I. Davydov, gathered detailed evidence of the severe repression of the islanders and tried to bring this to light by publishing a report, written by Davydov, in the *Dual Voyage*.

The Koniags suffered more than the others since they were assigned the task of supplying not only the Russians on Kodiak Island, but those in other locations as well. The most difficult of these duties was to set off in kayaks to the northwest coast of America and along the islands at distances of 1500 kilometers from Kodiak Island in search of sea otters; a large number perished from accidents during these expeditions which took place from April to August. The main hunting party consisted of approximately 500 canoes, and it proceeded along the northwest coast of North America to the Bobrovoi Inlet. The party was under the direction of a Russian *partovshchik* [group leader] with six or seven

Russian *promyshlenniki* as assistants. The other hunting parties were also under the direction of Russian *promyshlenniki*. The second party, named the Tugidakskai after an island off Kodiak Island, consisted of more than 200 kayaks, some of which then went on to Ukamok Island to trap sivodushkas for parkas. They supplied a group there with produce for an entire winter. The third party of forty canoes trapped sea otters in the estuary of the Kenai Bay. The fourth party, made up of fifty canoes, hunted otters along the shoreline of the Alaskan peninsula in Shelikhov Bay. In addition to Kodiaks, this party was made up of Koniags from the Alaskan peninsula and Eskimo-Alegmuts. Those who remained, approximately eighty in number, were decrepit Kodiakans who were sent in Company canoes [which, of course, the Kodiakans had built themselves] along the shores of the Alaskan peninsula in search of fowl. Later, the elderly Chugach and Kenai men would join with them. This hunting is also very dangerous, because it involved maneuvering among sharp rocks. Any person providing hides for seven parkas [thirty to forty hides went into each parka— R. L.] are given one parka; and may ask in its place five black foxes or eight so-called *sivodushka* and red fox.[58]

All those who remained behind, primarily women and children, were divided up to perform various tasks, among them catching and preparing fish, hunting for saranas and berries, stripping and sewing hides and products made from intestines, weaving animal threads and baskets made from grass, and preparing thread from nettle for weaving nets. Davydov also enumerates the duties of the Eskimo Kenai tribes of Alaska and the Chugach and Ugashinets.

As a result of their work for the company, the residents were unable to stockpile goods for the winter. As Davydov wrote: "If the Americans had suffered shortages of foodstuffs because of inactivity, they now have shortages for another reason." It is true that when the islanders were facing starvation, the company would help them with *iukol* (fish), "but it would be proper, according to the rules of honesty and wisdom, to employ moderation in using the labor of others, so that the durability of our profit will be linked to their prosperity. . . ." Such was Davydov's opinion.[59]

Iu. F. Lisianskii, one of the leaders of the first Russian circumnavigatory expedition, also voiced great alarm in his book on the fate of the islanders, who continued to decrease in number. Lisianskii enumerated the many tasks performed by the natives for the company that had already been described by Davydov. He also noted that: "the Kodiaks are extraordinarily obedient in carrying out Company orders and are pleased that the Company deigns to pay them for their labor." However, it should be "recognized," Lisianskii writes, "that such profitable trade for the Company may in time prove to be extraordinarily harmful to the natives."[60]

Lisianskii describes several meetings with the islanders, during which he attempts to explain to them the need to improve their lives by, among other things, introducing gardening, building better homes, and becoming accustomed to using perfected weapons. He proposed specific measures for maintaining the population and "these very profitable trapping industries":

(1) All articles (excluding valuables) necessary to clothe the natives which cost the Company virtually nothing, should be sold at a significantly lower price to the people, without whom the Company could not even exist

(2) Iron weapons should be introduced and should be used; without these weapons nothing can be accomplished without wasting a great deal of time

(3) Do not send (the natives) on extended canoe trips; rather, dispatch them in sailing ships to the fishing grounds and bring them back in these same ships

(4) Leave half of the young people at home, and do not use the elders for difficult tasks and those that they are not capable of doing because of their age, since their premature death often brings about the destruction of the entire family

Having presented these proposals, Lisianskii describes the present governor, Baranov, and his native assistants who, "having left behind their former customs, are condescending in their treatment of the Kodiak inhabitants."[61] I. F. Kruzenstern, commander of the *Neva* and director of the first Russian circumnavigatory expedition, also attacked in print the company's henchmen (the principal of whom he considered to be Baranov), for their treatment of the *promyshlenniki* and the local populace. Kruzenstern himself, as is well known, was never in Russian America. But in 1805, while in Petropavlovsk, he saw the

Maria, a company ship, witnessed the dreadful condition of the *promyshlenniki* aboard, heard several eyewitness accounts of the practices in the colonies as they applied to both the Russian *promyshlenniki* and the natives, and also heard accounts from Lieutenants Khvostov and Davydov, who were in Petropavlovsk at the time. He wrote:

> Lieutenant Davydov, during the time he spent on the Aleutian Islands, on Kodiak Island and the northwest coast of America, gathered crucial information on the Company's property there. He sent me a note from these locations reporting on the relations between the Islanders and their subjugators. Mr. Davydov intends to publish these remarks upon his arrival in St. Petersburg, and so a curious, valuable book will reveal the treatment the poor Islanders receive at the hands of the Company henchmen, which will engender compassion in everyone. Here I intend to outline the fate of seventy men who were employed as sailors on the sloop *Maria* in order to demonstrate their indifferent careless abandon even in dealing with the lives of their countrymen.[62]

Obviously, other officers on the *Nadezhda* were also indignant at what they had seen and heard about the practices in the colonies. Among them was a senior officer named M. I. Ratmanov. Documents held in the Commerce College file of the Central State Historical Archives, undoubtedly resulting from Ratmanov's interest, include a report "On the American Trapping Industry and the Life of the American Peoples that Rely on the Russian American Company."[63] This file contains a letter dated November 8, 1806, from Capt. 2nd Class M. I. Ratmanov to Count N. P. Rumiantsev, wherein Ratmanov requests that the information he has gathered during his stay on the Kamchatkan coast relating to the lot of the American peoples be given to the emperor. The Americans and the islanders, he reports:

> suffer at the hands of the local producers of the Company's goods and trades, in complete violation of the act agreed upon by the partners, where, in the second paragraph of the first article, they are solemnly bound: "to work towards increasing the number of settlers in the regions already inhabited by Russians and to settle regions that are still uninhabited, to maintain permanent, friendly relations with the Americans and Islanders, and to preserve this by introducing and expanding trade with them, which is to be

universally based on honor, truth, philanthropy and conscience and conform to the interests of the State and society."

A manuscript is attached to the letter detailing the exhausting labor the "Americans" are forced to perform and its consequences.

Also in the file is a letter addressed to Rumiantsev from Collegiate Assessor D. Sobolevskii, a stockholder in the company, in which he reports that after receiving information on the practices in the colonies, he contacted the company directors but was not permitted by them to initiate a revision of the company charter. To avoid allowing the state of affairs to meet a pernicious end, he brought his report directly to Rumiantsev. Two manuscripts are attached to Sobolevskii's letter: (1) A virtual reproduction of Ratmanov's manuscript above, and (2) "A description of buildings and artels."

The same file also contains a rough draft of a letter by Rumiantsev to Iu. F. Lisianskii, in which he requests that "as an eyewitness to the local conditions, please examine these two descriptions and kindly give me your comments on whether they are just, so that I may inform the Emperor of them as well."

And, finally, there is a signed letter from Lisianskii to Rumiantsev, dated December 20, 1806, containing a comment on Ratmanov and Sobolevskii's writings. Lisianskii correctly points out that they "came to conclusions based on a single original source," and that this source was an opinion on the severe labor bondage, scant compensation, and even the barbarism in the treatment of the natives. "However, he engages in exaggeration by dwelling only on the latter, on the rare cases . . . of the intemperance of a base individual," and he adds: "On the other hand, the present Governor is trying to do everything possible in his power to improve the position of the Russians under his control." Lisianskii notes that the starvation cannot be blamed entirely on the company, that in pre-trading days the natives went hungry, and that many pages of the manuscript are filled with a description of "the progress of affairs that must exist everywhere." In conclusion, Lisianskii writes:

I dare to conclude this work with the notation that the American Company needs to adopt measures immediately to insure that the population under its jurisdiction not only does not decrease, but that it expands, for a decrease in population will mark the demise of the entire sea animal trapping industry, since not a single Russian is capable of doing it himself; such a loss, I believe, under current circumstances, will be virtually unavoidable in twenty years, in view of the fact that since Kodiak Island was conquered by Shelikhov, no more than half the people still reside on the island; all of this in light of the fact that the distant hunting parties or industries, arose only a short while ago.

Further on, Lisianskii sets forth measures he considers essential for the colonies, the major elements of which are presented in his work.

Information from seamen and others visiting Russian America on the methods of rule employed in the colonies became public and thus came to the attention of higher government organs. Additionally, in Novo-Arkhangel'sk in 1809, a typical uprising of Russian *promyshlenniki* took place, resulting from the extraordinarily cruel leadership and the extremely difficult living conditions. During this uprising, a *promyshlenniki* conspiracy against Baranov and his assistants was uncovered. A local investigation was conducted at once; the accused were subsequently taken to Okhotsk and the case further pursued through the judicial organs. As a result of the prolonged judicial investigation the grounds for indignation became evident: hunger, thoroughly exhausting physical labor, cruel treatment, fleecing, and overall atrocious abuses perpetrated against the working people by the colonial administration. Eight years later the case reached the Senate, where, based on the reports of Pestel, the governor general of Siberia, it was decided "to establish a conclusion on Governor Baranov's cruel treatment of the American islanders." But the Senate "found no proof." It was decided that an official would be dispatched there to conduct an investigation. In August 1821 the Senate issued a decision "on the dismissal of the case of A. A. Baranov's abuses in the Russia's American Colonies in view of his death."[64]

Owing to the difficulty in communicating with the other colonial divisions, the Athinsk district (the Andreianovskii, Blizhnie, and Komandorskie islands) was under the direct control of the Okhotsk Office of the Russian American Company until 1823. It was governed by representatives elected from among *promyshlenniki* approved by the governing board. The Aleuts visiting Okhotsk on company ships were primarily from this region, and many arrived with complaints about *promyshlenniki* excesses directed at the Okhotsk port director. As a result, on August 14, 1814, the director issued the chief Aleut *toen* a "pronouncement" to protect the Aleuts from oppression:

I hereby instruct that all who engage in trapping in the Aleutian Islands be informed through this pronouncement that information has come to my attention via Aleuts of various islands under the control of the Russian monarchy regarding their enslavement, oppression and injustices at the hands of commanders from ships of the Russian American Company and *promyshlenniki* who came to these islands on ships to trap animals; these *promyshlenniki* used force in demanding various forms of property from the Aleuts, compelled them to work without any form of compensation, took their wives and children away, packed them together in living quarters and swore and ordered them about as though they were slaves. In order to put an end to such violent, insolent acts, by this pronouncement I am informing all who have occasion to appear on the Aleutian Islands that the Aleuts of all the islands under the control of the Russian monarchy and under the direct protection of the Emperor of All the Russias retain the right to enjoy their freedom and property on a par with all who are loyal subjects of the Russian State. So if henceforth someone . . . should perform an injustice against an Aleut, he will be prosecuted according to the laws and severely punished when caught. This will serve to stop forbidden acts against the peace-loving Aleut people inhabiting the outer reaches of the Russian Empire.

Reports on Aleut complaints were forwarded from the Okhotsk authorities to Pestel, the Siberian governor general, and from Pestel to the Ministry of Internal Affairs, which at that time supervised the company's operations. In June 1819 a directive was issued by the minister of internal affairs to the governing board of the company on the need to adopt measures aimed at eliminating "oppression" and "various injustices" perpetrated against *promyshlenniki* and Aleuts. Point two of this directive reads:

(1) The directorate of the Company is instructed that the measures taken to improve the treatment of the Aleuts shall be reflected not only in orders the Company issues to its directors, but in actual practice

(2) That the pronouncement issued to the Aleuts in 1814 by the Okhotsk authorities in response to the repeated complaints submitted to them by Aleuts with regard to various injustices perpetrated upon them by the *promyshlenniki* does not contradict the imperial privileges accorded the Russian American Company in articles 1, 2, 3, and 4, since these articles grant direct Company control over land only, not over the residents of this land

Thus:

All directors of the Company offices are strictly forbidden to abduct Aleuts and detain their wives under threat of prosecution under the laws. This is also applicable to the commanders on Company ships, as approved by the naval minister.[65]

V. M. Golovnin, director of the circumnavigatory expedition of 1817–19 on the *Kamchatka*, was issued a special order to investigate the situation of the colonial residents. Golovnin writes that Ratmanov's remarks provided the basis for sending him, Ratmanov, on the first *Diana* expedition of 1807 to conduct an unofficial local investigation of the company's affairs and present his conclusions personally. Ratmanov fulfilled the first half of the order, but his comments were never presented because "various changes took place." When the company ships sailed around the world for the first time in the history of Russian navigation "this was already more than enough to bring eternal fame to the Company, so Ratmanov found himself unable to speak out against it." When he was sent off on the second expedition on the *Kamchatka*, Golovnin was issued an official directive by the emperor. But it was 1861 before his writings appeared in print.[66]

In investigating the natives' situation on Kodiak Island, Golovnin concentrated primarily on the abuses that were already known from the writings of Kruzenstern and Lisianskii. He issued a request to the revered director of the Kodiak Ecclesiastical Mission, Father German, to verify the accuracy of Kruzenstern and Lisianskii's testimony, which Father German did in written form. In addition, Golovnin received several complaints directly from the Aleuts themselves. These complaints include the following:

(1) Work at any time and in any weather, and at places that are often attacked by American Indians

(2) Voyages to distant trapping outposts, and for periods of several years at a time, where personnel often perished at the hands of American Indians

(3) The elderly men and the women who remained at home were unable to stockpile provisions for themselves since they, too, were engaged in Company work

(4) Payment was made in goods that they themselves had produced, while the imported goods were extraordinarily expensive

(5) Complaints of persecutions and beatings. From year to year the Aleuts' numbers were declining and, as the population decreased, the work became more taxing for them

Complaints were also received from Aleuts of the Lise Islands who had been hired earlier by Shelikhov but had not yet been allowed to return home.

Golovnin demanded explanations from the director of the Kodiak office, G. G. Potorochin, who showed him the directives of the governing board in which there did indeed appear instructions not to overload the natives with work and to be kind when associating with them. There also appeared, however, strict instructions to produce a certain volume of produce, livestock feed, parkas, and so on. Other officers from the Kamchatka participated in this process and submitted their own reports.

Golovnin also received numerous complaints against the company when he was at Novo-Arkhangel'sk:

(1) From *toens* and from other Kodiaks who had been taken to Novo-Arkhangel'sk and for many years had been forcibly isolated from their homeland, wives and families

(2) That, in addition, the *toens* were isolated from their compatriots

(3) They were forcibly sent out to engage in hunting

(4) They were paid very little for their goods

(5) Even the women were overworked, and they were given neither food nor compensation, so that during the time they did not work for the Company they were forced to find food for themselves

(6) Many women lost their lives because of the difficult work, cramped living quarters and the lack of food and clothing, while others became ill

(7) The Kodiak *toen* Nakkan complained that they had been sent to hunt beaver on a French ship in 1817 in spite of the fact that they

protested this, since many Koniags on such hunts had already been killed by Indians, and this time virtually the entire hunting party of 24 men was killed. Baranov wanted to send out another party immediately, but the French sailors rebelled

(8) The Lise Aleuts complained that they were being held in Sitka (Novo-Arkhangel'sk) against their will

All of these complaints were confirmed by investigation.

Golovnin also wrote about the problem of the surrounding hostile Indian tribes of Novo-Arkhangel'sk, noting here the role of the American traders. Their generosity and honesty in trading attracted the Indians, and the latter convinced the Americans to supply them with firearms so they could protect themselves from the Russians, having promised in return that the entire trapping market would fall to the American merchants. "The energetic republicans did not fail to turn this favor to their advantage, and they began to sell the savages guns, gunpowder and lead at a high price; the savages quickly learned how to use the firearms and wreak havoc on the Russian *promyshlenniki*."[67] And, Golovnin writes, each year up to twenty American ships appeared within the boundaries of Russian territory in America, disrupting Russian trade. But what was even more evil was that "the overwhelming majority of *promyshlenniki* (and, of course, the Aleuts and Eskimos who were with them) perished at the hands of savage Americans, killed by gunpowder and bullets given to them by the educated Americans."[68]

Golovnin concluded from all this that Lt. Capt. L. A. Gagemeister, who assumed control of the settlements, "should take most energetic and serious measures to eradicate evil in the various aspects of the Company's activities, in spite of the Company's commitment to keep what had existed before, and make a special effort to eliminate oppression and persecution on the part of the *promyshlenniki* against the natives, and to improve their lives."[69]

In January 1818 L. A. Gagemeister (Hagemeister), commander of the *Kutuzov*, which had arrived in Russian America in November 1817, took over the position of governor general from the aged A. A. Baranov. From the time of Gagemeister's appointment through the abolition of the Russian American Company, only former naval officers were appointed as governors. Among them were such renowned scientists and explorers as F. P. Wrangell, A. K. Etholin, M. D. Teben'kov, and others. The complement of assistants and office directors was consequently eliminated.

Gagemeister's capable successors included the renowned conscientious and honest K. T. Khlebnikov, who left the colonies in 1832 only to serve at first as director of the office of the company's governing board in St. Petersburg, and from 1835 as one of its directors. During these years, the names of such scientists and explorers as I. Veniaminov, L. A. Zagoskin and others were associated with Russian America.

It may be assumed that the criticism aimed at company activities in the preceding years relative to their treatment of the natives did not disappear altogether. Government abuses in the colonies decreased without a doubt. However, the system for exploiting the natives that had been developed under Baranov continued to exist, inasmuch as it was the basis of the company's well-being. But there was a certain improvement in the position of the natives continuing down to the sale of Russian America. The roots of this system, as we have attempted to demonstrate, trace to Baranov and are the legacy of the period of private trading expeditions to America.

And, if nothing was said of the natives in the "rules" and "privileges" of the Russian American Company which were approved in 1799, the "rules" of 1821 contain a section entitled "On the Islanders" where the existing order is supplemented by several references to "humaneness." Along these lines, paragraph 51 of this section reads: "Islanders and others are to work for the Company by trapping marine animals. It is established that one half of all men between the ages of 18 and 50 may be called upon to serve the Company." In paragraph 52 it is stated that this is "to insure that as many selectees as possible are taken from families with more than one male, so that women and children will not be left without assistance or food." Paragraph 53 reads: "Islanders appointed to Company service shall be supplied with proper clothing, food and canoes by the Company, and above all they shall be paid a wage for the animals they catch amounting to no less than one-fifth that formerly received by Russians. The appointees need not remain in Company service for more than three years, after which they will be replaced by others." Paragraph 55 outlines woman and child labor: "If the Company finds it necessary to use women and available children under 18 for whatever tasks may need to be performed, this shall be permitted only by mutual consent and under a stipulated wage."[70]

The company's charter of 1844 repeats these rules in section 4: "The Settled Foreigners," which included "The inhabitants of the Kuril, Aleut and Kodiak Islands and the islands adjoining them, including the Alaskan peninsula, as well as the tribes living along the coast of America, such as the Kenai, Chugach, etc." Paragraph 267 specifies that "appointees shall not be isolated from their families for more than two years."[71] Also covered in the charter of 1844 are "foreigners who are not entirely dependent on colonial authority, but live within colonial territory" which included all the peoples that did not fit the category of "settled foreigners."

Ivan Veniaminov, the priest who served on Unalaska Island from 1824 to 1834, discusses the Aleuts of the Unalaska division of the 1820s and 1830s in his excellent monograph.[72] After serving ten years on Unalaska Island, Veniaminov was appointed archpriest at Novo-Arkhangel'sk, where he served from 1834 to 1838. All of these positive changes that came about in the lives of the Aleuts during the years of his service, particularly on Unalaska, to a significant degree were the result of his efforts. Veniaminov's activities are well known. He was more than a Christian priest. Having studied the oral Aleutian language, he created a written Aleutian language, translated an entire series of church and other texts, and compiled and published a grammar and a dictionary.[73] He taught the Aleuts Russian, and one-sixth of the Aleuts became literate under him. Being able at many professions, Veniaminov taught the Aleuts carpentry and joinery, shoe making, icon painting, and even watch making and imparted to them new cultural practices. The influence of Veniaminov's rich and brilliant personality was significant in Russian America overall.

Veniaminov wrote of the Aleuts of his time that they made up a single class, on the same footing as the Christian class, but were excused from any duties or taxes, in exchange for which they were bound to serve the company between the ages of eighteen and fifty "and, obviously, for Company wage." They were obligated to sell all their take in furs to the company exclusively for their taxes.

Veniaminov maintained that the Aleuts' present condition was a good one:

> For the Aleuts, aside from their service to the Company, enjoyed complete freedom; their service was temporary, and they were always paid. More and more the Company saw to it that the

director supervising the Unalaska division was a loyal man and a strict executor of order from the main colonial leadership. If the Aleuts' former freedom [which was, to be sure, more imagined than real] and their leadership [which was also imperfect] are not reinstated, then there is no need to alter the Aleuts' current administration, to which they have grown accustomed. Any change other than [return to their old] leadership will prove harmful and even fatal to them.[74]

The question of colonial administration greatly troubled Veniaminov. He spoke of it in a letter of August 16, 1829, from Unalaska to K. T. Khlebnikov in Novo-Arkhangel'sk:

> Wholly good intentions, the most useful institutions, and donations for this cause, will meet no success without an able administrator, or at least with administration that is insufficiently diligent. So the administrator is vitally important; if you fail to issue an order to your subordinate, or if it is not carried out properly, then all your intentions, institutions, resolutions, orders and efforts are in vain . . . what is needed is just administration. As the Aleuts (as I believe and am sure) could not exist without the Company . . . I am ready to act.[75]

For precisely this reason Veniaminov fought to have Khlebnikov installed as one of the company directors when he returned to St. Petersburg. Veniaminov wrote of this in a letter of August 13, 1831, from Unalaska to Khlebnikov in Novo-Arkhangel'sk:

> If when you return to Russia you could be the director of the governing board! . . . I don't dare speak of your enthusiasm for good deeds, of your capabilities and qualities of the heart and the soul, which are widely known to be excellent . . . I will only say that another man will not soon be found who would know as much about the local situations . . . so no one other than you could better know what is needed for improvement, what is not needed, what is insufficient, etc.[76]

In Khlebnikov's *Writings on the American Colonies of the Russian American Company* (which he occasionally referred to as the *Writings on America*), we find material on the positive changes in the residents' situation during the 1820s and 1830s. Of particular value is Khlebnikov's statistical material, which makes it possible to characterize the economic position of the aborigines during the years of his administration and the changes in their population.[77]

Unlike Veniaminov, Khlebnikov does not speak of sudden and significant changes in the natives' situation. In particular, he writes of the Kodiaks: "From 1818 they were afforded many privileges, were excused from Company labor and had their wages for their pelts increased significantly, but these privileges did not alter their situation. Idleness—a pernicious and rampant vice—must be eliminated through strict supervision."[78] It should be briefly noted here that the rebukes aimed at the aborigines for their "idleness" that are invoked in Russian America are actually evidence of their refusal of enforced, and to them nontraditional, forms of work.

In subsequent years the taxes on the payment the Aleuts and Kodiaks received for their pelts increased and their supply of foods improved, but there were no sudden changes in their fate: they remained in a semiservile state in relation to the Russian American Company: "the truly dependent" as they were appropriately referred to in company reports.

From the 1820s, Russian expeditions began to move into the islands of Alaska, areas that were entirely foreign to Europeans. After the coastal regions of Bristol Bay were explored during the expeditions of P. Korsakovskii and F. Kolmakov and following the establishment of the Alexandrovskii Redoubt at the mouth of the Nushagak River in 1820, Russians began to become acquainted with the residents of the Bering Sea coast and the Alaskan hinterlands. In 1832, a company trading post appeared where the Kuskokwim and Khulitnak rivers meet (the Khulitnaskii fort). In 1833, a Russian settlement was founded on St. Michael Island on the southern coast of Norton Bay, called the Mikhailovskii Redoubt. In 1845, the Kwikpak Ecclesiastical Mission was founded at an Eskimo settlement called Ikogmiut (along the lower Kwikpak River). The material gathered during the Russians' exploration of this region has great significance for the study of Russian relations with the populace of the Alaskan territory; the works of L. A. Zagoskin and F. P. Wrangell stand out in particular for their valuable information on the population.[79] The population of these territories is included in company documentation as "semi-dependents," and relations with it largely amounted to trade as well as attempts to introduce Russian influence through Christianity.

The "hostile Kolosh" who inhabited the Novo-Arkhangel'sk and the entire Northwest Coast of North America never submitted to the Russians and were a particular problem down to the sale of Russia's territories in America. True, a rapprochement with the Russians was progressing, albeit slowly; trade relations improved; Russian culture and the church gained influence; and some training in literacy occurred. Nonetheless, the Koloshes appeared in company documentation as "completely independent."

Data on the native population broken down according to tribes require special examination since the original information was partially exaggerated, and the subsequent data were not always divided among the separate peoples, but rather were more general in nature.[80]

Nonetheless, one conclusion seems warranted. At the time of its demise, the Russian American Company was subject within Russia to the accusation of having introduced slavery into its American possessions. It was vulnerable to this charge, but at the same time it had for long been under strict governmental orders to meliorate the condition of the native population, which it partially succeeded in doing. Under any circumstances, the true reasons for which the company was disbanded, as is well known, are completely unrelated to this issue.

PART FOUR
Cultural Life in Russian America

The Early Architecture and Settlements of Russian America

Anatole Senkevitch, Jr.

The colonial architecture of North America was an architecture of settlers who sought to adapt as best they could the familiar building traditions of the European mother countries to the unfamiliar circumstances of a new land.[1] The resulting architecture proved as diverse as the national traditions of the different peoples who settled the North American continent. Several colonial styles of architecture emerged. Of these, the best known are the relatively subdued English, Dutch, and German colonial styles of the Atlantic seaboard, the livelier French colonial style of the St. Lawrence and Mississippi valleys, and the exuberant Spanish colonial style of Florida and the American Southwest.

The least well known but no less significant of these colonial styles is that of Russian America, which evolved in the Russian colonial settlements along the southern coast of mainland Alaska, on the Aleutian Islands, and at temporary outposts in California and Hawaii. The Russian colonial style, stemming largely from Siberian adaptations of traditional Russian sources, extended chronologically from the establishment of the first permanent Russian settlements on the island of Unalaska in the mid-1770s to Russia's sale of Alaska to the United States in 1867. Aspects of that style have persisted in parts of Alaska and the Aleutians into the twentieth century, particularly in the design of Russian Orthodox churches. Thus, as with the other colonial styles of North America, the architecture of Russian America constitutes an important chapter in the architectural history both of America and of the mother country, Russia.

Russian settlement of the northwestern portion of the North American continent followed in the wake of Vitus Bering's voyage in 1741 to explore the still-uncharted "great land" to the east of Siberia. Successive expeditions by Siberian *promyshlenniki*, or fur hunters and traders to the Aleutian Islands, then to Kodiak Island, and finally to the southern shores of mainland Alaska led to the establishment of permanent Russian settlements in America. The building of these settlements, in turn, accounted for the gradual development of a distinctive colonial architectural tradition. This essay seeks to illuminate the early aspects and tendencies of that development from the early settlement at Illiuliuk through the enlightened colonizing efforts of Siberian fur entrepreneur Grigorii Shelikhov and those of his yeomanly successor, Aleksandr Baranov.

As had been the case with the other colonial styles of North America, the development of the Russian colonial variant had very crude beginnings. When the first wave of Russian *promyshlenniki* reached the shores of the Aleutian Islands, they had neither the time nor the means to build the substantial and picturesque log frame structures they had known in Russia or Siberia. In the early years they were compelled to put up flimsy temporary shelters in order to survive. The first more permanent structures were expedient adaptations of the native Aleut dwellings that dotted the landscape. As circumstances improved and the situation stabilized, there emerged a greater concern for erecting structures that would reflect as closely as possible the architectural traditions of the mother country.

Primitive Shelters of the First Russian Settlers

The Initial Temporary Forms of Habitation

The first Russian fur hunters in the North Pacific had no bases. Finding themselves on hilly islands often devoid of trees, they established temporary campsites along the shore, not far from where they had landed in their large open boats, or *baidaras*; these boats were made of sea animal skins stretched over a light framework of wooden strips fastened together by leather bindings.

The initial shelters built around these campsites proved very crude and expedient. In warmer weather the first Russian *promyshlenniki* often slept on the beach under their *baidaras* or in a tent, if they had sails or other suitable materials at hand for making one.[2] For greater protection from the sun and rain, these settlers transformed their *baidaras* and other available cargo material into a somewhat more substantial type of temporary shelter known as a *barabara*. Ivan Korovin, whose party of eighteen *promyshlenniki* landed on Umnak Island in April 1764 after a fierce battle with the Aleuts, described the makeshift nature of such a shelter. "After unloading the provisions from the vessel," Korovin wrote, "we made a *barabara* on the shore for our protection, placing the *baidara* along the ocean side and adding a few *lakhtaks* [sea animal skins] on that side, and placing *lakhtaks* on the opposite tundra side; around this we placed empty gun powder barrels and on top of them made a *barabara* out of the sails."[3] Such a shelter, of which no illustrations have yet been found, appears to have been roughly analogous to a crude yurt; the one devised by the Russians was fashioned out of a *baidara* turned over on its side to protect against sea breezes and covered by a makeshift tent to provide additional covered shelter around the boat.

Soon, however, the early Russian settlers endeavored to devise more permanent structures and places of habitation. At first, they simply occupied existing Aleut yurts and villages; before long, however, they built their own improved adaptations of these native dwelling prototypes. These efforts generally coincided with the Russian campaign begun in the 1770s to establish permanent bases of operation in Alaska's chain of islands.

The First Permanent Russian Settlement at Illiuliuk

The first permanent Russian settlement in northwestern America was founded on the northeast side of the island of Unalaska some time between 1772 and 1775 by the Russian seafarer Ivan Solov'ev.[4] Its beginnings had lain in virtual obscurity until recent times, thus bolstering the common assumption that the first permanent Russian settlements had been those founded by Grigorii Shelikhov on Kodiak Island in 1784–86, to be discussed below. However, publication in 1967 of the journals of Captain James Cook's third expedition from 1776 to 1780, which explored the Northwest Coast between Cape Fairweather and

Icy Cape, has confirmed that the settlement on Unalaska Island was already in existence by the time Cook's party landed there in October 1778.[5]

The settlement, known initially as Illiuliuk and Eguchshak and now known as the village of Unalaska, occupied a site overlooking Captain's (now Dutch) Harbor.[6] The first known Russian occupation of Illiuliuk occurred in 1768–69, when Captain Mikhail Levashev and his crew from the galiot *Sv. Pavel* (St. Paul) wintered there and erected a few temporary yurts.[7] Nothing is known of the settlement's appearance under Solov'ev's subsequent occupation some time in the early 1770s. The Russians who received Cook's party at Illiuliuk consisted of a group of *promyshlenniki* led by Gerasim G. Izmailov, who had arrived there in 1777. It may be that some form of linear development connects the structures built in the course of these three successive occupations, although no evidence has yet been found to illuminate the earlier phases of construction. The accounts contained in the several diaries published in the 1967 edition of Cook's journals do little more than describe the Russian settlement as it appeared to the respective members of Cook's party in the fall of 1778.

Thomas Edgar described the settlement as being laid out on a "low level spot about 2 or 3 miles in an Oval form" overlooking the west end of a harbor that was "well sheltered from wind and sea, being surrounded by high hills on all sides."[8] The settlement contained a large dwelling for the Russians measuring "about 70 to 75 feet long & about 20 to 24 feet broad & about 17 feet high in the middle." Built in an arched form, it was oriented east to west and had a door on the south side near the east end, with a fresh water river running nearby. In addition, the settlement also contained three large warehouses and another structure nearby under construction, as well as several dwellings for Aleut families. It also featured "two crosses opposite each other, painted white, about 10 or 12 feet high bearing east & west dis[t] from each other, about a quarter of a mile."[9]

The general layout, orientation, and building types of the Russian settlement described by Edgar and his companions on the Cook expedition bear a striking affinity with those employed in the Aleut settlements which these English visitors found nestled in the "deep sounds, bays, harbours & coves" of the island.[10] The Aleuts' maritime work dominated their choice of sites for a permanent settlement. A good landing, available fresh water, and suitable hunting and fishing grounds

Figure 1. View of Illiuliuk and Captain's Harbor in 1817 (from M. Louis Choris, *Voyage pittoresque autour du Monde* [Paris: Didot, 1822], pl. XI).

were prime prerequisites for locating a permanent place of habitation. That all these conditions appear to have been satisfied at Illiuliuk is indicated by Louis Choris's lithograph (fig. 1), which depicts the settlement as this Russian artist saw and rendered it in 1817.[11]

The prevalent Aleut dwelling type that the Russian settlers encountered at Illiuliuk and adapted for their own barrack was an oval structure that accommodated from four to six families, with about four persons per family. About twice as long as it was wide, the typical Aleut dwelling described by Cook and his associates was no more than fifty feet long and twenty feet wide[12] and was dug two feet into the ground. There being no timber on the islands, the structure used a framework of inclined driftwood poles stuck about four feet into the ground and lashed together to short cross pieces at the top to form a roughly oval roof. The framework was then covered with dried grass and a two-foot layer of excavated earth. A square opening in the middle of the roof served as the entrance to the dwelling, with a slanted post with steps notched out of it providing access to the floor level below. The roof opening admitted light into the interior and emitted the smoke from the fire within.[13]

In contrast to its rather squatty exterior, the Aleut oval dwelling proved rather spacious inside as a result of the added depth of two or so feet excavated within the structure. James King found that "there was tolerable Space left in the middle of the huts." This central space not only accommodated the landing area for the roof entrance overhead, but also served as "the common sewer of the different families that live round it."[14] The families had separate apartments "divided from one another by Mats & ... sunk a little lower than the middle space."[15] Cook noted that personal belongings were stored at the rear of each apartment. Each one was illuminated at night with a lamp that Samwell described as giving off "good light" and consisting of "hollow stone containing blubber & a little burnt straw heaped together at one end which serves as a wick."[16]

Not surprisingly, the appearance of these Aleut oval dwellings struck most European voyagers as bizarre. King noted that they looked "like a heap of dirt on a hillock very little higher than the common surface."[17] Georg Heinrich von Langsdorff, a German doctor and botanist attached to the Kruzenstern expedition of 1803–4, extended a more benign analogy in suggesting that such an aspect endowed Aleut villages with "the appearance of a European church-yard full of graves."[18] Cook's observations, far less flattering, asserted that the Aleut dwelling's "outward appearance is like a dung hill."[19] King ultimately dismissed most of them for being "meanly built & full of dirt & nastiness."[20]

Despite its primitive nature, the Aleut oval dwelling supplied the early Russian settlers at Illiuliuk and elsewhere on the island with a serviceable prototype that clearly was more permanent than the flimsy temporary shelters contrived by their predecessors. It was a structure that succeeded admirably in compensating for the dearth of timber on the island by exploiting the random supply of driftwood washed ashore. Yet, at the same time, as Captain Charles Clerke noted, the Aleut model was "somewhat improved upon" by the Russians at Illiuliuk.[21] Introducing rudimentary aspects of traditional Russian construction, these settlers raised the building to ground level and placed the entrance in the wall instead of on the roof. They covered the earth floor with boards instead of matting and glazed window openings with mica panes instead of oiled sea animal intestines.[22] In addition, they used a thatched roof of compacted layers of straw and dried grass, covered with netting to prevent wind damage, in place of the thick layer of excavated earth. The Russians also built mattress beds for the senior inhabitants to replace the mat bedding which the Aleuts placed directly on the floor; the lower ranks, however, still resorted to sleeping on the ground in traditional Aleut fashion.[23] The basic interior arrangement of the Aleut model was likewise modified somewhat. Separate apartments or sections, located along the perimeter, were concentrated at one end of the structure. The opposite end was divided off for a warehouse or pantry, recalling the basic arrangement of traditional Russian wooden barracks as well.

The Rise of a Colonial Russian Building Tradition

Illiuliuk, the first permanent Russian settlement in Alaska, became in time a major Russian-American fur trapping and fur trading center in the western Aleutians. However, a decade or so after Illiuliuk's founding, the center of Russia's campaign to establish permanent settlements in northwestern America shifted eastward to Kodiak Island and parts beyond. With that shift, moreover, the earlier Russian efforts to adapt Aleutian dwelling types and village patterns were gradually supplanted by attempts to establish settlements and erect structures whose essential aspects would approximate as closely as possible the traditional forms of the mother country.

These settlements were usually sited on promontories located at the heads of bays or at the mouths of rivers along the insular coast and mainland. Such locations reflected the exigencies of maritime hunting and native hostility. Although their close proximity to the sea was a feature that these later Russian habitations had in common with the pre-Russian Aleut villages, the use of promontories as a nucleus of fortified settlements proved an adaptation of established Russian planning practices.

The settlements of St. Paul Harbor (later Kodiak) on Kodiak Island and Novo-Arkhangel'sk (later Sitka) emerged as the successive centers of Russian America and so had the benefit of a somewhat more elaborate planning and architectural treatment. The majority of Russian settlements, however, were simple trading outposts. They contained the omnipresent Russian Orthodox church or chapel and an array of dwellings for the Russian *promyshlenniki* and storage buildings for their wares, as well as huts for the natives of the region who were the mainstays of the actual hunting enterprise.

In an illuminating account of his journey into the Alaskan interior from 1822 to 1844, Lavrentii A. Zagoskin described well the austere environment that marked most Russian settlements, ranging from villages to one-man posts. In the process, he also managed to seize upon those salient Russian aspects that distinguished these settlements during virtually all periods of their development. In assaying the organization and living conditions he encountered in these Russian-American settlements, Zagoskin noted that

> a Russian person is everywhere the same. No matter where he chooses to live, whether it be in the Arctic Circle or in the glorious valleys of California, he everywhere puts up his national log cabin, cook-house, and bath house, and provides himself with a house-keeper. However, the people who enter service in the colonies have not seen the world in style. Moreover, they are confined in semi-martial surroundings, and this is why the place where they live, enclosed by a heavy fence, is called a redoubt; the log cabin, a barrack, the batten window, a loop-hole; the detached cook-house, a mess; even the housekeeper has a different name.[24]

Precedents in Russian Wooden Architecture

The permanent settlements in Russian America were indeed built, as Zagoskin notes, almost entirely of wood. They thus perpetuated both a building tradition and a cultural metaphor that had long flourished in the mother country. Until the nineteenth century, not only most Russian churches, but also countless tiny villages scattered across the Russian countryside, as well as entire towns and cities had been constructed predominantly of wood. The picturesque image of wooden churches rising majestically over a cluster of log houses enclosed by a network of wooden walls and towers, which had been conveyed over centuries by native iconographers and foreign travellers alike, is emblematic of a "wooden Russia" whose abundant forests supplied material for farm and city, for house and church, and for street paving and eating utensils.[25]

The ancient town of Tsaritsyn on the Volga (later Stalingrad, now Volgagrad) captured in Adam Olearius's seventeenth-century view (fig. 2) epitomizes Russia's traditional wooden-built environment. Jacob von der Sandrart's seventeenth-century engraving of Tobolsk (fig. 3) indicates the transposition of this aspect eastward in the process of Siberia's colonization by Russia.[26] As numerous graphic representations of Russian American settlements illustrate, this same system of

Figure 2. View of Tsaritsyn in the mid-seventeenth century (from Adam Olearius, *Moskowitischen und Persischen Reise* [Berlin: Rutten und Loening, 1959]).

building in wood was brought over to northwestern America by the later waves of *promyshlenniki*. While an obvious common denominator links building developments in European Russia and Russian America, the more immediate source for the latter is to be found in the building traditions established in Siberia in general and eastern Siberia in particular.[27]

As in Russia proper, so in Siberia, wood was from the outset the fundamental building material. The wooden walls and bastions dating from 1683 which until modern times surrounded the city of Yakutsk reveal the early predilections for building in wood. This native preference had been duly recorded in the Siberian chronicle, which was accompanied by Semen Remezov's fanciful delineations of Russian wooden buildings in his naively rendered but descriptive plans of fortified Siberian settlements.[28] The chronicle likewise noted favorably the extreme speed with which log structures could be erected under the most adverse circumstances.

The Russian method of log construction, erecting a frame of logs laid horizontally on a rectangular or polygonal plan and secured at the corners through interlocking ends by either semicircular or angular cuts, had been perfected by the sixteenth century, if not earlier. Suc-

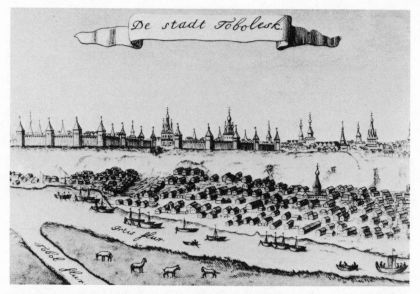

De stadt Tobolesk.

Figure 3. View of Tobolsk, ca. 1701 (by Jacob von Sandrart, from E. A. Ashchepkov, *Russkoe narodnoe zodchestvo v zapadnoi Sibiri* [Moscow: Izd-vo Akad. arkhit. SSSR, 1950], p. 15).

cessfully combining ingenious woodworking with the simplest structural techniques, this virtually prefabricated method of building permitted the development of expressive and elaborate building forms within the context of an underlying traditionalism.

The harsh Siberian environment gave rise to a more sober and severe mode of expression in architecture, as in other realms of Siberian culture. Just as Siberian folklore tends to be less vivid and fantastic than that of the Upper Volga region, Siberian costumes and embroidery less exuberant than those of the Russian south and northeast, so too the buildings erected by the Russian colonists in Siberia tended to be more austere than those found west of the Urals. This proved especially the case in eastern Siberia, where most of the fur trading settlements assumed a rather more utilitarian aspect and buildings evinced a more restrained manipulation of form and detail.

A number of villages and towns of log structures arose at various centers throughout this great fur empire. However, it was with the Pacific port towns of Okhotsk and Petropavlovsk, among the most unprepossessing of the eastern Siberian fur trade settlements, that the most direct links were established with Russian America. Founded in 1647 by a band of cossacks, Okhotsk had managed in the course of a century to grow from a minor outpost to a major seaport and trading center that attracted a large number of fur hunters and fur traders. Having pushed across Siberia in pursuit of sable, mink, and the otter, these *promyshlenniki* were lured to Okhotsk by the growing Chinese fur market and the anticipation of discovering new hunting and trapping grounds on outlying Pacific islands for the valuable fur seal and otter pelts.[29] By the end of the eighteenth century Okhotsk became a key staging area for commercial expansion to the east. Successive building programs had added scores of dwellings, administrative buildings, stores, warehouses, and several churches to its townscape. A plan of 1798 suggests that Okhotsk may, in the process, also have acquired a more regular layout, featuring a large citadel in the center and several streets aligned with structures extending westward.[30]

However, Martin Sauer, secretary of the Billings expedition to Siberia and northwestern America, conveyed a less than favorable impression of the Okhotsk that he encountered in 1788, a period coterminous with the founding of Shelikhov's settlements on Kodiak Island. The fortress looming so impressively in the plan of a decade later, noted above, was shown in the Sauer engraving (fig. 4) to be enclosed by little more than a meager gabion, or a series of loosely spaced vertical logs providing a primitive enclosure. To be sure, the church with its soaring belfry and other towered structures did serve characteristically to enliven the town's picturesque silhouette. Yet at the same time Sauer's account pointed to the town's basic unkemptness: "The city of Ochotsk [sic] is ... chiefly composed of sand, shingles, and driftwood, the whole town thrown up by the surf. ... The town occupies the space of about 1 verst [.66 miles] in length, contains 132 miserable wooden houses; a church and belfry; several rotten storehouses; and a double row of shops, badly stocked."[31] The image of Okhotsk conveyed by Sauer thus varies little from those of the early Russian American settlements conjured up by various eighteenth-century voyagers round the world. Sauer also complained, as Shelikhov himself was later to do, about the unwholesomeness of the prevalent fogs, mists, and chilling winds; the violent surf; and the shallowness and instability of the Okhotsk port harbor. Petropavlovsk, the other prime east Siberian reference point for settlements in Russian America, hardly conveyed a more auspicious picture.

Figure 4. View of Okhotsk in 1788 (from Martin Sauer, *An Account of a Geo-graphical and Astronomical Expedition to the Northern Parts of Russia* . . . [London: Cadell & Davies, 1802], facing p. 40).

Petropavlovsk was founded by Bering in 1740 on Avacha Bay along Kamchatka's eastern coast to provide a secondary port facility for his second expedition. Emerging as the second most important port on the Pacific after Okhotsk, it acquired numerous buildings and physical amenities. Judging by eyewitness accounts, however, its physical appearance and conditions during the time the first Russian settlements were being established in Alaska were, at best, unprepossessing (fig. 5). "Nothing is visible here," Captain Ivan Kruzenstern observed of Petropavlovsk in 1803, "that could at all persuade any one of its being inhabited by civilized people."[32]

Archibald Campbell, Scottish seaman and adventurer who docked at Petropavlovsk a bit later on his own journey round the world, observed that Petropavlovsk, "although the principal sea-port of the Peninsula of Kamchatka, is nothing more than a miserable village, containing 300 or 400 inhabitants, of whom about two-thirds are Rus-

Figure 5. View of Petropavlovsk and Avacha Bay, ca. 1765 (from [Stepan P. Krazheninnikov], *Voyage en Siberie* . . . , vol. 2 [Paris: Debure, 1768], pl. XI, opposite p. 209).

sians and the remainder natives [Kamchadals]."[33] Campbell also described the town's overall aspect: "It is situated on an eminence above the harbor, and, with the exception of the governor's house, consists of huts of one story high, built of logs and covered with thatch. In a few of them the windows are glazed with talc, but more generally the intestine of the seal supplied the place of glass."[34]

Campbell's observations regarding the siting of Petropavlovsk on a promontory above the harbor and the building forms, methods, and materials employed suggests a striking parallel to the scope of the first permanent settlements in Russian America.

In his lengthy diatribe on the squalid conditions in Petropavlovsk, Kruzenstern included an illuminating description of the building process employed there and of the problems involved in obtaining an adequate supply of building materials:

> The construction of a house at St. Peter and Paul [Petropavlovsk] is very expensive, no timber fit for the purpose growing in the neighhood of the town, and the people being obliged to bring it from

the interior. When any public building is to be erected, thirty or forty soldiers are dispatched under the command of an officer, and are employed for several weeks, and at imminent risk, in floating the felled timber down the rapid rivers. In this manner the whole garrison of Kamtschatka has been occupied during two years in building some barracks for ten or twelve men, nor were they yet completed; and the church on which they have been several years employed is in the same predicament.[35]

The predicament facing the building enterprise at Petropavlovsk is virtually identical to the one that was to plague so many coastal settlements in Russian America. In both places, the inherent advantages of rapid assembly ordinarily afforded by log construction were all but negated by the lack of nearby forests. Such, then, is the physical reality of developments in eastern Siberia that supplied the most immediate frame of reference for the establishment and construction of the first permanent settlements in Russian America.

The Shelikhov Phase of Settlement

The second phase in the establishment of permanent settlements in Russian America encompassed the gradual adaptation of familiar building methods and traditions utilized mainly in eastern Siberia. This contrasts with developments in the first phase, exemplified by Illiuliuk, wherein the settlement and building forms of the native Aleuts had been adapted to Russian use.

The second phase was effectively launched by the ambitious and enlightened Irkutsk merchant, Grigorii Shelikhov. A stockholder in most of the fur-trading expeditions of the 1760s to northwestern America from Siberia, Shelikhov had by 1770 become one of the wealthiest entrepreneurs of eastern Siberia. In 1781 he enlisted Ivan Golikov and his brother Mikhail as investors to form the Northwestern America Company, through which he proposed "to establish village and forts on the American coast and islands."[36] The establishment of these permanent outposts was intended to save time and money by reducing the number and length of voyages back and forth to Siberia while, at the same time, facilitating longer periods of hunting in the Alaskan waters. Not least, such an effort was conceived by Shelikhov as a major thrust in enhancing Russia's presence in Northwestern America and securing its colonization efforts there.

Figure 6. View of Three Saints Harbor in 1790 (from Sauer, *An Account of a Geographical and Astronomical Expedition to the Northern Parts of Russia* [London, Cadell & Davies, 1802], facing p. 182).

Three Saints Harbor. The first of Shelikhov's settlements was Three Saints Harbor, which was established on the southwestern coast of Kodiak upon the landing of Shelikhov's party there in September 1784. The earliest known view of the fledgling settlement (fig. 6) is found in Martin Sauer's published account of the Billings expedition. The harbor in question, where Billings's ships had anchored some six years later, was nestled "on the south-west side of the Bay formed by a low spot of land running from the side of the loftiest mountains."[37]

According to Sauer, the settlement numbered about fifty Russians, including the officers of the Company. As regards its basic scope and appearance,

> The buildings consist of five houses after the Russian fashion. Barracks laid out in different apartments, somewhat like boxes at a coffeehouse, on either side, with different offices: An office of appeal to settle disputes, levy fines, and punish offenders by a regular trial.... An office of receival and delivery, both for the company and for tribute: The commissaries' department, for the distribution of the regulated portion of provision: Counting-house, etc.: all in this building, at one end of which is Delareff's habitation. Another building contains the hostages. Beside which, there are storehouses, warehouses, etc. rope-walk, smithy, carpenter's shop, and cooperage.... Several of the Russians have their wives with them, and keep gardens of cabbage and potatoes, four cows and twelve goats.[38]

The legend beneath the view of Three Saints Harbor published by Sauer notes the presence of a "travelling church," an "astronomical tent," and "galliots haul'd ashore."

The image of Three Saints Harbor conveyed through Sauer's engraving and description is thus one of a fairly crude and temporary habitation. To be sure, some modest improvements were subsequently made: the first permanent church on Kodiak Island was built there in July 1796, and a school had opened a month before, indicating that the settlement would continue in use; these buildings may have been designed by Father Iuvenali, a member of the first Russian Orthodox mission to Alaska.[39] Still, the settlement's fortunes were eventually eclipsed by St. Paul Harbor, which was founded in 1791 on the northeast coast of Kodiak Island. In April 1805 Lisianskii observed that the shoreline along Three Saints Harbor had sunk precipitously following the earthquake of 1788 and sensed that the settlement itself, which "was a few years ago in a more flourishing state," was already in decline.[40] By 1880 Bancroft reported that "only one dilapidated log house and one native semi-subterranean hut" were on the site.[41]

The Forts on Afognak Island and Kenai Inlet. Given Shelikhov's almost obsessive concern for establishing elaborate "places of permanent Russian habitation," it seems rather unlikely that he would have conceived of this rather primitive settlement to be anything more than an initial and temporary base of operation. Even though Three Saints Harbor continued to be used as the company's headquarters for several years, Shelikhov quickly turned his attention to exploring the rest of Kodiak Island as well as neighboring islands and the mainland coast. In 1796 he founded the Fort of the Holy Three Saints, Basil the Great, Gregory the Divine, and John Chrysostom on Afognak Island; the Fort of St. Simeon the Friend of God and Anna the Prophetess on the Kenai (Cook) Inlet; and a small fortress on Cape St. Elias. The forts on Afognak Island and the Kenai Inlet provide the first evidence of the impressive scope of planning Shelikhov was willing to undertake in pursuing his company's objective to found permanent settlements.

Sailing back to Okhotsk later in 1796 in order to use his influence to gain a monopoly of the Russian American fur trade for his company, Shelikhov appointed K. A. Samoilov, a former Siberian fur merchant, as manager of his infant company. In a memorandum to Samoilov, Shelikhov outlined the intended scope of the two forts for which he evidently had prepared some sort of plans:

> The harbors and fortresses laid out by me on Afognak Island and in the Kenai should be laid out as sturdily as possible, according

to the plan; every kind of commodious and separate structure and fort; and a shed for the kayaks, and, beyond the fortress, for the newly arrived Aleuts, a good and warm bath house with a partition, in which the natives and hostages can bathe; a shed for drying fish in inclement weather; good warm stalls of various kinds for goats; and a large hayloft for the hay, as I am going to send over some cattle from Okhotsk. . . . And for garden produce, a fenced-in kitchen garden, for which my seed have been left behind, and more of which will be shipped from Okhotsk.[42]

It is evident that, even here, Shelikhov envisioned something more than just expedient fortified outposts. To begin with, his memorandum reinforces Gibson's argument that Shelikhov had acted from the outset to establish agriculture as the mainstay of his Alaska settlements.[43] At the same time, this quest for a more permanent sustenance base finds ample reflection in the plan for these two forts dating from 1787 (fig. 7).[44] Indeed, this plan reinforces the impression conveyed by the above instructions that Shelikhov had sought to project a degree of durability and decorum significantly beyond anything that would have been required simply to put up a pair of temporary fortifications.

It may be that, as the above memorandum suggests, the plan for these two forts was developed by Shelikhov himself. Commenting on it in his memorandum of November 30, 1787, to Catherine II, Irkutsk Governor-General Ivan V. Iakobi likewise referred to "Shelikhov's construction plan and building notes" for the two forts, thereby adding to the suggestion that Shelikhov was indeed the author.[45] At the same time, Iakobi's accompanying recommendation that Shelikhov be supplied with the "engineering expertise of a knowledgeable person, so that the fortifications would be built according to the rules of site selection and principles of fortification" may indicate a certain lack of confidence in Shelikhov's ability to carry off such a bold scheme on his own.[46] At the very least, it suggests that the venture was viewed by Iakobi as fairly important. Although he characterized the two forts as "nothing more than field fortifications with deep moats and elevated breastwork," Iakobi nonetheless made clear their strategic importance: "The fortress on the American mainland [in the Kenai Inlet] can defend the entire American coast that extends northeastward to Cape St. Elias," he explained, perhaps paraphrasing Shelikhov's report, while the one at Afognak "will have all the islands

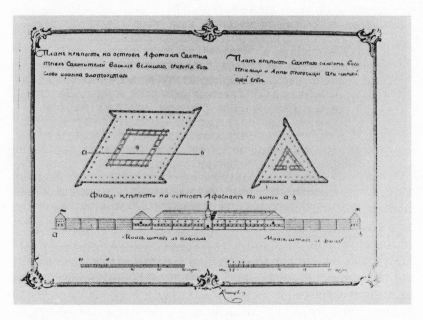

Figure 7. Plans of the Forts on Afognak Island and Kenai (Cook) Inlet (from *Russkie otkrytiia v Tikhom Okeane i Severnoi Amerike v XVIII veke*, ed. A. I. Andreev [Moscow: Izd-vo Akademii nauk SSSR, 1948], p. 256).

in the vicinity under its command, thereby discouraging other encroachments."[47]

Although it may well be that Shelikhov had indeed devised the actual plan, perhaps in consultation with specialists or books on the subject, one cannot exclude the possibility that the version reproduced here was rendered by a skilled draftsman, given its fairly refined presentation.[48] In any event, the pristine layouts of the Afognak and the Kenai forts, recalling the striking geometric regularity so favored by Russian neoclassical architects in the latter part of the eighteenth century, proved far more elaborate than those for any other Russian American posts. The plan for the Afognak fort, the larger of the two, is rendered as a 560-foot rhombus with demibastions at each corner and with a 14-foot high outer wall whose horizontal logs are reinforced by regularly spaced timber posts. In the center of the fort stands a citadel of similar shape, each side measuring some 210 feet, with a belfry in the central courtyard. The peripheral hip-roofed log structure contains barracks and storehouses. An open yard separates the citadel on all sides from the exterior wall of the fort. The smaller Kenai fort employs a similar structural and organizational scheme but is rendered as an equilateral triangle in plan.

The basic aspect of both fortresses, revealed in the elevation shown for the one at Afognak, is simple and straightforward. Yet, at the same time, it exudes a quiet formality and dignity that Shelikhov found conspicuously lacking at either Petropavlovsk or Okhotsk and which he must obviously have wished to impart to his outposts. The basic appearance of the Afognak fort also was similar to that of the ancient fortress walls and towers at Yakutsk.[49] Assuming that Shelikhov would surely have been familiar with this east Siberian town, it is not unreasonable to suppose that he should have considered adapting its venerable system of wood construction to a geometrically articulated neoclassical scheme.

Shelikhov's Plan for a Colonial Russian Capital. Among the most significant chapters in the early architectural history of Russian America is Shelikhov's ambitious but abortive attempt, thwarted by his untimely death in 1795, to build a full-fledged colonial capital worthy of the name "Glory of Russia" (Slavorossiisk). The "New Russia" (Novorossiisk) settlement subsequently built by Aleksandr Baranov in Yakutat Bay proved a very pale shadow, in both conception and fact, of the one for which Shelikhov had begun making elaborate plans on the eve of his death.

Shelikhov's determined campaign to petition the government for approval to set up a monopoly of the Russian American fur trade reflected his desire to obtain a franchise similar to those enjoyed by the English Hudson's Bay and East India companies. Anticipating a favorable reaction, Shelikhov moved confidently in 1794, a year before his death, to create a more stable and elaborate base for Russian settlement than the existing Russian trading posts, including Three Saints and St. Paul Harbors, could afford. He envisioned such a settlement as a fitting capital for his fledgling colony, one that would reflect both practically and symbolically the enhanced status of his own franchise and generally of the Russian presence in Northwestern America. There can be little doubt that Shelikhov intended to create for his colonial capital a more substantial and refined environment than had previously been achieved at either Petropavlovsk or Okhotsk. This new center, he insisted in a letter to Baranov, had to be "laid out with as much taste and building amenities as possible so that this settlement could, from its inception, pass for a town and not a village; so that . . . it would be possible to boast that Russians live comfortably with all the amenities, so that it could not be thought that Russians live as wretchedly in America as they do in Okhotsk, with its putrid air and lack of all the necessary amenities."[50]

Shelikhov did not live to see his dream fulfilled, and Baranov's subsequent efforts to carry it out proved largely in vain, but Shelikhov nonetheless left behind a building program of impressive scope and vision. Like Peter the Great, who had proceeded against incalculable odds to establish his new imperial capital of St. Petersburg as a practical and symbolic demonstration of his desire to break medieval Moscow's archaic dominance of Russia, so too Shelikhov appears to have been similarly driven by a grandiose dream. Shelikhov obviously was not a sovereign, yet the analogy does not appear entirely farfetched. His grand design for the colonial capital, though far more modest in scope and magnitude than that of St. Petersburg, may in a certain sense be seen as Shelikhov's "window to the east" in much the same way as St. Petersburg represented Peter the Great's "window to the west." Slavorossiisk appears, moreover, to have been inspired by two fundamental considerations that bear further upon the analogy: overcoming the *retardataire* situation of the Russian fur trading centers in northwestern America and eastern Siberia alike, and making Russia's presence in the north Pacific felt more forcefully as well as decorously in order to improve its competitive position vis-à-vis the other powers seeking to operate in the area.

Shelikhov had for some time given thought to establishing a "permanent Russian place of residence" on the mainland coast in the vicinity of Cape St. Elias. Given its more moderate climate, abundant forests, and fertile soil, he believed that this area afforded more favorable circumstances than either Kodiak or other nearby islands for diversifying the rudimentary economy of a fur trading post through the addition of farming, cattle raising, and shipbuilding activities.[51] Moreover, a mainland site also offered vital strategic and tactical advantages over an island site by yielding a more secure refuge from attack as well as discouraging foreign incursions into the fur hunting territory both staked out and coveted by the Golikov-Shelikhov company.[52] Accordingly, Shelikhov instructed Baranov to select the most suitable site available beyond Cape St. Elias for establishing the colonial center.

That Shelikhov had from the outset intended Slavorossiisk to be a grand and splendid place is suggested by his instructions to Baranov concerning the procedures to be followed in claiming the chosen site. The first task to be performed after selecting the site, Baranov was advised, was to claim it and the surrounding territory

> in the name of Her Imperial Highness, the Autocrat of All Russia, in a proper and well-organized procession accompanied by the firing of guns and the raising of loud cheers by those present with you, signifying that this land lies at the core of the holdings of the Russian empire. Along those points where the fortress is to be situated immediately raise a large Russian coat-of-arms; and on the site of the inhabitants' houses erect a large cross. Without doubt the Holy Archimandrite should also on this occasion conduct a proper religious ceremony and offer a special prayer for the health of Her Imperial Highness, of the entire Imperial family, and of all those faithful to the Russian throne.[53]

Shelikhov's overriding concern in conceiving of his Slavorossiik was not merely to erect a "commodious, well-built habitation," but to endow this new settlement with an architectural character befitting the status of a colonial capital. His intentions in this regard were clearly outlined in another memorandum of instructions to Baranov:

> In plan and in fact create squares for public gatherings as well as streets, though not very long ones, as they can be extended from the squares in several rows—but make them wide. And, if you settle on a very forested site, then, clearing the site according to plan, leave standing those trees which, for the sake of beauty and fresh air, would be suitable along the streets, in front of actual houses, and in the kitchen gardens. Orient houses lengthwise along the streets in such a way that there would be great distances from one house to another—you would thereby increase the size of the settlement—and, in addition, make the roofs of equal height and identical in all other respects. See that the kitchen gardens are identical for each house and that they are enclosed by good fences along the street. For public buildings, such as churches and monasteries, the office for the ecclesiastical administration of the Archimandrite, stores, a guard house for the office, and

warehouses where the village elders and clerks will store company and household goods, select proper sites and arrange them according to the style of fine cities, distinguishing these buildings as much as possible from the others.[54]

Also noteworthy is the fact that the houses which Shelikhov conceived for his colonial center were more elaborate than those typically built in Russian America prior to that date. In his memorandum to Baranov, he wrote:

> It seems to me that the houses erected for the settlers should be the kind where a white log cabin is connected to an adjoining vestibule and store room and a cold chamber or larder. Other service facilities such as granaries, cattle barns, and cellars would be housed in wings, but in such a manner that the exterior walls would not be vile but present a pleasant appearance to the streets.[55]

As Fedorova has pointed out, the house design specified by Shelikhov resembles the layout for the ubiquitous "connected house" and farmstead adopted in eastern Siberia.[56] What distinguishes Shelikhov's version from the more common vernacular Siberian prototypes, however, is its obvious concern for a formally refined, stylized design.

Shelikhov's plans for Slavorossiisk do not appear to have extended appreciably beyond the broad conceptual framework outlined in his memoranda to Baranov. These memoranda make no mention of Shelikhov's having prepared any sort of plans himself, as appears to have been the case with the forts on Afognak Island and the Kenai Inlet. Rather, they were aimed chiefly at elucidating the program that was to be followed by others in developing the actual plans for the settlement as a whole. That Shelikhov's confidence in Baranov's administrative abilities did not extend to architectural and planning matters is made abundantly clear in the memoranda in question. Indeed, despite Shelikhov's occasional indications to the contrary, they are replete with entreaties that Baranov defer to other individuals named in the memoranda in all decisions affecting the planning and design of Slavorossiisk. The individuals named were Ivan G. Polomoshnoi, whom Shelikhov designated to be the permanent manager of the new settlement; Archimandrite Iosaf, whom Catherine II had named to head the Russian Orthodox mission to the American colony; and Archpriest Iuvenalii and Archdeacon Stepan, who were among the seven clerics accompanying Archimandrite Iosaf to Alaska. Polomoshnoi was to aid Baranov in "the supervision of personnel, construction, and property management,"[57] as well as in "laying out the streets and houses" of the settlement.[58] Archimandrite Iosaf and the two priests were to serve as the architectural and planning consultants for the undertaking, as indicated in several passages in Shelikhov's memorandum; in the most telling of these, Baranov was advised that, in preparing plans for all the necessary buildings in the settlement, he should not fail to avail himself "of the counsel and views of the Holy Archimandrite and Fathers Iuvenalii and Stepan, who in this respect will be like tutors for you, as they are people engaged in geodetics and architecture."[59] The archimandrite's advice was to be sought in "establishing the general layout and confirming the selection of the site on which the aforementioned settlement is to be situated" as well as in determining which of the proposed buildings should be included in the final settlement.[60]

It is not clear to what extent the three clerics were ever actually involved in any design work for Slavorossiisk. Mention has already been made of the possibility that Father Iuvenalii may have designed the school and church erected at Three Saints Harbor in 1795 shortly before his death at the hands of the natives at Lake Iliamna. However, the only reference to any plans prepared for Slavorossiisk buildings appears in Shelikhov's discussion of the church projected for the new settlement. "Its plan, prepared in Irkutsk, has been entrusted by me to the Holy Archimandrite, along with sacred vessels, church plates, and vestments sufficient for two sanctuaries at the outset," he wrote Baranov, "and he will determine whether, contrary to plan, it should be reduced or enlarged, depending on the circumstances."[61] Shelikhov's rather ambiguous reference, although indicating Iosaf's involvement, would not seem to point to him as the designer. There is the possibility, of course, that the plan in question might have been prepared by Iuvenalii or Stepan in Irkutsk prior to their departure with the Iosaf mission to Alaska. At the same time, it is also conceivable that Shelikhov may have commissioned the plan from Aleksandr Ia. Alekseev, the first professional architect to settle in Irkutsk; Alekseev had become established there some thirteen years earlier, apparently as architect of the Irkutsk province. Also working for Alekseev at the time was another individual whom Shelikhov might have consulted for the purpose. This was Anton Losev, who subsequently became the provincial architect in 1799, the year in which he was also commissioned to design a barracks complex at Irkutsk for the newly formed Russian American Company.[62] Even though the plan for the church had presumably been prepared in Irkutsk, Shelikhov nonetheless outlined further instructions concerning its particular site orientation:

> The site for building the church should, as much as possible, be such that half of it lengthwise either stand inside the settlement or look out toward the settlers' houses, so that it would be possible to enter the church from their side without finding oneself on the other side, which would remain outside the settlement and would be enclosed by a tall, strong defensive wall of sufficient size to accommodate cells for the Holy Archimandrite and the other monks, with needed services, kitchen-garden, and a school for young [native] Americans.[63]

Significantly, a similar arrangement was subsequently employed for the church built in Novo-Arkhangel'sk for the Tlingit Indians, with half of it situated within the town proper (which was enclosed by a fortified wooden wall) and the other half standing in the Tlingit village located immediately outside the wall.

Although no accompanying plans have yet surfaced, Shelikhov's memoranda are sufficiently descriptive to make it possible to visualize the salient planning and architectural aspects he had projected for Slavorossiisk. His instructions to construct public buildings "in the style of fine cities," to create several formal and monumental squares for public gatherings where "it would be possible to erect obelisks honoring Russian patriots,"[64] and to build formally developed houses within the planned settlement all speak of his conscious emulation of Catherine the Great's ambitious town planning program. At the very beginning of her reign in 1762, Catherine had established the commission for the masonry building of St. Petersburg and Moscow (*Komissiia o kamennom stroenii S.-Peterburga i Moskvy*) which was active for the duration of her reign. This commission, whose jurisdiction was quickly expanded to include the planning of all Russian towns of any significance, and which thereafter came to be known simply as the Commission for the Building of Cities, accomplished an enormous amount of work in approving some 416 town plans. Its planning dictates were governed by the principle of imposing upon the fabric of old and new towns alike a neoclassical design conceived in strictly geometrical terms of a gridiron street pattern highlighted by wide radial avenues converging upon a monumental square or urban ensemble. Symmetrically articulated standard designs issued for various building types served to reinforce the stamp of neoclassical regularity thus imposed on Russian cities.[65]

Shelikhov's descriptive specifications for the planning and design of Slavorossiisk constitute a remarkable document in the history of Russian colonial architecture. They provide strong evidence of their author's farsightedness, energy, ambition, and, not least, keen planning and architectural sensibilities. In the process, they also reveal the conception of a fairly elaborate colonial capital that proved to have no equal before or after in Russian America.

After exploring several potential sites for Novorossiisk, Baranov settled on a site on the Phipps Peninsula, on the south side of the entrance to Yakutat Bay about four miles west of the present village of Yakutat. After several abortive attempts to begin construction in 1795, actual work on the site finally began in the summer of the following year. In the meantime, however, Shelikhov had died in Irkutsk on July 20, 1795, leaving Baranov to fulfill his dream of establishing a significant colonial capital. Baranov's efforts to do so, however, culminated in the construction of a far more modest settlement, which he named Novorossiisk (New Russia). That settlement lasted only a short while and was virtually extinguished by the brutal attack of the Yakutats in 1805. Baranov's founding of Novo-Arkhangel'sk in the preceding year may be seen, at least in part, as an attempt to extend the line of development charted by Shelikhov in his proposal for Novorossiisk. Yet here too, the end results obtained during Baranov's administration, though impressive in so many other ways, were to fall considerably short of Shelikhov's bold conception for a new colonial Russian capital.

The Baranov Phase of Settlement

The third discrete phase in the establishment of permanent settlements in Russian America was presided over by Aleksandr Baranov, whom Shelikhov had recruited in Okhotsk in 1790 to become the new manager of his company interests in Alaska. Baranov's initial efforts in this capacity included establishing St. Paul Harbor on the northeast coast of Kodiak Island, finding an acceptable site for Shelikhov's colonial capital of Slavorossiisk, and building a modest, short-lived settlement in the vicinity of the latter site. Following Shelikhov's death in 1795

Baranov continued managing the interests of what had become the Northwestern American Company until 1799, when the first charter of the Russian American Company was granted by the government of Emperor Paul I.

Baranov was made the first general manager of the new company, a position that came to be viewed as tantamount to being governor of Russian America. He served in this capacity until 1818, when he was relieved of his duties. The history of the development of Russian America during his tenure reveals Baranov to have been the most aggressive administrator connected with the Russian occupation of Alaska. His program of expansion, doubtless inspired at least partially by Shelikhov, encompassed the founding in 1799 of Novo-Arkhangel'sk, the establishment of Fort Ross and nearby sites in California in 1808–12, and even abortive efforts in 1815–17 to establish several enterprises in the Hawaiian Islands with company support. And yet the building activity for which Baranov was personally responsible generated little more than the same sort of expedient outposts that had marked earlier construction efforts in Russian America.

St. Paul Harbor. Baranov's first building activity was undertaken at St. Paul Harbor in Chiniak Bay, on the northeast coast of Kodiak Island. Obtaining Shelikhov's approval, he erected a temporary fort on the site, which he named in honor of the heir to the imperial Russian throne.

Shelikhov had encouraged Baranov to move the company's principal settlement from Three Saints Harbor to a more advantageous site. His reasons lay partly in the desire to obtain a better harbor, but chiefly in the determination to find more arable land for developing a viable agricultural base and to increase the timber supply for the construction of better ships and more substantial buildings and fortifications.[66] St. Paul Harbor proved satisfactory on all these counts. Hence, with Shelikhov's approval, the company headquarters were moved in 1792 to the new settlement, which is today the town of Kodiak. Before long, St. Paul Harbor became one of the largest settlements in Russian America and effectively its first colonial capital.

The first buildings erected by Baranov stood within and just beyond the temporary fort illustrated in the view of 1798 (fig. 8). The main structure was a two-story administration building and fur storage warehouse, extended in a J-shaped plan whose semicircular wing overlooked the harbor. The plain log wall structures, an archetypal Russian variant of utilitarian wooden building, had steep plank roofs

Figure 8. View of the Original Fort at St. Paul Harbor from the North in 1798 (from *Atlas geograficheskikh otkrytii v Sibiri i Severo-zapadnoi Amerike XVII–XVIII vv.*, ed. A. V. Efimov [Moscow: Nauka, 1964], pl. 170).

hipped at the ends. Emblematic of the fortified aspect of Baranov's initial complex were the crude lookout platform and octagonal watch-tower crowning the entrance bay of the administrative building, as well as the horizontal bands of loopholes articulating both structures.

That Baranov's initial fort was a temporary facility superseded by subsequent building activity that gave form to the later St. Paul Harbor is indicated by Father Gedeon's description of the settlement as it appeared in 1804. In it, Baranov's complex is already referred to as "the earlier wooden semi-circular fort" whose remains could be seen standing "opposite the church beyond a stream on a small hillock." According to Gedeon, the entire fort was badly deteriorated, and a third of it had already collapsed. All that remained standing, he wrote, were "the chambers of the company offices, the barracks for the hunters, the warehouses for fur goods, shops with cellars, and little else beyond the smithy and metal workshop."[67]

By 1795 a church was erected across the stream from Baranov's fort. Named the Church of the Resurrection, it was described by Lisianskii as "the only one to be found on the coast."[68] Judging by the same 1798 view, this church was the first structure in St. Paul Harbor to assume a more elaborate architectural character, employing the traditional three-part plan typical of most Russian wooden church architecture. In churches of this type, which had evolved from the simple shed structures resembling a peasant *izba*, the largest chamber in the center served as the sanctuary, with a small chamber added to the east for the apse, and another to the west for a vestibule. The addition of small bulbous domes on a tall drum enriched the silhouette of the tripartite mass, thus giving the simple wooden Russian shed church its inherently expressive form. In St. Paul Harbor's Resurrection, the central sanctuary chamber was surmounted by a large octagonal drum crowned by a bulbous (or "onion") dome, with the vestibule chamber to the west topped by a smaller variation of the emblematic form. The single apse chamber to the east was framed by hewn logs laid in a semioctagonal plan. The main floor of the church was elevated one full story off the ground, and an elaborate stairway employing a double flight of stairs led to the main entrance of the vestibule.

In 1796 a hospital was erected in St. Paul Harbor.[69] That it was the first built in Russian America attests to the growing importance of St. Paul Harbor as the center of the emerging Russian colony and its fur hunting and trading enterprise. Further improvements in the next decade or so encompassed the town's most significant period of growth. Father Gedeon's description of St. Paul Harbor in 1804 helps fix in time and space the array of structures that had been erected to supplement the initial fort:

> On the shore near where the boats lie anchored is a rigging shed, with several other large ones nearby for storing cargoes. Opposite it on the hill is the new administrator's house, with a library; and extending from it in the form of an elongated rectangle are eight various family dwellings. Across from the administrator's house, at the very end of the cape, stands a church and a bell-tower with dilapidated roofs. In front of the very entrance to the church, to the right, stands the general company cook-house and, to the left, is a large shed for the baidaras and various other articles. Behind the shed are store houses for foodstuff and a booth, i.e., a shed

on stilts for storing dried fish [*iukola*] and meat [*kachemaz*], in which the floor is built of poles to allow the free flow of air. In the store houses are kept the meats of whales, sea lions, and seals, as well as walrus and whale blubber, together with sarana and blueberries, whortleberries, and bilberries. All the food supplies are brought here from outlying artels. . . . Beyond . . . the remains of the earlier wooden semicircular fort . . . at the foot of the hill stands the old administrator's house, which now contains the Russian-American school; as well as the dilapidated quarters of the religious mission; the communal bath house; a round Aleut communal house [*kazhim*], where the native workers of the company and the sick live; and a new cattle yard. Not far away from all the latter is the house of the administrator's assistant, Banner, and visitors' chambers.[70]

Also in 1804 Capt. Iurii Lisianskii and the crew from his sloop *Neva* helped erect a redoubt with a battery of cannons to the east of Baranov's original fort to help guard the entrance to the harbor. Lisianskii's lithograph of the site, though featuring his crew's handiwork, also shows a number of other structures in the vicinity as well (fig. 9). The most apparent is a large circular building, topped by a clerestory drum and conical dome, standing well to the left of the redoubt. This structure is probably the Aleut communal dwelling, or *kazhim*, mentioned by Gedeon. Campbell, who anchored at St. Paul Harbor in 1808, noted that this barrack housed sixty Aleuts attached to the company settlement.[71]

Campbell's account also indicates that the scope and caliber of dwellings built in St. Paul Harbor had likewise been improved, suggesting in the process the apparent adaptation of a small-scale urban apartment prototype.

The town consists of about fifty houses, built of logs, the seams of which are caulked with moss, and the roofs thatched with grass; they are, in general, divided into three apartments below, and as many on the upper story. They are heated by stoves or ovens; when the wood is reduced to ashes, the vent is closed by means of a slide fitted for the purpose, and the heated air then diffusing itself through the room, renders it extremely comfortable. The windows, instead of being glazed, are covered with pieces of the

Figure 9. View of St. Paul Harbor in 1804 (from Yuri F. Lisiansky, *A Voyage Round the World* ... [London: John Booth, 1814], facing p. 191).

gut of a seal, split up and sewed together; this, after being well oiled, is stretched on a frame, and defended from the wind by cross-bars on each side. Talc is also used for the same purpose. This substance is found in flakes about the size of the palm of the hand, and several of these are puttied together to form a pane.[72]

The building campaign undertaken at St. Paul Harbor in this thriving period of its development was distinguished not only by its rapid tempo, but by its fairly impressive scope as well. Von Langsdorff's enthusiastic account asserted that, as a result of this concerted building activity, St. Paul Harbor had "by degrees assumed the appearance of a European village."[73] Von Langsdorff also indicated that Ivan L. Banner, the Deputy Commander of St. Paul Harbor, had assumed the task of planning the town and designing its latest group of public buildings. In his words, "M. Bander [*sic*] laid the plan of a new building to be begun the following spring [of 1809] for a library and permanent museum. At the same time he gave orders that in building this and all other new houses a certain regularity should be observed, so as to form a street; thus Kodiak may by degrees vie in this respect with the best-built European town."[74]

The establishment of a museum and a library offers more compelling proof that St. Paul Harbor had evolved from a primitive fortified settlement into a developing colonial town with an impressive number of cultural amenities (fig. 10). No other references have yet been found to support von Langsdorff's identification of Banner as a designer or planner. However, an 1808 plan of St. Paul Harbor drawn by Ivan F. Vasil'ev, a navigator aboard Lisianskii's sloop *Neva*, seems to reflect a measure of the concern for a more regular street and building layout that von Langsdorff had attributed to Banner (fig. 11).[75] Although its actual author is not identified, the plan itself reveals traces of an emerging sensitivity for greater regularity and, correspondingly, for the use of lot lines to regulate building activity. This device, first introduced in Russia through Domenico Trezzini's 1714 project for prototypical houses in St. Petersburg, was later applied on a broad scale in the massive town planning programs inaugurated by Catherine the Great and amplified by her grandson, Alexander I.[76] Indeed, the apparent use of lot lines—whether constituting the delineator's own proposal, or Banner's, or perhaps someone else's—tends to suggest a basic familiarity with Catherine and Alexander's planning programs and possibly even a conscious effort to emulate them in a nascent colonial capital. Such an effort would surely have been consistent with the intentions Shelikhov had earlier enunciated for his Slavorossiisk. In any event, the planning activity discernible in St. Paul Harbor, although still fairly rudimentary, had already reached a level of being on a par with, if perhaps not already exceeding, those of Okhotsk and Petropavlovsk.

With the transfer of the company headquarters to Novo-Arkhangel'sk in 1808, however, other administrative and service facilities followed suit, including the Russian Orthodox mission, which moved in 1816. The resulting decline arrested the town's earlier accelerated growth by removing the incentives for creating a physical setting appropriate for a colonial capital. Still, even though St. Paul Harbor was eclipsed by Novo-Arkhangel'sk, a panoramic view of the settlement drawn in 1842 by Ilia G. Voznesenskii suggests that its townscape had nonetheless acquired a moderately stylish neoclassical garb that was second only to that of the new colonial capital itself.[77] That aspect, however, was largely the product of those who succeeded Baranov as managers of the Russian American Company.

Novorossiisk or New Russia. The next significant phase of settlement undertaken by Baranov involved construction of the short-lived settlement of Novorossiisk, or New Russia, which he established on Yakutat Bay after Shelikhov's death in July 1795. It will be recalled that this

Figure 10. View of St. Paul Harbor in 1808 (from Georg H. von Langsdorff, *Bemerkungen auf einer Reise um die Welt* ... [Frankfurt: F. Wilmans, 1812], facing p. 50).

was the site on which Shelikhov originally had intended to found his envisioned colonial capital of Slavorossiisk. Ivan Polomoshnoi, whom Shelikhov had dispatched to Alaska for the purpose of overseeing the choice of site and the construction of the actual settlement, had reported on obstacles to establishing a settlement in the area, including the presence of hostile natives. Despite Polomoshnoi's negative report, however, Baranov settled on a site on the Phipps Peninsula, on the south side of the entrance to Yakutat Bay, about four miles west of the present village of Yakutat. After an abortive attempt to send colonists to the site failed in 1795, a ship carrying settlers led by Manager Polomoshnoi and a guard of twenty-five hunters headed by Stepan Larionov arrived there in the summer of 1796. Bad weather delayed construction work until the middle of August.[78]

Available firsthand accounts yield few adequate descriptions of the fledgling outpost. Tikhmenev's passing references, written after the fact, suggest that its scope did not represent any appreciable improvement over the other primitive Russian outposts that had been built over the preceding decade or so. The initial phase of construction involved the hasty erection of several barabaras that would enable the *promyshlenniki* and the settlers to establish residence at the new outpost. The barabaras built at Novorossiisk, according to Tikhmenev, were "usually built without a stove, with a large opening above." Tikhmenev's description suggests that these barabaras were roughly analogous to those built by the first Russian settlers at Illiuliuk. Instead of employing an outer covering of sea animal skin, however, their "front facade is covered with planking, [and] the remaining sides usually consist of staves covered with tree bark."[79]

In the next phase of construction Baranov, "with the help of the sixty men who had accompanied him, completed a barrack for the people and a warehouse for storing company merchandise." Before returning to St. Paul Harbor, he "instructed Polomoshnoi to continue building according to the delineated plan."[80] Tikhmenev does not identify the author of the plan in question. Shelikhov's detailed memoranda on Slavorossiisk had instructed Baranov to prepare such plans, but in close consultation with Archimandrite Iosaf and Fathers Iuvenalii and Stepan, and probably Polomoshnoi himself. Given that

Figure 11. Plan of St. Paul Harbor in 1808, drawn by I. F. Vasil'ev (from S. G. Fedorova, *Russkoe naselenie Aliaski i Kalifornii* [Moscow: Nauka, 1971], pl. 8).

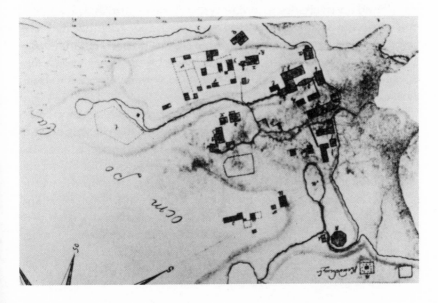

Archmonk Iuvenalii had been killed in 1795 and that Archimandrite Iosaf was recalled to Irkutsk in the following year to be consecrated a bishop, it is doubtful that Shelikhov's instructions were carried out.

The early phases of construction described by Tikhmenev were probably conceived solely as temporary measures to enable the settlers to occupy the site as soon as possible, with subsequent construction under Polomoshnoi's supervision of a more permanent planned complex of structures and amenities. This generally was the approach at St. Paul Harbor.

There was to be no further elaboration of any plans for Novorossiisk, however, as the Yakutat Revolt of 1805 laid waste to the settlement; the few Russian survivors managed to escape to St. Paul Harbor.[81] As a result, both Shelikhov's dream of a colonial Russian capital and Baranov's efforts to implement them at Yakutat Bay came to an abrupt and permanent end.

The Founding of Novo-Arkhangel'sk. Even as the Russian American Company was coming into existence, Baranov was preparing to carry out plans for the establishment of a new Russian settlement on Sitka (now Baranof) Island. Baranov evidently had begun cooling to the idea of establishing a viable settlement in the marginally hospitable area of Yakutat Bay even before the 1805 massacre had put an end to the endeavor. He was drawn instead by the prospect of establishing a settlement further south in a region that afforded an ice-free port the year round and a chance to circumvent American, British, and Spanish penetration of southeasterly Alaska by settling an area that had long been a rendezvous for traders. Hunting parties he had sent there after first visiting the area himself in 1795 had also brought back large bounties of valuable sea otter pelts. Thus in 1799 Baranov decided to build a new outpost there.

Vasilii Medvednikov, who had been dispatched ahead to select a site, had picked a spot about six miles north of the present town of Sitka. Although Baranov would have preferred the location where Sitka now stands, its occupation by a Tlingit village forced him to accede to the one chosen by Medvednikov. Work commenced in the winter of 1799–1800. By the spring, the new post, built entirely of wood and named St. Michael, was almost completed. It contained a large two-story warehouse, a blacksmith shop, barracks for the officers, a house for Baranov, a bath house, and a temporary kitchen.[82]

In a letter to Emelian Larionov, a company stockholder sent to become manager of Unalaska, Baranov described the experience of building the new post; that description also sheds light, in the process, on the primitive frontier conditions prevalent at the time. "Of the buildings," Baranov wrote,

we first erected a large wooden shed [balagan] into which we unloaded everything from the ships and placed all the ready foodstuff; next, we built a small modest bath house into which I moved in October, having lived until that time in a torn tent exposed to the elements; and here I suffered during the winter in the smoke and the drippings from the worn-out roof and the interminable foul weather until February. Then, we built a fine two-story barrack 8 sazhens [56 feet] long and 4 sazhens [28 feet] wide, with two sentry booths at the corners; a cellar under the entire structure for storing foodstuffs and provisions; and the manager's chamber, with outbuilding, into which I moved on February 15. . . . All the buildings were completed by a small work force; in fact, no more than 20 persons were engaged in the work over the winter.[83]

In June 1802 when Baranov was on Kodiak Island, a band of Tlingit Indians mounted a surprise attack on Fort St. Michael and massacred all but a handful of the Russian and Aleut inhabitants. The fort was set on fire, and only a few buildings were left "which had either escaped the ravages of the flames, or which probably the savages had not thought it worth while to destroy to the foundation."[84]

After struggling for some time to round up adequate supplies and men, Baranov launched an expedition in the summer of 1804 to recover Sitka from the Tlingits. At Norton Sound, he was joined by the Russian warship *Neva* under the command of Captain Iurii Lisianskii. The *Neva*'s guns helped assure the eventual surrender of the fort, although Lisianskii later observed that the fort "was constructed of wood so thick and strong that the shot from my guns could not penetrate it at the short distance of a cable's length."[85] After weathering a siege that lasted four days, the Indians took advantage of the nightfall to flee, leaving the site to the Russians. The Tlingit fort was demolished, and work on constructing a new fort on the site was begun immediately, with the aid of Lisianskii's crew. This new fort, which proved to be the nucleus of the new center for the Russian American colony, received the name of Novo-Arkhangel'sk to underscore its lineage from the original fort.

Among the most descriptive accounts of this fledgling outpost is the one conveyed in the lithograph and accompanying commentary published by Georg von Langsdorff, who assayed the scene not long after Baranov had completed work on the initial outpost. "The settlement of New Archangel," he wrote, "was at our arrival quite in its infancy." The description which followed made clear its primitive state: "Under such circumstances, nothing like the conveniences of life could be expected: the habitations were for the greater part unfinished, and consisted of small chambers without stoves, with so thin a thatch, that the rains, which we had continually, often came through. The Promuschleniks were kept constantly hard at work upon the barracks, warehouses, and other buildings, which were so exceedingly wanted."[86]

The fort depicted in von Langsdorff's lithograph (fig. 12) appears to have been no more advanced, and perhaps even less developed, than its immediate predecessor just up the coast. The fort is shown to be surrounded by a modest gabion of vertically spaced logs—an installation that is barely adequate for defense and that recalls corresponding aspects of Okhotsk and Petropavlovsk in eastern Siberia.

Nikolai Korobitsyn, a clerk with the Russian American Company who sailed into Novo-Arkhangel'sk aboard Lisianskii's ship *Neva*, supplied a description of the fort that seems to correspond most closely to the image conveyed by von Langsdorff's lithograph:

> The New Archangel fort is situated on a high promontory which, projecting out from the coastline into the sea, presents a pleasant view; and, considering its situation, is fairly safe from any kind of foe. Its fortification consists, because the settlement is new, of a gabion around the entire fort, interspersed with twenty canons. . . . Inside the fort is the Manager's [Governor's] residence with his office and kitchen . . . [and] a house, consisting of four rooms, for the officers and ship captains of the Company's maritime fleet. In the middle of the fort is a square, measuring 20 *sazhens* [140 feet] long and 10 sazhens [70 feet] wide. In the center of the latter stands a flagstaff on which the Company flag is hoisted on festival and ceremonial days, as well as upon the entry of vessels into the harbor.[87]

Figure 12. View of Novo-Arkhangel'sk in 1805 (from von Langsdorff, *Bemer-kungen auf einer Reise um die Welt* ... [Frankfurt, 1812], facing p. 76).

In addition to the fort proper, numerous structures had been raised beyond its walls. Nikolai Rezanov's report to the Russian American Company supplements Korobitsyn's description of the fort in providing a larger picture of the overall settlement that had begun emerging at this time.[88] Shelikhov's brother-in-law and high chamberlain to the emperor, Rezanov traveled to Novo-Arkhangel'sk and about the Russian colony in 1805 as special emissary of the company to report on its operations. In his report, Rezanov noted:

> The site of the fort is a high rock, or *kekur*, on a peninsula projecting into the inlet. On the left side, on a hill located on the same kind of peninsula that adjoins the kekur, is an enormous barrack with two booths or small towers for defending the place. The building is almost entirely of mast timber set on a larch log foundation reinforced with cobblestones, with cellars built inside it, extending down the slope of the hill all the way to the water. Beside it is a building consisting of two shops, a storeroom for provisions, and two cellars. To the side of this building stands a large shed [*balagan*]

on posts for storing foodstuffs; beneath the entire shed is a barnlike structure for processing the Company's wares. On the side opposite the fort is an enormous shed for storing cargo, with a log store on the water side and a wharf between it and the fort. On the right side, at the foot of the hill, is a chamber building containing a kitchen, bath, and several compartments for housing Company workers; along the shore is a large building complex [sviaz'] 9 sazhens [63 feet] long and 5 sazhens [35 feet] wide, in the center of which is a large smithy with three furnaces and with compartments for workshops along the sides. A cattleyard is located to one side. In addition to the above buildings, there is also a bath house, and another bath house with a light room below the fort.[89]

Both the fort and the town that began to spread out below it experienced significant growth and improvements following the transfer of the Russian American Company headquarters to Novo-Arkhangel'sk from St. Paul Harbor in 1808. A descriptive account by Peter Corney, a British seaman who stopped over in Novo-Arkhangel'sk in 1814 on his trading voyage to China, sheds some light on this improved aspect of the town's development. The gabion around the fort had by this time been replaced by a more substantial wooden wall. Corney found this wall to be "well calculated to defend them [the Russians] from Indians," although, judging by normal European standards, "a good ship would . . . soon destroy it."[90]

The town itself, by Corney's account, had grown to include sixty wooden houses and a church, as well as a shipyard and a complement of storage, service, and utilitarian structures. Like the fort itself, the town below it was also enclosed by a fortified wooden wall of "high paling, and look-out houses built at the distance of twenty yards from each other, where there are people on the watch, both day and night."[91] Other additions to Novo-Arkhangel'sk's townscape noted by Corney were the numerous kitchen gardens that had become staples of everyday life in the new colonial capital. According to Corney, "Every Russian has cleared a piece of ground, where they sow potatoes, turnips, carrots, radishes, sallads, etc., by which means, with plenty of fish and whale blubber, they live very comfortably."[92]

The planning aspects characterizing Novo-Arkhangel'sk's initial period of development, discernible from the above accounts, generally echoed those of most smaller provincial Russian towns in the first part of the nineteenth century. Although Emperor Paul had abolished the Commission for the Building of Cities upon succeeding his mother in 1797, his son Alexander I reinstated its authority shortly after his accession in 1801. The planning of cities, like all other internal planning in Russia, had to be subordinated to the political events surrounding the Napoleonic invasion of Russia in 1812. Significantly, a notable planning innovation of the period—the creation of a series of military settlements in Russia—suggests some interesting parallels, if not perhaps outright models, for the development of Novo-Arkhangel'sk and other contemporaneous settlements in Russian America.

Under the auspices of this program, certain territories were set aside for military administration under the purview of Count Aleksei Arakcheev and the Department of Military Settlements. Troops were to be settled on the land and combine soldiering with farming and to some extent with crafts and manufacture. A few small colonies were actually set up in 1810 in Mogilev province, but it was only after the Napoleonic Wars that they were instituted on a large scale, the period of their most energetic development occurring between 1816 and 1821.[93] Plans developed for these settlements, inspired by Alexander's penchant for cleanliness, symmetrical order, and efficient planning, placed great emphasis on extending the main thoroughfare along a straight line through the center of the settlement and creating an adjoining parade ground for military drills and reviews, bounded by various post and government buildings. The chief dwelling types employed in these settlements were the traditional *izba* cottages, clustered around small courts, with adjoining kitchen gardens.[94]

Although no evidence has yet been found to indicate that the Department of Military Settlements may actually have been responsible for any town planning schemes in Russian America, there is a marked resemblance between its rudimentary planning format and the basic layout discernible in Novo-Arkhangel'sk. Korobitsyn had noted the existence of a parade ground as early as 1804; Rezanov inventoried a corresponding array of administrative buildings and company barracks and warehouses; and Corney recorded the existence by 1814 of some sixty log houses with adjoining kitchen gardens and a complement of service buildings. All seem to reflect salient aspects of the plans for the Russian military settlements developed in this period. These same aspects, moreover, were subsequently found in the plan of Novo-Arkhangel'sk published in 1844 by Duflot de Mofras (fig. 13).[95] That

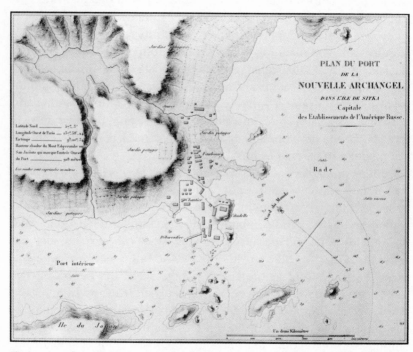

Figure 13. Plan of Novo-Arkhangel'sk around 1840 (from Eugene Duflot de Mofras, *Exploration de Territoire de l'Oregon, des Californies et de la mer Vermeille* . . . [Paris: A. Bertrand, 1844], pl. 21).

the aspect of a linear main street and adjoining parade ground enclosed by clusters of log dwellings and company and public buildings was to remain a dominant element in the townscape of the colonial Russian capital is indicated by the 1906 photograph of Sitka (fig. 14). Even if the Department of Military Settlements had no direct involvement in the planning of Novo-Arkhangel'sk, it is not inconceivable that the Russian American Company may have found it expedient to adapt the department's basic planning guidelines to the construction and expansion of its settlements in Russian America. But it is unclear whether there ever existed within the central offices of the Russian American Company a section or department charged with supervising the planning and construction of Russian American settlements. No evidence of such an entity has yet come to light, although all such actions undertaken in the colony would surely have had to receive prior approval from company headquarters. Too, as has already been noted, the company had approached Irkutsk provincial architect Anton Losev to design a barracks complex in that city in 1799. Whether the services of this or any other provincial architect might have been employed in subsequent years, either for the design of specific structures or for preparing "model" designs for various building prototypes in Russian America, likewise remains to be ascertained.

The state of building in Novo-Arkhangel'sk that Baranov bequeathed to his successors upon being relieved of his position as chief manager of the company in 1818 was effectively assayed by Captain Fedor P. Litke, whose discovery sloop *Seniavin* docked at the colonial capital for a month in the summer of 1827. Three exquisite lithographs, rendered by artist Baron von Kittlitz and published in the historical atlas accompanying Litke's account of his journey, provide the most descriptive views of building activity dating largely from the late Baranov period.[96]

Figure 14. View of Sitka in 1906 (from the Prints and Photographs Division, Library of Congress).

The first of these views is of the fort itself, perched on top of the Sitka *kekur* (fig. 15). The governor's house within it, still of the rather plain *izba* type, is doubtless the one Baranov had erected, perhaps with a few minor embellishments. Particularly striking are the two front towers, well proportioned two-story hewn-log structures which may have been built during the ensuing Hagemeister and Yankovskii administrations. The evocative dichotomy of primitive structure and powerfully expressive silhouette, so typically Russian, permeates von Kittlitz's lithograph of the fortress. A dramatic composition recalling something of the French eighteenth-century architectural and land-scape painter Hubert Robert's power to achieve dramatic, hauntingly evocative effects through the carefully orchestrated play of sunlight on selected elements looming in his pictorial space, this view ultimately conveys "environs qui sont extrêmement pittoresques, composés de

Figure 15. View of the Fort and the Manager's House in 1827 (from Frederic Lütke [Fedor P. Litke], *Partie Historique Atlas* [Paris: Engelmann et Co., 1835; atlas accompanying his 3 vol. *Voyage autour du Monde*, Paris: Didot, 1835–36], pl. 3).

Figure 16. View of the Main Road in the Center of New Archangel in 1827 (from Lütke, *Partie Historique Atlas* [Paris, 1835], pl. 7 [bottom view]).

hautes montagnes sortant de la mer et couvertes de magnifiques forêts d'arbres coniferes. Au milieu de ce tableau majestueux et sauvage, la citadelle presente un aspect très-riant."[97]

    The second lithograph by von Kittlitz provides an intriguing glimpse of the town's core rendered from the vantage point of the governor's house atop the fort (fig. 16). The road shown in the view, running more or less along the line of present-day Lincoln Street, was identified as the town's main thoroughfare. The bridge spans a stream that runs approximately where Marine Street occurs today. All but one of the structures lining both sides of the road are of the ubiquitous *izba* type, with the characteristic log walls and steep, hipped plank roof that predominated, as Zagoskin so aptly put it, everywhere that Russians chose to settle. Particularly noteworthy in this view is the striking octagonal building that dominates the nascent streetscape. Identified as a church but not by name in Litke's atlas, the building doubtless is the first Church of St. Michael built in Novo-Arkhangel'sk; the church probably dates from 1816 or 1817, although it is not clear whether it represents an entirely new structure or the refurbishing of an earlier building.[98]

Employing the basic format of the traditional octagonal tent-church so popular in Russian wooden architecture, this small structure commands the bold geometry of tiered octagonal forms with authority and grace. Underlying its bold manipulation of geometrical form is the most conspicuous effort yet uncovered in Russian colonial building at a stylish emulation of Russian neoclassical architecture, the effects of which are everywhere apparent: the simple octagonal blockwork of the base, framed by interlocking logs; the smaller octagonal dome, its walls probably of hewn logs with intersecting corners marked by corner boards; and the ridge boards of the "tent" roof, which act like ribs to articulate its geometrical aspect, terminating in a suave spirelet that originally would surely have been topped by a cross. The walls of the lantern-like dome are punctuated by handsome round windows that at once evoke an aspect of neoclassical geometry and of the more immediate nautical form of a porthole. Von Kittlitz referred to the interiors in passing as being richly decorated. Belcher, who visited the church in 1837, described them as "splendid, quite beyond conception in such a place as this."[99]

The third von Kittlitz lithograph of Novo-Arkhangel'sk published in Litke's historical atlas is a view of Sitka Bay, also from the governor's house (fig. 17). Apart from the dramatic rendering of the setting, what is particularly noteworthy from an architectural standpoint is the building at the bottom of the view; it is probably one of the fur warehouses built during Murav'ev's administration, although comparable structures may well have been built during Baranov's tenure. The building presents a charming image of the provincial Russian classical revival in wood. Its salient aspect of pediment gables supported by colossal columns and accented by lunettes, or semicircular windows in the gables, proved virtually as ubiquitous in the Russian provinces as did the provincial wooden variants of the Greek Revival that sprang up in the westward population centers of the United States in roughly the same period. Although the structural system employed in this building was probably traditional log construction, as indicated by the initial stages in the assembly of the adjoining structure to the right, the exterior appears to be sheathed with boards, as indicated by the rendering of the gables prominently in view. Such sheathing was a

Figure 17. View of Sitka Bay and the Russian-American Company Fur Warehouses in 1827 (from Lütke, *Partie Historique Atlas* [Paris, 1835], pl. 3 [bottom view]).

device prominently employed to achieve a more formal character for classical designs in wooden architecture and to simulate, in the more self-consciously developed designs, the severely plain neoclassic masonry walls. Symptomatic of the attempts by provincial Russian master carpenters to transfer salient elements of the classical revival from masonry to wooden architectural forms is the old company store (fig. 18), which may be the one mentioned in Korobitsyn's 1808 inventory as either the company retail shop or the company storehouse for merchandise, provisions, and materials.[100] The date of 1808 seems eminently plausible for its construction, though the structure itself may have undergone some modest transformations at a later date. Long known in Sitka as the Old Trading Post, this long and low building with a massive hipped roof and central gable became, after 1867, the Sitka Trade Company Building; it was torn down around 1920. Despite

Figure 18. View of the Old Russian-American Company Store in 1899 (from the Prints and Photographs Division, Library of Congress).

its modest stylish aspects, however, the structure clearly reflected a simple utilitarian building type long familiar in traditional Russian wooden architecture.

Such, then, was the overall character of the Novo-Arkhangel'sk that Baranov bequeathed to his successors in 1818 upon stepping down from his position of chief manager of the company. Although the settlement had progressed appreciably from its initial aspect of a crude, fortified trading post, it still does not appear to have been the equal of St. Paul Harbor. To be sure, Novo-Arkhangel'sk had remained throughout Baranov's tenure little more than a settled outpost in a new territory still in process of being fully assimilated. St. Paul Harbor had, on the other hand, been established in rather more secure territory. Moreover, it had been conceived and developed virtually from the outset as the center, if not a full-fledged capital, of Shelikhov's envisioned empire. Accordingly, its building activity had early on attracted the involvement of others, most notably Ivan Banner. In contrast, the building activity undertaken at Novo-Arkhangel'sk appears to have fallen entirely under Baranov's purview. If so, it did not prove the equal of his impressive record of accomplishments in other realms of administrative activity.

The rudimentary built environment that had arisen at Novo-Arkhangel'sk during Baranov's tenure, like the early nucleus of St. Paul Harbor before it, seems in many ways a manifestation of his apparent inability or disinclination to achieve anything more elaborate than an expedient enclave of utilitarian structures, save for a few noteworthy exceptions such as the first Church of St. Michael. That Baranov's overall architectural and planning legacy thus did not extend beyond the establishment of a primitive frontier building enterprise may be at least partially the result of his having had to confront the exigencies of survival in hostile territory. Too, the rather mundane character of the town's layout scheme may, as previously mentioned, have been suggested or dictated by a Department of Military Settlements format that, in its prototypical aspects, was likewise rather unprepossessing. Still, it seems rather clear that Baranov lacked the grand vision that Shelikhov had entertained and articulated for establishing more developed settlements in Russian America.

The reasons for this apparent state of affairs are not easily established. Available evidence seems strongly to suggest that Baranov had little inclination for building activity and that he regarded it simply as utilitarian. This, to be sure, has historically been the modus vivendi of most frontier situations in North America, and that of Russian America proved no exception. Baranov does not appear to have been particularly endowed with any conspicuous aesthetic instincts or sensibilities, even though he evidently was a devotee of Russian literature.

It is here, perhaps, that the gist of the matter may be traced to a fundamental trait which Baranov's biographer Kiril Khlebnikov detected in the first chief manager's personality. Although indicating that Baranov had proven effective in managing the affairs of the Russian American Company, Khlebnikov nonetheless referred to him, somewhat parenthetically, as a man who "had no love of fashion, and preferred the uniform he had worn when promoted (1805) to anything new, regardless of the fact that, in fourteen years, fashion had made it outmoded."[101] Thus, it may be possible to draw an analogy between Baranov's lack of concern for fashion in apparel and his apparent indifference to style in architecture. It may well be that Shelikhov himself had early on discerned this trait in his merchant manager. If so, this surely would account for the often gratuitous and condescending tone of those instructions bearing upon building activity contained in his otherwise congenial memoranda to Baranov. It would

Figure 19. View of Sitka from the Governor's Mansion ca. 1890 (from the Brady Photograph Collection at the Sitka Historical Society Museum).

also help explain his corresponding conspicuous efforts to divest Baranov of any real responsibility in planning and designing his abortive capital of Slavorossiisk.

There is, in fairness, another cause whose effects, though manifested by Baranov, also appear to have been fundamental to virtually all facets of the Russian-American enterprise after Baranov's enforced retirement as well. Almost everything about Russian America was perceived as being a "company" enterprise, with all the term implies. In his reflections on the last days in Novo-Arkhangel'sk before the official transfer of Alaska to the United States in 1867, M. I. Vavilov characterized the ambiance peculiar to the Russian colonies in Alaska as one where "all facets of life were circumscribed by the singular interests of the Russian-American Company."[102] Too, it must be said that, apart from the few more cultivated individuals stationed there, the predominant breed of *promyshlennik* whose raucous way of life set the tone for the town's, and indeed the colony's, ambiance as a whole might well have supplied little incentive for seeking anything but the most expedient improvements. As Clarence Andrews has noted, both the ambiance and the particular circumstances that nourished it made for a rather coarse and transient population:

> The *promishleniki* [*sic*] of the [Russian American] Company were a varied, turbulent body of men, gathered from all parts of the vast Russian empire. Exiles for political reasons, convicts sent to Siberia for punishment, fur hunters of the frontier, all passed on to the new colonies, for the company was continually sending out new men to take the place of those lost in the precarious business of fur gathering on these uncharted, rock-bound shores of the stormy north seas. In some instances this turbulence was promoted and encouraged by the intrigues of the naval officers in their efforts to discredit the work of the chief manager.[103]

The *promyshlenniki* had indeed represented a segment of Russia's population that, as Zagoskin had aptly put it, had simply "not seen the world in style." Beyond that, however, the picture yielded by Andrews and by available documentary evidence seems to bear out Vavilov's contention that the ills which historically had plagued the social as well as the cultural and built environments of Novo-Arkhangel'sk had stemmed inextricably from the company's almost obsessive preoccupation with fur trading as its great and all-absorbing pursuit. In this context, Shelikhov's earlier efforts, cut short by his untimely death, stand out in sharp relief as having been infinitely more enlightened, comprehensive, and farsighted. By contrast, the Novo-Arkhangel'sk that emerged during Baranov's term in office does not appear to have gone much beyond the aspect of a frontier "boom" town. To be sure, the situation appears to have improved somewhat under his successors. And yet this improvement must be measured more in quantitative than qualitative terms. For, as Novo-Arkhangel'sk and other towns in Russian America continued to develop, they tended to maintain their general aspect of frontier company towns, as evidenced by a photograph of Sitka taken some time before 1894 (fig. 19).

The Russian Orthodox Church in Alaska

Antoinette Shalkop

The history of the Orthodox church in Alaska[1] cannot be viewed as an autonomous phenomenon.[2] Down to 1867 it was closely linked with the Russian American Company, even though events in the church's history in Alaska do not closely correspond with the company's history. And if the mutual efforts of secular and ecclesiastical authorities overlapped only for a few decades, the brief history of the church can nonetheless be seen as part of the history of Russian colonization, for the clergy were missionaries of the Russian government as much as of the church. The church in Alaska was always part of the Siberian diocese, and never developed an independent structure. Such considerations make the church in Alaska difficult to evaluate. Perhaps the best way to measure its works before 1867 is by its impact on the lives of the native peoples it came into contact with and on the creole clergy. The year 1867 in effect marks the beginning of the more nearly autonomous history of the Alaskan Russian Orthodox church.

The Russian Orthodox church gained a formal structure in the New World only after the Russian American parishes were made part of the Kamchatka Diocese in 1841. Until 1855 developments in the new diocese were monitored by Over-Procurator Protassov and dominated by the monolithic figure of Ivan Veniaminov, known as Bishop Innokentii. In 1858 the bishop's headquarters were moved back to Siberia and the expansion of missionary activities in Russian America came to a halt. From the point of view of the imperial government, the church's function was to help Russianize the native population in areas occupied by the Russians, with the Russian American Company functioning as administrator, banker, and supplier. Twenty-six years after the establishment of the Kamchatka, Kurile, and Aleutian Islands diocese, the colonies were sold, leaving a number of creole clergy, trained to think and act like Russians, under a new government. These men continued to serve their religion but now found themselves in ambiguous circumstances.

The Administration of the Church

Prior to any organized effort on the part of the Russian Orthodox church, Russian laymen performed what religious rituals they could, principally baptism of the native peoples they encountered on the Aleutian Islands. In 1793, Catherine II authorized the establishment of the first mission which arrived in Kodiak on September 24, 1794. This initial experience created discord between secular and religious authorities in the colonies and made evident that it was necessary to designate one individual to whom all clergy would be responsible. One of the monks, Archimandrite Iosaf, was selected and consecrated bishop in April 1798. He was to assume responsibility for the "Kodiak, Kamchatka and American diocese" but perished in a shipwreck en route before he could.

Religious activities continued to be restricted by lack of personnel; there was, however, a chapel erected on Unalaska in 1806 that according to parish records stood north of the church built in 1825 by Veniaminov. A third building was erected at the end of the century, in 1894. A small church was erected in Novo-Arkhangel'sk, partially from timbers left after the shipwreck of the *Neva;* and the first priest, Aleksei Sokolov, began his service there in 1816.[3] In addition to keeping the vital statistics, Sokolov also kept the required confessional records. The latter are invaluable as the most complete extant census of the Russian Orthodox population in Russian America. Such record keeping continued through the nineteenth century, with priests recording not only the name of those who came to confession but also those who did not. Often, especially in the earlier period, many individuals made an effort to come to Novo-Arkhangel'sk to receive the Holy Sacraments during Lent or other church holidays. The records thus offer a fascinating parade of individual social profiles with each figure appearing year after year, until either death or departure removed him from this list. Father Sokolov kept his records in a democratic manner; all persons were grouped together without distinction. For each individual, Sokolov listed the name, patronymic, age, provenance, ethnic origin, social status, and in the case of women, relationship to the family. In 1834 Veniaminov changed the method of documentation to a complex breakdown based on social class, as Emperor Nicholas insisted be done in all areas of Russian life.[4]

Until the establishment of an Alaskan diocese, the clergymen in Russia's American colonies received their instructions from the Irkutsk diocese and sent their reports to the bishop in charge of parishes in eastern Siberia. On December 21, 1840, the over-procurator, Count Nikolai Aleksandrovich Protassov, issued an *ukaz* proclaiming that "the Ruler and Emperor has given his acquiescence to the suggestion made by the Most Holy Synod concerning the establishment of a special diocese formed by churches of the Russian-American settlements and other neighboring areas." The bishop of that diocese would be called bishop of the Kamchatka, Kurile, and Aleutian Islands; and Archimandrite Innokentii (formerly Ivan Veniaminov) was appointed to take charge of it. Regulations provided that (1) the Kamchatka and Okhotsk churches were to come under the supervision of this newly established diocese and were to be separated from the Irkutsk diocese; (2) this new diocese was to be classified as a third class diocese; (3) the new bishop was to take up residence in Novo-Arkhangel'sk.

The instructions following this *ukaz* are 160 pages long and state, among other things, that the Russian American Company was to assist in establishing the diocese and building the churches. An estimate made in 1838 determined that there were 10,313 Christians in Russian America and this qualified the new diocese to build eight churches, each serving an area of 1000 square *versts*. The Kodiak parish, with 6,338 Christians, was to be divided into two parts, encompassing Kodiak and Kenai. One priest was to be assigned to the northern part of the new territory and was to reside in Nushagak, which already had a chapel.

The salaries were also specified.[5] Prior to the establishment of this new diocese, clergymen were paid from funds of the Russian American Company according to the agreement the company made under Paul I to take care of the Russian Orthodox missionaries. Including transportation back and forth to Siberia, salaries for the clergymen and other expenses, the Russian government allocated a budget of 56,000 paper rubles, or 16,000 silver rubles, for the operation of the new diocese. This sum proved to be insufficient, and despite increases in the following years, financial support continued to be inadequate. The only clergymen who lived in relative comfort were those attached to the bishop's headquarters in Novo-Arkhangel'sk. Frequent pleas for help from those who served in other locations attest to their poverty.

The early period of the church's administration is characterized by rapid and frequent changes in local parishes and the centers of control over them.[6] The burden of this fluidity fell on individual priests, who were often moved without being given sufficient means to establish themselves in the new locations. Correspondence and reports from such individuals reveal the discomfort and genuine suffering they had to endure in carrying out their assignments during the period in which the new diocese was being developed.

The bishopric of the new diocese was oriented primarily toward Kamchatka and eastern Siberia; the Russian American colonies received only a small share of administrative attention. True, Veniaminov took three lengthy survey trips over that area while he resided in Novo-Arkhangel'sk. But there was much work to be done with the aboriginal tribes in Siberia where the imperial government was concerned with strengthening its base. Especially after the military failure of the Crimean War, the government found it necessary to fortify its positions south of Kamchatka, nearer to China, and determined to engage the church's participation by placing the bishop's headquarters on the Amur River.

The *ukaz* of January 31, 1858, gave new orders and described the changes to be introduced in the management of the church in Russian America. It stated that the see of the Kamchatka Diocese was to be transferred to the Amur River and was to manage the territory with the assistance of two vicariates, one in Iakutsk and the other in Novo-Arkhangel'sk. Since it would take some time to build the necessary establishments on the Amur River for the bishop and his entourage, he was to take up residence in Iakutsk and act at the same time as bishop of the diocese and vicar of Iakutsk until the appointment of someone else to this post. The consistory rights that had been held by the Novo-Arkhangel'sk bishop were now transferred to Iakutsk; Novo-Arkhangel'sk then was to become a vicariate, to be relieved of all responsibilities other than those concerning the parishes in Russian

America. The Novo-Arkhangel'sk seminary was also transferred and until its reestablishment on the Amur River was to be consolidated with the seminary of Iakutsk; the students attending it were also to be transferred to Iakutsk. In place of the seminary, a general school (*obshchee uchilishche*) was to be opened in Novo-Arkhangel'sk which would accept Russian American Company employees' children as well as those of the clergy.[7]

In June 1859, Archimandrite Petr,[8] who had been in charge of the Novo-Arkhangel'sk seminary, was promoted to the position of vicar general of Novo-Arkhangel'sk. Bishop Petr's period is characterized by order and consistency, and this is reflected in the church's records in the Alaska Russian church archives. He was, however, dependent on Veniaminov for all major decisions; a considerable quantity of instructions from the latter dealt with personnel and other matters. Bishop Petr was followed by Bishop Pavel,[9] who served in Novo-Arkhangel'sk from November 1866 to June 1870 and had the difficult task of handling the administration at the time of the sale of Alaska and facing the depressing consequences that followed it.

The period that followed cannot be separated from the earlier history of the Russian Orthodox church in Russian America. Politically, Russia was divorced from its colonies, but psychologically it continued to be present in the lives of the people who had been trained to think that through serving the church they also served the tsar. It also continued to be present in other ways. The diocese offices were moved to San Francisco, and Novo-Arkhangel'sk, now Sitka, was divested of its prestige, but the Russians did not relinquish entirely their foothold in Alaska. The imperial government retained the land on which the churches stood, since theoretically the church itself did not own any land. Russia did not, however, assume responsibility for those servants of the church and their families who remained in Alaska. On the contrary, the Russian government specifically washed its hands of this responsibility, asserting that all "civilized" people remaining in the land—among whom were the creole clergymen—would enjoy the protection of the laws of the United States, as citizens.[10] But such assurances rang hollow; Alaska was a territory and not a state, and nobody, including the newly arrived Americans, enjoyed firm rights in terms of land or property.

The movement toward San Francisco had been growing for a long time, since it was the residence of the Russian consul. As early as December 2 (14), 1867,[11] Consul Martin Klinkovstrom wrote about a group of Slavic immigrants who were seeking a Russian priest. Prince Dmitrii Maksutov also expressed his interest in these people. In a letter he described this potential new flow of Orthodox faithful and stated that he had personally attended their meeting and had been approached by them to establish a parish in San Francisco. The Russian ambassador to Washington, Baron Edouard de Stoeckl, also wrote to Bishop Pavel, reporting that the Greco-Russian-Slav Society of San Francisco had turned to him with a request to help it with the establishment of an Orthodox church. De Stoeckl stated that "the intention of our Government will probably soon be made clear concerning the establishment of a Russian Church in San Francisco, and even the move there of the Novo-Arkhangel'sk bishop's see, as the Most Reverend Innokentii, Metropolitan of Moscow has suggested." Innokentii Veniaminov, in making this recommendation, must have known what impact it would have on the people of Alaska.

Bishop Ioann Mitropol'skii moved the bishoprical see from Sitka to San Francisco in 1870. In a letter of December 12, 1870, to the diocesan office in Sitka, he wrote that "he decided to open a temporary administration in San Francisco...and that priest Nikolai Kovrigin and Deacon Vasilii Gavrilov Kashevarov were to serve under the chairmanship of Pavel Kedrolivanskii." The Sitka inhabitants, already despondent, were deeply dismayed; but the church's representatives felt that San Francisco had many attractive aspects, including its milder climate and the new congregation with assured incomes from mining and other industries. Sitka, by contrast, was destitute and had no prospects of economic improvement. This condition caused the local priest there to incur many debts, to sell various church objects, and even to trade church land. Such actions led eventually to a scandal and even to the sequestration of St. Michael's Cathedral in Sitka.

In 1877 an imperial *ukaz* announced that the Russian Orthodox church in America was to be placed under the diocese of St. Petersburg and was to receive its instructions from the Metropolitan of the Russian capital. The priests who moved to San Francisco were engaged in a bitter power struggle among themselves that ended only with the murder of one of them. The documents of that period indicate that disorder reigned in the lives of the former Russian citizens and conditions in Alaska became even more depressing.

Bishop Nestor Zass served from 1879 until June 1882. He took an interest in the people of Alaska but did not have enough time to accomplish what he set out to do. After a severe illness, he committed suicide by jumping off a ship near St. Michael Redoubt. After him two other men served as bishops of the Aleutian Islands and Alaska. The first, Bishop Vladimir Sokolovskii (1888–91) was notable for his intolerance toward other religious beliefs.[12]

The last representative of the Russian Orthodox church in nineteenth-century Alaska was Bishop Nikolai Ziorov (1891–98), who was in charge of the centennial celebrations of the Russian mission in Alaska. Commemorative events were organized in honor of the establishment of the first Russian mission in Kodiak. Ironically, the principal services were held in San Francisco and the official Russian Orthodox church letterhead of 1894 as well as all the invitations to celebrations in San Francisco had a picture of the newly built cathedral in San Francisco. The emphasis was on Russian Orthodoxy in northern America and not on past history in Alaska.

Bishop Nikolai's primary concern was with the development of new parishes in the United States, and he paid Alaska only as much attention as he felt was necessary. He traveled extensively and wrote copious poetic notes; he had a fine belletristic style, in fact, which may have had something to do with his popularity, for it enabled him to clothe harsh realities with a certain charm. He was responsible for the publication of the *American Orthodox Messenger*, which came out in September 1896.[13]

Social and Economic Conditions

The socioeconomic life of the clergy reflects the influence of Russian policies, social divisions, and the subordination of the church to the government. Here, too, the true attitude of the church toward the creole clergy was manifested, especially after 1867 when most of these people lost their functions and those who still rendered services were left with little or no remuneration. We should view the period as a single unit, however, since most financial matters were handled in the same manner before and after 1867. Money was collected in the form of contributions from the local parishes and was sent by the bishop or head priest to the Department of Ecclesiastical Affairs in Russia. In return, the Alaskan parishes were given operational funds allocated by that same department. Allocations were not necessarily in proportion to contributions, but theoretically according to need; sometimes the parishes that supplied the largest contributions received the smallest allotments, as occurred on the Pribilof islands. Although the money contributed by a given parish was credited to its church, the credit might never be reflected in goods or services received.[14]

From the very beginning of Russian Orthodox activities in Alaska, the support of the clergy was difficult, and it remained an unsolved problem to the very end. Prior to 1841, the Russian American Company paid all the salaries, giving clergymen in charge of parishes on the Aleutian Islands 1,200 rubles annually and providing an additional 850 rubles worth of provisions. After the establishment of the new diocese in 1841, the Russian government allocated 2,100 rubles for the same positions on the islands, but without funds for provisions. The end result was about the same, however, since the priests had to buy their supplies from the Russian American Company for the same price. The salaries were not sufficient even for upper ranking clergymen; almost every dossier contains requests for loans or help from the clergy care fund (*popechitel'stvo*). Even the most exemplary priests found themselves in this pitiful condition both during the Russian period and after the sale of the colonies, when the situation deteriorated even more.[15]

The classification of clerical posts was complex. The basic categories were the salaried (*shtatnye*), the retired or discharged (*za-shtatnye*), some of whom were entitled to a pension, and the unsalaried (*sverkh-shtatnye*) who were supposed to live on the income of the parish, the *dokhod*.

There were different kinds of salaried priests; some received a full salary, others only a portion. Members of the former groups were mostly of Russian origin and had had formal education; the latter were for the most part creoles who had been promoted through merit or necessity because of the lack of personnel in Alaska. During his service in Alaska, Veniaminov ordained several such priests, as did other bishops. A basic condition of such appointments was that the individual was to remain in the parish to which he was attached, and most of the time was dependent on that parish for all or a part of his income.

The second group, the retired or discharged clergymen, were those who had served a required period and were entitled to a pension. Theoretically, the pension was increased with the number of years of service. The beneficiaries of this program were mainly clergy of Russian origin who returned to Russia. Some, including the well-known monk Nikolai Militov of Kenai, died in the last years of their service. Among the creole clergy only those who took allegiance to the Russian tsar were entitled to receive a pension. The only such creole in the nineteenth century was Vasilii Shishkin who, although eligible to receive a pension, continued to work and died while in active service on the Aleutian Islands.

Most of the unsalaried clergy who lived entirely on the *dokhod* were from the Aleutian Islands. They served faithfully but remained in various degrees of destitution and sometimes faced actual starvation. Among these we should mention Pavel Shaiashnikov and Innokentii Lestenkov of the Pribilof Islands. These humble men must be credited with maintaining the Christian faith on the islands of St. Paul and St. George.

The practice of ordaining priests for a certain location and with the requirement that they live on the income they obtained from their parishioners was sanctioned by Veniaminov himself as a means of minimizing the expenses of Alaskan parishes. One such priest was Moisei Salamatov, who received his education in the Iakutsk seminary and returned to his homeland with the hope of becoming a priest. Just before leaving for Moscow to assume the rank of metropolitan in 1868, Veniaminov wrote to Petr Ekaterinovskii, then vicar bishop of Sitka, about the young seminarian Moisei Salamatov: "If the creole Moisei Salamatov agrees to remain in the Atka District permanently as a priest, and, even if his salary is stopped, to live on parish income only, and if he is at the same time deserving of this rank, then ordain him as a priest for the Atka parish . . ." (Instruction 1224).

Veniaminov participated directly in the sale of Alaska. According to his own correspondence, he did not regret this decision but shifted his interest to spreading Orthodoxy in the United States, a likely choice for a missionary as aggressive as he was. But what is difficult to understand is that no provisions whatsoever were made for the creole and native clergymen in Alaska. The Alaska Russian church documents contain a number of papers dealing with this subject; among them is an *ukaz* issued at the time the center of church administration was moved back to Siberia, on the Amur River. This decree, which concerns the rights of the clergy in the Kamchatka diocese, was issued by Over-Procurator Count Aleksandr Tolstoi "in accordance with the suggestions of the Right Reverend Innokentii, Archbishop of Kamchatka." It specified everything in detail, including the number of horses allowed for transportation from a Siberian seaport into the interior. But creole clergymen in Alaska were not even mentioned in this decree. Among clergymen serving in Alaska, only those who were either members of the diocesan office (*pravlenie*) or who were official "missionaries" enjoyed any defined rights. No creole clergyman could be in the diocesan office since it was being removed to San Francisco, where the coveted posts were fought over by priests from Russia. Creole clergymen were not considered "missionaries" because they worked in their home territory, although they surely performed the same duties and endured the same hardships as did those priests who were given the title. As a consequence, a large number of creole priests ordained to serve after the sale were designated to serve either for partial salary and additional income from the parish, or depended entirely on the *dokhod*. During the Russian period these people had lived more or less like serfs on a government-controlled estate.

Education and Cultural Life

Russians saw education as the necessary means of synthesizing old and new cultural patterns, and they applied in Russian America the same principle they used in other occupied countries: conversion of the population to Orthodoxy. A new convert through baptism became a Russian citizen, was given a Russian social rank (*soslovie*), and was entitled to receive elementary education.

The Russian government had long experience with such alien peoples as the Tartars of eastern Russia and the various Mongolian tribes of Siberia. They had learned that an expedient way to reach them was to learn the native language and translate religious material into it. The next step was to recruit students from among the new converts and to educate them to enter the priesthood in their own land. The responsibility of carrying out this task was assigned to the church, and rewards were given to those who applied themselves in the educational field. In Alaska, education was given special attention and was supported by the church as well as the Russian American Company. In addition to local schooling, the more gifted students were given an opportunity to go to Russia for specialized training in seamanship and other practical fields. The church considered education to be of the utmost importance, for Russian priests could rarely communicate with the native people and needed interpreters to perform services. The long term goal was to develop Russian speaking congregations.

The Alaska Russian church archives contain a variety of papers pertaining to education: school records, lists of books, inventories of libraries, and decrees outlining the rules for management. Education was centered on religion, writing, reading Russian and church Slavonic, basic arithmetic, and singing. Book lists and orders for material from Russia reveal much about the curriculum. No secular books were ordered, and if any came to Alaska, it must have been through private hands. There were many orders for the various periodicals that dealt with religious education.

The school in Novo-Arkhangel'sk developed a successful program before 1867; statistics show that there was no shortage of teaching personnel and that students of Russian origin as well as creoles attended the same school. There were also children from Siberia who attended on some sort of exchange program, and children from Russian America were sent to Petropavlovsk or Irkutsk to complete their studies. The seminary, however, was moved to Iakutsk in 1858 when administration of the diocese was transferred back to Siberia; the Russian American Company then operated a general school for clergymen's children as well as for those of its own employees.

Many problems arose after the sale of Alaska and the closing of the Russian school on November 20, 1874. There was a disastrous experiment in San Francisco, where the Russian school quickly failed because most parents there preferred to send their children to the local American school. Bishop Nestor then investigated conditions in Sitka to see how interested the local native people were in having a school reopen in their town. He recorded one specific incident as typical in his report of 1879. He asked an Indian in Sitka why he did not send his children to the Russian church school, to which he received the following reply: "If you will pay us money for my son's education, then he will go to school with the other children." In 1893, a new school named after Innokentii was opened in Sitka in the bishop's house in connection with an orphanage for ten boys. The program was revised, English was taught, and the school had relative success with the Orthodox parishioners. But the Russian priests by now faced competition from other denominations, especially the Presbyterians, who had an efficient school and attracted a large number of students.

The school established in Unalaska by Veniaminov in 1825 was still active after the sale, thanks to the work of Innokentii Shaiashnikov, who in 1880 recorded seventy-four students attending his classes. Although education was limited to religious subjects, Shaiashnikov was one of the rare survivors of the political transfer who knew the native language and was very effective among his people. As the San Francisco school brought no success, the over-procurator issued an *ukaz* on March 27, 1882 (no. 4291), in which it was ordered to transfer the funds, some 3,400 rubles, to Unalaska to open there a program that would prepare native boys for the priesthood. A number of girls also attended this school.

The church's educational program was useful so long as the Russians owned the land; it served the Russian American Company and helped to Russianize a substantial number of native people. Schools succeeded best in the Aleutians, where Russians had been the longest, had married local women, and where Russian was spoken in many homes. But on the Kenai Peninsula, around Nushagak, and in the interior on the Yukon and Kuskokwim, judging from the records kept by the priests, the schooling brought insignificant results. And after 1867, the weakened education effort did not reach far into the population and was further limited by the frequent conflicts between the lingering Russian culture and that of the United States.

Translations were a noteworthy contribution of the Russians in Alaska. With Russia's own Tartar population, the purpose of such translations went beyond religion: they were needed to foster communication. Veniaminov was the first to publish translations of religious works for Alaska, but he was not the only one to do so. In many ways Veniaminov was more fortunate than the men who followed him; he received his education during the brief "age of enlightenment" that Russia experienced during the reigns of Catherine II and Alexander I. It was Catherine who insisted that clergymen receive a broad education in various fields; tolerance and fascination with scientific discoveries penetrated all walks of life at that time, and students had access to a larger variety of books than they did later. Veniaminov benefited from this atmosphere and perpetuated it in his work.

Veniaminov's contributions to knowledge set an example that was followed by others; on the Aleutians Iakov Netsvetov, a creole priest, recorded ethnographic and other scientific information in his daily journal.[16] Salamatov and Innokentii Shaiashnikov continued translations of the Holy Scriptures into the Aleut language. On Kodiak Island Gerasim Zyrianov, Ilia Tyzhnov and Konstantin Larionov translated prayers and formulated a primer of the local dialect; Ivan Nadezhdin, a young Russian clergyman in Novo-Arkhangel'sk, made a translation of the Gospel of St. Matthew and some parts of liturgical works into the Tlingit language and compiled a Tlingit dictionary and a phrase book for the training of young clerical assistants. In spite of his achievements, Nadezhdin received no recognition for his work. In 1855 he was wounded during the Tlingit attack on the capital and eventually returned to Russia. In the interior of Alaska, the creoles Zakharii Belkov and Ioann Orlov should be mentioned for their work with the local languages, although the materials they left behind are not voluminous. There are undoubtedly others whose names have not been recorded.

In the artistic field, music was cultivated as an indispensable part of the liturgical service. Each bishop had his own retinue of choristers and a good voice being important for the ecclesiastical vocation, several men in Alaska rose to the priesthood through the choirs. Another artistic activity about which little is known was the art of icon painting, which, according to the records of the Alaska Russian church archives, was practiced in Novo-Arkhangel'sk at the seminary. The financial papers show an income from the sale of icons painted locally and indicate who ordered what sort of icons. Some of the icons that are still on the walls of the Russian Orthodox church in Kenai were painted in Sitka, and there were many in the Aleutians; some orders came from as far away as Petropavlovsk. In 1851 alone the financial reports show an income of 1,245 rubles from icon painting (*po operatsii ikonopisi*). The master painter of Novo-Arkhangel'sk was Grigorii Petukhov, who, as a young boy, had served in the personal retinue of Veniaminov. When he died in 1858, icon painting was discontinued and existing orders were canceled. There were other painters who worked in the studio at the capital, but once the seminary was transferred to Iakutsk, their work ceased.[17]

The church made other contributions that are valuable today to scientists in various fields. Much of the benefit derived incidentally from the compilation of parish records. The records that have survived describe the land and provide the names of places and people who lived at that time. Few priests ventured to describe the physical or cultural landscape for its own sake, but some left worthwhile records nonetheless. Others even in their routine reports give us incidental information on a variety of topics. Illnesses were usually identified by the symptoms, and it remains to scholars to determine what these ailments were in reality.[18]

One unexpected source of valuable information is the so-called church service journals (*Bogosluzhebnye zhurnaly*) in which, during the late nineteenth century, various clergymen recorded everything they considered newsworthy in their parish. Judging by the notes written on the margins of these journals by the bishops, priests were discouraged from penning irrelevant remarks and were instructed to record only the religious services they performed. But those who deviated from this rule left us useful information. Some Russian priests, such as Aleksandr Iaroshevich, documented their conflicts with the American authorities. Creole priests, more sensitive to native life, left some even more detailed narrations on local life.[19]

The church made a significant contribution in educating the native and creole parishioners and in raising some of them to the rank of priesthood. But the creoles and natives repaid this favor amply with their dedication and long service. The natives who were given the task of "upholding the banner of Russian Orthodoxy," as the over-procurator of the Holy Synod put it, carried on their work in a remarkable manner. Parish work outside Novo-Arkhangel'sk was done by creole priests, for the most part underpaid and without the status that the Russian-born priests enjoyed. Many of these men knew local dialects and perpetuated that tradition of performing services in the native language. Some of them were truly remarkable men, and the opinion held by some historians that the creole was not able to cope with life after the Russians left is not entirely correct. Many men were crushed by difficulties, but some, the creole clergymen among them, survived and quietly nurtured the graft of an alien religion upon their native culture.

Discipline of the Clergy

The records of discipline problems among the Orthodox clergy of Alaska reveal much about life in Russian America, the Russian American Company, the church, and the clergy. For example, rank was an important factor in determining appropriate punishments. High-ranking clergymen were more likely to receive official cooperation in concealing their indiscretions, lest a shadow be cast on them. Complaints against the upper clergy were viewed as vilifications, whereas a simple *prichetnik* or deacon could get into difficulties over minor offenses.

The Russians made sin a public matter in order to discourage it through the punishment of public contempt. Some convicted individuals were made to stand on their knees at the church door throughout the service, or were obliged to leave a service at a certain point as unclean beings. Yet these punishments were not as damaging as being fined, demoted, or defrocked. Fines could deprive the individual of basic necessities. Judging from the documents, Veniaminov used this method frequently. Demotion meant disgrace and loss of income also, but defrocking put the offender on the street. And since the Russian class system was so rigidly controlled, a clergyman from the lower classes who was defrocked had nowhere to find employment.

Offenses were ranked according to their gravity. The most unpardonable crimes were irreverence toward the imperial authority, blasphemy against the church, and insurrection. Any sign of liberalism could have been interpreted as one of these. Surprisingly, while fornication was treated as a serious transgression, it was usually handled in such a manner as to put the blame on the woman or on some other party who was responsible for the gossip. Matters were normally thus smoothed over and the clergyman went ahead with his work. Another frequent offense was mismanagement of church funds, for which the guilty clergyman had to repay the amount from his own resources. Many problems were the consequence of alcohol abuse. Although liquor was rationed throughout the Russian period, records of deliveries list wines of different sorts. Under Veniaminov, the bishop's headquarters received substantial shipments of champagne, marsala, and other delicate wines. Drinking and belligerent behavior were frowned upon since it was usually public, but if the individual repented (*raskaialsia*), he was forgiven and given another chance. With the exception of a few exemplary priests most had an incident or two of this nature in their records.

Certain tipplers showed great ingenuity. After the sale of Alaska, the territory came under the Indian law that prohibited the import of liquor, but not of molasses, from which a very potent beverage was distilled. In addition, the church was authorized to receive shipments of wine and liquor for ritual purposes and for the "health of clergymen." The customs officers reported witnessing irregularities on many occasions. Several priests were reported to have used cranberry juice for communion and then to have drunk all the wine themselves.

During the Russian period there existed a dual disciplinary system, under both the Russian American Company and the church. The sacrament of confession was apparently used as part of this control system. To make matters worse, one was not permitted to miss confession without a good excuse. Many who went did so unwillingly, and the surviving records tell of several individuals who attended to this duty regularly before the sale of Alaska but stopped once they felt they could get away with it.

A tendency toward greater independence and even a spirit of political unrest became more evident after the sale of Alaska. Several clergymen reflected this new mood after 1867. Most were creoles, with the exception of one Iosif Levin, Russian born of Jewish origin (*iz evreev*). Levin's case is well documented and is of particular interest because he worked among the Tlingit Indians. Pavel Levin, son of Moishe Levin, converted to Russian Orthodoxy and became a monk in 1889, taking the name of Iosif. Together with his brother, a musician who had also converted, Iosif was sent to Killisnoo to work among the Tlingits. In Killisnoo, a small settlement dominated by the herring industry, Iosif Levin promptly ran into problems. Local residents circulated a petition calling for his removal because of his harshness towards the Indians. Local Russian leaders and the resident Orthodox priest, Aleksandr Iaroshevich, also accused Iosif Levin of irreverence and blasphemy.

The accusations were handled in the customary manner: people in Killisnoo were asked to submit their accusations in writing, and Vladimir Donskoi, the chief priest at Novo-Arkhangel'sk, prepared a questionnaire to be administered orally among illiterate Indians. According to his accusers, Iosif Levin took his work very seriously and tried hard to learn the Tlingit language, but he criticized the Tlingits' mores and especially their family customs, calling them "thieves, profligates, and drunks who sell your wives and daughters." His devotion was acknowledged, and it was said that he shouted in his zeal and even wept in church. But he was accused of being a Talmudist.[20] Levin was quoted as having said that the Virgin Mary and Christ were both Jews; that the teaching of love among men was practiced 3,000 years before the birth of Christ; and that Russians were baptized under threat of death. He was also quoted as having said "that everything in Russia is done under the stick, Orthodoxy itself was spread among the Russian people through coercion." The worst accusation came at the end of the summary of the eleven-point questionnaire, where Levin's own words were quoted: "Twelve senile blockheads sit in the Holy Synod and they are ruled by a secular power in the person of the Over-Procurator. The head of the Church, however, is the Ruler, the Emperor himself. And the day will come when the young monks will overturn the yoke of monarchy and will rule the Church independently." Faced with such charges, Iosif Levin was returned to San Francisco where an American doctor determined that the monk was on the verge of a nervous breakdown.

The Lives of the Creole Clergy

The lives of the creole priests provide a particularly vivid mirror of the Orthodox church in Alaska. The creole clergy were in effect living testimony of the church's work in the new land; they also provide evidence of the continuing role of Russian Orthodoxy in the New World after 1867.

The line between the Russian and the creole clergy, although imperceptible in some cases, was always present. The principal difference was that a Russian priest could seek a transfer if he did not like his situation, whereas the creole could not. The creole priests remained, regardless of the conditions and the state of their health, and some were forced to endure unbelievable hardships. Very few creole clergymen received any ecclesiastical training prior to the establishment of the Kamchatka, Kurile, and Aleutian Islands diocese. After Veniaminov became bishop at Novo-Arkhangel'sk, the Russian American Company built two substantial buildings, one for the bishop's residence and the other for a seminary school. Thus by the time of the sale of Alaska, many creoles had already finished their apprenticeship and were just beginning to serve as clergymen.

Let us look at the well-documented lives of two creole priests, each representative of his period and social level. Both were sons of employees of the Russian American Company; both were born on Atka and received their initial training by assisting other priests before the establishment of the seminary at Novo-Arkhangel'sk. The difference between the two is that the first died before the sale of Alaska and the second in 1886.

The first clergyman, Iakov Netsvetov,[21] is well known as one of the contributors to Veniaminov's translations of religious books into the Aleut language. He also left a long journal in which he gave descriptions of the Aleutian Islands that he serviced while based in Atka. He was a dedicated worker and was thoroughly Russianized, which was not the case with all creoles.

Iakov Netsvetov's father was a Russian coachman (*iamshchik*) from Tobolsk employed by the Russian American Company. He reared a family on the Aleutians. In the years before his death in 1837, the Russian American Company made him keeper (*sluzhitel'*) of the church at Atka. Iakov was born in 1804 of a native mother. Like his two brothers, Iakov was employed by the Russian American Company, and in 1825 he was in Irkutsk, whence he wrote to Bishop Mikhail, the head of the Irkutsk Diocese. His letter, dated September 10, 1825, states: "In 1823 I was relieved by the Russian American Company from my duty as a scribe and, not being part of any class, found myself without work. And as I have a desire to enter the clergy class, to which I find no obstacles, I would like to ask permission to serve." Bishop Mikhail of Irkutsk noted at the top of this petition that because the applicant had audited classes at the Irkutsk seminary, he considered him as eligible, provided Netsvetov "planned to serve in his native land."

On October 1, 1825, Netsvetov was given his first clergyman's rank, and on January 31, 1826, he married in Irkutsk. During his early priesthood, Netsvetov worked in the Aleutian Islands and spent most of his time in Atka. After Veniaminov became bishop and returned to Russian America, he planned to expand missionary work and decided to bring Netsvetov to the Kenai Peninsula where the Russians had several small posts. An *ukaz* to that effect, on February 3, 1844 (no. 21), gave Netsvetov detailed instructions for his transfer. Netsvetov arrived in Novo-Arkhangel'sk in September 1844, only to find that the plans had been changed. He was destined to go to St. Michael Redoubt and was assigned the task of building a new mission in an area that was foreign to him.

Iakov Netsvetov started his work on the Yukon in 1845. Many difficulties lay in his path. The territory was too large for one priest to manage with few helpers. He did not know the local language and had to rely on interpreters, and the local seminomadic people were wild and not inclined to cooperate. Indeed, the Russians feared them because they had killed several Russians during attacks on their outposts.[22] Netsvetov's health began to fail, and he requested medical books and various medicines in his list of supplies. In 1852 he wrote a petition for relief:

> I entered service in this land already afflicted with physical handicaps, which in the first years I could endure with effort. ... But during my seven years in this severe and cold climate, my illnesses and attacks have increased so much that now I find myself unable to serve in this part of the country. The difficulties that arise daily in my work here, in the church, and in my travels, are too great for me to bear with my weakness and illness. Therefore, I dare most respectfully to ask Your Grace to relieve me from an extended stay here and to permit me to depart. ... (No. 262, August 8, 1852, St. Michael Redoubt)

Veniaminov responded with the following notation written at the top of Netsvetov's letter:

> No. 30. Received August 13, 1853, to the petitioner: There have been no examples of Apostles who requested and received release to retire or to rest, and you are a true Apostle; therefore, I do not dare to take upon myself to discharge you from the Apostolate and by so doing—among other things—to deprive you of the crown for your labor and your illnesses; it is through them that you will carry on your task and you must carry on so as to proclaim Christ. In the meantime God will send you helpers.

This was the first of several fruitless appeals for relief by Netsvetov. None of the monks assigned to him was of any real assistance except for the last, Ilarion Peremezhko, who served from the early 1860s to the time of the sale and left some fairly literate and comprehensive reports. The other helpers could not cope with life in the wilderness. Two of them also had problems with the authorities, one for permitting a Russian laborer without a passport to marry a native woman, the other for shooting at some natives. The third was accused by an angry native husband of being involved with his wife.

Netsvetov was not spared the humiliation of being reprimanded for spending more than his salary. A defeated man, on July 18, 1862 (no. 632), he responded to an *ukaz* of December 29, 1861, stating that the remote missions had demanded great expenditures for travel. The 450 *versts* between St. Michael Redoubt and Ikogmiut could be traversed only with the assistance of at least ten native men, each of whom required twenty rubles a season, plus provisions. He thereafter asked for deductions to be made out of his salary to pay for these debts. Bishop Petr Ekaterinovskii finally took pity upon Netsvetov and released him from his assignment. Netsvetov arrived in Novo-Arkhangel'sk late in 1863 and died there in 1864, leaving a debt of 6,573 rubles which Veniaminov ordered to be paid from the church treasury.[23]

Our second creole clergyman, Vasilii Shishkin,[24] is representative of the lower ranks of creoles who made up the majority of the ecclesiastical class in Alaska. He never reached the rank of priest and was engaged a part of his time in manual labor of some sort. He was born in 1812 in Atka, son of Dmitrii Shishkin, a Russian petit bourgeois (*meshchanin*) from St. Petersburg. Vasilii began to serve as an assistant to the priests at the newly built church in Atka in 1829 and in 1841 was transferred to Nushagak, where he remained until the death of his wife in 1859. Hoping for promotion, in 1846 Shishkin petitioned Veniaminov regarding the departure from Nushagak of Ilia Petelin, Veniaminov's son-in-law, who found the climate too harsh for his health. Shishkin declared that he would like to take the post. He had learned the native dialect but he had no formal training. Every applicant was supposed to write a composition in which he was expected to state his convictions and beliefs. Veniaminov found Shishkin's text inadequate to warrant promotion. Failing to obtain a promotion, Shishkin then tried to obtain a transfer, stating that his health had begun to deteriorate, but he was again refused. After the death of his wife, Bishop Petr Ekaterinovskii transferred him to Novo-Arkhangel'sk and gave him his first promotion. In 1860, Shishkin was finally made deacon.

Shishkin's decline, like that of many others, began in 1867, when the entire Russian system in the New World began to crumble. Creoles watched Russians leaving in large numbers. Native women remaining with small children saw their husbands sail away. Shishkin, who had a son in school in Iakutsk, decided to leave also. Again he wrote a petition stating that he wanted to be near his son and to find employment in Russia. But he was refused, not being an ethnic Russian. Like several other Russianized clergymen in his situation—Vasilii Shabalin and Vasilii Gavrilov Kashevarov, for example—Vasilii Shishkin turned to drink.

In October 1868 a report was submitted to the Ecclesiastical Office in which it was reported that Deacon Shishkin "roams drunk in the port ... he got drunk and was beaten in an American bar." Shishkin, facing possible demotion, responded to the accusations with a letter to Bishop Pavel on December 14, 1868:

> After having read the ukase from the Most Holy Synod of March 19, 1858, I did not find in it any kind of rights for me to receive either a pension or travel funds, if I should want to go somewhere. This in spite of my service since 1829 on the island of Atka where I began first with Father Iakov Netsvetov—a total of 40 years of service. I found only one single favorable word for my creole calling (*moemu kreolskomu zvaniu*): clergymen, natives of the Kamchatka diocese[25] upon completing their indicated service, that is, ten, fifteen or eighteen years, would be entitled to not half, but only one third of the salary last received by them. Now, I dare to turn to your Grace to decide as you please, considering of course that men serving in the Russian American Company for a period equal to my service, receive such a generous settlement that they are even entitled to a pension for the rest of their lives, that is, without having to serve any longer because of old age or due to the sale of these colonies. One's heart sickens when one sees that clergymen cannot have the same rights as the civilian and citizen classes do.[26] But I leave this to God's judges and strengthen myself with the words of Jesus Christ who promised his followers not temporary blessings and worldly well-being but sorrow, suffering and so on. . . .
>
> But for all this, I dare to burden your Grace with the following: 1) I am asking most respectfully to be permitted to go to Iakutsk where my son is, so that I could personally watch after his conduct, his studies and his life and as much as possible help him with financial support. 2) Most mercifully give your orders to allow me to travel and per diem funds for my voyage to Iakutsk. I do not refuse to work in the Ecclesiastical Department if work can be found for me; and I am ready to serve my God wherever it is, but I cannot serve any longer in Sitka because its damp climate does not agree with my old age.
>
> Vasilii Shishkin, most
obedient servant, Deacon of the
Novo-Arkhangel'sk Cathedral.

A note inscribed on this letter by Bishop Pavel states that the original was to be forwarded to Innokentii Veniaminov. We do not know what the latter's reaction was, if any, but we do know that Shishkin was still not permitted to leave. His situation deteriorated further. He was cheated out of his savings by Russian colleagues; he was told that he had many debts which he claimed he had paid off; his superiors reduced his income to six dollars a month; and he was forced to beg. He wrote again, but was by now a broken man. The Sitka priest, Nikolai Mitropol'skii, tried to intercede in his behalf but without results.

Shishkin symbolizes the end of the Russian American period in Alaska and the church's experiment with the natives of the new land. The creoles who were born during the Russian period and survived into the 1880s soon slipped away from their Russian heritage; sadness and pain were replaced by tales that transformed reality into legend. The Russian Orthodox church continued its activities in Alaska, and a missionary effort even began in the 1880s. For example, Tlingit Indians, who had resisted Russian influence earlier, were now proselytized. For this initiative, as for all others before and after 1867, the church depended entirely on the Russian government and received all of its direction from Russia. Local church authorities were never permitted to develop solutions that would have been more suitable to their peculiar situations. The church never had sufficient personnel or means to develop the area. In Novo-Arkhangel'sk, the Russians lived sealed off by natural barriers, mountains and sea, and although there was considerable activity behind the stockade, it affected a limited number of people. In other places the church was understaffed and often placed its missionaries in impossible situations where they could only earn martyrdom.

The impact of the sale of Alaska on creole members of the clergy was traumatic. They had accepted Russian religious and political beliefs, were dependent economically on the Russian American Company, and had learned to think of themselves as Russians. With the transfer of the land to the new owner, they were left to face a new world on their own.

Science and Education
in Russian America

E. A. Okladnikova

Russian scientific endeavors in America, which played a direct role in the education of the indigenous populace of the Aleutian Islands, the American Northwest, and Kamchatka, evolved in several directions. This study deals principally with geography, ethnography, and linguistics, but the Russian American Company also initiated systematic mineralogical and botanical surveys in North America. Particular successes were achieved in the fields of astronomy and meteorological and magnetic research, and there were limited attempts to introduce agriculture, gardening, cattle breeding, and forestry techniques.

Scholars from the Academy of Sciences were not the only ones to pursue research in these fields. Others to play a role included nonacademy intellectuals, the clergy, officials of the Russian American Company and such Decembrists as D. I. Zavalishin and Romanov. *Promyshlenniki* figured prominently in the field during the early period. Later, creoles who had been educated in the schools of Russian America and Russia were instrumental in science.

The early history of Russian-American geographic and ethnographic discoveries was linked to Russian expansion in the Pacific.[1] The works of such Soviet historians and archivists as L. S. Berg, A. I. Andreev, A. V. Efimov, D. M. Lebedev, M. I. Belov, V. M. Pasetskii, and B. P. Polevoi have demonstrated that Russian maps and Russian geographic data laid the groundwork for many European maps of the Pacific and America that appeared before 1758.

In the words of the Soviet scholar L. I. Sternberg, "the reports of Cossacks and *promyshlenniki* included in their naive, lapidary, and laconic log books have made it possible for scholars to extract priceless information on the original geographic configuration, the population and the character of the peoples of Siberia and the Pacific coast, whose ethnographic features have long since undergone drastic changes. All of this would have been lost to science in the absence of such reports."[2]

The contributions to geographic knowledge on Russian America in the late eighteenth and early nineteenth centuries occurred as a result of explorations by the Russian merchantry, who went to great lengths in reconnoitering the unknown region. Vitus Bering's Kamchatkan expeditions, particularly the great Northern expedition of 1733–34, played a major role in the development of Russian geography and ethnography, especially as it concerned the ethnography of the peoples of the Pacific.

G. W. Steller was already making arduous preparations when he was selected by the Academy to serve as *ad'iunkt* natural historian for the Kamchatkan expedition. Thanks to his reports and dispatches to the Senate, the academy and the synod, we are familiar with Steller's scholarly and organizational efforts for the period between September 1740 and June 1741, when on Bering's invitation he finally set off for America.

Steller was more than a researcher: he was also the coordinator of the scholarly activities of his fellow specialists on Siberia. His biography and scholarship are richly interlaced with the lives and works of his associates, which at various times included S. P. Krasheninnikov, A. P. Gorlanov, and I. I. Lindenau, among others. They were the pioneers in the study of many regions of Eastern Siberia and Kamchatka, although their names and works have been forgotten or have been incorporated, often without citation, into the works of others. Such otherwise modest and industrious scholars as the "scribe" Osip Argunov and the soldier Aleksei Danilov have been guilty of this.

Professor G. Müller, author of the first *History of Siberia*, drafted detailed and extensive instructions encompassing all ethnographic areas, including linguistics, for the expedition's members. The Academy of Sciences was not confined to the role of expedition director. It also named its own talented members as participants, including Müller himself, Krasheninnikov, and Steller. Materials preserved in the third file of the archives of the Academy of Sciences are particularly valuable since they relate to the history of Steller's American voyage.

Steller, the *ad'iunkt* of the Petersburg Academy of Sciences who had assembled and been the first to analyze this valuable data, can therefore be considered the pioneer student of the natural history of Alaska and North America. His principal works were published in Germany between 1770 and 1793, and include significant studies in the field of natural history and in "political history," e.g., geography, ethnography, linguistics, and history.[3]

Steller and Krasheninnikov were among the first to pose the question of the origin of native American Indians. This issue was resolved when their ethnographic and geographic findings supported the hypothesis of the transmigration of American aborigines from Asia. Krasheninnikov was also the first scholar to determine the relationship between the Kamchadalian and Chukot languages. The Russian scholar L. I. Sternberg wrote of the linguistic research of Krasheninnikov and Steller: "It is generally striking how much importance these ancient scholars attached to linguistic material. We discover that for each people they not only provided lexicographic material, but comparative-dialectal material as well. Three dialects are clearly distinguished by Steller in Kamchadalian and by Krasheninnikov in Kodiak, while Steller provided lexicographic material together with a valuable text: a translation for the Kamchadalian 'Our Father.'"[4]

Steller was at sea from June 4, 1741, through August 26, 1742. A detailed report on the voyage to the Senate was signed on November 16, 1742.[5] At the conclusion of the report Steller wrote:

> While on the voyage I recorded the history of the ongoing expedition and the lands we observed; where we happened to go ashore I made and noted botanical and other observations. Regarding natural history, I described a few animals that had been previously unknown, namely the sea cow, seal (*sivuch*), a sea bear and a sea beaver; all of which I made sketches of. I described all the birds and fishes encountered on the voyage as well as the birds and fish found on the [Bering's] island where we lived.

Especially noteworthy among Steller's works are his writings on botany and zoology: "A Survey of the Grasses Collected from Iakutsk to Okhotsk in 1740," "A Survey of the Grass Collected in America," "A Dissertation on Fishes,"[6] "A Survey of Fishes," "A Survey of Birds,"[7] "A Survey of Marine Animals,"[8] "A Survey of Insects," "A Survey of Objects that Fly Out of the Sea," "A Mineral Survey,"[9] "A Survey of Medicines that Originated with the Russian Peoples," "A Survey of All that Was Seen and Examined on the Sea Voyage, in German," and "A History of Kamchatka, in German."

Following Steller's death, the academician Müller drew up a report for the academy based on the "reports on the Kamchatkan expedition" which provided a complete listing of all that Steller had done for the academy for the period 1739–46.[10]

The works of Krasheninnikov and Steller were the fruits of a decade of systematic effort. The second volume of Krasheninnikov's work, entitled *A Survey of the Land of Kamchatka*, which is 500 pages in length including Steller's contribution, is a substantial piece of research on both the ethnography of Kamchatka and a wide range of peoples of the Pacific, the Far East, and America.

Information relating to Russian voyages and geographic discoveries in the Arctic and Pacific oceans between 1640 and 1670 "based on the actual memoirs of the voyagers themselves and the maps they drafted" was later assembled and interpreted by P. S. Pallas in 1781.[11] At the request of Catherine II, Pallas also published a "comparative dictionary of all languages and dialects."[12] The first two volumes of this edition were published in 1780. The first volume includes a comparison of the languages of the peoples of Europe and Asia. The dictionary itself contains material on the Aleut and Kodiak languages as well as short listings of the languages spoken by the Cherokee, Iroquois, Oneida, and Seneca Indian tribes.

A government expedition under the command of P. M. Krenitsyn and M. P. Levashev was sent out from 1764 to 1769 to identify the discoveries of Russian *promyshlenniki* and to naturalize the inhabitants of the newly-discovered islands. This effort was concentrated in the vicinity of the islands of Unalaska and Unimak and along the Alaskan coastline.

Beginning in the 1770s, particularly following the expedition of Capt. James Cook, the Pacific became an arena for the long rivalry between Russia, Great Britain, and France. Amidst this competition, the figure of G. I. Shelikhov appeared on the historical stage. As early as the 1770s the Rylsk merchant Shelikhov had taken steps to claim the Kuril Islands. In the 1780s he expanded into America, which not only led to the creation of the Russian American Company but also brought about major changes in the life of the indigenous population. It also led to the systematic exploration of the Alaskan islands. At the same time new territories were being claimed for the Golikov-Shelikhov company, previously unknown Pacific islands were also being discovered. The *St. Georgii*, a vessel dispatched to the Aleutian Islands under Pribilov's command, returned with an abundant bounty and also information on two new islands: St. Gregory and St. Paul. The following other islands along the American coast were discovered by the Golikov-Shelikhov company: Shelidak, Ugak, Sukliu, Hlikahlik, Nikakhta, Hluk, Thalha, St. Constantine and St. Helena, Achaku, Kayak, Yukutat Gulf, and L'tua Bay.[13]

Shelikhov himself authored a comprehensive survey of the American islands.[14] He noted that the islands lying west of Kytak Island and in "Northwest America" were fertile enough to support small-scale farming; moreover, there were many hay fields to facilitate cattle breeding. Shelikhov concentrated on describing the inhabitants, particularly their physical attributes and customs. The latter included burial practices; "ceremonies" performed when greeting guests; methods for producing clothing, including those made from the stomachs of wild animals; underground abodes; communal residences for men (*kazhims*); shamanism; the use of dogs in transport; and the practice of tattooing.

Operating on the directives of Catherine II, Shelikhov instructed all his people in new claimed lands "to concentrate on trapping and on prospecting for any metals, minerals and rare gems."[15] He also ordered the purchase of various locally made items for shipment to Okhotsk: "parkas; wooden sloops; woolen rugs with interlaced strips of beaver hide; fine quality chests; and any other curios, Kenai or local, that can be exported."[16] He was interested in ores, crystal, natural dyes, and fine quality clay, as well as such ethnographic items as "ceremonial costumes, masks, headgear, besoms, drums, hand-held rattles and the like."[17]

Shelikhov showed interest in hiring qualified researchers to go to the New World. In addition to the people indispensable to the operation of the company, such as founders, gunsmiths and blacksmiths, he requested that an "officer with a knowledge of mining be sent to Russian America to record the natural history."[18] He himself continued to gather data in many fields, including notes on a "solar eclipse lasting an hour and a half that occurred on August 4, 1787."[19]

Russian influence also spread in the field of agricultural science. An order issued to Shelikhov by I. A. Pil', governor general of Irkutsk and Kolyma, specified that "durable residential structures are to be built beyond the walls of the established fortifications for the ploughmen, artisans and all who are to take up residence here."[20] Shelikhov was assigned responsibility for seeing to it that assets be channeled into developing agriculture as well as into constructing sea vessels.[21]

The agricultural development of the region began under Shelikhov as part of the overall plan to build up the economy of Russian America and to enhance the independence of her residents. According to the plans of Shelikhov and Pil', the company was to see to "the sowing of hemp and flax, in which the unskilled will be trained, while the skilled shall produce linens and other essential items."[22]

The founding of the Russian American Company and the need for an efficient system for organizing its operations and for outfitting the trading stations required a knowledge of the local ethnography, as well as of the hydrography, geography, astronomy, and natural resources. As a result, the expeditions outfitted for America and Kamchatka took on the character of scientific voyages.

The circumnavigatory expeditions of Russian seafarers in the 1810s and 1830s comprise the second major stage in the history of the study of America. The age of maritime scientific expeditions begun by Bering and Chirikov was continued in the expeditions of Krenitsyn and Levashev (1764–65) and I. I. Billings and G. A. Sarychev (1785–93).

According to the instructions issued to the Billings-Sarychev expedition by the Academy of Sciences, Billings's geographic and astronomical expedition was to survey the Chukot coastline from Kolyma to the Bering Strait and study the seas lying between the Irkutsk *guberniia* and the American coast situated on the opposite side. Signifying the beginning of the crucial second stage of the expedition, the vessel *Slava Rossii* set forth from Petropavlovsk harbor en route to America. The voyagers were at sea for a total of five months. On this voyage Sarychev, making his way by Aleut canoe, gave an account of the major Unalaskan straits, including the Bobrovoi Inlet and the Kapitan Harbor; surveyed the bay of the Three Saints Harbor on Kodiak Island; and visited the Chugach Inlet on the American coast between the Kenai Peninsula and the estuary of the Atna (Mednyi) River. That Sarychev's observations and the maps he drew are marvelously precise is noted by all who have since had occasion to use them. In addition to hydrography, Sarychev's materials illuminate several aspects of Aleut life and provide valuable information on the island's natural phenomena. Such work laid the foundations for the scientific study of the islands, which was subsequently completed by I. Veniaminov, D. M. Teben'kov, and other scholars.

Sarychev has left an account of the customs and practices of the local populace on Kodiak and the Aleutian Islands, concentrating on the Aleuts' ceremonies. Included in his atlas are reproductions of the masks worn by the ceremonial dancers. The lyrics of their songs are also reproduced in his text. The Billings-Sarychev expedition was the first to provide a portrait of Chukchi life, together with more detailed information on the Yukagir, Okhotsk Tungus, and such indigenous American tribes as the Kenais, Aleuts, and Chugach. At Pallas's direction, Dr. Robek compiled a dictionary of twelve native language dialects on this expedition. The kinship of Asian and American Eskimos was established as a result of Billings's efforts.[23]

In addition to Sarychev's writings, the expedition's findings were also published in the works of Billings's secretary, M. Sauer. Billings's own diaries contain valuable ethnographic material as well.[24] A variety of specimens of various sorts was also collected in the course of the expedition. Documents in the Army-Navy Archives' Billings collection include the instructions issued by the Academy of Sciences "on the collection and shipment to the Academy of rare specimens from the mineral, animal and plant kingdoms,"[25] The ethnographic materials brought back in 1794 by voyagers on the Billings-Sarychev expedition are still preserved in the Museum of Anthropology and Ethography in Leningrad.[26]

I. F. Kruzenstern and Iu. F. Lisianskii were the first to open a sea route from Kronstadt to Russian America by sailing around the world on the *Nadezhda* and *Neva* sloops in 1803–5. Lisianskii subsequently produced one of the most comprehensive works ever written on life and culture in Russian America. In examining the development of Russian scientific activities in America, it is impossible to ignore the works of Georg Heinrich von Langsdorff, who devoted his brilliant and extraordinary life to the Imperial Academy of Sciences in St. Petersburg. Between 1803 and 1805 he sailed as a naturalist on the first Russian circumnavigatory expedition. In the company of N. P. Rezanov, he visited Unalaska, Lisi, St. Paul, St. Gregory, and Kodiak Islands. In addition to his zoological, mineralogical, and botanical research, von Langsdorff left memoirs which describe the homes, diet, dress, finery, and tattoos of the Unalaskan Aleuts as well as the sea bear trapping industry on St. Paul Island. He also gathered data on their kayaks, weapons, whale-hunting practices, women's crafts, marriage traditions, customs, entertainment, and religion. This scholarly work contains references to the culture of Kodiak Island, and the living conditions of the Aleuts, the Koniag, and the Russian residents of the island.

Von Langsdorff spent the winter of 1805–6 in Novo-Arkhangel'sk in the company of N. P. Rezanov, A. A. Baranov, N. A. Khvostov, and G. I. Davydov, travelling with this group to the northeastern sector of the island inhabited by the Tlingit Indians. He studiously recorded his travel impressions of such Indian institutions as the family, diet, dress, fishing practices, weapons, weaving crafts, finery, and life-style in general. In Novo-Arkhangel'sk he produced a drawing of several ceremonial Indian group dances.

During this period von Langsdorff also visited California and Kamchatka. While in Kamchatka especially he worked prolifically. In 1812 he published his *Remarks on a Voyage Around the World, 1803–7*, which was written on the basis of materials from his diary. Von Langsdorff's work can be numbered among the most important sources on the ethnography of North American natives.[27]

From 1807–9 V. M. Golovnin commanded a circumnavigatory expedition to Russia's American lands on the sloop *Diana*. The need for essential supplies in Russian America was so great that even the Patriotic War of 1812 did not hinder the "distant voyages" about the seas. From 1813 to 1816 M. P. Lazarev repeated Kruzenstern and Lisianskii's voyage on the vessel *Suvorov*. The first circumnavigatory expedition to explore northern routes originating from the Bering Strait was outfitted by the Russian government under the command of O. E. Kotzebue; it took place from 1816 to 1818 on the brig *Riurik*. Kotzebue's was the third scientific expedition "in search of a route around Alaska" to follow the expeditions of Sarychev, Krenitsyn and Levashov.

One of the most renowned geographical expeditions of the nineteenth century was launched in Russia in 1818 "in order to acquire a comprehensive understanding of our planet." The expedition consisted of two detachments, one for northern waters and the other for the south. The director of the southern detachment and commander of the sloop *Vostok* was F. F. Bellinhausen. The second vessel—the *Mirnyi*—was under the command of Lazarev. The northern detachment, consisting of the sloops *Otkrytie* and *Blagonamerennyi*, was commanded by M. N. Vasil'ev. One of Vasil'ev's tasks was to find a northern pass from the Pacific to the Arctic and to determine the direction of the shoreline north of the Bering Strait. The second detachment's mission was to proceed as close as possible to the South Pole and to explore unknown lands. One of the tasks of the expedition was to reach the South Pole itself.

According to the orders drafted by the admiralty, the explorers were instructed to "conduct scientifically useful tests" involving oceanographic, meteorological, and magnetic observations. A large-scale research project was planned to study polar radiance and the condition of the upper and lower levels of the atmosphere, as well as ice, icebergs, oceanic and tidal currents, and the temperature and salinity of ocean water. The collection of ethnographic, botanical, zoological, and mineralogical samples was given a special priority.

Voyagers in the northern detachment were eminently successful in surveying the American shores, studying the natural resources and populace of the Far North, updating maps previously drafted by other explorers, and conducting research on the Arctic Ocean and sailing conditions in these waters. The Aleutian Islands—including the island of Unalaska—were surveyed, and an ethnographic description of St. Lawrence Island completed. Expedition members visited California, and the navigator Rydalev produced sailing directions for the San Francisco Bay.[28]

V. M. Golovnin, another Russian seaman who sailed on a circumnavigatory expedition and spent time in America, completed his study upon his return to St. Petersburg. This book contains meteorological data later republished separately by the Navy Department in 1873 in a book entitled *Meteorological Observations Conducted During the Circumnavigatory Voyage of the "Kamchatka," under the command of Captain Golovnin: 1817–1819.* Comprehensive ethnographic material on Kodiak Island, Novo-Arkhangel'sk, California, and the Californian Indians was also included in Golovnin's book. Golovnin's work is also valuable today for the historical insights it contains on the activities of officials of the Russian American Company and on missionaries such as Father German; it also highlights the lives and customs of the creole population of Russian America, as well as many other topics.[29]

Accounts of California and the ethnographic details relating to the life and culture of her native populace can be found in the diaries of F. F. Matiushkin and his associate Golovnin from the voyage of the *Kamchatka* and in F. P. Wrangell's diary, *A Voyage from Sitka to St. Petersburg.*

Two other officers of the imperial navy, N. A. Khvostov and G. I. Davydov, also made several valuable observations on the history and ethnography of the Aleuts and the inhabitants of Kodiak Island, Kenai Bay, and the Mednyi River.[30] These authors pointed out that all the "Americans" did not possess sacerdotal skills; rather, only a select group were so endowed.

The second section of their book begins with a geographic survey of Kodiak Island and a more precise rendering of the island's location. It also describes in detail the fish, wildlife, and climate on Kodiak Island.[31] An important chapter is devoted to the custom of tattooing, a practice which staggered the Europeans' imagination. What seemed to them no less exotic and inhumane was the practice of gathering oyster shells off the corpses of slaves that had been lowered into lake water.[32]

Yet another chapter deals with the "Americans'" historical, geographical, and astronomical conceptions. In the section on mythology Khvostov and Davydov render the Kodiakan myth of the creation, where they cite the legend of the unruly daughter and the dog; also mentioned is the continental American legend of the Raven-Creator.[33] The "Americans'" geographical conceptions were, in the authors' words, "very peculiar." On the basis of long-distance voyages the aborigines had come to believe that the world never ended: "People set off on voyages at a young age, only to return very aged; even then they had never seen the end of the world."[34] Davydov and Khvostov also report that in addition to a calendar (whose twelve months the authors enumerate), the Eskimos had a limited knowledge of the stars, which included references to the Pleiades and the Big Dipper.[35]

One of the most significant works written by an official of the Russian American Company from the standpoint of the history of science in Russian America were the memoirs of K. T. Khlebnikov. The memoirs are comprehensive in scope, examining all six regions of Russian America, including Sitka, Kodiak, Unalaska, Atkhinsk, and the Northern and Ross territories.

In the field of descriptive anthropology, Khlebnikov, proceeding from personal observations, supported the hypothesis of the Asiatic origins of the Aleuts inhabiting Kodiak Island.[36] He published materials on the population of Kodiak Island from 1792 through 1825.[37] Throughout his memoirs Khlebnikov describes the customs and life-style of the aboriginal populace[38] and gives special treatment to a discussion of the soil texture on the Aleutian Islands. In addition he made frequent trips to Russian California from 1817 through 1832.

Ivan (Popov) Veniaminov (later Archbishop Innokentii) made a significant contribution to the study of the geography, history, and ethnography of the peoples of the Aleutian Islands and the Northwest Coast of North America. His important *Writings on the Islands of the Unalaskan Region* marked the zenith of the study of Aleutian culture achieved by Russian scholarship in the second half of the nineteenth century. Literally everything captured the bishop's interest: the islands' origins; the history of their discovery; the process by which they were settled and the appearance of the islands' first inhabitants (he believed the Aleuts were natives of Mongolia);[39] volcanoes; earthquakes; marine and land wildlife. He made climatic and meteorological observations and studied the influences behind the formation of the islands' special climate. In Alaska he continued producing meteorological studies while surveying the mountains, rivers, gulfs, flora, and fauna. But above all it was man that fascinated Veniaminov; his anthropological scholarship is absorbing for its depth and philosophical curiosity.[40] He characterized the Aleuts and described their natural abilities and qualities which he admired, particularly their visual acuity, fortitude, endurance, and vigor. Veniaminov's works are exceptionally valuable because they contain his detailed descriptions of Aleut customs associated with childbirth, marriage, death, ceremonies, and armed conflicts; such items of material culture as homes, clothing, kayaks, and hunting tools; and their views on moral principles, time, the universe, language, and medicine. Beyond all this, the bishop was significant in his fight to establish the system of education and to build schools.[41]

His writings on the Koloshes comprise a large segment of his scholarly legacy.[42] Veniaminov wrote of the origins of the Koloshes and their names, and he cited all the occasions where their ceremonies were performed. He also described their rituals, their customs for imparting resolve (thrashings), their ceremonies involving human sacrifices, and their mythology. Veniaminov was the first to approach the study of the rich and ancient heritage of the indigenous Indian populace of Alaska with affection and devotion. A series of tales of the Raven, the legendary forefather of the Indians of the North American Northwest, were recorded by his pen almost seventy years before Emmons and fifty years before the American scholar Niblak first published a few such legends in English translation. Veniaminov translated legends on the creation cycle (the Raven cycle), on the thunderbird and the antedeluvian humanity of birds, as well as a series of cosmogonic legends (about the brother and sister who turned into the sun and moon), and ursine myths, among others. He described shaman rituals, the variety of shaman spirits, demonstrations of the power of shamans' hair, healing ceremonies, and the practice of cathartic vomiting to cleanse one's self when undergoing the initiation into shamanism, along with much more.[43] Veniaminov also reveals himself in his work as an important authority and discriminating connoisseur of the Indians' applied art. The fieldwork of Veniaminov the ethnographer yielded a large quantity of vivid and useful material, such as references to the significant role played by old women and mothers in Indian society.

On March 20, 1841, the botanist F. von Fisher wrote of Veniaminov's practical efforts toward educating the Aleutian natives and introducing the islands to modern amenities:

> The Right Reverend Innokentii, renowned for his extensive philanthropy on behalf of the inhabitants of northwest America and the Aleutian Islands, particularly the island of Unalaska, told me of his desire to cultivate a forest on that island and thereby provide its residents with a valuable resource . . . and indeed, some trees transplanted from Novo-Arkhangel'sk to Unalaska by Right Reverend Innokentii at no small effort have taken well and demonstrate that a forest can be cultivated on that island.[44]

In addition to proposing that certain species of trees be used for transplanting, including fir, silver fir, Sitka pine, cedar, larch, birch, alder, Siberian acacia, aspen, and poplar,[45] Fisher himself recommended specific planting methods and the requisite care for the saplings.

The Russians in America were involved in forestry, agriculture, and gardening in both their practical and scientific aspects, as manifested by the early missionaries' attempts to train the natives in small-scale farming and forest cultivation, the Russian American Company's efforts to introduce plow farming in order to provide the colonies with bread, and the development of farming and cattle breeding in Russian California. This research assumed a systematic form in the 1840s with the works of Veniaminov, G. E. Chernykh,[46] and I. G. Voznesenskii.

Between 1830 and 1860 a third stage of scientific research in Russian America began to take form. The third stage coincides with the crisis in serfdom and the growth of national self-consciousness in Russia. The Russian navy, concentrated in the Black Sea, was now almost entirely excluded for use in exploring either the Arctic seas or America. The expeditions of this period were outfitted instead primarily by the Academy of Sciences, a group of independent mining engineers, and by the Russian American Company.

Il'ia Voznesenskii's expedition to Russian America is a landmark of this period in the ethnographic and biological study of northwest America and California. In the mid-nineteenth century the first serious and concerted effort to study the culture and life of Californian Indians was undertaken by Russian scholars, as reflected in their collection of ethnographic materials. It was at the hands of Russian scholars that at the turn of the nineteenth century many unique items of Indian culture were preserved for both Americans and Russians. The ethnographic and zoological collections which he assembled in California are still preserved in the special collections of the Museum of Anthropology and Ethnography and the Zoological Museum in Leningrad.[47]

Immediately following his arrival in the Russian American capital of Novo-Arkhangel'sk, Voznesenskii was met by I. A. Kuprianov, who had worked on hydrographic projects and had been instrumental in the development of scientific research in Russian America. During his tenure as director of the colonies, Kuprianov had assembled abundant zoological, botanical, and ethnographic samples. He assigned Voznesenskii the task of preparing these collections for shipment. After completing Kuprianov's assignment, Voznesenskii set off on a voyage to California in 1840–41 with the principal purpose of collecting zoological and botanical samples for the Academy of Sciences. The fruits of this voyage exceeded all expectations.

As P. M. Kozhin recently pointed out: "Voznesenskii's field work in effect marked the genesis of the scientific study of California."[48] Voznesenskii proceeded "south by sea along the California peninsula to the southern bank of the San Francisco Bay and up the Sacramento River to the Per'evaya River. The explorer's itinerary also encompassed the Fort Ross region, and although his stays there were brief, they nonetheless enriched his collection with a plethora of ethnographic material, including the names of common household items from the southwest Pomoan dialect.[49]

Voznesenskii began collecting materials as soon as he arrived in California. His initial samples were collected from the region inhabited by the Miwok Indians, or more accurately the Coastal Miwok, a tribe which had settled in the Bodega Gulf region just where Voznesenskii put ashore on the *Elena.* During his extended "excursions" to Sonoma (the Coastal Miwok), Napa (the Vintu), and up the Sacramento River (the Miwok), Voznesenskii assembled extensive collections of wicker crafts[50]—the most traditional and in their own way the most original of Indian arts.

Voznesenskii's trip to southern California lasted a mere forty days. In the Port Loretta region his attention was focused solely on collecting botanical and zoological specimens. Frequently he drew precise sketches of the specimens he found, revealing himself as a talented artist in the process.

During his stay on the Northwest Coast of North America and Alaska, Voznesenskii worked on geological and mineralogical research and made a visual survey of the Alaskan peninsula. He also devoted time to the study of botany, zoology, and ethnography. From the "Lesnov Toen" he purchased eleven samples of various masks.[51]

During the winter he spent in Novo-Arkhangel'sk in 1834, Voznesenskii obtained several valuable specimens both by purchasing them from the natives and by searching them out in the hills. During this time he also made notations on earthquakes in his journals. Voznesenskii also conducted important scientific research on Kamchatka, along the Okhotsk coastline, and on the Kuril Islands. During this same period the Russian American Company made repeated efforts to explore the inland territories adjoining the northwest coastline of North America. The famous kayak expedition of Kashevarov and Serebrennikov was organized for this purpose; it explored the Mednyi and discovered the Tlishitna River.

Between 1842 and 1844 what was by every measure the most significant expedition to the Alaskan interior took place under the direction of L. A. Zagoskin. The purpose of this expedition was to survey the basins of Russian America's two great rivers—the Yukon and the Kuskokwim. This expedition revealed a virtually unknown world of Indian and Eskimo tribes and gave rise to a famous book on history, ethnography, and geography entitled *A Cross-Country Survey of a Sector of Russian Possessions in America.*[52]

Zagoskin, the first Russian specialist in the field of American Eskimo spiritual culture, ritual, and shamanism, concentrated on the Athapaskan Indians and the Eskimos. On the basis of his field work, he established the tribal continuity of various Athapaskan groups.[53] Zagoskin's ethnographic observations began with linguistic notes together with an anthropological classification of the tribes; later he added ethnographic material. Zagoskin strove to examine systematically all aspects of the material and spiritual culture of the tribes that had captured his eye. His work is characterized by a "critical view," an attempt not only to produce definitive conclusions but also to substantiate them scientifically with the material he presented. Today his ethnographic collections are among the unique exhibitions at the Museum of Anthropology and Ethnography of the Academy of Sciences of the USSR in Leningrad and at the Museum of Anthropology of Moscow State University. His specimens constitute a valuable supplement to those gathered by Voznesenskii; the more so since there are no items from the inland regions of Alaska in Voznesenskii's voluminous collections.

Another Russian seaman and scholar on America—F. P. Litke of Sitka, St. Georgii—also collected ethnographic material along the coast of the Norton Gulf and the Kwikpak and Kuskokwim rivers during a circumnavigatory expedition on the sloop *Seniavin* between 1826 and 1829. He also produced important geographical, climatic, botanical, geographical, and some ethographic work.[54]

Litke's book contains data on the geological makeup of Sitka, St. Gregory, and the Great Baranov and Aleutian islands, as well as lists of useful minerals extracted at these locales, such as tufa, a mineral used by the Aleuts in the construction of stoves, as well as amber and brimstone, which were also mined by the natives.[55]

On the Alaskan peninsula the expedition found furruginous sand, cinder, pumice, chalcedony, jasper, quartz, and more.[56] Litke also described three new Alaskan mountain ranges: the Morzhov, Ivanov, and Pavlov[57] ranges and concluded that "it appears the Aleutian archipelago cannot be anything other than the remains of a land which formerly lay to the west of America and broke away violently from the continent. It is likely that volcanic forces and oceanic currents played equal roles in this cataclysm."[58] Of the Diomedes Islands Litke wrote, "These islands are likely the remains of a natural dam unifying America and Asia that was dissolved by the sea."[59]

While sailing the Bering Sea Litke mapped important navigational points lying along the Kamchatkan coast north of the Avachin Inlet. Systematic magnetic observations were performed and abundant collections of grasses, mammals, birds, fishes, and minerals were also gathered here. The expedition's bird collection was to go to the Academy of Sciences.[60]

Litke focused his attention on producing a census of Kodiak Island, the island of Unalaska, and the islands of the Atkhinsk region. According to his calculations approximately 11,000 natives resided here. Armed with this data he attacked the censuses worked out before him by Sauer, von Langsdorff, and Shelikhov wherein the populations were deliberately exaggerated. In Litke's opinion the most accurate and impartial census had been produced by Baranov.

Litke's book contains descriptions of social relationships within families, the rites associated with birth,[61] child-rearing, and death; the social status of women,[62] slavery,[63] tribal organization,[64] battles,[65] and games (such as the stick game, which was played along the entire Northwest Coast).[66]

The islands of Sitka, Unalaska, St. Matthew, and the Pribilovs were described by Litke both in terms of their natural history and ethnography. The kayaks and earthen abodes of the American natives were also examined.[67] At the conclusion of his work, Litke outlined his hypothesis on the genetic kinship among the tribes of the Northwest Coast of North America.[68]

In 1862 an overview of Russian America was written by Lt. Capt. P. N. Golovnin of the Department of the Navy. This report by Golovnin, who had been responsible for revising the colonies' operation, describes Russian America's soil, climate, vegetation, and useful minerals, particularly coal.[69] Golovnin wrote of coal strata that could be found from the coastal region to very far inland; he also named gold as one of the significant mineral resources of Russian America's Northwest.[70] In discussing the customs and practices of the Aleuts and other Indians, Golovnin did not confine himself simply to enumerating the objects that were characteristic of their material culture; he also made notations regarding various of their ancient rites, including the ritual of sacrificing slaves. Golovnin's negative views on the institution of slavery among the Indians were those of a nineteenth-century intellectual.

Engraved and printed in Novo-Arkhangel'sk in 1852, I. Teben'kov's *Atlas of the Northwest Coast of America from the Bering Strait to the*

Korrientes Cape and the Aleutian Islands, with an attached rendering of Several Regions of the Northeast Asian Coast appeared after Kashevarov's *Atlas of the Eastern Sea.* Teben'kov's atlas summarized the results of many years of Russian geographic exploration in Russian America. Between 1845 and 1850 he had surveyed the west coast of Sitka Island, the American coastline between the Kenai Peninsula and Kodiak and her adjoining islands. The Aleutians were also carefully explored.

Novo-Arkhangel'sk boasted a museum in which were housed various items brought over from St. Petersburg by A. S. Stroganov. Included among its collection were "various portraits, drawings and pictures from the Academy of Arts, sketches of different vessels from P. V. Chichagov, naval minister, and a prayer book from the Most Reverend Amvrosii."[71] The museum also contained cartographical materials and scientific instruments.[72] In 1837 the governor's residence also contained a library, a study with naval maps and instruments and a "museum of birds and animals living on the lands and in the seas of the Russian American colonies and the garments of the primitive tribes inhabiting the northwest coast of America."[73]

At the behest of the Academy of Sciences, the Russian American Company in 1841 began constructing an observatory to conduct magnetic measurements on Japan Island, not far from Novo-Arkhangel'sk. This observatory became the American link in the world's first regular geophysical network, established by Russia in the second quarter of the nineteenth century. The project to create such a network of meteorological observatories across all of Russia, including the Far North and Kamchatka, with scientific analysis to be concentrated in a special scientific committee of the Academy of Sciences, was proposed as early as the beginning of the century by V. N. Karazin. Meteorological data produced by the observatory on Japan Island was to contribute significantly to this international geophysical collaboration.

In much the same spirit, the Imperial Botanical Garden approached the heads of the Russian American Company with a request for samples of certain varieties of American animals and vegetation. The Botanical Garden sent the company instructions setting forth not only which species of animals and vegetation should be collected, but also the methods to be used to collect and prepare them.[74]

Systematic geological research was undertaken in Russian America beginning in 1848 with the works of P. P. Doroshin, an engineer who was sent to Russian America that year by the board of directors of the Russian American Company. Doroshin conducted research and examined the type of soil in the Sitka region, on Kodiak Island, and along the Eastern bank of the Kenai Bay. Of Doroshin, P. Tikhmenev has written:

> A mining engineer who joined the Company in 1848, Doroshin conducted geognostic research and surveyed Sitka Island to the Arctic Cape, along with Kodiak Island and the eastern side of Kenai Bay. On Sitka he found limestone; on Khuntsevo he uncovered coal as well as soils that most probably contain diamonds. Coal and graphite were discovered in several regions on Kodiak Island. Coal samples whose quality was recognized to be significantly higher than that of the coal found on Kodiak Island were uncovered along the coast of Kenai Bay. In the Kaknu River he turned up evidence of gold.[75]

A joint Russian-American project to study the mineral resources found along the Northwest Coast of North America was organized in 1865 as a result of a letter written by a mining engineer named de Stoeckl to the director of the Department of Mines.[76] From a private conversation with Romanovskii, colonel of the Corps of Mining Engineers, de Stoeckl had learned of the discovery of gold, silver, mercury, and copper in the Sierra Nevada region by an American geologist named E. Whitney.[77] De Stoeckl therefore contacted Whitney and proposed that a joint Russian-American expedition across Russian America be organized, with support from the Russian Ministry of Finances. The Ministry of Finances in turn, through Lieutenant General Gildstern, stipulated that "all reports, maps, and materials from Whitney's expedition are to be turned over to Russia."[78]

So on the eve of the year 1867 Russia was again preparing to employ scientific technology to gain mastery of the natural resources of the Aleutian Islands and North America, just as she had done when Russians first became active in America in the eighteenth and early nineteenth centuries.

Although published literature on Russians' efforts in the field of education in America is not as extensive as the materials on science in Russian America, the information contained therein, coupled with abundant archival materials, make it possible to portray in some detail the history of Russian education in America.[79] The very fact that schools of various types existed—elementary, secondary, and special schools, such as seminaries—and that they were available for both the creoles and aborigines, as well as for the children of officials of the Russian American Company, was significant for the history of Russian America, for it reveals a concern on the part of the company for the education of the native populace.

From the first steps taken to convert the Aleutian natives to Russian Orthodoxy through the planning for a medical institute and the founding of both a seminary and a colonial "academy" in Novo-Arkhangel'sk, each generation of Russians in America strove to do its part in educating the natives on the continent and the islands, not always motivated strictly by political or economic considerations, but inspired by the progressive ideas of the enlightened thought of their day.

Russians' educational programs in America were patterned along two principal lines, clerical and secular. Native children were drawn into the schools by associating with the Russians. On the Kenai Peninsula a settlement established by the Lebedev-Lastochkin company maintained a school where the Russian language was taught; simple *promyshlenniki* functioned as teachers there.[80] Largely as a result of these schools on Kenai and Kodiak, a great deal of progress was made in eliminating the language barrier.

Indeed, Russian traders gradually came to employ what L. D. Starr calls the practice of "instructing" the natives by familiarizing them with Russian culture, customs, and religion. The *promyshlennik* Ivan Glotov became the pioneer in this cause as early as 1759 when he first began baptizing the Lisii Aleuts into the Russian Orthodox church. Andrian Tolstoi carried on Glotov's work.

Extensive plans to expand trade and local industry in Russian America as well as to explore and conduct scientific research in new territories all gave rise to the need to educate a local work force.

Progress in the field of education in Russian America became clearly evident with the arrival of Shelikhov, who himself taught Amanat children Russian, mathematics, and scripture. Shelikhov's wife, Natal'ia Nikolaevna, taught needlework to young creole girls. A special sewing workshop was set up in her home. In all there were twenty-five students. The Kodiak school offered training in navigation, mathematics, and "the arts." A plan to send several particularly gifted students from this school to Japan "for navigational training" was also considered.

On December 11, 1775, a resolution by Shelikhov was adopted on Kodiak Island which contained, among other items, the following reference to the school: "The children's school I have founded (to provide) a Russian education for the locals is to be expanded."[81] Shelikhov delivered books to Kodiak Island and made a great effort to spread literacy in the native communities: "These people must be given the opportunity to improve their minds," he wrote, "Their children are able to grasp their lessons quickly, in fact, by the time of my departure several had learned to speak Russian so well that they could be understood without difficulty. I have provided twenty-five young students with such an education, all of whom frankly prefer to associate with Russians rather than with their primitive elders."[82] In a report to the Irkutsk Governor I. A. Pil', Shelikhov wrote of the natives' innate nature: "However savage they may be in their customs and manners, the islanders are in fact rational as well, given their profound and extensive ignorance. I believe that the sincerity of their peaceable disposition outweighs any possible heathenism in it."[83] Pil' advised Shelikhov to make an effort to "be kind and obliging in your contacts with the Americans," to familiarize them with Russian culture and life-styles in an "educational residence," and to "draw out the most talented youth from the Indian and Aleut communities." Vancouver has written of the Russians' prescient policy: "in all their colonies (the Russians) draw the natives into their communities and house them in specially-constructed residences where they are trained in the Russian language. No doubt they also try to teach them practices that in time would serve the interests of both peoples."[84]

In Murav'ev's time a school was established at Novo-Arkhangel'sk. The school that had been founded earlier by Shelikhov on Kodiak Island continued to operate, but was now used primarily to educate orphans.

The historical archives in Leningrad contain the draft of a document drawn up in the name of the director of the Russian American Company that refers to "a gift from the Grand Duchess Mariia Fedorovna in the amount of 2,000 rubles to be used to establish an academy of commerce."[85] And indeed, the school on Kodiak Island opened its doors under Baranov, and later operated under Rezanov. The latter believed that "in order to develop this region, three foundations must be laid: one in agriculture and one in education, together with a program to encourage population growth."[86]

The first secular school on Kodiak Island to be operated by the Russian American Company was opened during Baranov's tenure as commandant. Lt. Aleksei Chistiakov was appointed director of the school. The curriculum was designed to teach the students spelling, arithmetic, and scripture. This school was subsequently converted into an academy, and part of it transferred to Novo-Arkhangel'sk. A boys' school was founded on St. Paul Island as well, of which the following was written by F. P. Wrangell:

> Rezanov issued instructions to build an agricultural school under the supervision of Fathers Herman and Afanasii. In 1805 twenty boys were selected from a group of eighty and were sent to Afognak, where they worked in farming with the Fathers. Some of these boys left the school, but a few remained up to 1825 . . . all of these various efforts to establish schools were not fruitless, however, and in the colonies today there are numerous bookkeepers and accountants among the Creole labor force who were students of that era.[87]

A school for creole girls was also founded where the girls were taught basic housekeeping and needlepoint by the wife of the island's governor, Banner. Wrangell recalled that

> Bander's [Banner's] wife selected ten young Creole girls to be trained in needlepoint and housekeeping, but she only lived for two years and [after her death in 1804] the school disbanded. In 1821 Murav'ev directed the administration to provide charity support for orphans and see to their education: six were found, but there was no one to teach them. I found seven and unfortunately saw that there was no woman who could get along with the children as needed. I nonetheless tried to support this institution as much as possible.[88]

A school for girls was opened in 1839 and by 1847 all vacancies there were filled. The girls, both creoles and daughters of company officials, were taught in the same manner as in Shelikhov's school. The curriculum included housekeeping and needlepoint; those who wished to could study spelling and arithmetic as well.

In the 1830s the Baranov-Rezanov school was turned into a colonial academy for officials of the Russian American Company as a result of the efforts of A. K. Etholin. All the children of company officials, without regard to rank or title, studied in this all-colonial academy. Those who attended this academy at the company's expense were required to work in a colonial position for a period of ten years. This way the company made every effort to secure a work force for the colonies by attracting a locally educated labor force, including creoles.[89]

In 1837 seventeen graduates of this colonial academy, having completed the scientific curriculum, became company officials, sailors, traders, and ship boys. In general, the course of study followed two lines, one providing workers for the navy and the other training priests.

The Novo-Arkhangel'sk boys' academy for the sons of company officials functioned as a preparatory school for the colonial academy. The children of company officials of the "lower ranks," together with workers' children and orphans, were accepted here. All graduates of the Novo-Arkhangel'sk school had the option of automatically matriculating at the colonial academy. Several of them joined the ranks of the company as fully qualified clerks and artisans after graduation. The creoles A. Kashevarov and R. Serebrennikov are known to have been particularly successful after graduating from the Novo-Arkhangel'sk school, achieving success not only in their work for the company, but for Russian learning as well.

In a report entitled "On the Progress of Popular Education in the Kamchatkan Region of 1866" the following is recorded:

Academies have been founded at the Company's expense in America, the port of Novo-Arkhangel'sk and on Kodiak, Unalaska and Atka Islands. In America and Novo-Arkhangel'sk the archpriest Pavel Kurolivanskii and a Company official, Vasilii Shishkin, do the teaching and are paid by the Company. Another official, Vasilii Kashevarov, teaches the Kolosh children on a volunteer basis in a Company building. Petr Kashevarov, a priest, teaches the children scripture at the Kodiak academy and is paid by the Company. Father Innokentii Shaiashnikov and both deacons do the volunteer teaching on the islands of Unalaska and Atka. The priests' wives from the Atka chapel provide instruction for the girls. In addition, the children at the Nushagak and Kenai missions—creoles, Alegmutes, Kuskokwims and Kenais—are taught by the missionaries, arch-priest Feofil and Father Superior Nikolai, the former in the school that already exists there, the latter in his home.[90]

In 1854 a temporary school for the sons of Russian American Company officials was founded in Novo-Arkhangel'sk. Four years later the Russian American Company, acting on behalf of the governing board, submitted a proposal to the "Holy Ruling Synod" to establish a common colonial academy at Novo-Arkhangel'sk in which children of the clergy would be educated alongside the children of company officials. The following guidelines were proposed by the board of directors of the company:

1. An academy to be called the General Academy of the Russian-American Company shall be established for young men in Novo-Arkhangel'sk.
2. The responsibility for overseeing this academy shall fall on the colonial administration, with direct supervision assigned to a single teacher who shall be chosen for this task by the governor.
3. Curriculum: (1) biblical scripture, ecclesiastical and church history; (2) the Russian language; (3) geometry, including stereography; (4) geography; (5) history of the Russian state and general history; (6) penmanship and drawing; and a program of ecclesiastical training deemed by the church to be sufficient in depth for clerical students planning to enter a seminary.
4. The construction of the school, the teachers' salaries and housing for the students, etc. shall be paid for by the Company.[91]

In August 1858 the board of directors of the Russian American Company presented to the Ministry of Finances its case for the need to establish such a general colonial academy in Russian America:

> In the Russian-American colonies, the administration of which is entrusted to the Russian-American Company, the education of youth has been limited to an existing ecclesiastical seminary in Novo-Arkhangel'sk ... where children are given a secular education, and to primary schools for boys and girls established at the Company's expense.

With the sphere of Company operations expanding significantly and the attendant increase in the local population, the need to establish such an educational institution in Novo-Arkhangel'sk is quite evident. This institution would provide the children of Company officials with an education sufficient to enable them to occupy positions in the Company apparatus, which are now filled primarily by individuals on temporary assignment from Russia . . .

It would be good if this school could provide an education for the children of Company officials who cannot afford to pay for their own children's education. This could facilitate an end to the need for consigning people from Russia to fill these posts and the expense of their return trip following the end of their tenure.[92]

In response to this appeal in 1859 this General Academy of the Russian American Colonies (for boys) opened its doors. On this institution P. A. Tikhmenev observed:

The re-opening of the boarding school in Novo-Arkhangel'sk can be expected to play no small role in the education of the daughters of Company workers. A similar boarding school was founded by the Company during the time I. A. Kuprianov ran the colonies and was upgraded significantly during Etholin's time. It is clear from the colonial Governor's most recent report that there were already fifteen female students enrolled in the school. The curriculum consisted of courses in the scripture, the Russian language, geography and history. The girls were also trained in sewing.[93]

In tracing the evolution of secular education in Russian America, L. D. Starr writes that a colonial institute was formed from Baranov's 1805 school (later, the Etholin Academy of the mid-nineteenth century). In the tsar's directive to the board of directors of the company on the establishment of the general school, special attention was given to the development of studies pertinent to commercial affairs.

From the company schools the creoles went on to Irkutsk and St. Petersburg to continue their education. Each year there were between five and twelve students in Russia studying maritime, commercial, and medical sciences. The renowned Alaskan explorers A. I. Klimovskii, A. F. Kashevarov, P. F. Kolmakov, and P. V. Malakhov were all creoles and graduates of the famous Kronstadt Navigational Academy in St. Petersburg.[94]

With regard to the educational efforts of the Russian Orthodox church in America, it might be noted that the mission that arrived on Kodiak Island on the *Three Saints* galiot soon expanded its activities into the sphere of popular education. On Kodiak Island a school for native children was established in the home of the archimandrite. A member of the archimandrite's retinue who remained on the island after the former's return to Russia described the school as follows: "[Fathers German and Iosaf] were not only responsible for the orphans left at our home for upbringing and education, but for each of us as well, as we were making every attempt to educate the natives. Hence, it was important for us to maintain cordial relations with the people."[95] There follows a complaint about A. A. Baranov, who was hindering the educational process by overloading the children with work. Archimandrite Iosaf, sent by the Holy Synod to America to head the ecclesiastical mission, wrote upon his return to Russia that the natives of these regions "are capable in both philology and art."[96]

F. P. Wrangell described the mission's first experiences with this school:

> The original missionaries remained on Kodiak Island and limited their educational efforts to the [Pavlov] harbor region itself. They worked to establish an agricultural school and a school for the creole children. But, unable to gain the respect of the local leadership, with whom they waged an incessant battle in demanding absolute independence, and being to a large degree restless and morally reprehensible, members of the mission did not succeed in establishing a school with a solid foundation, nor in spreading agriculture, nor in giving these people a taste for such activity.[97]

Wrangell also wrote the following on the history of the Kodiak school:

> Soon after the mission's arrival, Archimandrite Iosaf established a school in his home for fifteen creole children. Father Nektarii was the teacher. When the Archimandrite departed, he put Father Herman in charge of the school. This school remained in a mission building until 1802, when it was taken over by the Company and a certain trader by the name of Iudin provided training for the students under the supervision of the Kodiak boarding school. With the arrival of Father Gedeon on the *Neva*, a school was re-established there for eighty boys. Their teacher was again Nektarii.[98]

Father German operated his own school for Aleut children on Elovii Island in 1823.[99] He was assisted by the Aleut Christian Zyrianov, who functioned as a translator of prayers into the Kodiak language. Father German, who practiced gardening at his home, worked diligently to impart agricultural techniques to the natives.[100]

Father Gedeon and V. F. Lisianskii arrived in Russian America in 1804. Of his activities there, Gedeon wrote: "In my remaining spare time I engaged in writing and preaching. I also prepared the arch-deacon Nektarii to assume teaching duties in the Kodiak school. Nektarii demonstrates a strong interest in and aptitude for science, particularly mechanics. I showed him some of the basics of the other sciences: arithmetic, history, and geography. The French language was also covered."[101] Gedeon's efforts in the field of education found expression above all in the establishment of a school for the Kodiak natives, which was opened in 1805, offering two class levels of instruction. Originally, thirty people studied reading, writing, and elementary catechism in the first class level; in the second, twenty boys studied Russian grammar, arithmetic, geography, and church and social history. Nor were the practical arts neglected, for "in their free time the students were taught to plant gardens, to sow and reap vegetables and weeds, to gather the necessary grasses and seeds and to fish; there was also a shoe-producing section."[102]

Father Gedeon's contribution here is indisputable. He founded the school on Kodiak Island, trained the school's teachers from among the local creoles and organized and directed the preparation of a dictionary and a grammar of the native language.[103]

The efforts of these missionaries laid the groundwork for Veniaminov's work. Innokentii Veniaminov's activities in the Aleutian Islands and northwest America have been discussed in sufficient detail in a series of books, although his significance by virtue of the volume of his achievements and his colorful personality warrant monograph-length treatment.[104]

In discussing Veniaminov's contribution to the education of the natives of the Aleutian Islands it is important to cite his school on the island of Illiuliuk, where he trained church workers from among the aboriginal populace; his efforts to develop a phrase book; his translations of evangelical texts into the Aleutian language; and his work in producing an Aleutian grammar for a people with no written language. Beginning in 1840, Veniaminov also devoted special attention to developing commercial education in Russian America.

In 1825 an academy for Aleuts was founded on the island of Unalaska. The establishment of this academy, which in 1860 claimed forty-three female and fifty male students (principally Aleuts) coupled with the efforts of Veniaminov and his predecessors, were instrumental in the St. Paul Aleuts' ability "virtually to a man" to read.[105] Tikhmenev states:

> The foundation for educating the local children was laid by the archpriest himself, who, beginning in January of 1844, gathered together young boys and girls on appointed days and personally taught them scripture there. Other colonial parish priests followed this example, so that in 1844 upwards of 400 children were being trained throughout the entire diocese. Subsequently, schools were formed in all churches and many chapels where children were taught the Christian Code, along with grammar.[106]

In 1836 the tsar issued a directive establishing a system of primary education in the Russian American colonies.[107] The directive specified that church property was to be used in support of the educational system; likewise, the church was responsible for providing books, and prayer books. Attached to the directive was a list of books to be used for instruction, including Dmitrii Tikhomirov's "spelling book," a Kodiak dictionary, and Veniaminov's catechism. In 1841 schools providing an education up to the second grade level were in operation on Nushagak, Kenai, Amlak, and Kodiak islands, as well as in the village of Chipak. In 1860 the school on the island of Amlia had thirty students. Attempts were made to found a school at the Kwikpak mission as well. Grammar and arithmetic were also being taught in a school on Bering Island. Information on the condition of diocesan schools for creole children and foreigners of both genders is contained in the reports entitled: "The Permanent and Monastic Academies," 1844–45.[108]

In 1860 Father Vikarnyi, who had been dispatched on a special mission to Russian America by the Holy Synod, issued a critique on the condition of the missions. On educational work among the Koloshes he wrote that "the foundations have been laid for the study of the Kolosh language; numerous prayers have been translated into this language . . . and many common colloquial words have been assembled."[109] Regarding the further education of the graduates of the Novo-Arkhangel'sk academy, he wrote that "the children should enroll in the Blagoveshchensk seminary."[110]

In the report delivered to St. Petersburg on "the diocese's condition," Vikarnyi wrote that:

1. Since 1825 an academy for boys and girls has been in operation in America, on Unalaska. In 1860 there were about ninety students here. A sexton, a deacon and a priest and his wife provide volunteer instruction for the children.
2. A school at the Atkhinsk parish has been in existence since 1850. It is located in the main building of the settlement on Amlia island. Occasionally the Aleuts themselves do the teaching here; at other times the deacons from the Atkhinsk parish teach the students.
3. In the distant settlements on the island the Aleuts teach each other.
4. At the Nushagansk mission a deacon under the supervision of a missionary provides instruction for the children from October to May, i.e., until the natives wander out to more distant places in search of food and game. In 1860 there were thirteen boys and four girls from the creole and Indian communities in this school.
5. A Kwikpak missionary is also working to spread literacy among the converts.
6. A general school for company officials and the clergy is to open soon at the Novo-Arkhangel'sk school, which was founded by the company for boys from the lower classes, along with an institution for female orphans, also of the lower classes.[111]

Father Vikarnyi concluded that "it can be said that all the churches in America, with the exception of one on Kodiak Island, maintain parochial schools."[112]

A small theological school was opened at the capital in 1841, as Starr has described.[113] In 1844 it became the Novo-Arkhangel'sk Theological Seminary; before its conversion a petition was sent to the Holy Synod. In 1843 the senior procurator of the synod wrote that Veniaminov had informed him of the run-down condition of the Kamchatkan academy and proposed that the Kamchatkan and Novo-Arkhangel'sk theological schools be merged.[114]

As early as 1842 Archpriest Prokopii Gromov, director of the school on Kamchatka, presented a draft of the curriculum for a unified Kamchatka–Novo-Arkhangel'sk seminary. On the quality of instruction at the Novo-Arkhangel'sk school he concluded that "The depth [of the students' knowledge] is, from an academic point of view, on a par with that of a district school or seminary in Russia."[115]

A full course of study was to occupy a ten-year period. The first four years were to be used to teach "ecclesiastical history, Orthodox catechism, arithmetic, Russian civil history, rhetoric and the principles of geometry."[116] The second four years were to include "scripture, physics, medicine, psychology, astronomy, and mathematics," and in the final two years the program would concentrate on "scripture (through *Ecclesiastes*), geometry, and stereometry, physics (properties of solid objects, hydrodynamics, aerodynamics, acoustics, pneumatics), medicine, psychology (philosophy), logic, physics (properties of light, electricity, magnetism, and electromagnetism), astronomy and geology."[117] It is evident from the list of subjects that the largely native-born students would be exposed to courses conducted on a very advanced level.

Even more systematic and extensive plans were laid for medical training in Russian America.[118] The staff doctor of the Russian American Company proposed that "in order to provide training in the medical sciences at the Novo-Arkhangel'sk academy a special department be founded there, which shall be called the Medical Institute."[119] Students were to meet the following requirements for admission: "(1) possess a sufficient knowledge of scripture, arithmetic, Russian, geography and history; (2) possess a healthy body and a strong intellectual aptitude; and (3) be between 15 and 18 years of age."[120]

The author of this proposal, A. Romanovskii, presented a detailed curriculum, which included the following subjects: anatomy, botany, zoology, mineralogy, geology, chemistry, pharmacology, and midwifery. It was suggested also that a doctor be invited to Novo-Arkhangel'sk to conduct a special advanced lecture course designed to hone the students' abilities still further.[121] The principal quality Romanovskii attempted to impart to his students was not technical proficiency but sympathy, as well as self-sacrifice and an ability to apply knowledge in practice, "so the students may be able to render assistance at any time."[122]

The opening of the Novo-Arkhangel'sk seminary occurred thanks to a directive from the tsar issued on April 22, 1844.[123] This parochial institution was to be supported by the interest from the seminary's assets, as proposed by Veniaminov.[124] The Central State Historical Archives in Leningrad contain numerous documents relating to the Novo-Arkhangel'sk theological seminary's early years of operation, including financial reports, a syllabus,[125] a document on the appointment of a rector to the recently opened seminary,[126] and a document on the faculty.[127]

A Siberian priest, Petr Listivinishchev, was chosen to be the inspector for the seminary as well as instructor for two of the company schools. Ilia Tyzhnov, another Siberian, taught the class in theology; he had earlier been sent to Kodiak Island "to teach the [Russian] language and perform his own translations." In 1845 he was named inspector of the Novo-Arkhangel'sk academy.[128]

The sacristan Emel'ian Molchanov, a creole, studied reading, writing, ecclesiastical history, and catechism at the Novo-Arkhangel'sk school. After completing his course work at the company school in 1837, he served as deacon for the local Novo-Arkhangel'sk parish until 1841, when at the request of Innokentii Veniaminov he was transferred to the Nushagak mission to serve as sacristan there. He subsequently worked as a clerk in the capital, and then served as a priest in the first grade level of the Novo-Arkhangel'sk school.[129]

Seminary reports provide some concept of the number of Russian and "foreign" students enrolled in the Novo-Arkhangel'sk theological seminary. In the period December 1, 1845, through May 1, 1846: "In the third grade level there are fifteen students, including nine Russians and six creoles; in the second grade level there are nineteen: nine Russians and ten creoles; in the first grade level there are eighteen: ten Russians, eight creoles and one Alegmut from the Mikhailovsk Redoubt."[130] The report for 1849–50 provides for the following listing: "Fourth grade level: three students, one of whom is a creole. Third grade level: sixteen students, two of whom are creoles. Second grade level: fifteen students, no creoles. First grade level: sixteen students, three of whom are creoles."[131]

Bishop Innokentii (Veniaminov), reporting on the diocese for the period 1842–43, wrote about the theological school at the colonial capital and about the four company schools,[132] noting with satisfaction that "the students know the basics of medicine and can function as doctors and serve as midwives."[133]

Some 490 books were purchased in St. Petersburg for the library of the theological seminary, among them Karamzin's *Russian History*, maps of Russia and all regions of the world, Anaragov's general history and others.[134] Books were also donated to the library from individual sources.[135]

Regarding the education of the native populace of California, efforts were made during the eras of I. A. Kuskov and K. T. Khlebnikov not only to develop agriculture and cattle breeding and to turn the Indians from nomads into settlers, but also to develop handicrafts locally by employing "regional strengths."[136] Plans were also made at Fort Ross to build children's schools patterned after the academies at Novo-Arkhangel'sk and Kodiak and for the use of children of Russian American Company officials.

PART FIVE
Russian America and the United States

Russian America and
International Relations

N. N. Bolkhovitinov

Alaska's grim climate and remoteness from the main centers of world civilization might seem to have been insuperable barriers to foreign influences. Nonetheless, Alaska was never isolated; its history, like the history of any other region of our planet, is part and parcel of world history. This was true even in those remote prehistoric times when the settlement of the North American continent proceeded via this region. It was also true of the era of modern exploration in the first half of the eighteenth century, and during the 125-year-long Russian period of Alaskan history (1741–1867).

Studying the history of the discovery and development of the northwestern part of the American continent by Russia, A. V. Efimov of the Academy of Sciences of the USSR noted with justification: "America entered the sphere of Russian foreign policy not in 1809, when formal diplomatic relations were established with the United States, and not during the War of Independence, but much earlier, after Peter I shattered Sweden's might ... and Russia became broadly involved in the world politics of the time."[1]

When Peter I sent Vitus Bering's expedition to the region in 1725, he wrote an instruction in which he not only raised the question of "discovering the joining point between Asia and America," but also set the task of carefully exploring the northwestern part of the American continent.[2] For our study it is particularly important that he wished to gain international recognition as far as possible. Peter instructed

Bering to "go to any city of European possession or, if you can see any European vessel, find out from it what the coast is called and write it down, and go ashore yourself."[3]

As a result of explorations over many years, Russian navigators, fur hunters and explorers mastered the boundless expanses of eastern Siberia, discovered the straits separating the Chukotsk peninsula from Alaska, and were the first to launch exploration of the mainland of America's northwestern coast. Russia's discovery of America was not only the result of the government's policy, but first and foremost the consequence of popular efforts. After 1742, when Bering's companions returned with a rich cargo of beaver furs from the island bearing his name, enterprising Siberian merchants and fur hunters began equipping regular expeditions to the Aleutian Islands. It was there that the first Russian settlements were founded.[4]

The long-standing geographical problem of whether Asia joins with America was solved definitely, clearly and finally: Asia does not "join" with America. But this was just one and by no means the main result of early Russian geographical discoveries. Their more significant consequence was to establish links between Asia and America. In this sense we are fully justified in saying that, as a result of Russian expeditions sponsored both by the tsarist government and privately, Asia was "joined" with America and more or less stable contacts established between the two continents. Russia became not only a European and Asian power but, to a certain extent, also an American power. The term "Russian America," which later gained wide recognition, appeared. In the first half of the nineteenth century, Russian America included the territory of modern Alaska as well as the Fort Ross settlement in California.

Neither Bering nor other Russian navigators succeeded in reaching "any city of European possession" in America during the eighteenth century (Peter's successors no longer set this task).[5] This international meeting took place finally on the territory of Russia's own possessions when in October 1778 the ships of the third expedition of the famous English navigator James Cook reached the shores of Unalaska Island. Entering Captain Bay, Cook discovered a Russian settlement there, got acquainted with the Russian sailors and fur hunters and in particular held numerous meetings with Pilot G. G. Izmailov, Navigator Ia. I. Sapozhnikov, and others.

The first to be dispatched by Cook to the shore on October 8, 1778, was the "quick-witted" American, John Ledyard, who discovered on the island about thirty Russians and seventy "Kamchadals or Indians from Kamchatka." The small sloop *Sv. Pavel* (St. Paul), which belonged to the merchant company of A. Orekhov, I. Lapin, and V. Shilov and was sent in 1776 under the command of G. G. Izmailov to the Lisii Islands,[6] was mistaken by the American for the ship which Bering used in making his outstanding discoveries. Ledyard acknowledged, however, that Bering's discoveries not only substantially facilitated Cook's voyage but also deprived the English captain of the glory of being "the sole discoverer of the northwest of the continent of America."[7]

Let us recall that along with other materials, James Cook had in his possession P. Chaplin's map of 1729, which reflected the results of the first Kamchatka expedition of Bering; G. F. Müller's map of Russian discoveries (1758); "A Description of the Kamchatka Land" by S. P. Krasheninnikov (1755); and, last, I. Stahlin's map (1774) which contained, though in a distorted form, information about the Aleutian Islands.[8]

During the several meetings which James Cook had with the Russian sailors and fur hunters between October 10 and 21, 1778, he made a few corrections in his cartographic materials and received two new maps from G. G. Izmailov. One of them showed Kamchatka and the Kuril Islands, where the Russians had a settlement on Marikan Island (Samushir) at 47.5° N, and the other contained all the discoveries made to the east of Kamchatka in the direction of America.

It is noteworthy that the English navigator had a high regard for the abilities and knowledge of his Russian interlocutors, first of all G. G. Izmailov. "I became convinced," James Cook wrote in his diary, "that he has excellent knowledge of the geography of these places and that all the discoveries made by Russians were known to him. He immediately pointed out mistakes on the new maps."

From his talks with the Russian navigators, Cook obtained reliable information about the position of a number of Aleutian Islands and also about voyages to the Alaskan peninsula, Chukotka, Kodiak Island, and so on. "From Izmailov," Cook wrote, "we learned the name of Kodiak, one of the biggest of the Shumagin Islands. ... The names of other islands were taken from the map [of Izmailov?] and written down in the way he pronounced them. He said that all these names were Indian. ... I have already pointed out that the Indians and Russians here called the American mainland Alaska ... and it is well known to them that it is a big land."[9]

"This Mr. Izmailov," Captain Cook concluded, "deserves a higher position for his endowments. ... He is sufficiently versed in astronomy and other essential fields of mathematics. I gave him a Hedley octant and, though this was probably the first instrument of this kind he came across, he knew it so well that he could use it shortly afterwards."[10]

The materials of Cook's third expedition are highly important also for determining the date of the foundation of the first Russian settlement on Unalaska Island. On the basis of these materials, the Soviet ethnographer S. G. Fedorova came to the conclusion that a permanent settlement on this island existed already in the 1770s, or prior to the foundation of G. I. Shelikhov's well-known settlements (1784–86).[11] Indeed, the participants in the expedition (J. Ledyard; pilot R. Edgar; assistant surgeon J. Samwell and others) gave detailed descriptions of this settlement. According to Edgar, the site of the settlement was "an oval area two or three miles long" and "a river with very good water" flowed near the houses. The small bay was well protected from winds. The dwelling was seventy to seventy-five logs long, twenty to twenty-four logs broad and about eighteen logs high. Not far from the house there were "three large storage premises" with dried fish, skins, and provisions. "After we got acquainted with the Russians," Cook wrote in his diary, "some of our gentlemen visited their settlement at different times, always receiving a warm welcome. The settlement consists of one dwelling and two storage premises; apart from the Russians there are Kamchadals and natives." Cook and his companions also reported that the Russians had "small settlements on all main islands of the Anadyr Sea and in many places along the American coast," putting the total number of inhabitants, including Kamchadals, at five hundred.[12]

The importance of this information is quite obvious. The participants of one of the most outstanding and prestigious sea expeditions saw for themselves that Russian settlements existed near the shores of North America and obtained valuable additional material on the discoveries made by Russian navigators. Of course, these settlements were small at that time and had few inhabitants. Most of them arose as temporary support bases of fur hunting. Hunting teams alternated every four or five years. However, the Unalaska settlement, the founding of which is dated by S. G. Fedorova between 1772 and 1775, may be regarded as more or less permanent. On the other hand, the attempts of the Russians to settle on the American continent itself failed at that time. The mainland was settled later, as a result of the activity of G. I. Shelikhov and the Russian American Company. That the discoveries of Bering and Chirikov and the subsequent activity of the Russians in the Pacific North embraced the most remote part of the Northwestern Coast of America did not pass unnoticed in European capitals, causing special concern in Madrid. Spanish diplomats in St. Petersburg—Marquis de Almodovar, Viscont de Herrera, and Conde de Lacy—dispatched patently exaggerated reports that Bering and Chirikov sailed as far as 45° N and that new Russian expeditions might pose a threat even for Mexico. In consequence the Spanish authorities hastened to take measures to settle the territory of modern California. In 1768 a naval base was set up in San Blas, followed by the founding of San Diego the next year, Monterey in 1770, and San Francisco in 1776. Numerous expeditions were sent to the Northwestern Coast of America and in 1788 one of them, under the command of E. J. Martinez and G. L. Haro, reached Russian settlements where they were welcomed by E. I. Delarov, chief manager of the "Northeastern Company."[13] The results of this meeting were reported in an interesting dispatch received in St. Petersburg from Russian diplomats in Spain in the spring of 1789:

From a dispatch of the Russian Minister in Madrid S. S. Zinov'ev to Vice-Chancellor I. A. Osterman
Madrid, February 26/March 9, 1789
Most Illustrious Count, Dear Sir!

Herewith I have the honour of forwarding a dispatch (relation) on the voyage to California of a Spanish ship, which I received from Consul Brandenburg who, I believe, has for his part sent the dispatch to Your Excellency. For my part, I intend to seek an explanation from Count Floridablanca and immediately to send my report to Your Excellency ... "[14]

I have the honour ...
Stepan Zinov'ev

This report was supplemented by the following statement:

Report on the voyage of a Spanish ship to California (*Relation d'un Voyage en Californie par un batiment espagnol*)

The letters received from San Blas in California report that the *San Carlos* packet-boat under the command of Mr. Haro, a pilot of the Royal Fleet in the rank of junior lieutenant, sailed from the said port on a secret mission on January 24, 1788, along with frigate "*Princesa*" commanded by Captain Martinez. Arriving together with the frigate at the port of Prince William, the packet-boat separated and continued along the coast alone. A port was noticed from the "*San Carlos*" and Mr. Haro sent a boat for reconnaissance; a small boat with a Russian crew left the port to meet it and, drawing level with it, sailed on together with it to the port, where the Spaniards were heartily welcomed by the Russians settled there. From that moment on most friendly relations were established between the Russians and the Spaniards. They gave parties to one another on the shore and aboard the ship and exchanged presents. In particular, the Russians gave the Spanish captain a detailed map of all their settlements on this coast, the number of which reaches now eight, and also supplied the most complete information about them.

The Spanish packet-boat "*San Carlos*" left the port, which was not named, on July 1 and sailed for Unalaska, where it joined the frigate, "*Princesa*".

Judging by the results of this expedition, the Russians have eight settlements in this part of the coast, lying at 48 and 49° N; each is inhabited by sixteen to twenty Russian families, or 452 people in all; they have cultivated their morals and customs among approximately six hundred savage Indians and exact a tribute from them for the benefit of the Russian Empress.

Apart from the mentioned eight settlements, the Spaniards sailing up to 62° N, discovered, it appears, three other less significant Russian settlements at 59°. It is said that the Russians began to found various settlements on the coast of North America nearly nineteen years ago, and their trade with the indigenous population is confined to the exchange of shirts, cloth, and vodka for wolf skins and moccasins.[15]

This report was subsequently used by the main directorate of the Russian American Company as one of the arguments for extending the southern boundaries of Russian possessions in North America down to 51° and even 45° N.[16] Some investigators believed that the information set forth in the dispatch was deliberately falsified by officials of the Russian American Company and that this document did not exist at all.[17] While the data on the location of Russian settlements were distorted in this document (in reality they were situated in the area of Unalaska Island and the shore of the Prince William [Chugatskii] Bay or approximately 10° to the north), the report itself and, most important, the settlements, actually existed. It is not unlikely that the Spaniards shifted their location to the south so as to make the "Russian threat" look more formidable in Madrid.

Reviewing the first visits of foreigners to the Russian possessions in the Pacific North, we must also mention John Ledyard's bold attempt to travel across Siberia by land to the Northwest Coast of America. In the course of his trip Ledyard met in 1787 with a number of Russian merchants who were linked with fur hunting on the shores of North America, including G. I. Shelikhov. He also had a talk with the Irkutsk governor-general, I. V. Iakobi, and others. In February 1788 Ledyard was expelled from Russia to the West on the order of Catherine II. The circumstances of Ledyard's Siberian travels are well known today and there is no need to dwell on them in detail. Let us note only that S. D. Watrous's full and reliable publication points out that the real circumstances of Ledyard's expulsion from Russia remain unclear. "Catherine, of course, gave the order for Ledyard's arrest," Watrous writes, "but it is yet impossible to determine who advised her on his activities and whereabouts, or urged her to take this measure."[18] On the basis of archival materials, the present author has determined who those persons were and why they insisted on the expulsion of a foreign competitor from Russia. The Manuscript Division of the Library of Congress in Washington and the Central State Archive in Moscow both contain copies of undated "Notes from a Conversation" of G. I. Shelikhov with an unknown "voyager of the English nation named Ledvar," i.e., John Ledyard. The "Notes" were written after Shelikhov's talk with Ledyard in Irkutsk on August 18 [30], 1787, and served as the basis for Iakobi's secret report to A. A. Bezborodko on November 7 [18], 1787, the result of which was the "unexpected" decision taken by Catherine II.[19] (At present these two documents and a number of other important materials on John Ledyard are published in the joint Soviet-American collection *The United States and Russia: The Beginning of Relations, 1765–1815* ([Washington, 1980]).

In concluding his detailed report to Bezborodko, the governor general of Irkutsk and Kolyvan wrote: "Previously I had not considered it necessary to burden the august person of Her Imperial Majesty with this matter, fully knowing how busy our Most Gracious Sovereign is with the most important affairs of state, but now, letting Your Excellency judge regarding the journey undertaken by this squire Ledyard, I take the liberty to report that, if necessary, sending him back to St. Petersburg will pose no difficulty, for there is sufficient time for this." There is also a notation on the original copy of Iakobi's report: "Regarding this, orders were issued to Iakobi, Eropkin, and Passek on December 21, 1787 [January 1, 1788]."[20]

As can be seen, the appearance of foreign competitors in the area of Russian settlements in the Pacific North worried not only Siberian merchants and local authorities, but also the tsarist government in St. Petersburg. These fears increased as more and more foreign ships engaged in fur hunting appeared off the shores of Northwestern America: 1785—one, 1787—six, 1788—eight, 1789—ten, 1790—six, 1791—eleven, 1792—twenty-one, 1793—seventeen, 1794—twelve, and so on.[21] The best known of these incursions were George Dixon's voyages aboard the *Queen Charlotte* (1787); the voyages of Nathaniel Portlock aboard the *King George* (1787); John Meares's travels aboard the *Nootka* (1787–89); Robert Gray's expedition aboard *Columbia* (1788–92); not to mention the expeditions of La Perouse, Vancouver, Malaspina, and others.[22]

The Russian monopoly of geographical discoveries and fur trade in the Pacific North was obviously coming to an end. Foreign competition intensified the tendency toward association among rival Russian trading companies, and led to the formation in 1799 of the monopolistic Russian American Company under the "august protection" of the crown. For guidance and "for special facilitation and encouragement of the said company" Paul I approved in July 1799 "rules" and "privileges" pertaining to "the entire expanse of lands and islands described above," and granting to the company "the exclusive right to all acquisitions, fur hunting, trade, establishments and discoveries of new territories."[23]

A secret instruction from the directors of the Russian American Company of April 18 [30], 1802, directed A. A. Baranov, the chief manager of Russia's American settlements:

To affirm Russia's rights not only up to 55° but beyond that limit, relying on the sea voyages of Captains Bering, Chirikov and others and referring also to the annual voyages and fur hunting expeditions by private persons since that time. Try also to substantiate certain rights to Nootka Sound so that, in the event of a demand from the English court, it would be possible to draw the boundary up to 50° or at least half way to 55°, if it proves impossible to set it beyond. This region is not yet occupied by [the British] and Russia has a predominant right to it. And to this end you must work with the utmost energy and haste to begin settling along the 55th parallel by building a fortress, for now you will have enough people. If you find it convenient to resettle Russified [native] Americans there, you can do this, too, but only with their kind consent, which you may secure by granting certain benefits.

To assure success, it is proposed to discontinue all exploration to the North in these places and turn all attention to the areas nearer the English when we shall build up our possessions. To this end you must annually supply the Main Directorate with all possible information so that it can support your plans and needs and, without losing time, extend to you all possible aid. The Main Directorate, however, is paying you to avoid meetings with the English and thereby evade the need to enter into talks with them concerning the boundaries. The Main Directorate hope that, being prudent and experienced, you will continue to do this. But should the need for such a meeting arise, you must invoke the rights of Russia and declare that you do not dare deal with so important a matter, and that the British court may approach the Emperor directly. From the maps attached to this letter you will see that Vancouver and Puget [the British voyagers] have themselves marked the places occupied by our hunting parties, calling them Russian settlements.

Vancouver has great praise for the Russians' treatment of [native] Americans, saying that Russia gained dominance over the savage peoples not through victories but by finding the way to their hearts. This comment by foreign navigators will bring you special honor, and, by affirming the justice of your humble and sensible methods, has brought your name to the attention of the Emperor. . . .

Seeing from the Second Volume of Vancouver's voyages[24] that some of your hunters gave the maps of your sailings to the English,

the Main Directorate finds it necessary to reprimand you and to
say that you should be not only more discriminating in your trust,
but also avoid all such impermissible services harmful to the fatherland.[25]

This "Instruction" received the approval of "the committee, composed of the honorable stockholders," and "His Excellency the Minister
of Commerce, Privy Councillor and Cavalier Count Nikolai Petrovich
Rumiantsev, April 8, 1802." In the person of Rumiantsev the company
had an influential and firm defender in the government. The company's
activities were also promoted by N. S. Mordvinov and N. P. Rezanov.
Thanks to his energy, initiative, and skill as an observer, Rezanov was
able, during his comparatively brief stay in Russian America, to get a
full picture of the situation there and to chart concrete ways of
expanding Russia's influence throughout the Pacific North. One of the
most interesting testimonies to Rezanov's fruitful and extensive
activities is his own secret memorandum to Baranov of July 20 [August
1], 1806, written so that "in case of our (your and my) death, our
successors might see what we intended doing."[26]

Leaving the "northwestern coast of America," Rezanov stressed the
need to establish a permanent population in the colonies and recommended that anyone signing contracts with the company should be
encouraged to agree to a long residence there.[27] To encourage the
building of houses, kitchen gardening, and so on, it was proposed to
give settlers land "for perpetual and hereditary possession." Rezanov
planned also to give the Russian settlements "the protection of a
military garrison." To this end he intended to start by sending "57
cannon and four mortars with a decent quantity of war shells" and
then to send annually, "with every transport from St. Petersburg 250
puds of powder and 600 puds of lead." He also suggested to the directors of the Russian American Company that they build a sawmill, a
hospital, a church, and other public buildings. And by special order
of February 15 [27], 1806, the actual chamberlain, chief procurator of
the Senate and Russian American Company plenipotentiary also instituted an elective "court of inquiry into conflicts between fur hunters
and [native] Americans"; in its work, this court was "to combine the
administration of justice with meekness."[28]

Of particular interest are Rezanov's practical steps and considerations to procure food from California, Japan, the Philippine Islands

and a number of other places and to develop commercial ties with them. "The most reliable source" of ensuring a supply of food for the Russian settlements in America he saw in gaining a foothold on "the coasts of New Albion." The same aim was to be promoted also by obtaining from Boston the required quantity of grain, which would cost at all times less than half of Okhotsk prices (point 7); and by purchasing vessels from the "American States" (point 4). In view of the lack of funds, Rezanov suggested that the company's directors, "over and above the promised notes ... mint a special coin for the local area." He expected this step to cause a "multiplication" of fur hunting, agriculture and trade. "Foreign vessels wintering [in Russian America] will likewise pay for the labor of the inhabitants. In a word: everything is dead now, but the whole area will come to life through the circulation of coin" (point 10).

Rezanov's sweeping projects were not destined to materialize (he met an untimely death in Krasnoiarsk on March 1 [13], 1807), though both A. A. Baranov in Novo-Arkhangel'sk and the company's directors in St. Petersburg took various practical steps to put them into effect. Noteworthy in this regard is Rumiantsev's report to Alexander I, in which he discussed in detail the international aspect of the activity and in particular made the following points on the basis of reports by its directors and by Baranov.[29]

The American states intended to found a settlement on the Columbia River in New Albion in the summer of 1808 unless the Russians had settled there first. To keep them away, Baranov sent a detachment of Russians and loyal natives with Commerce Councillor Kuskov to occupy a place for settlement between Trinidad Bay and the fortress of San Francisco. He instructed Kuskov to barter for expensive furs with the savages, which formerly only the Bostonians had done. In addition, he sent a Bostonian vessel with a contingent of Russians and islanders to California to purchase provisions, which, despite the prohibition of the Spanish Court, the California authorities and especially the missionaries found it profitable to sell secretly (point 3).

Slobodchikov, the commander of a detachment of Russian *prom-yshlenniki*, sailed to the Sandwich Islands in 1807 in a small vessel bought from the Bostonians, befriended the local king, and brought back to Baranov as a token of the king's friendship a helmet decorated with many-colored feathers. Baranov considered Slobodchikov a smart, enterprising man who brought honor to the Russians, even if he was illiterate (point 4).

Baranov, upon the arrival of the ship *Neva*, did not want her kept idle and dispatched her to the Sandwich Islands to try to establish commerce with them. Lieutenant Gagemeister, the captain of this ship, reached the islands in January of the next year. There he learned that King Kamehameha ruled over the islands of Maui, Hawaii, Molokai, Lanai, and Kahoolawe; that the products of the land had become exorbitantly expensive on account of the Bostonians, who recuperated there on the way to Canton to obtain various necessities, bartering their goods for trifles; that the king of these islands had arrogated this trade to himself alone and the majority of his European goods rotted idly in warehouses; and, finally, that the king not only would not be against the settlement of Russians on the island of Molokai (which was very fertile, though less so than the others), but even needed such a settlement to protect himself against the king of the other Sandwich Islands. Gagemeister considered twenty men sufficient for the settlement, and as many for its defense, with one cannon. He noted that these islands, having the best climate, can furnish all Asiatic Russia abundantly with their products, which consisted of coconut and bread trees, breadfruit, yams (from which good rum was made), sugar cane, rice, wild tobacco, pineapple (from which an excellent wine was made), sandalwood and other woods similar to guaiacum, wild horned cattle, and pigs (point 5).

Concerning Baranov's request for a "government-sponsored settlement" on "New Albion," the chancellor suggested that Alexander I "leave it up to the directorate of the American Company to establish this settlement by itself. It can in any case, hope for the merciful protection of Your Majesty."

Regarding the company's proposals for "remonstrances to the Bostonians on the sale of weapons to the islanders," Rumiantsev found it sufficient to charge Count Palen, Alexander's envoy in Washington, "with soliciting the cessation of such harmful commerce," and announced his intention of raising the issue with the American minister in St. Petersburg, John Quincy Adams. The chancellor's report was approved by Alexander I, but on the diplomatic talks in Washington Rumiantsev reported to St. Petersburg in July 1810: "I have become more and more convinced that the government of the United States has just as little desire as it has the power to put an end to this illegal commerce."[30]

In the meantime, the number of foreign vessels off the Northwest Coast of America continued to increase, but their composition changed substantially at the turn of the nineteenth century. In the last decades of the eighteenth century the Northwest Coast (including the Russian possessions) was visited by forty-three Spanish, seventy-four English, and fifty-three American vessels. Although from 1800 to 1820 no Spanish vessels visited the area, and only nineteen English ships were registered during this period, the number of American vessels reached 222![31] According to the data compiled by J. Gibson, from 1801 to 1841 American vessels concluded over one hundred "trade deals" in Novo-Arkhangel'sk; the English vessels, six; and the French, one.[32]

As has already been pointed out in connection with the general appraisal of the Russian American Company's ties with foreigners, care must be taken to avoid one-sidedness. The "Bostonian ship owners" violated the company's monopoly by competing with the Russians on the Chinese market and by selling armaments to the Indians, among other things. At the same time the Russians' business contacts with the "Bostonians"—the purchase of food, vessels, and the organization of joint hunting ventures—enabled the Russian settlements to meet a considerable part of their food requirements and even to make certain profits later on. For their part, the "Bostonian ship owners" were quite satisfied with their contacts with the Russians. Not only did they acquire the furs necessary for the China trade, but also, through access to Novo-Arkhangel'sk, gained use of a reliable base which was essential in the grim conditions of the Pacific North.

Typical of this relationship were the activities of Captain John D'Wolf who in 1806 not only sold goods but also his vessel *Juno*, for cash, notes, and pelts worth $68,000. For the transport of his crew, Wolf was given the fully equipped ship *Ermak* and provisions for one hundred days.[33]

From 1800 to 1840 the trade deals of captains Winship, Davis, Ebbets, Ayres, Hunt, Meek, Bennett, Pigot, Blanchard, McNeill, Snow, Barker, and others in Novo-Arkhangel'sk ran into tens of thousands of dollars. Joint beaver hunting also proved mutually beneficial. An example of this was Baranov's contract of May 19 [30], 1808, with Captain G. W. Ayres of the *Mercury*. Ayres, with twenty-five boats with Aleutian crews at his disposal, worked under Shevtsov's command. Though the benefits of joint hunting were shared with "foreigners," the advantage of such an arrangement was that it facilitated hunting beyond the limits of Russia's waters, where the sea otter population had been depleted, and extended it to areas lying as far south as California. In conclusion the "contracting parties" expressed a desire "to maintain in the future between ourselves and our fellow-countrymen mutual ties and advantages based on good faith in the profitable commerce of these remote areas."[34]

We should not think, of course, that the relations between the two parties were always as idyllic as they appear in this contract. Other relations are suggested by the testimony of V. M. Golovnin, the captain of the sloop *Diana*, who knew both English and French and helped Baranov to sign an agreement with Ebbets and Davis in 1810. "A mere chance" showed to Golovnin that the intentions of John Jacob Astor, who sent his vessel

> for trading with the Company's colonies, were not so pure and did not pursue [our] mutual benefit, as he and Mr. Dashkov had made it out to Mr. Baranov. This happened in the following way. Ebbets, the commander of Astor's vessel, wishing to show me how much effort it cost its chief to build, load, and send it to America, produced three rolled papers from his desk and gave them to me to read. Two of them contained different accounts referring to the subject but the third, which he undoubtedly gave me by mistake, was a supplement to his instructions. Among other things, this stated that on his way he should call at the Spanish harbors on the shore of North America indicated in the instruction, and at wharves visited by savage people, and conduct trade there should it be profitable. With the remaining goods or with no goods at all, should he manage to sell them, he was to sail to the Company's settlements in order to discuss future trade with Baranov. Should Mr. Baranov ask why he did not bring the goods mentioned in Mr. Dashkov's and Astor's letters, he was instructed to invent an excuse; for example, he might say that on the way he met a vessel and was informed that a multitude of ships had already visited the Company's colonies and supplied them in abundance with every manner of goods, and that the Company could not now be expected to buy anything from him, and the like. Then Astor instructed his agent to have a closer look at the Company's affairs in America; to find out its strengths, its methods of defense, and the condition of its fortresses; to learn more reliably how much public trust is enjoyed by the Company in Russia and what the government thinks of it; to find out about Baranov's ties in St.

Petersburg and whether he has any support at court, whether he is really the chief governor of all the Company's possessions, the extent of his power in the local region, allowed by his position, etc.

At the same time, Golovnin, who can hardly be suspected of any sympathies for the Russian American Company's foreign rivals, also pointed out positive aspects of Baranov's ties with the "Bostonian ship owners":

Sailing to America, we were afraid that we would find the Company settlements in the most wretched state due to food shortages. This would indeed have occurred had it not been for the citizens of the American Republic. Their vessels were sent for trading along the local coasts, but they carried with them many provisions (wheat flour, hard tacks, grits, corned beef and pork, etc.) that they exchanged them for Mr. Baranov's fur goods at great advantage to the Company. In Sitka [Novo-Arkhangel'sk], we found all the stores filled with vital necessities. Some American ships called at the Sandwich Islands and brought back large quantities of salt and a root called *taro* which, when dried and ground, looks like flour and is no less nourishing. When mixed with ordinary flour, bread and cakes baked from this mixture are very tasteful. Apart from the three American vessels which we found in Sitka, one of which departed shortly after our arrival, two more vessels laden mostly with food products arrived during our stay. ... For this accidental and temporary abundance, officers of the Company must not thank their governors but the commercial spirit and enterprise of the Americans, that is, those traders whom the Company's sponsors wanted to keep off the northwestern shore of America....[35]

At one time it seemed that "temporary abundance" might become permanent, that the provisioning of the Russian settlements would depend not on episodic deliveries and accidental visits of individual ship owners but would be placed on a firm contractual basis. After prolonged and complex talks, a convention was concluded between John Jacob Astor's fur company and the Russian American Company in St. Petersburg on April 20 [May 2], 1812. This agreement might have signaled the beginning of a new stage of Russian-American relations in the American Northwest. But in fact it had no significant effect on the subsequent development of events. Its implementation was prevented by the Anglo-American war of 1812–15 and by Napoleon's invasion of Russia in June 1812. Instead of the expected era of cooperation, a new round of mutual rivalry began after 1815.

The history of the restitution of the privileges of the Russian American Company and of the decree of September 1821, the connection between these events and the genesis of the Monroe Doctrine, and, last, the conclusion of the conventions of 1824–25, are all discussed in detail in my monograph on Russian-American relations in the years from 1815 to 1832. Let us here recall only that these decisions were under preparation over a long period of time and were no mere accident. And Golovnin was not, as some historians have claimed, the company's "virtual dictator" who could at his own discretion shift the southern boundary of the Russian possessions from 55° to 51° N.[36]

A number of institutions and individuals took part in the preparation of the September decisions: the Russian American Company, the ministries of internal affairs, finances, foreign affairs, and others. But the archive materials indicate that the leading role fell to the minister of finances, D. A. Gurev, who took charge of the company at the end of 1819.[37]

Study of the archival sources has helped revise or substantially adjust other traditional views on the history of Russian America. Thus, after the publication in 1939 of Professor S. B. Okun's well-known book, historians generally held that the Russian American Company was merely a convenient screen for the expansionist policy of tsarism, that its practical activity was carried out under strict governmental control and was identical with or, at any rate, very close to the official line of the imperial cabinet.[38] In general terms this is correct, but certain corrections must be entered. Not only was there no unity between the leadership of the company and the tsarist government on many questions, some of them fundamental, but also open and serious disagreements arose between them.

The trading interest and practical activity of Russian colonists in America came increasingly into conflict with the conservative policies of the tsarist government in St. Petersburg. The leaders of the tsarist government, adhering to the principle of legitimacy and to a generally conservative foreign policy after 1815, did not pursue active expansion in the Northwest of America and did not intend to disturb the status quo in any serious way; by contrast, the main directorate of the company was not averse to seizing opportunities to expand its possessions, to taking advantage of the benefits opened up in connection with the founding of Fort Ross in California, and to establishing permanent trade ties with Mexico, Hawaii, Haiti, and others. The company was persistent in its efforts to maintain its monopoly rights in the North Pacific and sought to protect its possessions from the penetration of foreign rivals.

A. A. Guber of the Academy of Science of the USSR justifiably drew attention to the fact that, in contrast to the colonial policy of the western European powers, which had "a naval, oceanic character, the colonial policy of the Russian Empire was mostly continental. The Far East and Pacific played an immeasurably smaller role in Russian policy at that time and were subservient to the general political situation in Europe."[39] Count Ia. O. Lambert, an influential tsarist expert, emphasized back in 1817 that "in consequence of her geographical position, Russia is not destined to develop her naval forces on a grand scale" and that she therefore should be circumspect in developing trade at a great distance from the center and the main ports. The conservative character of feudal Russia's policies in the Pacific and American Northwest was fully manifested in several events: the skeptical reception given P. Dobel's projects for the development of trade ties between Kamchatka and Russian America and the Philippines, California, and Canton, for example; the decision to reject the application for Russian citizenship received from Kaumaulia, the "Owner of the Sandwich Islands," and in the categorical refusal to support Dr. Schaffer's proposal for the annexation of Hawaii in 1818–19.[40]

Disagreements between the tsarist government and the Russian American Company were revealed with particular clarity during the signing of the conventions of 1824–25, when the company, in which the dissident Decembrists and especially K. F. Ryleev had gained influence, came into open conflict with the Ministry of Foreign Affairs. Numerous notes and protests were forwarded to the tsarist government pointing out that the convention of April 5 [17], 1824, by granting the Americans free trade and fishing rights in the Russian possessions for a period of ten years, violated the privileges of the company and posed a threat not only to its welfare but to its very existence.[41]

Let us recall also that in 1825 the company's leadership informed the tsarist government of its intention to "set up fortresses on the northwestern shore of America along the Copper River from the seashore inland." In response, Alexander I had gone so far as to issue instructions calling the directors of the Russian American Company "to strictest account for the impropriety of the proposal itself and to indicate that they must unfailingly abide by the decisions and plans of the government without going beyond the boundaries of the merchant estate."[42]

The supporters of greater Russian influence in the Pacific basin and North America (N. P. Rumiantsev, N. S. Mordvinov, I. B. Pestel, and others) had lost ground by the early 1820s, at the same time as such conservative figures as K. V. Nesselrode and Ia. O. Lambert gained influence. Accordingly, Russia's policy in the American Northwest began to reflect the prevalence of conservative or protective tendencies, which explains why the complaints of the Russian American Company were actually disregarded in most cases.

It is indicative in this connection that when in 1826 Nesselrode forwarded to the tsar the Russian American Company's repeated complaints regarding the terms of the 1824–25 conventions, he wrote that: "Many of [the company's] proposals, such as the confiscation of ships with cargoes and peacetime inspections at sea by merchant ships, are contrary to the mutual rights and conditions of the treaties with England and America. These remarks have led the company's directors to express their dissatisfaction and to lodge the old complaints again." The minister of foreign affairs took the view that the apprehensions expressed by the company contradict its own interests and "the dignity of our court."[43] The negative stance of the foreign affairs minister decisively ruled out any possibility of altering the conditions of the 1824–25 conventions to any degree in the company's favor.

This review leads to a few concluding words about the historiography and above all about the views of my American colleague, Professor Howard I. Kushner. I should stress at the outset that on the whole I hold in high regard Professor Kushner's contributions to the study of Americans' activities on the Northwest Coast. Particularly worthy of note is his detailed analysis of the expansionist plans of both the American government and private citizens, which show that New England business circles were interested in trade in the Northwest, in organizing whaling there, and in other ventures.[44] Elaborating William A. Williams's view that the incorporation of Alaska was viewed by the Secretary of State William H. Seward and his colleagues as a "stepping stone" to Asia's market, Kushner adds with full justification that this territory was also seen as a valuable acquisition in its own right.[45]

The questionable element in Kushner's research lies not in such valuable secondary insights as these, but in the main thesis of his book, namely, that relations between Russia and the United States in the Northwest were a "history of conflict" and, at times, open hostility. It was "conflict and rivalry over the Pacific Northwest, not amity that led the tsarist government to cede Russian America to the United States." This purchase was the "culmination of the [United States'] continental expansion," which not even a water barrier could halt.[46]

Over two decades ago, when my first works on the history of the Monroe Doctrine were published, I held to a certain extent analogous views and turned my attention primarily to the conflict and rivalry of the United States, tsarist Russia, and England in the Northwest of America.[47] Later, I realized that this constituted only one aspect of the problem. In the American Northwest, Russia and the United States were not only rivals but also partners in cooperation.[48] It is gratifying to note that in recent years this view has been gaining currency; it is reflected in particular in an interesting article by Professor Mary E. Wheeler.[49]

Putting forth his "new interpretation," Professor Kushner remarks that the supporters of the "amiable character" of relations between Russia and the United States based their case mainly on the analysis of European problems. Yet the study of relations in the American Northwest makes it possible to introduce substantial adjustments. But only adjustments! To assess the general character of Russian-American relations solely in the context of the Northwest is as erroneous as it is to consider them exclusively in the context of European problems.

The basic significance of the U.S. expansion is evident. The participants of a "special meeting" at the building of the Russian Foreign Ministry on December 16 [28], 1866, particularly the Grand Duke Konstantin and Edouard A. de Stoeckl, made direct references to a serious menace to Russian settlements from Americans. Such a menace was especially evident in the 1850s. But at this time of decision (1866–67) this menace was more potential than real. During and immediately after the Civil War, from 1861 to 1865, the United States was occupied by much more important problems than far away Alaska. G. V. Fox's mission to Russia in 1866 was a culmination of a long period of friendly relations between two countries. In this connection the Russian government considered the cession of Alaska first of all in the light of liquidation of mutual contradictions and strengthening the factual alliance of two great powers. A long idea of continental (not naval) destiny of Russia, consolidation and strengthening position in the Far East (especially in the Amur region) became for Russia more and more important.[50]

In advancing his argument, Professor Kushner classed Frank A. Golder, Victor J. Ferrar, and Thomas A. Bailey as "consensus historians." I have written on the "consensus school" on many occasions, most recently in a special study in which this school occupies a central place.[51] Naturally, I take issue with the views of different representatives of this influential trend in postwar American historiography. But I cannot bring myself to include any one of these three authors in the "consensus school." Golder died long before the first symptoms of the new trend appeared in American historiography. Perhaps only Bailey's works could with some stretch of the imagination be assigned to the "conservative consensus school." But to defend any notion of the "amiable character" of relations between Russia and the United States was scarcely characteristic of him; on the contrary, Bailey's book *America Faces Russia* (1950) stands as one of the clearest examples of the influence exerted by the cold war on the study of Russian-American relations. It would perhaps be more correct to speak of a generally accepted or traditional view of the character of Russian-American relations, but in this case, too, we are running the risk of simplifying the blurring divergences in the views of many of our predecessors.

And the last consideration. I have already warned against the danger of one-sidedness. The history of Russian America cannot be studied solely on the basis of Russian or American sources, as was done so often in the past.

The pleasant conference of students of Russian America held on Baranof (Sitka) Island in the very heart of the former Russian territory, where the land is saturated with the spirit of the old traditions, provided scholars the opportunity to discuss, compare, correct, and supplement old conceptions. Such joint discussions will doubtless help to evolve a more accurate conception of the complicated and contradictory history of Russian America.

The Sale of Russian America to the United States

James R. Gibson

Just before dawn on March 30, 1867, in the Department of State in Washington, D.C., a treaty was signed whereby

> his Majesty the Emperor of all the Russias agrees to cede to the United States, by this convention, immediately upon the exchange of the ratifications thereof, all the territory and dominion now possessed by his said Majesty on the continent of America and in the adjacent islands, and in consideration of the cession aforesaid, the United States agree to pay at the treasury in Washington, within ten months after the exchange of the ratifications of this convention, to the diplomatic representative or other agent of his Majesty the Emperor of all the Russias, duly authorized to receive the same, seven million two hundred thousand dollars in gold.[1]

So for two cents an acre the United States acquired an area twice the size of Texas for a comparable sum (the federal government had assumed the Texan debt of $7.5 million after annexation in 1845). To Washington's embarrassment, however, the ten-month deadline for payment had to be extended. Ratification was swift, with the Senate approving the Alaska Treaty by a vote of thirty-seven to two on April 9. But appropriation was delayed by prolonged and acrimonious debate in the House of Representatives over the value of President Andrew Johnson's "polar bear garden" and Secretary of State William Seward's "ice-box." The House was miffed at not having been consulted until after ratification by the Senate, and it was also embroiled in the issue of impeachment of the president; upholders of the fraudulent Perkins claim further delayed proceedings. Finally, on July 27, 1868, amid charges of bribery, the appropriation bill cleared Congress and Russian America legally became the Territory of Alaska, although the formal transfer of authority had already taken place at Sitka (Novo-Arkhangel'sk) in the previous October.[2]

Why the United States bought Russian America, and why Russia sold its only overseas colony, are quite different questions. The answers to the former are fairly clear, in spite of American preoccupation with domestic affairs and the abeyance of American expansionist sentiment in the postbellum period. Massachusetts Senator Charles Sumner, chairman of the Committee on Foreign Relations, explained in his widely acclaimed pro-ratification speech the motives that impelled him and his government, namely: to expand American commerce to the Far North and the Far East ("Not only does the treaty extend the coasting trade of California, Oregon, and Washington Territory northward, but it also extends the base of commerce with China and Japan"); to enlarge American dominion ("With increased size on the map there is increased consciousness of strength, and the heart of the citizen throbs anew as he traces the extending line"); to extend republican institutions ("We dismiss one other monarch from the continent"); to preempt a British purchase ("Sometimes it is said that Great Britain desires to buy, if Russia will sell"); and to cement American-Russian friendship ("It attests and assures the amity of Russia").[3] Above all, Secretary Seward was moved by the ambition to aggrandize his country and enhance its "geopolitical centralism." He hoped also to gain popularity within his divided party and improve the stature of President Johnson, who was facing impeachment over his Southern Reconstruction program (and who, incidentally, was "not inclined" to the purchase).[4] An ardent expansionist, Seward saw Alaska as a pincer for squeezing British Columbia into American hands and securing the entire West Coast as a bridgehead for American penetration of Asian markets. Should Canada prevail, Alaska would still serve as a commercial drawbridge between Asia and North America.[5]

The Russians' reasons for selling are less clear and much disputed. Howard Kushner, for example, has argued that the sale of Russian America was the result of seventy years of pressure by American commercial expansionists who valued the colony's resources and that relations between Russia and the United States in the Northwest during the first two-thirds of the nineteenth century were characterized more by conflict and rivalry than by amity and cooperation.[6] This interpretation is questionable on several grounds. First of all, Alaska was Russia's to sell, not the United States' to buy. If Russia chose not to sell, there was nothing that the United States could do about it short of outright seizure, which was unlikely in view of the predictable reactions not only of Russia, a friend, but of Great Britain, a foe and the preeminent military power. Also, if American pressure on Russian America were so irresistible, why did the colony not fall into American hands earlier in the century rather than later, when the Russian population and fleet were both larger, the American threat (in the form of offshore whalers) less serious, and American empire-building less popular? The answer is that Russia had not wanted to sell earlier, whereas she was willing to do so after the Crimean War and, more importantly, once the Amur Valley had been annexed. In addition, the United States had no need to buy Russian America for American merchants to get its resources—sea otters, fur seals, whales, fish—for these were all marine resources, readily accessible even without territorial control. All that was required was access to the inshore and offshore hunting and trading grounds, which American skippers had always enjoyed, despite Russian protestations. Moreover, those American businessmen with exclusive trading rights in Russian America, such as the American Russian Commercial Company, stood to lose their monopolies through cession.[7]

Finally, Americans did not lobby for the acquisition of Alaska in the manner that they had earlier campaigned to win Texas, Oregon, and California. And for good reason. Most Americans probably did not feel strongly about remote and wild Alaska. No American settlers had migrated there, as they had to the Spanish and British borderlands. And, to repeat, American entrepreneurs could get what they wanted from Russian America without possessing it. Conflict did occur, but so did concord, which actually predominated. In the final analysis, however, the perspective of the Northwest Coast is too narrow to explain fully the sale of Russian America. Commercial pressure and resource appreciation by American businessmen may have been factors in the willingness of the United States to buy Alaska but they do not explain the willingness of Russia to sell.

The surviving evidence suggests an explanation. In his three-hour Senate speech, Sumner asserted that the tsar was motivated by the same factors that had induced Napoleon Bonaparte to dispose of Louisiana: "First, he needed the purchase-money for his treasury; secondly, he was unwilling to leave this distant unguarded territory a prey to Great Britain, in the event of hostilities, which seemed at hand; and, thirdly, he was glad, according to his own remarkable language, 'to establish forever the power of the United States, and give to England a maritime rival that would sooner or later humble her pride'."[8] Edouard de Stoeckl, the Russian minister to Washington, in what the tsar called a "very remarkable" memorandum of 1867 to Foreign Minister Prince Aleksandr Gorchakov, summarized his explanation of the transaction that he had long sought by pointing out that: (1) other European colonies in the Americas had already become independent; (2) the Russian American Company had failed to develop the territory over several-score years; (3) nonreciprocity in trade (arising from the company's monopoly) had incurred American displeasure, while, at the same time, American freebooters threatened the Russian colony; (4) Russian America was too remote and too large for the motherland to defend effectively; and (5) Russia's Pacific future lay not in unproductive Alaska but in the Amur basin, whose fertile soil and splendid harbors held more promise and which would be easier to defend.[9]

Russia's motives for selling Alaska have traditionally been attributed to the needs of economics, strategy, and politics. It has commonly been argued that Russian America was what the New York World called a "sucked orange,"[10] an unprofitable and hence dispensable wilderness that was unloaded onto an unsuspecting United States. Unquestionably the Russian American Company was on the verge of bankruptcy by the mid-1860s. The value on the Russian stock market of the more than 7,000 company shares rose from 224 silver rubles in 1842 to 500 in 1854 and then fell to 150 in 1862 and 75 in 1866; well before the sale the stock was worth less than its nominal cost.[11] By then the tsarist government was providing 200,000 rubles of direct and indirect subsidy annually, a figure that represented more than one-quarter of the company's income.[12] On the eve of the sale, the firm was 1,000,000 rubles in debt, including 725,000 rubles owed to the Russian treasury, and it was unable to pay any dividends in 1862 or 1863.[13] Beginning in 1862 the company attempted to secure a loan in London and St. Petersburg, but in vain.[14] Its head office was forced to conclude "with utter frankness that without money to pay its debts, nothing can save this concern from a complete cessation of operations."[15]

This financial crisis was hardly surprising, but it arose artificially from governmental interference rather than naturally from the economic worth of Russian America itself. When the company's third charter expired at the end of 1861, it was not automatically renewed (as had been the case previously) by the Russian government, which instead established a review committee and sent two inspectors, State Councillor Sergei Kostlivtsev of the Ministry of Finance and Captain Pavel Golovin of the Naval Ministry, to tour the colony from 1860 to 1861. Such an inspection had been suggested in 1856 in order to determine the value of the colony in case it were offered for sale and, short of that, to determine what changes, if any, should be made to the company's charter before it was renewed.[16]

Kostlivtsev and Golovin eventually submitted their incriminating findings to the review committee of fourteen bureaucrats, stockholders, and scientists.[17] In 1863–64 the committee issued a lengthy and critical report;[18] the company countered with a slanted two-volume history of its operations, written by a shareholder.[19] Noting that the natives of Russian America, especially the Aleuts, had been mistreated and that the colony had been weakly settled and developed, thanks to the immobility of serfdom and the monopolistic complacency of the company, several government departments recommended that the franchise be renewed for another twenty years but that the Aleuts and creoles be freed from the obligation of working for the company and be allowed to live wherever they wished; that the company's monopoly be limited to the fur trade only, freeing the firm to concentrate on its primary duty of administration; that Novo-Arkhangel'sk in the Alaska panhandle and St. Paul Harbor on Kodiak Island be opened to free trade; and that the colonial governor be appointed by, and subordinated to, the government, with the colony being transferred from the jurisdiction of the Ministry of Finance to the Naval Ministry. The government discussed these recommendations and finally, in 1865, offered the company a new charter lasting until 1882 under the new conditions. The head office of the company agreed to accept most of the new terms, provided that the government would subsidize it in the amount of 200,000 rubles annually. The government concurred, even offering to cancel the company's debt to the treasury of 725,000 rubles. But a general meeting of the more than 200 stockholders—the company's last—rejected the new terms, and the company remained in limbo, existing by virtue of an imperial decree of 1861 that empowered it to function in accordance with previous privileges.

Meanwhile, the insecurity and criticism had taken their financial toll, so much so that the company was unable to pay dividends in 1862 or 1863, and the value of its shares plummeted. However, before governmental backing became uncertain and publicity became unfavorable the company remained profitable. Grand Duke Konstantin, head of the Naval Ministry and younger brother of Tsar Alexander II, exaggerated when he told Minister of Foreign Affairs Gorchakov in 1857 that "this colony brings us a very small profit."[20] In fact, the Russian American Company's profits were still sizable. During the period of the third charter (1842–61), the Russian population increased slightly.[21] By the late 1850s the value of the company's capital had doubled since the early 1840s, the annual cost of upkeep of the colony had decreased, and the company's annual dividend had increased from 15 to 20 rubles.[22] This is not to say that Russian America was thriving, especially by comparison with the rest of the Pacific coast of North America. As de Stoeckl informed Gorchakov in 1860: "The increase in population on the Pacific coast of the United States, resulting from the conquest of California, instilled new life into those lands, which hitherto were deserted, and raised the hope that the trade of our colony would in turn undergo a similar development. But this hope has been largely dashed, and the affairs of the company, as far as I have been informed, are scarcely more flourishing today than they were fifteen or twenty years ago."[23]

Nevertheless, Alaska was still in the black; during the 1850s the Russian American Company's annual net profit ranged from 46,000 rubles in 1851 to 322,000 in 1856 and averaged 171,000 (80 percent of which was paid out in dividends).[24] The fur trade, based mainly upon sea otters and fur seals, had stagnated in the wake of the depletion of furbearers on the Northwest Coast and the loss of fur buyers in China, which was disintegrating under domestic discord and foreign encroachment. But the company adjusted. It tried marketing its furs elsewhere—San Francisco, New York, London. More importantly, it spread its commercial risk by diversifying its activities. By the middle 1850s the company was paying as much attention to the catching of fish, the felling of timber, the cutting of ice, the mining of coal (all for export to the growing markets of California and Hawaii), the hunting of whales, and the importing of tea (from Shanghai into Russia) as it was to the hunting and trading of furs. The tea trade was particularly successful; during the period of the third charter the company derived more revenue from the sale of tea than from the sale of pelts, and it accounted for about one-third of Russia's imports of Chinese tea.[25] The company also profited handsomely from the sale of imported goods in Russian America itself. The surcharge on such goods amounted to 77 percent and the company's net profit to 35 percent, which was ensured by the absence of competition.[26] By 1860 the firm was making more money from this traffic than from the fur trade.[27]

Even its fur business was showing signs of recovery, thanks to the replenishment of the sea otter, fur seal, and fox populations by means of strict conservation measures and to the receipt of higher prices for the scarcer skins (for example, the prices paid by the company to the colony's natives for adult sea otters increased fivefold between 1804 and 1850).[28] From 1839 additional revenue was provided by a series of leases to the Hudson's Bay Company of the *lisière*, the mainland panhandle of Alaska. The rent was paid first in land furs and then in pounds sterling. And the company cut costs by improving efficiencies through administrative consolidation and tighter accounting, by importing provisions more cheaply from California in the last half of the 1850s, and by employing more and more creoles in lieu of costlier Russians.

Thus, by the end of the period of the third charter the Russian American Company was not in financial straits. It had indeed experienced a slowdown, but that had started long before in the first half of the 1820s. The heyday of the maritime fur trade had been the period of the first charter (1799–1818), when sea otters and fur seals were still plentiful and windfall profits were made. By 1820 the market value of company shares had reached nearly 600 rubles.[29] Thereafter fewer pelts, higher wages, better services, expansion inland, stiffer British competition, and several expensive around-the-world voyages of supply raised costs and lowered profits. The company was really no better off during the period of the second charter (1821–40) than during that of the third; if anything, it was worse off, but it was not liquidated because it was still needed for noneconomic purposes. Fur exports from Russian America totalled 1,555,000 during the first, 900,000 during the second, and 825,000 during the third charter period, and as many sea otters (the most valuable fur bearers) were exported during the third as during the second period.[30] Total company income was even one-third higher for the third than for the second franchise period,[31] thanks to the aforementioned adjustments.

It has been said that the period of the first charter was marked by much peltry and little order, the second by less peltry and more order, and the third by little peltry and much order.[32] In other words, from franchise to franchise Russian America's *economic* raison d'être became less compelling, and if a time had to be picked when the colony ceased to serve a significant economic purpose, that time would be the first half of the 1820s, when overhunting had almost eradicated the fur bearers, not the last half of the 1850s, when reorientation and consolidation had arrested and even reversed the economic slowdown. It was not until the 1860s that critical financial difficulties arose, and these were primarily generated—if not engineered—artificially (for political reasons) by governmental investigation, accusation, and procrastination.[33] That is why Foreign Minister Gorchakov had warned in 1856 that a colonial inspection would make it difficult for the Russian American Company to obtain credit, which was "so necessary in commercial matters."[34] And sure enough, once the inspection began, the company had difficulty floating a bank loan. Similarly, in 1857 the Russian Ministry of Foreign Affairs had cautioned that negotiations with the United States should be conducted with "the utmost secrecy in order not to harm the business of the company."[35] But Russia's willingness to sell did become known and the company's business suffered accordingly.[36]

Another economic argument that has often been advanced to explain the Russian relinquishment of Alaska has to do with the desire to replenish the Russian treasury, which had been drained by the Crimean War (1853–56). Indeed, Russia's financial resources were severely strained throughout the last half of the nineteenth century by heavy expenditures on military ventures, railroad construction, and industrialization; and foreign capital was welcomed to compensate—along with state capital—for the feebleness of the Russian entrepreneurial class. At the end of the Crimean conflict Grand Duke Konstantin wrote Gorchakov that "because of the straitened condition of state finances ... the thought occurred to me that we ought to take advantage of the surplus of money in the treasury of the North American United States and sell them our colony."[37]

The sale price of Russian America, however, was much too small to lighten appreciably the empire's financial burden. The Russians estimated that the colony was worth at least 7,500,000 silver rubles ($5,000,000) or at most 20,000,000 rubles ($13,333,333).[38] The United States initially offered $5,000,000 but eventually paid $7,200,000 in gold. The Russian American Company received part of this sum as compensation for the loss of its territory. The rest—$6,526,666 or 9,790,000 rubles—went to the Russian treasury, but its share represented only three-fifths of the annual budget of one ministry (the Naval Ministry), two-thirds of the government's annual deficit, and less than one-fortieth of the government's annual budget.[39] In 1866 Baron Theodor Osten-Saken, an official in the Asiatic Department of the Ministry of Foreign Affairs, pointed out in a memorandum on the proposed sale of Alaska that "in case the sum which we might receive for our colony were great enough to cover a certain portion of our state debts, then of course, the temptation would be strong, but a few millions or even a few tens of millions of rubles will hardly be of any state importance in an empire which has about half a billion of annual income and expenditure and more than one and a half billion of debts."[40] The reasons for the sale of Russian America were not economic.[41]

The colony was more of a strategic than an economic liability. It had always been undermanned and undersupplied,[42] and it was difficult enough keeping at bay the natives, let alone enemy powers. Indeed, natives attacked the post of Nulato in 1851 and the colonial capital of Sitka (Novo-Arkhangel'sk) itself in 1855. But it was the Crimean War that underlined the indefensibility of Russian America. Russia's fledgling Pacific fleet was preoccupied with the Taiping Rebellion of 1850–65, which threatened to topple the ruling Manchu dynasty of China. Russia's possessions on both sides of the North Pacific, particularly on the more distant eastern side, lay hopelessly exposed to superior British and French sea power. The Russian American Company contemplated a fictitious sale of its colony to the ice-trading American Russian Commercial Company of San Francisco in order to forestall its seizure by the allies.

Although this deal was not consummated, it publicized the possibility of purchasing Russian America. The British for their part feared that in the event of war the Russians would cede Alaska to the United States rather than see it taken by their prospective Anglo-French enemies, and in that case the Hudson's Bay Company would be unable to renew its profitable lease on the *lisière* that expired in 1854. So at the beginning of that year, just before Great Britain and France declared war on Russia, the Russian American and Hudson's Bay Companies signed an agreement that exempted the North American territories (but not the shipping) of the two concerns from the hostilities. The Russian American Company circumvented the shipping exclusion by chartering foreign vessels which flew the flags of their own countries. Russia also took the precaution of stationing a Siberian line battalion of some two hundred men at Sitka, but they proved unnecessary.

The value of the neutrality pact was demonstrated later in the same year when an Anglo-French squadron bombarded Petropavlovsk and Ayan on Siberia's Pacific coast. These attacks underscored Russia's vulnerability in the North Pacific. The Russian navy was simply no match for allied sea power.[43] As Grand Duke Konstantin acknowledged after the war in 1857, "in the event of war with a naval power [i.e., Great Britain] we are not in a position to defend our colony."[44] He reiterated his belief in Russian America's indefensibility in 1866, declaring that "the condition of our colony worsens from day to day, and being so remote from the motherland it is of no importance to Russia, whereas the necessity of defending it will continue to be as difficult and as expensive in the future as it has been in the past."[45]

Konstantin was, in fact, the most avid high-level proponent of cession, partly because his overtaxed navy was responsible for the protection of colonial waters, as well as sometimes for the provisionment of the colony. Regular patrols by Russian cruisers did not begin until 1850, when one ship of the Pacific fleet was stationed off Russian America.[46] Konstantin, who was put in charge of the Naval Ministry towards the end of the Crimean War in 1855, resisted the reinforcement of the colony's naval contingent because of the high cost. Following the Crimean debacle, retrenchment and economy were the order of the day in defeated Russia. "I am now looking for ways of reducing our naval appropriation and would like very much to reduce the estimated requirement by one quarter of the total estimated sum," said Konstantin to Gorchakov in 1857.[47] The remote exclave of Alaska, difficult and costly to defend, was expendable. In 1864 the Naval Ministry calculated that the deployment of two or three corvettes in Russian-American waters would cost from one to one and one-half million rubles yearly, a sum that was, in its own words, "too burdensome for the annual budgetary estimate of the Naval Ministry."[48] However, "without the maintenance of regular cruising," concluded the review committee, "it is difficult, if not utterly impossible, to support, extend, and consolidate Russian colonization in our American posses-sion."[49] In other words, the colony would have to be sacrificed.

Russia was unable to defend Russian America not only from enemy navies in wartime but also from rival merchant marines in peacetime. Particularly troublesome were American "filibusters"—freewheeling Yankee traders who aggressively and often clandestinely trafficked in a variety of goods and products like Hawaiian sandalwood, Caribbean rum, English firearms, Pacific whales and fur seals, and Californian tallow and hides with little regard for foreign authority and little restraint from their own government. Shrewd traders as well as adept seamen, these spearheads of American capitalism had long plagued Russian America, as they had New Spain. In the first third of the nineteenth century they took sea otters along the Northwest Coast under the very noses of the Russians, even trading guns and liquor to the Tlingits and inflaming them against the tsar's men; in the second third they domi-nated whaling in the Okhotsk and Bering seas and the Gulf of Alaska, which were de jure if not de facto Russian. In the middle 1840s at least two hundred foreign whalers, mostly American, were hunting these waters; by the middle 1850s there were up to six hundred.[50]

The Russian government could do little but protest these forays, since its navy was not strong enough to patrol effectively all of the offshore waters of its far-flung empire. The protests were equally inef-fective, since the laissez-faire American government was not prepared to restrict what it considered the legitimate and even laudatory busi-ness activities of private citizens. De Stoeckl, the head of the Russian legation in Washington, D.C., asserted in 1860 that:

> In case of war this colony will be at the mercy of every hostile power and even in time of peace it is not protected from American freebooters, who are swarming over the Pacific. To the complaints that the Imperial mission in Washington has repeatedly made on this subject, the federal government has invariably replied that it is up to us to take the necessary precautions against these marauders and that the United States cannot undertake surveil-lance of our shores. These disputes, which are always disagreeable, can to a greater or lesser degree harm the maintenance of good relations between the two countries.[51]

Strategically, then, Russian America was vulnerable and hence dis-posable. But political considerations were even more important. As

Frank Golder, an early American specialist on Russian America, noted, "to the Russian government . . . Alaska was from the beginning more of a political . . . problem."[52] Whereas by the time of the expiration of the third charter, the Russian American Company was still serving its economic purpose in spite of the indefensibility of its territory, it was no longer serving its political purpose, namely, to facilitate Russian imperialist expansion. As de Stoeckl told Gorchakov in 1860, "from the political standpoint our possession is hardly of even secondary importance."[53] The company had long operated under the aegis and in the interests of the Russian government. Chartered in 1799 as a private joint-stock venture along the lines of the British East India and Hudson's Bay companies, the Russian concern had soon come under increasing state control. By the late 1810s it was a crown corporation, with naval officers serving as governor of Russian America and governmental officials, including the tsar himself, holding shares. The company was, in its own words, the government's "most loyal, reliable, and conscientious agent, which is indispensable to it in all special cases when it finds it awkward to act in its own name."[54]

The political significance of the company's territory was specified by the review committee at the end of the third charter period:

> In spite of the small value to us of the American territory in terms of hunting and trading, there are nevertheless political considerations that make its firm retention by us necessary. Only by strengthening our presence in America's north can we consider ourselves masters of the northern part of the Pacific Ocean, the possession of which in many respects bestows great advantages on a powerful state. By virtue of circumstances Russia was prompted to assert its naval presence on the eastern frontier of Siberia; with the subsequent development there of our naval power and—under its protection—our merchant marine, the fate of this borderland will be linked more and more with the interests of our American territory, but only if we succeed in strengthening the Russian element in the latter. Our strong influence on America's north will give us the right to influence in the affairs of this part of the world, which is already of particular importance to the European states; it also offers a means of rapprochement with Japan and enhancement of our power in the Far East in general. Finally, possession of our American colony can be turned to

undoubted advantage for the development and strengthening of our navy, giving it the opportunity and the pretext for showing the flag in distant seas equally with other maritime powers and offering it excellent practice for training skilled and experienced seamen.[55]

Baron Osten-Saken expressed a similar view. He felt that rivalry between the United States and Great Britain guaranteed the integrity of Russian America, whose real worth should not be judged by the operations of a "lifeless company," and that cession of the colony to the United States would alter the precarious balance of power in the North Pacific by strengthening the American position at the expense of the British and make the United States a closer and stronger rival and even a potential enemy of Russia in the Far East. He concluded that "it would seem that the present generation had a sacred obligation to preserve for the future generations every clod of earth along the coast of an ocean which has world-wide importance."[56]

But Osten-Saken and the review committee were outranked and outargued by Konstantin, de Stoeckl, and other influential officials who believed that there was little or no future for the Russian empire in North America in the face of increasing and encroaching American muscle. To them, the United States seemed bound to acquire all of the continent, and Russia was powerless to prevent this manifest destiny. As an anonymous Russian official[57] put it in 1860:

Whatever they may say in Europe about the cynicism of the dogma known in the political encyclopedia as the "Monroe Doctrine" or the doctrine of "manifest destiny," anyone who has lived the North American life cannot fail to understand instinctively that this principle is entering more and more into the blood of the people, and that new generations are sucking it in with their mothers' milk and inhaling it with every breath of air. Even one who has not lived in America, if he can free himself for the time being from the conceptions of a Europe long since bound up by artificial conditions, will understand that a people which has developed so rapidly and so successfully was bound to appreciate that the main reason for this development was the absence of the restricting influence of neighbors. These people try to maintain this invaluable advantage by all the means at their disposal and the question of the destruction of the influence of neighbors leads in practice to the principle of not having any.[58]

The Russian neighbor and its designs on North America had already been stymied in the middle 1820s, when American and British resistance had compelled the tsar to revise his 1821 decree that had unilaterally proclaimed Russian dominion as far south as 51° and had closed the Alaskan coast to foreign ships. In the wake of the Monroe Doctrine of 1823 and by conventions in 1824 and 1825, St. Petersburg retreated to 54° 40' and reopened colonial ports and waters. However, it aspired to expand its North American beachhead, most hopefully from Fort Ross, which had been established in 1812 just north of San Francisco Bay as a farming base and hunting station. But this exclave failed to prosper and was sold to New Helvetia's John Sutter in 1841. Meanwhile, increasing American and British settlement and exploitation engulfed the intervening Oregon Country. American determination culminated in the acquisition of the lower Columbia in 1846 and upper California in 1848, as well as Texas, and British resolve in the creation of the crown colonies of Vancouver Island in 1849 and British Columbia in 1858. The United States even appeared destined to gain British North America. No imperialist opportunities remained in the continent for Russia, which was rightly preoccupied with weightier European affairs anyway. Indeed, it seemed that Russia would be fortunate to hold Alaska. Eastern Siberia's Governor-General Nikolai Murav'ev, an admirer of the United States and a "continental isolationist" who envisioned Russia's Pacific destiny in Asia rather than in America, put the situation this way in 1853:

Twenty-five years ago the Russian-American Company turned to the government with a request to occupy California, which virtually nobody owned then, and it expressed its fear that this region would soon fall prey to the United States. In St. Petersburg they did not believe this fear and they asserted that this would hardly happen within one hundred years. The company contended that this would occur within twenty-five years, and it has already been more than a year since California became one of the United States. It was impossible to foresee the rapid spread of American dominion in North America, and it was also impossible then to foresee that these states, once ensconced on the Pacific Ocean, would quickly surpass all other naval powers there and would have need of all of the northwestern coast of America. The sway of the United States over all of North America is so natural that we should not be very sorry that we did not become entrenched in California twenty-five years ago—sooner or later we would have had to cede it; but in ceding *peacefully* we could have in exchange obtained other advantages from the Americans. Now, however, with the invention and development of railroads it is more evident than ever that the United States will inevitably spread over the whole of North America, and *we can expect that sooner or later we will have to cede our North American possession to them* [Murav'ev's italics].[59]

Grand Duke Konstantin, likewise a continentalist, concurred, telling Minister of Foreign Affairs Gorchakov in 1857 that "we should not delude ourselves and we should foresee that the United States, striving constantly to round out its possessions and desiring to dominate North America undividedly, will take the said colony from us and we will be unable to regain it."[60] In the same year this forecast was reiterated— albeit obliquely—by Admiral Ferdinand von Wrangell, a former governor of Russian America, when he advised Gorchakov that the government might even want to sell the colony for less than its full value out of *"fears of the future"* and *"anticipatory prudence"* (Wrangell's italics).[61] So Konstantin proposed that Alaska be sold to the American republic, "thereby resolving amicably and for us profitably a question that may otherwise be decided in our disfavor by conquest."[62]

Also in 1857 it was rumored that some Mormons intended to migrate from the United States to British Columbia or Russian America, whereupon, de Stoeckl feared, Russia would be faced with the alternative of armed resistance or territorial cession.[63] He added that there loomed the possibility that Alaska's auriferous river bars, which were well known to the Russians, might spark an uncontrollable gold rush that would bring an embarrassing end to the Russian American Company's rule, just as the Fraser River strike of 1858 had within weeks attracted from 4,000 to 5,000 American gold seekers who helped to overturn the Hudson's Bay Company's control of British Columbia and even threatened to wrest the colony from Great Britain in the same way that they had usurped California a decade earlier.[64] British traders and Anglican missionaries were already encroaching upon Russian America along the upper Yukon River. De Stoeckl warned Gorchakov of Russian America's precarious political position vis-à-vis the United States in a letter of 1867:

> Whatever will be the limits of the confederation of the United States, they will [not] restrain the feverish activity and enterprising spirit of Americans. In their eyes this continent is their patrimony. Their destiny (or manifest destiny, as it is called) is to expand constantly, and in this expansion, which the nation has pursued with as much perseverance as success, adventurers have played the role of capturer on more than one occasion. It was they who little by little overran Texas, which later became a state of the union. New Mexico and some other parts of the south have been acquired in the same way.
>
> It was hoped that the few resources of our colony would protect it from the rapacity of freebooters, but it has been otherwise. The fish and furs and some other products of relative insignificance to our possession, which are certainly not equal to the rich valleys of the Mississippi and Rio Grande or the gold-bearing plains of California, have nevertheless not escaped the cupidity of Americans.[65]

Russia was simply not strong enough to maintain its empire overseas, particularly in the face of growing American might. The belated and halfhearted emancipation of the serfs (1861) and the late and lame industrial revolution (after 1860), plus the conservative and stifling autocracy, meant that Russia was long severely handicapped as a great power by internal economic weakness.

More important to the fate of Russian America than the realignment of political forces in North America was the revision of power relations in Asia and the resultant reorientation of Russian imperialist policy. This shift was prompted by Russia's traumatic defeat in the Crimean War. That struggle, in Lenin's words, "demonstrated the rottenness and impotence of feudal Russia."[66] This was to become a recurring leitmotif: a military disaster revealing the economic, military, political, and social backwardness of the ancien régime and inducing overdue reforms in its domestic and foreign policies. Thus, the Crimean War led to Alexander II's "great reforms," including the abolition of serfdom, the Russo-Turkish War of 1877–78 to economic reforms for the promotion of industrialization, the Russo-Japanese War of 1904–5 to rural reforms and the creation of a parliament, and the First World War to revolution. The Crimean conflict, besides producing the heroics of the Light Brigade and Florence Nightingale, ended Russia's dominant role in southeastern Europe, where she had long sought to gain the Straits (the Dardanelles and the Bosphorus, which control navigation between the Black and Mediterranean seas). With the acquisition of Latvia and Lithuania in 1795, Finland in 1809, Bessarabia in 1812, and much of Poland in 1815, Russia had reached her western limits; further expansion was blocked by the other great powers.

In North America growing American might seemed irresistible. That left Russia's southern frontier across the plump waist of Asia as the only arena of promising imperialist opportunities. And here the decline of two longtime foes eased Russian advancement. In the southwest the disintegration of the Ottoman Empire from the eighteenth century fostered the Eastern Question and facilitated Russian penetration of the Balkans and the Transcaucasus in the wake of Persia's decline. In the southeast the deterioration of the Manchu dynasty loosened China's suzerainty over the steppe pasturelands, cultivated oases and valleys, and fabled caravansaries of Western Turkestan (soon to be rendered Russian Turkestan by Gorchakov's "civilizing mission") and her direct control over the reputed breadbasket and fur reserve of the Amur River valley. More importantly, the Amur represented a rapid and cheap route between the heart of ice-bound and mountain-rimmed Siberia and the huge, untapped markets of the Orient.[67] Certainly the contiguous Far East of Asia now offered Russia much more— and closer to home—than the overseas Far West of North America, and her eastern policy changed accordingly.

Toward the end of the eighteenth century Russia had already tried to annex Amuria but had been repulsed by the powerful Manchus. By the middle of the nineteenth century, however, their power had waned in the face of foreign intervention and internal turmoil. The first blow was the Opium War of 1839–42, caused by Great Britain's attempt to end China's restrictions on foreign trade. The conflict was resolved by the Treaty of Nanking, which opened several Chinese ports to British vessels and surrendered Hong Kong. This was the first of a series of "unequal treaties" imposed upon a hapless China by Western imperialist powers. As one of them Russia was determined to share in the easy spoils. But she had to proceed carefully in order not to provoke Great Britain, which opposed St. Petersburg's three-pronged thrust into the Balkans, Inner Asia, and the Far East. In the Far Eastern theater the Russian American Company was now used as a cover to avoid alarming Russia's rivals, masquerading as a private concern to camouflage state aims in the manner of the East India and Hudson's Bay companies. In 1844 the Russian government ordered the company to reconnoiter the estuary of the Amur River with a view to determining its navigability.[68] This was accomplished in 1849, when Captain-Lieutenant Nevel'skoi demonstrated that the river could be entered by seagoing vessels. From 1851 under the forceful direction of Governor-General Nikolai Murav'ev, who was granted viceregal powers by the tsar, the company helped to explore and settle the Amur Country. In 1853, on the eve of the Crimean conflict, the government assumed control of the Amur venture, and the company was given jurisdiction of Sakhalin, the island commanding the entrance to the Amur.

Here in what was to become known as the Maritime Territory lay, in the opinion of many Russian statesmen, the empire's Pacific future. De Stoeckl, for example, believed firmly that Russia had its own manifest destiny but on the Asian rather than the American side of the ocean. In 1869 he advised Gorchakov that:

> It is on our Asiatic shores that our interests lie and it is there that we should concentrate our energies. There we are on our own ground and have the resources of a vast and rich territory to exploit. We will take our part in the extraordinary activity that is developing in the Pacific; our establishments will rival those of other nations in prosperity and, with the solicitude that our august monarch has shown to the lands along the Amur, we cannot fail to gain in this vast ocean the important position that befits Russia.[69]

De Stoeckl repeated his advice to Gorchakov in 1867, declaring that:

> It is in the lands of the Amur and especially in the territories to the south of this river that we must concentrate our resources and energies. These areas are fertile and will readily attract emigrants.[70] They have magnificent [sic] harbors, and the vicinity of Japan and China assures them a profitable commerce. It is here that our power in the Pacific must be based. These areas are contiguous to the empire, and from that they will become even easier to defend.[71]

Grand Duke Konstantin agreed, asserting that with respect to Russian America "it is urgent to abandon it by ceding it to the United States and to render all of the government's solicitude to our Amurian possessions, which form an integral part of the empire and which by all accounts offer more resources than the northerly shores of our American possession."[72]

Konstantin's agreement was critical. Intensely patriotic and energetic, he was one of his ruling brother's ablest and closest advisors. Russia's Crimean defeat taught Konstantin that the war-torn country must reform and retrench and the far-flung empire must reorganize and consolidate. This became his idée fixé and his country's idée-force. It meant, to Konstantin, the abolition of the anachronistic monopoly of the Russian American Company and the abandonment of its exposed and neglected colony. In 1857 he told Gorchakov that Russia

> must do its utmost to become stronger in its center, in those solidly and natively Russian regions which in nationality and belief constitute its real and main strength, and it must develop the strength of this center in order to retain those extremities that can bring it real benefit. The North American [United] States, following the natural order of things, is bound to strive to possess all of North America and therefore sooner or later they will confront us there, and there is no doubt that they will even acquire our colony without much effort, and we will never be able to regain it.[73]

Konstantin envisioned both Russia and the United States becoming mighty empires at the expense of their common foe, Great Britain, but within their own continental land masses. Asia was to be Russia's, and North America the United States', domain.

Konstantin's Weltanschauung was shaped by the geopolitical outlook of his subordinate and friend Murav'ev. Described by the novelist Ivan Goncharov as far-sighted, quick-thinking, hyperactive, and daring and as a "courageous fighter" against obstacles in his path (including Gorchakov's own ministry),[74] Murav'ev believed that it was Russia's Far Eastern frontier, not its European border, that should be reinforced and extended. He expressed his viewpoint in 1853 in a confidential note to Konstantin:

> I only make bold to say not that the events underway to the south and west of our European borders are unimportant or that war with Turkey, England, and France would not alarm us, but Russia is so strong in its singlemindedness and in its absolute devotion

to the Tsar that no danger can threaten it from that side, and its domestic material strength and resources are so solid and great that the longer this war would last, the more terrible it would be for our enemies, especially England, even if they succeeded in inflicting some damage to our towns on the European frontier. But in the Far East our situation is different: Avacha Bay in Kamchatka and the mouth of the Amur (Sungari) and navigation on this river can be taken from Russia by force. Neighboring, populous China, now helpless in its ignorance, can easily become a danger to us under the influence and direction of the English and French, and then Siberia will cease to be Russian; and in Siberia, besides gold, there is space, which is vital to us and is sufficient for all of the excess agricultural population of European Russia for an entire century. The loss of this expanse cannot be compensated by any victories and conquests in Europe; and in order to keep Siberia it is necessary now to retain and strengthen Kamchatka, Sakhalin, and the mouth of the Amur and navigation on it and to gain a strong influence on neighboring China.[75]

Murav'ev, who opposed all monopolies like that of the Russian American Company, was convinced that Russia had to abandon Russian America to the United States and regroup in Asia astride the Amur, the only waterway that links the Pacific Ocean and the Siberian interior. To him the Pacific and the Amur formed the "natural boundaries" of the empire. And without the Amur Russia would be barred from the Pacific; indeed, the river was regarded as essential to the supply of Siberia's Pacific coast during the Crimean War. Murav'ev feared that if Russia did not occupy the Amur valley, Great Britain or the United States would.[76] "China and Japan are gradually falling prey to the British and the Americans," he warned Konstantin in 1854.[77] Both men had more fear of British commercial encroachment in the Far East than American commercial encroachment in the Pacific Northwest, and they were determined to counter British and French efforts to expand at China's expense. They wanted their country to become a ranking sea power in the Pacific, with the Amur and the Sea of Japan becoming Russia's Mississippi and Gulf of Mexico.

Murav'ev moved swiftly to resolve the "Amur question" in Russia's favor. He led three expeditions down the river: in 1854, when he opened it; in 1855, when he defended it; and in 1858, when he acquired it, to borrow the words of his biographer.[78] By the Treaty of Aigun of 1858, Russia gained the left bank of the Amur; two years later the right bank of the tributary Ussuri was won by the Treaty of Peking. Also in 1860 Vladivostok (boastfully meaning "lord of the east") was founded on Peter the Great Bay; it soon became Russia's principal port on the Pacific and the home of its Pacific fleet. Murav'ev, having achieved his ambition to annex Amuria as the locus of Russia's Pacific strength, retired in 1861 to Paris in failing health but with an ample pension and the honorific and fitting title of Count of the Amur, his surname becoming Murav'ev-Amurskii. China was helpless to resist Russia's advance, being racked by the internecine Taiping Rebellion.

By the early 1860s, then, the Russian American Company had fulfilled its political purpose on the Asian side of the Pacific. And on the American side its political role had been usurped by American and British might. Little wonder that the Russian government balked at renewing the company's franchise, for it no longer needed the venture. All that it needed was a buyer for the company's territory. The two likeliest customers were the United States and Great Britain, and the United States was the logical choice politically, as well as the only interested party.[79] As Minister of Finance Mikhail Reitern told Gorchakov in 1861, "the transfer of our colony to the U.S. seems to me to be especially desirable politically."[80] For one thing, Russia and the United States were on friendly terms, and they shared a common antipathy towards Great Britain. Despite the aggressive enterprise of American skippers in the North Pacific (whose impact had been exaggerated by de Stoeckl), there had been no really serious friction between Russia and the United States. In the words of Tsar Alexander II in 1866, "the Russian and American peoples have no injuries to forget or to remember."[81] And the United States had sympathized with Russia during the Crimean War. Great Britain, by contrast, vigorously opposed Russian expansion in Eurasia, and she had sympathized with the Polish rebels of 1863 in their vain attempt to become independent of Russia. Relations between the United States and Great Britain had deteriorated during the Civil War (1861–65), and American expansion in the Pacific Northwest had been resisted by Whitehall.

Also, Russia needed a closer ally to help her press for the abrogation of the humiliating terms of the Treaty of Paris of 1856, which had sealed her ignominious defeat in the Crimea by stripping her of part of Bessarabia, neutralizing the Black Sea, and depriving her of any claim to protection of the Orthodox Christians in the empire of the Porte. The United States was seen as that ally. Furthermore, in the eyes of anglophobic Russia, the cession of Alaska to the United States would undermine British power in North America by enhancing the American grip on the Pacific Coast at the expense of British North America, and perhaps even provoke a clash between Great Britain and the United States. In the words of a letter from Karl Marx to Friedrich Engels in 1867, "the Russians . . . are making trouble for the lordly English in the United States."[82] An American Alaska would sandwich Canada, which was struggling towards nationhood. De Stoeckl acknowledged in 1859 that "if the United States were to become master of our possession [Russian America], British Oregon [Columbia] would be squeezed by the Americans on the north and south and would with difficulty evade aggression on their part."[83] And Reitern admitted that cession would make the United States "a neighbor of the English colonies not only on the south but on the northwest as well." This, he added, "cannot but result in the strengthening of our friendly relations with the United States and the furthering of the possibility of disagreement between these States and England."[84]

Following the sale, Marx asserted that "thereby England is cut off from the sea on one side through the Yankees and the reversion of the whole of British North America to the U.St. [United States] is accelerated. That's the secret of the whole affair!"[85] St. Petersburg was well aware that, in de Stoeckl's words, "the plan for the cession of our colony, if it is realized, will greatly perturb the British government."[86] This was in Russia's interests. Gorchakov realized that a weaker British presence in North America would mean a weaker British position in the North Pacific and therefore in the Far East, and it was undoubtedly this prospect that persuaded him to agree to the sale of Russian America to the United States.[87]

The sale of Russia's only overseas colony, then, was motivated primarily by political considerations, secondarily by strategic factors, and least of all by economic concerns. In 1854 Secretary of State William Marcy and Senator William Gwin informed de Stoeckl that their country might buy Alaska, but the Russian chargé d'affaires declined and told them to forget the matter.[88] Three years later, when Alaska's indefensibility had been demonstrated by the Crimean War and Amuria's promised land had been secured by Murav'ev's aggression, Grand Duke Konstantin proposed to Gorchakov that Russian America be sold. The conservative minister of foreign affairs, however, who favored a policy of caution and restraint (his *politique de recueillement*), feared that an American purchase at that time would overly antagonize Great Britain so soon after its Crimean victory.[89] But the proud Gorchakov had little choice but to execute his sovereign's reform-minded policies, although his ministry insisted that liquidation of the colony be postponed until the expiration of the Russian American Company's franchise at the end of 1861. Meanwhile, de Stoeckl was instructed in 1857 to plumb discreetly American official opinion on the subject; his feelers became concrete and specific in 1859.[90] President James Buchanan favored a purchase, but Russia then decided "to postpone this matter until a more favorable time."[91] Such a time was the close of 1861, when the company's third charter expired and the American presidential election ended; by then, too, the Amur Country had been incorporated into the Russian Empire. But then the Civil War intervened, and Washington was preoccupied with the preservation of the Union and the assertion of federal authority. This conflict worried Russia, since a break between the North and the South would weaken the stature of the United States as a foe of Great Britain, Russia's arch enemy. De Stoeckl warned Gorchakov that "the disintegration of the United States as a power is a deplorable event. The American confederation has been a counterweight to English might, and in this sense its existence is an element in the worldwide balance of power."[92] Gorchakov himself declared in 1862 that Russia desired "the preservation of the American Union as an undivided nation."[93]

Meanwhile, Russian America was being inspected by Kostlivtsev and Golovin and discussed by the review committee. By now the Russian American Company had in political terms succeeded in Amuria but failed in Alaska, where, moreover, it was finally losing money in the wake of official prying and stalling. The company could not continue without large subsidies,[94] and for the government to assume control of the colony would cost the Russian treasury at least 250,000 rubles annually. As the review committee concluded, "the financial resources of the territory could hardly ever be sufficient to repay the cost of its defense or even administration."[95] So the only sensible course was to sell. And that was precisely the decision reached by Tsar Alexander II on December 28, 1866, after consultation with Konstantin, Gorchakov, Reitern, de Stoeckl, and Naval Minister Nikolai Krabbe at the Winter Palace. With this in mind, de Stoeckl returned to

Washington from St. Petersburg in early 1867 and approached Seward. It was an opportune time, for the Hudson's Bay Company's lease of the *lisière* was due to expire on June 1. Probably in order to save political face, the tsarist government insisted that the negotiations be conducted in such a way as to make it appear that the United States had taken the initiative. Seward gladly complied, for he egotistically wanted all of the credit for the transaction. Seward also insisted on secrecy so that he could present a fait accompli to Congress, which was hostile to the Johnson administration. De Stoeckl agreed, and Russian America became American Alaska.[96] Ironically, the tsar's offer was telegraphed via Cyrus Field's new transatlantic cable, whose successful laying in 1866 aborted Western Union's much longer overland telegraph line linking Russia, Canada, and the United States via the Bering Strait; it would have greatly eased Russian management of Alaska and perhaps have prolonged Russian tenure.[97]

The year 1867 was fateful for the political geography and history of the lands bordering the North Pacific. On the American side the confederation of the eastern colonies of British North America brought into being the unlikely Dominion of Canada in the face of the burgeoning United States. The American Union, reconsolidating itself after a searing civil war, hastened the end of the continent's colonial era (and heralded the end of its westward movement) by purchasing Alaska from tsarist Russia. On the Asiatic side, the Meiji restoration substituted the mikado for the shogun and generated Western reforms that were to transform Japan from a feudal, isolationist state into a modern industrial and military power. And Russia withdrew from the Western Hemisphere to solidify its newly found position in Asia at the expense of the Chinese. These events had far-reaching and long-lasting consequences, namely, Japan's rise to power, Canada's distrust of the United States, and China's aversion to Russia. Those legacies are still very much with us.

The Significance of the Alaska Purchase to American Expansion

Howard I. Kushner

Although in the past thirty years nineteenth-century American expansion has been reinterpreted in terms of the relationship between external factors and the requirements of domestic political, social, and economic forces, the acquisition of Alaska continues to be explained by North American scholars in terms of the notion that "Europe's distresses were America's successes."[1] The United States proved able to purchase Russian America, this argument runs, only because the Russians desired to "unload this bothersome liability" of ice-covered real estate.[2] In fact, according to one version, if it weren't for Secretary of State William H. Seward's unrequited lust after territory,[3] or, according to another, his desire for Asian markets, Alaska might have remained a Russian possession.[4]

Soviet historians, on the other hand, have insisted that the story should be revised substantially. Writing in 1939, S. B. Okun disputed "the legend which grew up later" that the tsarist government was unaware of the economic value of Russian-America. "The presence of gold-fields in Alaska was not only known to the government in the 1860's but was also discussed over and over again in the press. ... Tsarist Russia knew very well what she was selling, and the United States knew equally well what it was buying." It was, in part, the fear that Alaska's great resources would bring "an army of [American] prospectors" soon followed by "an army of soldiers armed with guns" that persuaded the Russians to part with their possessions. Thus, Russia sold Alaska because of her "inability to defend her colonies in the event of war" and her "inability to protect them even in a period of formal peace." Moreover, the "shift of Russian interests to the continent of Asia" played an important role in the tsar's decision.[5]

Although, Okun concluded, England would have paid more for the colonies than the United States did, "it was much more important for the tsarist government to win an ally, especially one whose interests went counter to those of England." Therefore, "in her aim to undermine English power in North America, and, at the same time, bring about a clash between the United States and the British empire, Russia decided to sell Alaska, and the aspiration of the United States to dominate the American continent induced" them to buy it.[6]

All future Soviet scholarship on the Alaska Purchase would be influenced deeply by Okun's arguments and conclusions. However, certain aspects of his thesis—particularly conflict between the United States and Russia—would be emphasized at the expense of others as the cold war progressed. Thus, A. V. Efimov, the dean of Soviet Americanists, suggested that Seward played upon Russia's post Crimean War weakness by threatening an invasion of American filibusters if Russia refused to relinquish its colony.[7] In 1953 T. M. Batueva argued that the sale of Alaska was due directly to American expansion in the Pacific.[8] Specifying that this particular expansion was the result of Seward's combining with other U.S. capitalists, A. L. Narochnitskii alleged that Russia, financially and militarily too weak to resist, agreed to the sale.[9]

These views were brought together in the mid-1960s by Mikhail Belov. Belov attempted to tie the Alaska purchase to what he saw as the combination of nineteenth-century imperialism and tsarist degeneracy. "American pressure upon tsarist Russia, which was weakened by the Crimean War ... was the decisive factor. The United States," Belov maintained, "compelled tsarist Russia to cede Alaska." Belov rejected Okun's earlier suggestion that Russia ceded its possessions to the United States in an attempt to "cause a clash" between the United States and Great Britain: "American capitalism proved to be more adroit, more aggressive, and more powerful than the old, experienced British capitalism, which was weaker in the given region."[10]

Later Soviet scholarship tried to temper Belov's interpretation. Influenced by their nation's détente policies of the 1970s, Soviet historians now tended to stress the amicable nature of relations between the United States and Russia in the first half of the nineteenth century.[11]

The most influential and prolific among them is Nikolai N. Bolkhovitinov. Although Bolkhovitinov's earlier works elaborated the
antagonisms between the United States and Russia, his more recent
publications have revised this earlier emphasis. Nevertheless, while
his conclusions underscore the peaceful nature of Russian-American
relations, Bolhovitinov's works (which will be discussed below) offer
evidence which tends to support the view that American expansionist
policies played a key role in the cession of Alaska.[12]

We have reached the ironic historiographical situation which finds
Soviet historians suggesting that the United States acquired Russian
America because it was shrewd, while American historians, by and
large, attributed the purchase to their nation's mindlessness.[13] Nevertheless, a détente consensus seems to have emerged with both Soviet
and North American scholars agreeing that the cession of Alaska took
place in a context of mutual goodwill.[14]

Those few studies by North Americans which suggest that the Alaska
Purchase was the result of expansionist pressures by the American
government and special business concerns remain in the distinct
minority.[15] Like Okun, they argue that Russia parted with Russian
America reluctantly. By focusing on relations in the Pacific Northwest,
rather than on Europe, they claim to uncover "a history of conflict
and, at times, near hostility between Russia and the United States."[16]

Two critical views of such an interpretation have emerged. The first,
suggested in the works of Dr. Bolkhovitinov, is that a conflict thesis is
reminiscent of the cold war rhetoric of an earlier generation of American
historians who attempted "to prove the existence of ominous 'danger
from Moscow' to the western hemisphere as early as the first half of the
nineteenth century, and to portray the relations between Russia and
the United States of America as a chain of original 'dramatic confronta-
tions.'"[17] Bolkhovitinov cites Thomas A. Bailey's *America Faces Russia*
(1950) as arguing that "from the day of its emergence until our day, Russia
has taken an extremely hostile position toward the United States." In
other works Bolkhovitinov finds an overstated picture of "the anti-Russian aspect of the Monroe Doctrine," and a tendency to "exaggerate
Russia's expansionist intentions in California." Moreover, he argues that
"advocates of the 'natural hostility' between Russia and the United
States" can be uncovered long before the cold war period.[18]

Certainly Bolkhovitinov is correct in noting that studies of Russian-
American relations by U.S. scholars were influenced by cold war

rhetoric and assumptions, but it does not follow that those studies tended to characterize pre-1867 relations as hostile. Rather, the thesis of Bailey and others was that naive Americans were deceived by Russian policymakers into believing that Moscow's intentions were friendly. The actual relations between the two nations were not pictured as antagonistic. The only exceptions, which are discussed below, were the tsar's *ukaz* of 1821 excluding U.S. nationals from Russian America and the issuance of the Monroe Doctrine. Though Bailey refers to the reports of various United States ministers who found tsarist Russia to be "the calm of despotism," he writes that "diplomatically speaking, the years from 1832 to 1848, and even to the outbreak of the Crimean War in 1854, are barren in Russian-American relations." Certainly Bailey discovers no tensions in the Pacific Northwest, for he explains, while "American pioneers were pushing west under the propulsion of Manifest Destiny; the Russian people were tending to their own affairs." In fact, he sees this as a period when the United States "had relatively little business with Russia and most of that was of third-rate importance." The Russians were "determined to cultivate our [U.S.] friendship."[19]

The second criticism, mainly by North American scholars, revolves around the interpretation of evidence. Like Bolkhovitinov, they find relations in the Pacific Northwest more suggestive of cooperation than conflict. For instance, Richard A. Pierce argues that "a case might as easily be made for a long-standing friendship. The Russian-American Company colonies also worked with the American traders to mutual benefits; the ice trade and the telegraph venture were pursued in harmony, and there were many expressions of goodwill by individuals."[20] Similarly, Basil Dmytryshyn notes that "while on numerous occasions some Russians as well as some Americans voiced concern over their respective intentions and activities, from 1790 to 1867 Russian-American relations in the Pacific Northwest also abounded in close and continuous cooperation." The Russian American Company relied upon food, transport, and American-made vessels and thus, Dmytryshyn concludes, "the list of American-Russian cooperation in the Pacific Northwest is quite long, indeed longer than the list of conflicts."[21] Mutual distrust of Great Britain, suggests C. Bickford O'Brien, played a more important role in unifying Russia and the United States than "tensions, rhetorical attacks, and complaints on both sides" did in dividing them.[22]

Nevertheless, to suggest that mutual dependence did not exacerbate tensions ignores the contradictory nature of the relationship. The more that the Russian American Company allowed itself to rely upon the Yankees, the greater American interest grew in the resources of the area. The result was almost always an increase of tensions.

This pattern of dependence leading to tensions can be traced back as far as Russian-American Governor A. A. Baranov's first contract with Yankee Captain Joseph O'Cain in 1803. The Russian company could not ship its sea otter furs to Canton because of Chinese treaty restrictions. Baranov agreed to provide sea otters in return for supplies and the shipping of Russian otters to the China market.[23] News of O'Cain's successful dealings quickly spread. By 1805 enough Yankee ships were in Russian-American waters for Nikolai Rezanov to warn the tsar that his possession "would be an unexhaustible source of wealth . . . were it not for the Bostonians," and thus it was "necessary to take an stronger hold of the country else we shall leave it empty handed."[24] Baranov persuaded Rezanov that the contract system was worth maintaining if only because it forced the Yankees to deal directly with the Russian company rather than with the Aleuts and Tlingits. Nevertheless, both agreed that the eventual goal was the self-sufficiency of the colony and the termination of reliance on the Boston traders.[25]

In 1808 the Russian government issued the first in a sixty-year series of protests about Americans trading illegally in Russia's North American possessions.[26] And, as always, the United States government not only refused to act against its nationals, but also it questioned Russia's jurisdiction over Indians and unsettled areas of Russian America.[27] And, as almost always, the Russians backed off, believing, for instance during the Napoleonic Wars, that national interest would be better served by avoiding conflict with the United States.[28] The result was increased American penetration of Russian America, leading to additional complaints like those of naval captain Vasilii Golovnin, who, upon returning from a voyage to Russian America in 1811, persuaded the directors of the company to petition the tsar to halt "any further interference with Russian business on the part of private North American hucksters."[29]

Of course, there were also internal factors that could account for the complaints of Golovnin who wished to see a stronger Russian navy take a firmer control of the colony. Also suspect were the motives of the governing board in St. Petersburg, some of whom personally invested in the outfitting of ships for around-the-world expeditions to supply the colonies.[30] Nevertheless, even if one remains suspicious of the warnings and fears of Rezanov, Golovnin, the governing board of the company, and the Russian Ministry of Foreign Affairs, Baranov's dependence on the Yankees for supplies and transport of sea otters had not led to a reduction of tensions. The more that U.S. citizens become involved in the Northwest coast, the more they pursued goals which threatened Russia's sovereignty over its possessions.

By the early 1820s Congressman John Floyd warned that Russian "forts, magazines, towns, cities, and trade, seem to arise ... as if by magic." While Floyd urged American expansion, he projected his own hostile plans on the tsar, who "with an army of a million of men ... menaces ... even the king of Spain's dominions in North America." He warned that Russia's expansionist designs, if left unchecked, would allow them to "command the whole northern part of the Pacific Ocean."[31]

Not surprisingly the Russian minister to the United States, Pierre de Poletica, was concerned about the increasing hostility he perceived vis-à-vis Russian America. He had refrained from submitting reports of these "instances of political madness" because he "noticed no disposition on the part of the American government to preoccupy itself seriously" with Russian America. But, Poletica warned, "all this may radically change, especially now when Congress is preoccupied with these settlements."[32]

Poletica's dispatches and the reports of Captain Vasilii Golovnin added weight to the constant pleas of the main directorate of the Russian American Company that the activities of United States nationals be restricted. On September 16, 1821, Emperor Alexander I issued a *ukaz* which proclaimed that "from the Bering Strait to 51° northern latitude" (extending to the Aleutians and the eastern coast of Siberia) was "exclusively" Russian territory and foreigners were excluded from "the pursuits of commerce, whaling, and fishery, and all other industry" there. The *ukaz* claimed a one-hundred-mile territorial water right, warning that foreign vessels in these waters were "subject to confiscation along with the whole cargo." Nine days later the tsar issued a second *ukaz* authorizing the company "to annex ... newly discovered places to Russian dominion" south of the fifty-first parallel, "provided that they have not been occupied by any other European nation, or by citizens of the United States."[33]

The tsar's *ukaz* according to the minister of foreign affairs, Count Nesselrode, was issued because "foreign adventurers and smugglers" continue to participate in "fraudulent trade in furs and other articles exclusively reserved for the Russian-American Company. These traders," Nesselrode complained, "appear often to betray a hostile tendency," for they "furnish arms and ammunition to the natives in our possessions" exciting them to "resistance and rebellion" against Russian authority.[34]

The *ukaz* of course, stimulated further anti-Russian sentiment among landed expansionist circles in the Congress and the press.[35] Soon spokesmen for the maritime Northwest Coast trading and whaling interests added their voices in support of immediate federal action to pressure the Russian government to withdraw its *ukaz*.[36] Whether John Quincy Adams's subsequent strong reaction to the *ukaz* was motivated by his presidential ambitions, or by his own fears that Russia might indeed present a danger to his expansionist hopes for the United States, is less important than the impact that his reactions had on American-Russian relations. The secretary of state's protests against the *ukaz* are well known, and the record of his meetings and correspondence concerning it are available in so many places that there is no need to repeat them here.[37] Several points, however, must be emphasized. Adams took a very hard line in opposing the *ukaz*. In July 1822 Adams and the American minister to Russia, Henry Middleton, warned that the correspondence relating to the *ukaz* showed that "a state of war between the two powers exists" lacking only "a declaration or act of violence, which latter cannot be long in coming."[38] Second, although the Russian government agreed to negotiate further before a final decision would be reached regarding the implementation of the *ukaz*, the Monroe administration continued in its tough public and private pose until those negotiations were completed in April 1824.[39]

During this period Adams announced his "no future colonization principle." He informed the Russian minister to the United States, Hendrik Tuyll, on July 17 that the United States would "contest the right of Russia to *any* territorial establishment on this continent, and that we should assume distinctly the principle that the American continents are no longer subjects for any new colonial establishments."[40] And when in November 1823 Tsar Alexander I emphasized to the United States that he and his monarchical allies would aid Spain and

Portugal in retrieving their lost Latin American colonies, Adams's private reply to the tsar was harsh and direct.[41]

Given the political, diplomatic, and rhetorical context, it would be difficult to characterize the period 1820 to 1824 as one of amicable relations between the United States and Russia. Although the issues engendered by the *ukaz* and the Monroe Doctrine were settled by the negotiation in April 1824 of a convention opening the Russian possessions to U.S. traders for a ten-year period, the agreement itself led to an increased American presence in Russian America and, eventually, to threats and near hostilities when the Russian government refused to renew the treaty in 1834.[42] The seeds of future conflict were rooted in the intentions of the foreign ministries of both nations when the convention was negotiated. Nesselrode viewed the pact as the only way to limit U.S. penetration of Russian America because "by signing this agreement, the Americans have just as solemnly admitted that, at the expiration of a few stipulated years, we shall have the legal power to forbid them absolutely to trade or fish in that whole area."[43] Adams and his negotiator in St. Petersburg, Henry Middleton, had very different expectations. They believed that the Russian settlements would become so dependent on United States trade that the continuance of the free access clause of the treaty would prove indispensable to the Russian American Company.[44] Company officials in St. Petersburg shared Adams's interpretation, although in their case with trepidation rather than with hope. Konrad Ryleev of the company's St. Petersburg office predicted that if the pact were ratified, "the Company has every reason to fear that not alone within ten years, but within a much shorter period the foreigners ... will bring the Company to a state of complete destruction."[45] "Only one thing could assure the security of Sitka [Novo-Arkhangel'sk]," warned another company official, "the complete removal of the citizens of the United States from its shores."[46]

Even though this period witnessed the rapid decline of the sea otter trade, Yankee interest in Russian America intensified. Boston traders continued to be the chief suppliers of necessities for the Russian colony, while increasing numbers of Yankee whalers followed their prey into Pacific Northwest waters, often landing on the shores of Russian America.[47] But when the Russian government attempted to close its colonies to American traders in April 1834, the United States government vigorously protested. Secretary of State John Forsyth informed the Russian minister that the treaty applied only to those areas where the company had settlements; Americans could not be excluded from unoccupied areas.[48] The suggestion of the United States minister to Russia, William Wilkins, that "the only way in which you can avoid collision and difficulties there, will be to throw the entire coast open to the fair competition of . . . the United States, England, and Russia," found little support among Russian government and company officials.[49]

Nesselrode found himself in a tough position. On the one hand he hoped to use American-Russian diplomatic amity to offset British commercial and political power in Europe while on the other, he was under great pressure to protect Russian America from further assaults. The inevitable confrontation occurred in August 1836 when the American brig *Loriot* was seized by the Russian company on an uninhabited stretch of the coast.[50] Claiming that nothing in the 1824 convention gave Russia the right to interfere with American vessels, Forsyth asserted that the United States never intended to abandon its rights on "any unoccupied coast of North America."[51]

Harsh words continued to flow, with United States minister to St. Petersburg, George M. Dallas, suggesting to Washington that it protect its "lawful commerce by forceable means," while warning Nesselrode that "armed opposition to American trade" would bring results he could not "venture to foresee."[52] Although neither side backed down, the Russians intercepted no other ships and American traders and whalers continued to sail in Russian-American waters. Meanwhile (in 1838), partially in an attempt to halt Yankee activities, Nesselrode approved a ten-year lease of a strip of territory running from Cape Spencer south to the 54° line to the Hudson's Bay Company in return for payment of rental in furs, foodstuffs, and supplies. This agreement, Nesselrode hoped, would do "away with all rivalry in the fur trade, . . . putting an end to the frequent occasions of friction with England and with the citizens of the United States of America which have already led to unpleasant correspondence with those governments."[53] When Forsyth learned of the grant he told the Russian minister to the United States that he hoped it was not true, for "such a lease means renunciation of possession."[54]

While war had not broken out, it would be difficult to view events during the 1830s as tending to bolster the Russian colony. In fact, the 1824 treaty, rather than settling claims, served to intensify differences. The same was true of commercial contacts such as whaling, which boomed along the Northwest Coast in the thirties, forties, and fifties. During this era hundreds of Yankee whalers annually hunted the leviathan in Russian-American seas, often landing along the coast. Adolf Etholin, manager of the Novo-Arkhangel'sk settlement, complained in 1843 about "whaling vessels which threatened to ruin the fur trade by scaring the sea otters away and . . . whaling captains, who despite the convention and Russian orders, continue to enter harbors, etc., in the Russian possession."[55] And the protests continued for the next decade alleging that the Yankees stole oil as well as food and women from the Aleuts and Tlingits, leaving behind bad liquor and syphilis. This behavior was ruining trade and company officials demanded armed cruisers to keep Yankee vessels out of the Russian domain. Ships were dispatched but, remembering the U.S. government's reaction to earlier attempts to enforce the convention of 1824, captains were instructed to "be very careful in their actions and so far as possible avoid occurrences that can lead to complaints."[56]

As usual the Russian government could do little to protect its North American colonies. Yankee whaling should not be dismissed as a one-shot enterprise whose threat to Russian America might end as it grew less profitable by the later 1850s. First of all, whaling was a complex commercial industry whose investors were always willing to diversify to meet changing demands, whether it was the manufacture of cotton textiles, the exploitation of new fisheries, or other more specialized ventures. The leaders of the whaling industry were also the fathers of American manufacturing, industrial, and technological capitalism—and they had political influence as well. When the whaling captains brought back reports of valuable fisheries, minerals, furs, or other potentially profit-making resources, ship owners often attempted to diversify into these areas.[57]

Although each American commercial enterprise in Russian America did not inevitably lead to the next, they were not unconnected. Equally important, the increasing collaboration between maritime and landed commercial forces in the United States made Russian America less secure. Whether the Russian American Company was forced to depend upon American commercial interests in some instances, or to resist them in others, the result was the same—the weakening of the colony's ability to resist what Nikolai Murav'ev foresaw in 1853: "The ultimate rule of the United States over the whole of North-America is so natural that we must sooner or later recede."[58]

The political power of the Northwest Coast trading and whaling interests is evident from their successful opposition to the Polk administration's desire to form an alliance with Russia in order to put increased pressure on Great Britain to cede all of Oregon to the United States in 1845 and 1846.[59] And, in the 1850s when most other expansionist plans were doomed as the result of increasing national disunity, landed and maritime factions from all regions continued their drive not only to protect American interests in the Pacific Northwest, but also to annex Russian America. The men who pushed in this direction were not obscure businessmen or unimportant politicians. They included in their midst prominent political leaders of both parties such as Senators William McKendree Gwin of California and William H. Seward of New York. Hiram Sibley of Western Union headed the list of business leaders who invested in the potential wealth of Russian America. The speeches, letters, arguments, and plans of these men did not appear in a vacuum. Their analyses connected the Northwest fur trade to whaling and to the other resources of Russian America— coal, ice, timber, and fisheries.[60]

Also, they viewed Russian America as the stepping-stone to Asian markets, which it had been since the first Boston traders took sea otters from Baranov and sold them in Canton. Of course, like all those Americans concerned with the Northwest Coast, they desired cooperation, not conflict, with the Russian American Company. Nevertheless, their goals were the exploitation of the resources of Russian America, and if cooperation failed to gain results, they were open to other means of persuasion. When Seward proclaimed to an American audience in 1860 that he would advise the Russians to "go on and build your outposts all along the coast, even to the Arctic Ocean—they will yet become the outposts of my own country—monuments to the civilization of the United States in the Northwest," he was not only predicting the future, he was also recapitulating the history of American expansion.[61]

While there is no need to repeat the story of the American Russian Ice Company of San Francisco here, it is important to remember that the tsar was reluctant to sign the original twenty-five year contract with the ice company because it "exceedingly reduced the value of our possession in North America." Yet Russia had no choice but to agree to the ice company's terms since there was no other way to guarantee the colony's supply of necessities during the Crimean War.[62]

Whatever the final results of the Collins telegraph line, the McDonald fisheries scheme, or the Goldstone-Cole trading and fur proposals, they all combined to remind United States leaders and the Russian government of the actual inability of the colony to sustain a concerted American commercial drive in that area.[63] Even though these ventures all were based upon cooperation with the Russian American Company, none had the effect of bolstering it. Rather, in combination, they delivered the final blows to a colony that for seventy years reeled under the impact of dependence, cooperation, and conflict with United States nationals and their government. Perhaps this dialectical process was best understood by Edouard de Stoeckl, the man who negotiated the sale of Russian America to the United States. Beginning with the 1824 convention, he noted how time and again the United States government pushed to keep Russian America open to Yankee commerce. "But another problem menaced our possessions. I am speaking of American filibusters who swarm in the Pacific. ... It was hoped that the little resources of our colonies would shelter them from the rapacity of the filibusterers, but it has been otherwise." For while American citizens had many rich areas of their own to exploit, "the fish, the forests, and several other products ... have not escaped the lust of the Americans."[64]

Even if Professor Dmytryshyn is correct that "the list of American-Russian cooperation is quite long," the initial cooperation or even cooperative intentions did not avoid conflicts; rather, more often it led to them. Even mutual distrust of Great Britain never drove American commercial ventures or the federal government to ease their pressures for trading and commercial rights in Russian America. On the other hand, distrust and fear of British power in Europe did have a limited impact on Russian policy in the Pacific Northwest in that, at times, the Russian government resisted American demands with less vigor than it might have otherwise.[65] Nevertheless, the relations between the United States and Russia in regard to Russian America had more to do with the nature of American expansion than with British or Russian policy. For, as Admiral Ivan Popov concluded in 1860:

> Whatever they may say in Europe about ... the "Monroe Doctrine," or the doctrine of "manifest destiny," anyone who has lived in the North American life cannot fail to understand instinctively that this principle is entering more and more into the blood of the

people, and that new generations are sucking it in with their mother's milk. .... [Americans] try to maintain ... advantage by all means at their disposal and the question of the destruction of the influence of neighbors leads in practice to the principle of not having any.[66]

The continuing tension between dependence and conflict suggests that American political and commercial expansion played a formidable role in the Russian decision to part with its North American possession. Recent scholarship, however, continues to assert traditional notions to explain the purchase. While most admit, along with Richard Pierce, "that the fears of Murav'ev-Amurskii and Grand Duke Konstantin did help bring about the sale,"[67] they, nevertheless, emphasize four other factors as crucial: (1) the company had proved unprofitable for many years and showed no likelihood of ever being so;[68] (2) from a strategic point of view Russian expansion along the Amur had made the retention of the North American colonies less important;[69] (3) "far from acting out of fear or hostility, the St. Petersburg government chose to cede Alaska in order to maintain cordial relations with Washington";[70] and (4) de Stoeckl was able to play upon "Seward's eagerness" to expand American territorial holdings in the Pacific in order to persuade the United States to "purchase the unwanted land," for "apparently only Seward cared much about Alaska."[71]

To argue that Russia sold Russian America because it proved to be an unprofitable venture and to stop there, neglects two more pressing considerations: why had the company proved unprofitable, and was unprofitability alone enough to convince Russian decision makers to sell such a vast territory? As we have seen, the Russian American Company, Russian naval officers, and various government officials insisted that the activities of Yankee traders and whalers directly interfered with the ability of the company to achieve financial success. No doubt, as James Gibson demonstrates, problems of supply contributed to the financial condition of the colonies.[72] Nevertheless, prior to 1853 key officials blamed American commercial and expansionist policies for obstructing and retarding the economic potential of Russian America. Of course, some of these analyses were rhetorical, while others masked self-serving explanations for company failures. However, the complaints about the Yankees as well as the attempts by the St. Petersburg government to keep traders and whalers out of Russian

America were too frequent and sustained to be passed off as mere oratory. Even if some cliometrician could demonstrate that Russian America's economic position actually were enhanced by the American presence, it would be irrelevant because company, government, and naval officials *believed* that the impact of the United States was detrimental to the survival of the colony.

To these earlier fears were added, after 1853, the growing conviction that Russian America could not be defended against American annexationist desires. Interestingly, many of those who urged the cession of Russian America to the United States considered the territory to be of actual and potential economic value, but a strategic liability. On the other hand, many of those who urged retention of the possession concluded that the colony's economic value was insignificant but believed it essential from a strategic point of view.

Thus, urging cession to the United States in 1853, Murav'ev argued that "due to its present amazing development of railroads the United States will soon spread over all North America. We must face the fact that we will have to cede our North American possessions to them."[73] In 1854, at the outbreak of the Crimean War, the Russian American Company considered a fictitious sale of Russian America to the ice company of San Francisco in order to avoid a British seizure. The Russian Ministry of Foreign Affairs rejected the plan fearing that once the colony was in U.S. hands, it would never be relinquished.[74]

When federal officials learned of the possible Russian willingness to sell, they immediately informed de Stoeckl of the Washington government's eagerness to buy. De Stoeckl worried that once American leaders believed that Russia's commitment to its territories was weak they would press for its cession. "They are dangerous neighbors," he cautioned, "and we must avoid giving them the least quarrel."[75] By the end of 1857 the tsar's brother, the Grand Duke Konstantin, warned that the Russian American Company could not continue its efforts to exclude United States nationals "without involving our Government . . . in controversies with the Americans" which would "harm not only the company's trade, but all Russian trade in North America." The United States, Konstantin predicted, "is bound to aim at the possession of the whole of North America. . . . No doubt they shall take possession of our colonies without much effort and we shall never be in position to regain them."[76] Like Murav'ev, the grand duke urged his brother's government to concentrate its energy on preserving the new acquisitions along the Pacific coast of Asia.

Others, like the former Russian American Company Governor Ferdinand von Wrangell, advocated a cession to the United States *because* of the colony's wealth of "rich coal deposits, ice, construction timber, fish, and excellent seaports," as well as its potential for "the development of industrial activity." For Wrangell believed that while "even twenty million silver rubles" could not be regarded as a fair price for Russian America, "*anticipatory prudence*" dictated a sale to the United States.[77] Konstantin and Wrangell's memorandums convinced both the tsar and the foreign ministry that negotiations should begin with 1861 as the goal for cession. Reports from de Stoeckl in the United States and urgings from Admiral Ivan Popov reinforced the decision. Only the impending American civil crisis interfered with a sale to the willing Buchanan administration.[78]

In 1863 the tsar convened an Extraordinary Commission headed by Minister of Internal Affairs Butovskii to reevaluate the future of Russian America. The commission, alleging that the colonies were of "small value ... as far as industries and trade are concerned," nevertheless concluded that there were "political reasons which make their preservation by us an absolute necessity." Russian America must be retained "as a support to our power in the Far East" and "for the revival and reinforcement of our navy."[79]

During the Civil War, Americans continued to push for concessions in Russian America, and requests accelerated at the war's termination. The impact of the American Russian Ice Company of San Francisco, the Collins Overland Line, The Goldstone-Cole proposals, and the McDonald plans are discussed at length elsewhere.[80] These ventures, plus the continued warnings of de Stoeckl, convinced the minister of foreign affairs, Prince Aleksandr Gorchakov, that the findings of the Extraordinary Commission of 1863 should be reevaluated. In December 1866 Gorchakov submitted to the tsar the opinions of Grand Duke Konstantin, Minister of Finance Mikhail Reitern, and Asia Department Head Theodor R. Osten-Saken. Konstantin, consistent with the position he had advocated since 1857, urged cession of the territories before the United States seized them. Reitern agreed, noting that because the colonies remained indefensible against the Americans, they would continue to be a financial failure.[81]

Osten-Saken, however, disagreed. Accepting the logic of the 1863 Extraordinary Commission, he urged retention of Russian America because cession to the United States would place Russia's Asian holdings in the same peril to which its North American possessions had long been exposed. "Are we in a position to oppose them [the United States] in the Eastern Siberian territories?" Osten-Saken warned that, armed with the possession of Russian America and with the Collins telegraph, the United States would have a "sufficiently strong motive for gaining access to Japan and China along the chain of volcanic islands connecting America with Kamchatka, Kamchatka with Sakhalin etc." He disputed that the sum Russia would receive for its colony would be a significant inducement for a sale since "a few millions or even a few tens of millions of rubles will hardly have any State importance in an empire which has about half a billion annual income and expenditure and more than one and a half billions of debts." Osten-Saken concluded that "it would seem that the present generation had a sacred obligation to preserve for future generations every clod of earth along the coast of an ocean which has world-wide importance."[82]

Gorchakov and Alexander II rejected Osten-Saken's pleas and opted for a sale to the United States. However, they did not do so because they considered the colony to be worthless, but rather because they feared that Russian America's value to the United States made the territories indefensible against the Americans. As Gorchakov concluded: "The means of defense are insufficient to protect them against American filibusters who swarm the Pacific." For Gorchakov the fall of Russian America was the inevitable result of American expansion: "The Americans bought Louisiana and Florida from France and from Spain and quite recently Texas from Mexico" and now they will "do the same for our colonies." No doubt Gorchakov and Alexander II understood the irony of American purchases in the past, for they must have realized that the United States had acquired Louisiana, Florida, Texas, and California by a combination of force and cash.[83]

As the debates within Russian policymaking circles demonstrate, Russian expansion to the Amur did figure significantly in the considerations which led to the sale. However, this was not so much because they made the Russian-American colonies less important, but rather because both those who advocated and opposed the cession feared American penetration of the Amur region would inevitably follow that of Russian America.[84] Murav'ev and Osten-Saken argued that retention of Russian America was essential for the protection of Russia's Amur possessions, while Butovskii, Konstantin, and others insisted that the only way to secure eastern Siberia from U.S. expansion was to consolidate Russian power in Asia by no longer attempting to resist the United States's drive to acquire Russian America.

This takes us to the third point, that Russia desired cordial relations with Washington and that "Russian-American rapprochement during the 1860s" led to the American willingness to buy Alaska. The possibility that Russia desired the United States as a makeweight against Great Britain does not contradict the reality that Russia was, nevertheless, forced to cede her possessions to the United States. In fact, it demonstrates how vulnerable Russian America proved even to minimal expansionist threats on the part of official and private American forces.

Actually, so far as relations in the Pacific Northwest are concerned, a stronger case can be made for Russia's attempting to use cooperation with the British to offset the American thrust. The 1839 agreement between the Russian American Company and the Hudson's Bay Company provides one clear example of this policy.[85] More important than unspecified fears about Great Britain were Russian policies aimed at growing U.S. power in the Pacific. Increasingly after 1858, the Asiatic section of the Ministry of Foreign Affairs worried that if the United States obtained Russian America the result could be "various misunderstandings, disadvantages, further seizures, etc., to which we should be subject if we were to receive a new next-door neighbor in the power of the United States of North America." Osten-Saken warned that with such a cession "the distribution of the North American continent between the three great powers ... will be disturbed," because "at the present time there is one important hindrance to a further movement of the Americans farther and farther to the west along the coast of the Pacific Ocean: the possessions of the strong naval power— England." But, Osten-Saken predicted, "by purchasing our colonies the Americans will jump over this barrier with one step. Are we in a position to oppose them with any counter actions on the Eastern Siberian territories?" Clearly, for Osten-Saken the British supplied the makeweight against United States expansion. Remove British power and "the existing—and for us advantageous—equilibrium in the northwestern corner of America will be destroyed beyond repair."[86]

Notions of a rapprochement rest finally upon the belief that Americans were deceived into interpreting the visit of the Russian fleet to the United States in 1863 as an act of support for the Union cause. While Russia, fearful of a war over Poland, sent the fleet to avoid its being blocked up in Kronstadt harbor during the winter of 1863–64, the Union leaders were, the story goes, naively led to view the visit as an act of friendship.[87] However, American leaders, particularly Seward and Sumner, knew why the vessels had come and consciously used the fleet's appearance to persuade the French and the British that intervention or even recognition of the Confederacy might bring about a European war with Russia in alliance with the United States.[88] Moreover, much of the American press remained hostile to Russia because of its suppression of the Polish rebellion of 1863. In any case, it is the height of historical naiveté to believe that United States leaders would have purchased Alaska because they desired to show their appreciation to Russia. [89]

Finally the suggestion that Washington purchased Alaska only because Seward wanted it fails for several reasons. What is astounding about the 1867 purchase was not that there was minimal opposition to it, but rather given the domestic political situation, that it so easily passed through the Congress. Those who controlled the Senate were in the midst of a bitter and protracted battle with the Johnson administration over Reconstruction policy. Secretary of State Seward's continued support of Johnson's positions earned him the lasting enmity of congressional opponents of the administration. For as de Stoeckl realized, the opposition to the purchase treaty "is not aimed at the transaction itself as from a passionate animosity which reigns in the Congress against the President and even more against the Secretary of State."[90] Even so, on April 9, 1867, only ten days after Seward submitted it, the Treaty of Cession was ratified overwhelmingly by the Senate. And while Seward must certainly be credited with orchestrating the campaign in its favor, the treaty found wide national support among influential newspapers. Many of those newspapers which ridiculed the purchase of "Walrussia" nevertheless urged Senate approval in their editorial columns. Even a cursory reading of articles and editorials in March and April would demonstrate that the press believed Alaska would prove a valuable asset to the United States. Aside from Horace Greeley's rabidly antiadministration *New York Tribune*, no substantial press opposition appeared. Also, the treaty had other important supporters inside and outside the government including former Assistant Navy Secretary Gustavus Fox, Quartermaster General Montgomery

Meigs, Julius Hilgard of the Coastal Survey, Professor Spencer Baird of the Smithsonian Institution, Commander John Rogers, Congressman Thaddeus Stephens, Perry M. Collins, and Hiram Sibley of Western Union.[91] The most important advocate was Senate Foreign Relations Committee Chairman Charles Sumner, whose initial opposition turned to enthusiastic support thanks to Seward's efforts. Sumner guided the treaty through the Senate, delivering a remarkable three-hour speech which reviewed American commercial and political dealings with Russian America. For Sumner there was no question of the economic and strategic advantages that the treaty offered to the United States.[92]

It is true that the House of Representatives did not approve the appropriation of the money for the purchase for over a year. However, this was due less to opposition to the purchase than to other factors. First, the House could not have approved the bill prior to December 1867, since it was not in session when the Senate ratified the treaty and was not scheduled to convene until December. Second, as a money bill, the appropriation would, as a matter of routine, have to go through committee—not generally a speedy process. Third, there was no sense of urgency (although de Stoeckl was somewhat anxious) because the United States had taken actual possession of Alaska on October 18, 1867. Finally, the Congress had suspended all business in the spring of 1868 for President Johnson's impeachment trial. Even so, on May 18, while the impeachment proceeding was in progress, the House Committee on Foreign Affairs approved the appropriation of $7.2 million and in July it passed the House by a large majority. While much has been written about de Stoeckl's use of Robert Walker allegedly to bribe unsympathetic congressmen, the appropriation never was in doubt. More important, those in the House who spoke in favor of the purchase urged acquisition for the same reasons that Seward and Sumner had—its value to the United States.[93]

It would be foolish, of course, to deny that Seward was an ardent expansionist, but it is crucial to recall that while during this period he pushed for the annexation of British Columbia, the purchase of the Danish West Indies, and the abrogation of the Clayton-Bulwer Treaty limiting the U.S. right to construct an isthmian canal, Seward succeeded only in Russian America.[94] The reason for this one success rests upon the fact that it was the culmination of seventy years of American-Russian competition along the Northwest Coast. Perhaps the story was best summed up by Edouard de Stoeckl, who in 1867 concluded that in the final analysis Russia had been forced out of its North American territory: "Menaced by American neighbors our possessions would entangle us in serious disputes with the Federal Government and finish by becoming American property."[95]

While for many traders, whalers, and commercial schemers Russian America offered *actual* financial gain, for many others the *idea* of the potential of the Russian colony—be it economic, political, or strategic—served as a driving force. Thus, ideology played at least as important a role in the purchase of Alaska as material interest. Like all nineteenth-century expansionist visions, the latent rather than the actual value of Russian America sustained a seventy-year private and federal drive. And, like other expansionist perceptions, a good deal of Russian America's potential value lay in the fact that it led to other expansionist projects—in this case the markets of China and Asia.

At a very minimum scholars must no longer view the cession of Russian America as a curiosity, but rather as an integral part of nineteenth-century expansion. Since the annexation of Alaska took place after the Civil War, historians must revise, as well, worn out notions of a "Civil War synthesis" that have assumed that landed expansion virtually disappeared from American life and thought after 1848.[96] They must revise also their conclusions that because of the Civil War, American expansionism turned from continentalism toward commercial, insular expansion. For continentalism did not die with the Civil War, and if a transition took place from landed expansion toward commercial expansion, the turning point was more likely the Alaska Purchase and not the Civil War.

Since the history of American-Russian relations in the Pacific Northwest is almost always examined piecemeal, if at all, the Alaska Purchase is almost always explained exceptionally, and thus, ahistorically. Yet, when viewed from the perspective of more than a century, the annexation of Russian America may prove more important to our understanding of the history of the United States than usually is imagined. While the interests which traditionally concerned themselves with Russian America—supply, fur trade, whaling, fisheries, ice, coal, and timber, for example—were premodern in many ways, they were also, in much more important ways, transitional enterprises that underlay American industrial capitalism. First of all, they tended to be corporate rather than individual undertakings. Shipping and whaling required large capital outlays, and investors, reluctant to risk large sums on any one voyage, limited their liabilities and maximized their profits by shareholding. Moreover, the men who invested directly and indirectly in Northwest Coast enterprises diversified their investments in many projects and simultaneously risked capital not only in shipping, fishing, fur trading, and whaling, but also in cotton textile factories, banking, and insurance companies.[97] These were the men who laid the foundations for Northeastern corporate capitalism. Thus, while some of their financial enterprises seemed premodern, they pursued them in modernizing ways.[98]

The political and strategic visions aimed at Russian America were modern as well, in that they reflected the requirements of an evolving American empire—natural resources and markets in underdeveloped areas for an expansive American economy. Thus, it is not strange that the purchase of Alaska, more than any other expansionist event of the nineteenth century, attempted to resolve the contradictions that had divided landed and maritime expansionists since the 1780s, if not before. Of course, this resolution led to new contradictions. Columbus had stumbled on the New World on his voyage for Asian markets and, with the purchase of Alaska, America's Columbian paradox took another giant step.

PART SIX

Russian America: The Documents

Published Sources on Russian America

Patricia Polansky

The period of Russian settlement in Alaska and the American Northwest has given rise to a considerable documentary and scholarly literature. The purpose of this essay is to provide an introduction to materials published in the last ten years by surveying bibliographic sources, collections, voyage materials, dissertations or theses, and monographs.

Bibliographic Sources

There is no single bibliography of works on Russian America, although several broader bibliographies contain much material on this topic. Most researchers start with James Wickersham's *Bibliography of Alaskan Literature, 1724–1924* vol. 1 (Cordova: Miscellaneous Publications, Alaska Agricultural College and School of Mines, 1927). Dedicated "to the Pioneer Mothers of Alaska," this is an impressive list of 10,380 "printed books of history, travels, voyages, newspapers, periodicals, and public documents in English, Russian, German, French and Spanish" (p. vii). The bibliography grew out of the need of the compiler, who represented Alaska in Congress, to acquaint himself with the literature of Alaska. Laws and maps are not included in the materials covered. There are 670 items in the section on Russian America.

Because Wickersham did not read Russian, he had to enlist the aid of researchers who did. It is not clear whether the Russian items were ever examined *de visu*, and there is no list of sources consulted.

Various lacunae and inconsistencies exist; some titles are not correctly cited. Inconsistencies occur particularly in citing foreign language titles. For instance, the title of a work may be given in English with the note (in Russian) following. Unauthored articles are cited by the name of the journal, and then the title of the article. These discrepancies, though disconcerting, do not limit the usefulness of this still standard compilation. The coverage is thorough, and subject arrangement is quite useful. The list of 3,548 government documents is a welcome aid for beginning researchers.

A specific example of bibliographic problems which are perpetuated is Wickersham's citation (no. 5996) for the *Otchety* (Reports) of the Russian American Company, recorded as 1843–63, nineteen volumes. This has remained the standard reference for years. However, a more complete bibliographic description is needed. There were, in fact, *Otchety* issued in 1842 and from 1864 to 1871. Richard Pierce notes that the annual reports prior to 1842 were published in journals and did not appear separately.

One can only feel relief on turning to Valerian Lada-Mocarski's magnificent *Bibliography of Books on Alaska Published Before 1868* (New Haven/London, 1969). This annotated, critical work is a model of correctness and detail. It is a chronological list of 161 books, and in spite of the title, includes only 1867 imprints. Although all languages are covered, the majority of the items are in Russian. Unfortunately, this work is not comprehensive, nor does it list periodical literature. A comparison of this with other Northwest bibliographies can be found in an article by William R. Hunt, "Northwest bibliography from Dall to Lada-Mocarski," (*Pacific Northwest Quarterly* 62, no. 3 (1971): 117–20).

Elsie Tourville's *Alaska, A Bibliography 1570–1970 with Subject Index* (Boston, 1974) is an unsuccessful attempt to fill the void of a comprehensive bibliography. The introduction does not explain why documents, serials, dissertations, manuscripts, and diaries were omitted in favor of promotional literature (travel guides and commercial brochures), cookbooks, photo albums, and fiction. Its reference value is diminished by a lack of consistency in entries and a disregard of standard formats. There are numerous typing errors and inconsistent transliterations. From the high rate of inaccuracies in Russian and English citations, one assumes that items were not examined. There are insufficient access points for a bibliography of 5,040 items, arranged alphabetically by author and title. The subject index is almost unusable—the headings are too broad and there is no index heading for Russian America. This work, like Wickersham's, has no title access. Finally, a review of Tourville in *Library Journal* (1975: 100, 468) by Dorothy Lunsford mentions a *Basic Bibliography of Alaskan Literature* by Melvin Ricks (4 vols. [Juneau, 1961]). This unpublished manuscript listing 5,227 items is similar in scope to Tourville, but is not cited as a reference that she consulted.

The posthumous editing by Stephen and Betty Haycox of *Melvin Ricks' Alaska Bibliography: An Introductory Guide to Alaskan Historical Literature* (Portland, 1977) provides yet another source for Russian America materials. This unique work lists topical entries in an encyclopedic presentation. Under "Wickersham," for instance, is a description of his bibliography in addition to his other works; there is an alphabetical list of explorers who came to Alaska under "Exploration;" even journal titles appear with a publication history. Especially significant is the attempt to update and supplement Wickersham, Lada-Mocarski, Tourville, and the *Arctic Bibliography*. Ricks cites monographs, articles, and government publications which are not listed elsewhere. Although he states that this work is not exhaustive and that it is intended primarily for those unfamiliar with Alaskan historical sources, it is nonetheless a useful source for the researcher. Unfortunately, although there is much coverage of Russian involvement in Alaska, only a few items in the Russian language are cited, and then they are translated into English. Moreover, there are blind cross-references on certain authors who are well known in the field, e.g., Svetlana Fedorova and James Gibson are missing entirely; and there are various bibliographic errors.

The Arctic Institute of North America, in cooperation with the United States Department of Defense, produced the fifteen volume (101,599 items) *Arctic Bibliography* (Washington, D.C., 1953–71). This source covers the years 1949–67. Although most of the material included is scientific and technical in nature, there is a subject entry under "Russians in Alaska." The descriptive annotations are good, and reviews and articles are included, as well as books; and information is provided on the location of libraries. Russian journals are treated extensively, and considerable material on the voyages of exploration is described.

Harry Majors discusses sources for "Russian Alaska, 1800–1841; as chapter 38 of his lengthy *Science and Exploration on the Northwest Coast of North America, 1542–1841* (Seattle, 1969). But there are many omissions, such as the annual reports of the Russian American Company and the special investigative report of 1860 and 1861.

Even less comprehensive is the section on "Russisch-Amerika" (pp. 486–88) in Klaus Meyer's *Bibliographie zur Osteuropäischen Geschichte* (Wiesbaden, 1972), which covers the years 1939 to 1964 and lists only thirty-eight items.

The involvement of the Russian American Company in Alaska lacks definitive bibliographic treatment by Russian and Soviet scholars. The following works are a beginning point. A. Arkad'ev, "Russkie na Tikhom okeane (obzor literatury)" (Russians in the Pacific Ocean: A survey of the literature) in *Nauka i zhizn*, no. 3 (1949): 41–45, although very short and barely adequate, emphasizes the major Soviet works on Russian America. A. G. Adamov's bibliographic essay, *Pravda o russkikh otkrytiiakh v Amerike* (The truth about Russian discoveries in America) (Moscow, 1952), discusses the northern voyages, James Cook, Russian America, George Vancouver, California, and Alaska. V. V. Tomashevskii's *Materialy k bibliografii Sibiri i Dal'nego Vostoka, XV–pervaia polovina XX veka* (Materials on the bibliography of Siberia and the Far East, fifteenth to first half of the nineteenth century) (Vladivostok, 1957) lists over 3,500 items including books, journal and newspaper articles, documents, and manuscripts. Materials on early exploration and Russian America can be found on pages 103–33. Russian and Soviet imprints are included, although, as with many Soviet publications, citations should be checked against another source for verifying or completing bibliographic data.

In the reference section of Soviet libraries one often finds in-house bibliographies prepared by the staff. Three such unpublished bibliographies at the Academy of Sciences Library in Leningrad contain interesting titles and reveal some esoteric materials, yet are superficial in nature and contain no annotations. They are A. D. Aleksandrova, *Ekspeditsii russkikh promyshlennikov na Aleutskie ostrova v 70-e-80-e gody XVIII veka* (Expeditions of Russian *promyshlenniks* in the Aleutian Islands during the 1770s to 1780s) (Leningrad, 1962; 2l. 18 items); G. N. Pankova, *Materialy k istorii Rossiisko-Amerikanskoi Kompanii* (Materials on the history of the Russian-American Company) (Leningrad, 1966; 13l. 105 items); and M. V. Tsvetkova, *Russkie issledovaniia iuzhnoi chasti Tikhogo okeana (konets XVIII-nachalo XIX v.) i deiatel'nost' Rossiisko-Amerikanskoi Kompanii* (Russian research on the southern part of the Pacific Ocean [end of the eighteenth to beginning of the nine-

teenth centuries] and the activity of the Russian-American Company)
(Leningrad, 1961; 171. 144 items). Moscow State University's Scientific
Library has produced *Spisok russkoi literatury o deiatel'nosti Rossiisko-
Amerikanskoi Kompanii i russkikh poseleniiakh v Kalifornii* (List of Rus-
sian literature on the activity of the Russian American Company and
of the Russian settlements in California) (no other data given). It was
sent to the Library of Congress and is mentioned by Robert Allen in
"Russian Documents about the United States," *Quarterly Journal of
Library of Congress* 21, no. 3 (1964): 217–33.

Works that reflect the Russian American Company's activities in
Hawaii and California can be found in two bibliographies. A preliminary
edition of *Russian Writings on the South Pacific Area*, by Patricia Polansky
(Honolulu: Pacific Islands Program, University of Hawaii, Miscellaneous
Work Papers, no. 5, 1974), lists only Russian language books and journal
articles, along with a section on archival locations in the Soviet Union.
In the preliminary edition the sections on the voyage materials and
Hawaii are the most useful, while a final edition in progress will be
annotated and will include sections on the northern voyages and the
Russian American Company. John A. Hussey has published *Notes
toward a Bibliography of Sources Relating to Fort Ross State Historic
Park California* (Sacramento, 1979). This is a very good guide to sources
for Russians in California and the most important materials for the
study of the Russian American Company. However, Hussey cautions
the reader that the work is not complete and excludes Russian language
material. Sources are organized into bibliographic aids, manuscript
materials, and printed and processed materials covering both monographs and articles. Many items are annotated, but there is no index.

Concerning the Orthodox church, there is Barbara S. Smith's excellent *Preliminary survey of Documents in the Archive of the Russian
Orthodox Church Alaska* (Boulder, 1974). Smith surveys the history and
location of Alaska Orthodox records, provides a history of the church,
describes and evaluates the Alaska archive, recommends topics for
further research, and includes an annotated bibliography. Parts of this
were published also in *Orthodox Alaska* (5, no. 5 [1975]: 13–30).

Another important collection of church records is at the Library of
Congress. Often called the Alaska Russian Church Archives, or the
Alaska Papers, the official entry in the Library of Congress catalog is
Russian Orthodox Greek Catholic Church of North America, *Diocese
of Alaska Records, 1772–1936*. There are over 150,000 items. Various

descriptions of these materials have appeared over the years: *Report of the Librarian of Congress*, 1927, 27–28; V. Basanoff, "Archives of the Russian Church in Alaska in the Library of Congress" (in *Pacific Historical Review* 2, no. 1 [1933]: 72–84, and also reprinted in *Orthodox Alaska* 1, no. 5 (1970); John Dorosh, "The Alaskan Russian Church Archives" (in *Quarterly Journal of Current Acquisitions of the Library of Congress* 18, no. 4 [1961]: 193–203); A. Shalkop, "The Travel Journal of Vasilii Orlov" (in *Pacific Northwest Quarterly* 68, no. 3 [1977]: 131–40). Recently a four-volume *Index to Baptisms, Marriages, and Deaths in the Archives of the Russian Orthodox Greek Catholic Church in Alaska* (Manuscript Division, Library of Congress, 1964–73) appeared, which refers only to the Alaska Papers' section on vital statistics, as well as the seven-volume *Russian America Collection* gathered for H. H. Bancroft.

Voyage Materials

Descriptions from the many Russian circumnavigations beginning in 1803 are important storehouses of information. Captains like I. F. Kruzenstern, I. F. Lisianskii, V. M. Golovnin, F. F. Bellinghausen, F. P. Litke, as well as others on the ships, kept journals and diaries and often maintained correspondences. Artists usually sailed with the explorers and left a visual record. Information can be found on biology, zoology, botany, climate, ethnographic descriptions of local inhabitants, architecture, linguistics, and other subjects. In the course of their explorations, the Russians visited South America, the Antarctic, Australia, the Pacific Islands, and Russian America. Maps are often included with new islands charted, named and sketched. These voyage accounts provide the only eyewitness descriptions in existence.

Fortunately, with the appearance of Ella Wiswell's excellent translation of V. M. Golovnin's *Around the World on the Kamchatka, 1817–1819* (Honolulu, 1979), the major Russian voyages are now available in English, with the exception of Litke. Golovnin makes observations on Russian America and California in chapters 5–8. Many of M. T. Tikhanov's watercolors reproduced in black and white, with a color frontispiece of a Kolosh chief from Baranof Island, a very good introduction, notes by Golovnin and the translator, plus a bibliography, make this a welcome volume for those who do not read Russian.

An article by Rémy Dumond-Fillon, "Historique de l'exploration scientifique du Pacifique par les Russes" (in *Cahiers d'histoire du Pacifique*

[1978]: 13–37), presents a general survey of voyages by Russians in the Pacific, including Russian America.

In addition to the sources discussed earlier there is a 952-leaf manuscript in the Northwest Collection of the University of Washington by Harry M. Majors entitled *Science and Exploration on the Northwest Coast of North America, 1542–1841* (Seattle, 1969). This lengthy historiographic analysis of Russian, American, British, and Spanish voyages enumerates major primary and secondary works with annotations, library locations, source of the reference, and often recent sales prices. This is a good introduction at the foundational level of historical research. Included are books, maps, periodicals, and manuscripts. Two particular weaknesses are the lack of Russian secondary sources and the statement that Golder's archival locations are nonexistent (l. 137) since Soviet archives have been reorganized. A careful reading of Patricia Grimsted's *Archives and Manuscript Repositories in the USSR: Moscow and Leningrad* (Princeton, 1972) will identify present-day locations.

The work of Soviet scholars who have access to archival materials and are able to publish their findings must also be consulted. L. A. Shur's chapter "Dnevniki i zapiski russkikh puteshestvennikov kak istochnik po istorii i etnografii stran Tikhogo okeana (pervaia polovina XIX v.)" (Diaries and notes of Russian travellers as sources for the history and ethnography of the Pacific Ocean countries [first half of the nineteenth century]) in the collection of essays *Avstraliia i Okeaniia; Istoriia i sovremennost'* (Australia and Oceana; past and present) (Moscow, 1970) discusses the voyage materials and provides library and archival locations in the Soviet Union.

Dr. Svetlana Fedorova has done much to make scholars aware of archival documents. Her article about Ivan Kobelev, a participant in the Joseph Billings expedition, who recorded observations on the island Eskimos in the 1770s, is presented with the reproduction of three archival documents in "Isslevovatel' Chukotki i Aliaski kazachii sotnik Ivan Kobelev" (The investigation of Chukotka and Alaska by the cossack 'sotnik' Ivan Kobelev) in *Letopis' Severa*, no. 5 (1971): 156–72.

The contributions of two navigators with the same names, both of whom worked for the Russian American Company and both of whom made important cartographic contributions on the areas of Alaska and the Aleutian Islands, are highlighted in another article by Dr. Fedorova.

While these two are often confused, careful research in the K. T. Khleb-nikov Archive in Perm shows the two men to have had different patro-nymics (Filippovich and Iakovlevich) and thus to be unrelated. Her well-researched article has the title "Shturmany Ivany Vasil'evy i ikh rol' v izuchenii Aliaski (pervaia polovina XIX v.)" (The navigators Ivan Vasil'evs and their role in the study of Alaska [first half of the 19th century]) in *Letopis' Severa*, no. 9 (1979): 167–210. A large format map, which is a reproduction of one prepared by I. I. Vasil'ev and, it is believed, used later by the explorer-ethnographer Lieutenant Zagoskin, accompanies this article.

F. A. Kul'kov, a Vologda merchant, recorded notes on a variety of topics in his manuscript, which is published in the chapter by R. G. Liapunova, "Novyi dokument o rannikh plavaniiakh na Aleutskie ostrova ('Izvestiia' Fedora Afanas'evicha Kul'kova 1764 g.)" (A new docu-ment about early sailings to the Aleutian Islands ['notes' of Fedor Afanas'evich Kul'kov, 1764]), in *Strany i narody Vostoka* 20, no. 4 [1979]: 97–105).

Chapters in A. I. Alekseev's new work *Russkie geograficheskie issledovaniia na Dal'nem Vostoke i v Severnoi Amerike* ... (Russian geographical investigations in the Far East and in North America ...) (Moscow, 1976) survey the following: "Raboty ofitserov i sluzhashchikh Rossiisko-Amerikanskoi Kompanii. Puteshestvie v severnuiu Ameriku N. A. Khvostova i G. I. Davydova" (The works of officers and employees of the Russian-American Company. Voyages to North America by N. A. Khvostov and G. I. Davydov); "Issledovaniia I. G. Voznesenskogo" (The investigations of I. G. Voznesenskii) and "Dal'nevostochnye issledovaniia uchastnikov krugosvetnykh plavanii" (The Far Eastern investigations of the participants of the round the world voyages).

Carol Urness relates an account by a Russian fur hunter in 1774 on the ship *St. Michael* in her article "Dmitri Bragin's Voyage in the North Pacific" (in *Terrae Incognitae*, no. 2 [1970]: 87–93). This account is unusual because the original documents prepared by Bragin in 1772 were left intact and not edited. Peter S. Pallas, the German naturalist, translated these observations into German and English, but they lan-guished unknown until 1948.

Richard Pierce and Mary Sadouski translated "The Aleutian Exped-ition of Krenitsyn and Levashov" by I. V. Glushankov (in *Alaska Journal* 3, no. 4 [1973]: 204–10; originally in Russian, "Aleutskaia ekspeditsiia Krenitsyna i Levashova," in *Priroda*, no. 12 [1969]: 84–92), which tells about the archival discovery of an atlas from their secret expedition of 1769.

The logs of the *St. Peter* and *St. Paul* under Bering's command are reexamined by Gil Mull and George Plafker, who describe the sites of "The First Russian Landings in Alaska" (in *Alaska Journal* 9, no. 3 [1976]: 134–45). In connection with these two ships Vasilly Ushanoff attempts to paint their "portraits." In his article "St. Peter and St. Paul: Ships of Alaskan History" (in *Alaska Journal* 9, no. 2 [1979]: 16–17), the artist explains how he reconstructed the images of these ships from two miniatures in a charter awarded by Catherine II to Sven Waxell.

Two Russian travel accounts are available in English as a result of David Kraus's translations. They are *V. S. Khromchenko's Coastal Explorations in Southwestern Alaska, 1822*, vol. 64 of *Fieldiana:Anthropology* (Chicago, 1973), and *A. F. Kashevarov's Coastal Explorations in Northwest Alaska, 1838*, vol. 69 of *Fieldiana: Anthropology* (Chicago: Field Museum of Natural History, 1977). Both works are edited by James Van Stone, have illustrations, introductory materials, the translated journals, notes, bibliographies, and indexes.

Biographies of four major Russian voyage captains are now available. They are A. I. Alekseev's *Fedor Petrovich Litke* (Moscow, 1970); V. M. Pasetskii's *Ivan Fedorovich Kruzenshtern* (Moscow, 1974); V. M. Pasetskii's *Ferdinand Petrovich Vrangel' 1796–1870* (Moscow, 1975); and V. A. Divin's *Povest' o slavnom moreplavatele* (A story about a famous seafarer) (Moscow, 1976). The last work is the biography of V. M. Golovnin. Ia. M. Svet presents a nicely illustrated account of the life and voyages of *Dzhems Kuk* (James Cook) (Moscow, 1979) that is intended for a lay audience.

British Columbia hosted the Simon Fraser Conference at Vancouver in 1978 in honor of the bicentennary landing of Capt. James Cook at Nootka Sound. Two papers have been published—James Gibson's "The Significance of Cook's Third Voyage to Russian Tenure in the North Pacific" (in *Pacific Studies* 1, no. 2 [1978]: 119–46), and Yakov Svet and Svetlana Fedorova's "Captain Cook and the Russians" (in *Pacific Studies* 2, no. 1 [1978]: 1–19). Svet discusses Cook's efforts to find the Northwest Passage in an earlier essay, "Novye dannye o prebyvanii na Kamchatke tretei ekspeditsii Dzh. Kuka (1779 g.)" (New information on the stay in Kamchatka of James Cook's third expedition, 1779), located in *Novoe v izuchenii Avstralii i Okeanii* (New studies about Australia and Oceania) (Moscow, 1972), 219–27.

Reprints make available works long out of print: Archibald Campbell, a Scottish seaman sailing with the Russian American Company, resided over a year in Hawaii and recounts his observations in *A Voyage Round the World, from 1806–1812* (Honolulu, 1967; reprint of 1822 ed.), and Madame Charlotte Bernhardi's *Memoir of the Celebrated Admiral John de Krusenshtern*, SJS no. 53 (Seattle, 1964; reprint of 1856 ed.).

The Soviets have published shortened versions of two voyage accounts unavailable since 1947 and 1950: Iu. F. Lisianskii, *Puteshestvie vokrug sveta v 1803, 4, 5 i 1806 godakh na korable "Neva"* (Voyage around the world 1803–1806 on the ship "Neva") (Vladivostok, 1977), and I. F. Kruzenstern, *Puteshestvie vokrug sveta v 1803, 1804, 1805 i 1806 godakh na korabliakh Nadezhde i Neve* (Voyage around the world in 1803–1806 on the ships *Nadezhda* and *Neva*) (Vladivostok, 1976). Both have introductions by A. I. Alekseev.

Dissertations / Theses

Unpublished doctoral dissertations provide a rich source of information, including translated Russian American Company documents and useful supplementary appendices. Surprisingly, several studies have been written without using Russian language primary or secondary sources. The majority are on historical-political subjects. Three dissertations, which devote attention to the purchase of Alaska, indicate the desire to answer the eternally enigmatic question of why it was sold by Russia and bought by America.

"The Purchase of Alaska: Backgrounds and Reactions" (McGill University, 1969) by Joseph Tarnovecky, discusses the military considerations, financial pressure, and friendship with the United States which occasioned the offer to sell by Russia, and the desire for expansion and appreciation of the value of Alaska which induced America to accept. Ronald Jensen's "The Alaska Purchase and Russian-American Relations" (Indiana University, 1971) examines negotiations for the sale through U.S. documents, making the point that the national interests of both countries determined the fate of Alaska. Richard Neunherz's "The Purchase of Russian America: Reasons and Reactions" (University of Washington, 1975) uses U.S. newspapers, debates from Congress, and the private papers of senators and representatives. He concludes that only a plurality supported the purchase and that it was a fortunate accident that the United States decided to buy what had become a Russian liability.

For background on "The Origins and Formation of the Russian-American Company" (University of North Carolina, Chapel Hill, 1965), Mary Wheeler surveys the Siberian fur trade, the role of China-Japan relations with Siberia, and the commercial and business history of the area. She discusses primarily Grigorii Shelikhov. Realizing that the fur trade would need a permanent company and would ultimately be involved in the colonization of the region, he founded the Joint Stock Company, which later became the Russian American Company.

Other research concentrates on economic factors to explain the fate of Russian Alaska. George Elliott notes the sharp competition for the fur trade among the Russian American Company, and Spanish, British, and Yankee entrepreneurs in his "Empire and Enterprise in the North Pacific, 1785–1825—A Survey and an Interpretation—Emphasizing the Role and Character of Russian Enterprise" (University of Toronto, 1957). He claims it was economic, not political factors, that accounted for the Russian America successes and failures. Anthony Hull makes a very interesting and thorough presentation in "Spanish and Russian Rivalry in the North Pacific Regions of the New World, 1760–1812" (University of Alabama, 1966). Using both Spanish and Russian documents and sources, Hull emphasizes economic factors as the major cause of events. He appends a useful list of Spanish and Russian ambassadors. This thesis is an informative complement to the excellent survey of Russian and Spanish sources by Stuart R. Tompkins and Max L. Moorhead in their article "Russia's approach to America" ("Pt. I: From Russian Sources, 1741–1761"; "Pt. II: From Spanish Sources, 1761–1775") in *British Columbia Historical Quarterly* 13, no. 2 (1949): 55–66, 13, nos. 3–4: 231–55. Howard Kushner explores *American-Russian Rivalry in the Pacific Northwest, 1790–1867* (Cornell University, 1970). He assigns as a strong motive for the Alaska purchase the influence of American whaling interests centered in Boston. The Alaska purchase was a transitional phase of U.S. expansion—a link between the past quest for land and the emerging commercial enterprises.

The tenure of Baron Ferdinand Petrovich von Wrangell as governor of the Russian American Company is researched in the well-documented thesis by Stephen Johnson called "Baron Wrangel and the Russian-American Company, 1829–1849: Russian-British Conflict and Cooperation on the Northwest Coast" (University of Manitoba, 1978). Wrangell, an explorer, scholar, admiral, and statesman, was a firm leader and worked toward providing the company with a stable, regular source of supplies, as well as a market for its products. The ten-year trade contract which he won from the powerful Hudson's Bay Company enabled the Russian American Company to remain longer on the North American continent than the tsarist government might have wished.

Other topical approaches are of interest. Winston Sarafian's excellent study, "Russian-American Employee Policies and Practices, 1799–1867" (University of California at Los Angeles, 1970), discusses the Russian employee and native conditions. He points out that while the Russian American Company tried to keep the employees healthy and supplied with basic needs, it paid such minimum wages that those hired were in constant debt. Sarafian states that he translated over 10,000 company documents in preparing his work. One finds here, for instance, Zinovii Govorlivyi's report "A short review of the diseases in the territories of the Russian-American Company from 1851 to 1859" (translation of "Kratkii obzor boleznoi vo vladeniiakh Rossiisko-Amerikanskoi kompanii, s 1851 po 1859 god" from the *Otchet* [Report] of the Russian American Company for 1860). Henry Coppock studies "Interactions between Russians and Native Americans in Alaska, 1741–1840" (Michigan State University, 1969), looking at the cultural changes of the Tlingits and Aleuts during this period. "The Cultural and Educational Developments of the Aborigines and Settlers in Russian America" (New York University, 1961) by Jerome Starr studies the ethnic composition and educational activities of the area. An interesting analysis is made of the few materials that were available for study in schools. He also appends a useful chronology of Russian voyages around the world. Michael Kovach examines the "Russian Orthodox Church in Russian America" (University of Pittsburgh, 1957) and appends a glossary of Russian and English terms which is quite thorough.

Of the several masters theses written, three are particularly interesting. David Strausz, "The Russian American Company to 1825" (University of Washington, 1962), is noted for its appended translations from the Sitka archives. One is on Dr. G. Sheffer's (variant spellings Shaeffer, Schaffer, Scheffer) adventures in Hawaii. Janice Smith's archaeological analysis in "Pomo and Promyshlenniki: Time and Trade Goods at Fort Ross" (University of California at Los Angeles, 1974) extends to a history and description of Fort Ross, which she based on Russian sources.

Mary Sadoŭski's study on "The Sitkine Incident: A Russo-British Confrontation on the Pacific Northwest Coast in June 1834" (Queen's University, 1975) is a comprehensive doctoral dissertation which includes translations of correspondence from and to Sitka preserved in the Russian American Company records in the U.S. National Archives.

Material Published in the 1970s

In the past decade a substantial body of publications, both scholarly and popular, reflects a continued interest by a broad audience of readers.

Primary Sources. A significant contribution by the late V. A. Divin with the assistance of K. E. Cherevko and G. N. Isaenko is the publication of *Russkaia Tikhookeanskaia epopeia* (The Russian Pacific epic) (Khabarovsk, 1979). This work presents Russian geographical discoveries through documents, showing not only the position of Russia in the Far East, but its role in opening Japan, China, India, and the Northern Pacific. Nine major archives supplied the documents for this publication. Of the six sections, the third one pertains especially to Russian America, presenting thirty-seven documents on Shmalev, Chichagov, Krenitsyn, Levashev, Billings, Sarychev, Shelikhov, and others. The book is illustrated, has definitions of archaic and naval terms, introductions and references for each section, as well as a list of prominent persons with biographical data.

Observations on America by Kiril T. Khlebnikov, chronicler of the Russian American Company, are now translated with notes and bibliography by Basil Dmytryshyn and E. A. P. Crownhart-Vaughan in a beautifully illustrated and extremely informative volume entitled *Colonial Russian America: Kyrill T. Khlebnikov's Reports, 1817–1832* (Portland, 1976). The reports included deal with Novo-Arkhangel'sk and Fort Ross. This translation is based on a report which originally appeared in *Morskoi sbornik* in 1861. Leonid Shur in his review (in *Russian History/Histoire Russe* 5, no. 2 [1978]: 225–26) mentions many discrepancies between this and the original manuscript, of which he states the Oregon Historical Society has a microfilm copy. The translators note in their introduction that they are preparing a second volume with the heretofore unpublished parts on "Kodiak; Unalaska, the Alaskan peninsula and the Fox Islands; Atka, the Andreanov, Komandorskie and Near Islands; and the Pribylov Islands, St. Matthew Island and part of North America" (p. iv).

In the meantime Soviet scholars Svetlana Fedorova and Roza Liapunova have brought these unpublished materials together in the monograph *Russkaia Amerika v neopublikovannykh zapiskakh K.T. Khlebnikova* (Russian America in the unpublished notes of K. T. Khlebnikov) (Leningrad, 1979). This volume, the first of three, is an indispensable contribution to the study of Russian America and is valuable not only for the publication of the archival manuscript, but also for all the supplementary materials—an introduction which reviews the literature by and about Khlebnikov; annotations throughout the text; a list of drawings in the published records of Khlebnikov's work; a glossary of special terms, places, and obsolete words; separate indexes of geographic, ethnic, and personal names; and a large fold-out page with three maps from Tikhmenev's history. Volume 2 will cover Novo-Arkhangel'sk and volume 3, California.

Professor James Gibson has also made parts of Khlebnikov's materials available in English. "Russian America in 1833: The Survey of Kiril Khlebnikov" (in *Pacific Northwest Quarterly* 63, no. 1 [1972]: 1–13), is a statistical survey of the Russian American Company under Wrangell's governorship. A translation of an unpublished manuscript, "Russian America in 1821" (in *Oregon Historical Quarterly* 77, no. 2 [1976]: 174–88), concerns the bureaucratic structure of the company and other observations that are attributed to Kiril Timofeevich Khlebnikov.

"Puteshestviia i issledovaniia K. T. Khlebnikova v Severnoi Amerikke" (K. T. Khlebnikov's travels and investigations in Northern America) by L. A. Shur appears in a volume prepared for the sixth congress of the Geographical Society of the USSR, *Propaganda geograficheskikh znanii, geografiia v srednei i vysshei shkole* (Leningrad, 1975), 51–56.

The fourth volume in the North Pacific studies series provides an official account of the colonies just prior to Russian withdrawal from North America. Translated from *Morskoi sbornik* and edited by Basil Dmytryshyn and E. A. P. Crownhart-Vaughan, the work is entitled *The End of Russian America, Captain P. N. Golovin's Last Report, 1862* (Portland, 1979).

The important Russian language series issued from 1960 by the Ministry of Foreign Affairs, *Vneshniaia politika Rossii XIX i nachala XX veka* . . . (Russia's foreign policy of the 19th and beginning of the twentieth centuries . . .), publishes documents relating to the history of Russian America. For example, the latest issue, vol. 2, no. 9 (Moscow, 1976), contains fourteen relevant documents—six of these concern Sheffer and Hawaii.

At last there is a new translation by Richard Pierce and Alton Donnelly of Petr A. Tikhmenev's extremely important *A History of the Russian-American Company* (Seattle/London, 1978), which "balances fidelity to the original text with readability and consistency with common sense" (p. vii). There exist several earlier translations into English of varying quality. The new translation benefits from these earlier versions and presents the original work in its entirety. Tikhmenev based his history on primary materials which have since been lost. Extensive notes by the translators, many illustrations, and a glossary of terms are included in a departure from the original. The appendixes of the Russian edition are not included here, but have been published separately as volume 2 with the title *Documents* (see next section). Professor Pierce has published extracts from Tikhmenev's work in P. A. Tikhmenev's *Historical Survey of the Formation of the Russian-American Company and Its Activities to the Present Day* and in the *Russian-American Company Charters*. These were done for the Alaska Division of State Libraries, translation project of material relating to Alaska natives, 1974, nos. 4 and 11, respectively.

In 1963 Melvin Ricks translated parts of Shelikhov's voyage to Alaska, 1793; Berkh's history of the Aleutian islands; and Khlebnikov's life of Baranov, 1835, under the title *The Earliest History of Alaska*, which has been reprinted in a limited edition (Anchorage, 1970).

History and Politics. Many of the studies in this broad area have at their core the desire to explore or explain the sale and purchase of Alaska and to discuss whether cooperation or conflict was the basis of Russian-American relations.

An introduction to historical sources is provided by Winston Sarafian's "Alaska Bibliography of History Sources" (in *Alaska Journal* 6, no. 3 [1976]: 181–82; no. 4: 253–55; 7, no. 2 [1977]: 60–63), which lists Russian and Western materials in five sections—bibliographies, published documents, unpublished documents, dissertations/theses, and selected books.

Robert Kerner argued in his "Russian Expansion to America: Its Bibliographical Foundations" (in *Papers of the Bibliographical Society of America* 25 [1931]: 111–29), that the study of Russian America must be seen in the perspective of Russian eastward movement and Russian foreign policy as a whole. Frank Golder's *Russian Expansion on the Pacific 1641–1850* . . . (New York, 1971; reprint of 1914 ed.) may be viewed as a forerunner of Kerner's idea, but it is not broad enough in scope, covering essentially Dezhnev and the two Bering expeditions. L. N. Neatby covers the Bering expeditions and Chirikov's voyage to American (Alaskan) shores in his *Discovery in Russian and Siberian Waters* (Athens, Ohio, 1973). A review of voyages through the Aleutians and Bering Strait is available in a reprint of William Coxe's 1787 edition *Account of the Russian Discoveries between Asia and America* (New York, 1970). The work of J. Arthur Lower, *Ocean of Destiny: A Concise History of the North Pacific, 1500–1978* (Vancouver, 1978), attempts to survey Russian America in the context of European discoveries, the fur trade and the past 400 years of trans-Pacific contacts. Although it is very readable, Lower's volume tries to cover too much in a limited space.

Soviet scholars have also undertaken studies from this broader perspective. In the section discussing Chukotka as an organic part of the Russian state, there is an examination of the discovery routes from Kamchatka to Alaska and the Russian American Company's role in the development of North Pacific trade relations in the book edited by N. N. Dikov, *Ocherki istorii Chukotki s drevneishikh vremen do nashikh dnei* (Essays on Chukotka's history from ancient times to the present) (Novosibirsk, 1974). A textbook prepared by Raisa Makarova entitled *Vneshniaia politika Rossii na Dal'nem Vostoke: vtoraia polovina XVIII v. 60-e gody XIX v.* (The foreign policy of Russia in the Far East: The second half of the eighteenth century to the 1860s) (Moscow, 1974) examines the Russian American Company activities within a broader context. A study which discusses the early explorations between Asia and America and voyages up to Shelikhov's time within the context of Russia's economic and political goals is found in V. A. Divin's *Russkie moreplavaniia na Tikhom okeane v XVIII veke* (Russian voyages in the Pacific Ocean in the eighteenth century) (Moscow, 1971). Present-day political and economic relations between the Soviet Union and America in the Pacific area are examined in the new volume *SShA i problemy Tikhogo okeana* (USA and problems of the Pacific) (Moscow, 1979). The chapter (pp. 10–39) by A. I. Alekseev "Osnovnye vekhi amerikanskoi ekspansii v basseine Tikhogo okeana" (Basic landmarks of American expansion in the Pacific basin) provides a historical background for the Russian American Company development.

The purposes of Vitus Bering's two voyages of 1728 and 1741 had not been examined satisfactorily until the appearance of Raymond Fisher's excellent research on *Bering's Voyages: Whither and Why*

(Seattle, 1977). The instructions for the 1728 expedition are controversial in nature, but Fisher argues that the Russian objective was to find a sea route to the American shore and explore it. The second expedition was clearly to annex territory and to exploit resources. The two voyages, he argues, were a continuation of Russian eastward expansion across Siberia.

Bering's first expedition is treated by E. G. Kushnarev's *V poiskakh proliva: pervaia Kamchatkaia ekspeditsiia 1725–1730* (In search of the straits: The first Kamchatka expedition, 1725–1730) (Leningrad, 1976).

The work by G. I. Shelikhov, entrepreneur and founder of the predecessor company to the Russian American Company, has been reissued with the title *Rossiiskogo kuptsa Grigoriia Shelikhova stranstvovaniia iz Okhotska po Vostochnomu okeanu k amerikanskim beregam* (The Russian merchant Grigorii Shelikhov's travels from Okhotsk across the eastern ocean to American shores) (Khabarovsk, 1971). The introduction is by Boris Polevoi, who is also the editor.

French historian Michael Poniatowski has revised his 1958 study *Histoire de la Russie d'Amérique et de l'Alaska* (Paris, 1978), which presents Russian America from 1725 to 1898 within a broad scope of trade, foreign relations, and postsale Alaskan history.

The year 1975 produced three American and one Soviet study on Russian-American relations, which debate whether it was rivalries and constant conflicts or basic desires for cooperative efforts that shaped events for the final sale in 1867.

Nikolai N. Bolkhovitinov's careful work in Soviet and American archives has produced substantial evidence of Russian-American cooperation. He discusses diplomatic, cultural, and trade contacts, which fostered closer relations. He does not ignore the conflict which occurred, but stresses the desire for friendship as a basis of the relations between these two countries. Of primary interest among Bolkhovitinov's extensive works are *The Beginnings of Russian-American Relations, 1775–1815*, trans. Elena Levin (Cambridge, Mass./London, 1975), originally in Russian, *Stanovlenie russko-amerikanskikh otnoshenii, 1775–1815*); and his second volume, *Russko-amerikanskie otnosheniia, 1815–1832* (Russian-American relations, 1815–1832) (Moscow, 1975). Both of these works contain a thoughtful presentation of new material. Both books have been widely reviewed with their errors, gaps, and deficiencies pointed out. The appendix in the 1775–1815 volume, "Writings and Sources on Early Russian-American Relations" and the bibliography of archival and printed sources in the 1815–32 volume are very useful for indicating the contents and locations of Soviet archival materials.

The argument for cooperation has been stated from the American side by Mary Wheeler in her "Empires in Conflict and Cooperation: The 'Bostonians' and the Russian-American Company" (in *Pacific Historical Review* 40, no. 4 [1971]: 419–41). It was cooperation with the Bostonian Yankee traders which enabled the Russian American Company to continue operations. A companion to this article about the company's role in the maritime fur trade is the chapter "Bostonians and Muscovites on the Northwest Coast, 1788–1841," by James Gibson in the book edited by Thomas Vaughan, *The Western Shore: Oregon Country Essays Honoring the American Revolution* (Portland, 1975), 81–120.

Perhaps the single most controversial book of the past decade is Howard Kushner's expanded dissertation published as *Conflict on the Northwest Coast, American-Russian Rivalry in the Pacific Northwest, 1790–1867*, Contributions in American History, no. 41 (Westport/London: 1975). Kushner uses a wealth of American primary source materials to build his case that Russia only reluctantly sold its Alaskan territory rather than wait for America to seize it. He discusses the influence of the whaling industry, traders, settlers, and business interests in the outcome of events. A major flaw in this otherwise well-presented work is the paucity of Russian sources, even those available in English translation.

Kushner continues his arguments of an aggressive United States in "The Russian-American Diplomatic Contest for the Pacific Basin and the Monroe Doctrine" (in *Journal of the West* 15, no. 2 [1976]: 65–80). Using both American and Russian sources he argues that the Monroe Doctrine was a deterrent to further Russian expansion in the Northwest.

Ronald Jensen's *The Alaska Purchase and Russian-American Relations* (Seattle/London, 1975) is also based on a dissertation. Jensen has reviewed the existing literature, noting its omissions. He analyzes the international setting, relates the history of the cession within the context of Russian-American relations, and describes the extent of intrigue in persuading the U.S. Senate to ratify the purchase treaty.

Sud'ba Russkoi Ameriki (The fate of Russian America) (Magadan, 1975) by A. I. Alekseev uses archival materials from, among several, the

Central State Archives of the RSFSR of the Far East (TSGADV) and the State Archive of the Irkutsk Oblast (GAIO), and surveys the literature of the early voyages, including maps and atlases. Alekseev echoes S. B. Okun in the belief that the Russian American Company was an instrument for expansion of the tsarist government. The economic situation of the company is discussed with the problems of food-producing bases brought out in a chapter on Fort Ross. Finally, the author addresses the question of the sale pointing out the conflicts between Russia, the United States, and England, and concludes that the tsar's government had been prepared to sell to the United States many years before the actual event.

Kushner and Alekseev agree that conflicts led to the sale. However, the former argues that the Russians were hesitant to relinquish their hold on the American land, while the latter argues the Russians were ready to sell, perhaps even earlier than 1867.

Two additional works that focus on the sale are James Gibson's "Why the Russians Sold Alaska" (in *Wilson Quarterly* 3, no. 3 [1979]: 179–88), and T. M. Batueva, *Ekspansiia SShA na severe Tikhogo okeana v seredine XIX v. i pokupka Aliaski v 1867 g.* (U.S. expansion in the North Pacific in the mid-nineteenth century and the purchase of Alaska in 1867) (Tomsk, 1976).

Richard Pierce has contributed a series of articles on the governors of the Russian American Company. Each one provides as much bio-graphical data as are known. All were published in the *Alaska Journal*. Their titles are as follows: "Two Russian Governors: Hagemeister and Yankovskii" (1, no. 2 [1971]: 49–52); "Russian Governors: M. I. Murav'ev, 1820–1825" (no. 3: 41–43); "Alaska's Russian Governors: Chistiakov and Wrangel" (no. 4: 38–45); "Alaska's Russian Governors: Ivan Kupreianov" (2, no. 1 [1972]: 21–24); "Alaska's Russian Governors: Etholen and Teben-kov" (no. 2: 19–27); "Alaska's Russian Governors: Rosenberg, Rudakov, and Voevodskii . . ." (no. 3: 40–48); "Alaska's Russian Governors: Johan Hampus Furuhjelm" (no. 4: 21–24); and "Alaska's Russian Governors: Prince D. P. Maksutov" (3, no. 1 [1973]: 20–30).

Other items of interest include M. Huculak's *When Russia Was in America: The Alaska Boundary Treaty Negotiations, 1824–25, and the Role of Pierre de Poletica* (Vancouver, 1971). Poletica was chief negotiator for Russia in the discussions which produced the Ukaz of 1821 and defined the boundaries of Russian America. Stephen Johnson's "Russia on the Pacific Northwest Coast in the 1830's: Baron

Wrangel Versus the Government of Russia on Colonial Policy" (in *Musk Ox* 17 [1975]: 14–21) is a well-researched study of the administrative problems between the Russian government and the Russian American Company. Also on this topic is a reprint of a Frank Golder paper on "The Attitude of the Russian Government Toward Alaska" (in *Alaska Journal* 1, no. 2 [1971]: 53–55, 59). Another aspect of Baron von Wrangell's governorship of the Russian American Company is presented in a paper given at the Third North American Fur Trade Conference in Winnipeg, Canada, May 5, 1978, by Stephen Johnson, entitled "Wrangel and Simpson . . . a Unique Relationship." Philip Ault details the abortive attempt in 1864 to link the United States to Europe via Alaska and Russia in "The (Almost) Russian-American Telegraph" (in *American Heritage* 26, no. 4 [1975]: 12–15, 92–98). Interesting highlights are provided in "Alaska's First Russian Settlers" (in *Alaska Journal* 7, no. 3 [1977]: 174–77) by Winston Sarafian, who describes the first fifty-one people sent by the Shelikhov-Golikov Company in 1794. Available again is Hector Chevigny's *Lord of Alaska, Baranov and the Russian Adventure* (Portland, 1971; reprint of 1942 ed.). A territorial dispute resulting from the sale of Alaska is clarified in B. D. Lain's "The Fort Yukon Affair," 1869 (in *Alaska Journal* 7, no. 1 [1977]: 12–17).

Economy. No economic history of the Russian American Company per se exists; however, several articles can be cited. Nikolai Bolkhovitinov reveals the activities of a colorful American trader in "Vydvizhenie i proval proektov P. Dobella (1812–1821 gg.)" (The Promoting and Failure of P. Dobell's Projects, 1812–1821) (in *Amerikanskii ezhegodnik* [1976]: 264–82). Glynn Barratt discusses an unsuccessful project to explore the Arctic from Bering Strait to Hudson's Bay that would have benefited the economy of the Russian American Company in "The Russian Interest in Arctic North America: the Kruzenshtern-Romanov Projects, 1819–1823" (in *Slavonic and East European Review* 53, no. 130 [1975]: 27–43). The fur trade and supply problems were the basic economic reasons for the rise and fall of "Russia in the Pacific Basin," according to Oleks Rudenko (in *Journal of the West* 15, no. 2 [1976]: 49–64). A closer look at the men and events which led to the formation of the Hutchinson Kohl company is made by Frank Sloss and Richard Pierce in "The Hutchinson-Kohl Story: A Fresh Look" (in *Pacific Northwest Quarterly* 62, no. 1 [1971]: 1–6). This was the company that bought the assets of the Russian American Company from Prince Maksutov. More details are presented in Frank Sloss's article, "Who

Owned the Alaska Commercial Company?" (in *Pacific Northwest Quarterly* 68, no. 3 [1977]: 120–30). Social and economic changes are discussed in B. D. Lain's "The Decline of Russian America's Colonial Society" (in *Western Historical Quarterly* 7, no. 2 [1976]: 143–53). W. L. Ostenstad studies the arrangements made with the Russian American Company for "A Lucrative Contract: The HBC and the Pacific Ice Trade" (in *The Beaver* [1977], outfit 308.3: 36–40). The history of a trading post and later salmon cannery site is given by James Van Stone's "Nushagak" (in *Alaska Journal* 2, no. 3 [1972]: 49–53).

Historical Geography. James Gibson's *Imperial Russia in Frontier America: The Changing Geography of Supply of Russian America, 1784–1867* (New York, 1976) is an excellent, well-documented, and indispensable addition to understanding events in the development of these northern territories. This coherent narrative examines the geographical influences on the history of this region and concludes that one of the major reasons for Russia's eventual withdrawal from America was the inability to secure a stable food supply.

Excerpts from the diary of Sir George Simpson, who was governor of the Hudson's Bay Company, record an outsider's (non-Russian) impressions of the Russian American Company and of the Indians of southeastern Alaska and Sitka, and may be found in the article "A Journey to Southeastern Alaska" (in *Alaska Journal* 1, no. 1 [1971]: 34–42).

In the volume *European Settlement and Development in North America: Essays on Geographical Change in Honour and Memory of Andrew Hill Clark* (Toronto, 1978), James Gibson edits and also contributes a chapter entitled "Old Russia in the New World: Adversaries and Advertising in Russian America" (pp. 46–65).

Ethnography. James Gibson provides a succinct description of "Russian Sources for the Ethnohistory of the Pacific Coast of North America in the 18th and 19th Centuries" (in *Western Canadian Journal of Anthropology* 6, no. 1 [1976]: 91–115). He points out that many anthropological works have not made use of the numerous descriptions recorded by Russian voyagers, ethnographers and traders. He provides excerpts from these accounts and a bibliography.

A survey of the literature, both Western and Soviet, on the problems of resource development in Russian America is given by G. A. Agranat in his "Ob osvoenii russkimi Aliaski" (The Opening by the Russians of Alaska) in *Letopis' Severa*, no. 5 (1971): 180–93.

The *Records* of the Russian American Company in the U.S. National Archives are a little-used source for anthropologists on the Eskimos, Indians, and Aleuts. Winston Sarafian and James Van Stone annotate 123 items in their study of "The Records of the Russian-American Company as a Source for the Ethnohistory of the Nushagak River Region, Alaska" (in *Anthropological Papers*, University of Alaska, 15, no. 2 [1972]: 53–78).

"Mercantilism and Societal Change: An Ethnohistoric Examination of Some Essential Variables" (in *Ethnohistory* 22, no. 1 [1975]: 21–32) by J. B. Townsend examines aspects of the Russian American Company's trade goods as an index to social changes.

Dorothy Ray's excellent cultural history, *The Eskimos of Bering Strait, 1650–1898* (Seattle/London, 1975), presents a chronological description of the Eskimo peoples in the context of Siberian expansion, European explorations, the Russian presence, and later American acquisition of Alaska. This well-written study is the result of twenty years' research and has a very good bibliography of the sources consulted. She engaged a translator for the Russian materials.

Because of their access to archival material, a number of Soviet works in this field should be noted. L. A. Fainberg discusses the Arctic peoples in his work *Ocherki etnicheskoi istorii zarubezhnogo severa (Aliaska, Kanadskaia Arktika, Labrador, Grenlandiia)* (Essays on the ethnic history of the non-Soviet North [Alaska, Canadian Arctic, Labrador, Greenland]) (Moscow, 1971). R. S. Vasil'evskii investigates several primitive peoples in his study *Drevnie kul'tury Tikhookeanskogo Severa* (Ancient cultures of the North Pacific Ocean) (Novosibirsk, 1973), devoting almost half of the book to the Aleutian natives. The first scientific expedition sent to the Northwest American coast by the Russian government is detailed by R. G. Liapunova in "Etnograficheskoe znachenie ekspeditsii Kapitanov P. K. Krenitsyna i M. D. Levasheva na Aleutskie Ostrova (1764–1769 gg.)" (The ethnographic significance of captains P. K. Kenitsyn's and M. D. Levashev's expeditions to the Aleutian Islands, 1764–1769) (in *Sovetskaia etnografiia*, no. 6 [1971]: 67–80). Reproduced are the eight sheets of ethnographic drawings in Levashev's album. These drawings copied by Frank Golder are also available at the Northwest Collection of the University of Washington (see Collections), and can be found under the title *Alaska Scenes*.

Diaries, notes, journals, and reports of participants describing the customs, culture and forms of social relationships concerning

Chukotka, Alaska, and the Aleutians are gathered in Z. D. Titova's compilation *Etnograficheskie materialy Severo-Vostochnoi geograficheskoi eskpeditsii: 1785–1795 gg.* (Ethnographic materials of the northeastern geographical expedition, 1785–1795) (Magadan, 1978). Included in this work are manuscripts concerning Joseph Billings's expedition, primarily translated from the notes of Carl Merck.

An analysis of the history of the Aleuts based on archaeological, ethnographical and anthropological factors may be found in R. G. Liapunova's *Ocherki po etnografii Aleutov (konets XVIII-pervaia polovina XIX v.)* (Essays on the ethnography of the Aleuts [end of the eighteenth to first half of the nineteenth centuries]) (Leningrad, 1975). Although there is no bibliography to this thorough study, manuscript materials, including illustrations, are used and referenced in footnotes. A similar contribution is the study "The Aleut Social System, 1750 to 1810, From Early Historical Sources" by Margaret Lantis in the monograph *Ethnohistory in Southwestern Alaska and the Southern Yukon: Method and Content,* Studies in Anthropology, no. 7 (Lexington, Kentucky, 1970), 139–301. Lantis uses Russian accounts which are available in Western languages. G. I. Dzeniskevich has searched the writings of various voyagers and travellers for materials on the Athapaskans in "Vklad russkikh puteshestvennikov v etnografiiu atapaskov Aliaski (XVIII–XIX vv.)" (Contributions of Russian travellers to the ethnography of Alaska's Athapaskans, eighteenth–nineteenth centuries) (in *Ocherki istorii russkoi etnografii, fol'kloristiki i antropologii,* no. 7 [1977]: 77–88, *Trudy, novaia seriia AN Institut etnografii,* vol. 104). R. G. Liapunova presents a brief survey based on Levashev and Veniaminov "K voprosu ob obshchestvennom stroe aleutov serediny XVIII v." (On the question of the social structure of the Aleuts in the mid-18th century) in the collection edited by A. M. Reshetov, *Okhotniki, sobirateli, rybolovi* (Hunters, gatherers, fishermen) (Leningrad, 1972), 215–227.

In a continuation of the same theme, A. P. Okladnikov and R. S. Vasil'evskii have published the results of a Soviet-American expedition *Po Aliaske i Aleutskim ostrovam* (Through Alaska and the Aleutian Islands) (Novosibirsk, 1976). This anthropological survey examines the life and traditions of natives who crossed from Siberia and settled in North America. Okladnikov discusses more of these findings from Anangula in the Aleutians in "Asia-America: the Ancient Bridge" (in *Alaska Journal* 9, no. 4 [1979]: 42–45).

A *Festschrift* volume dedicated to Aleksei Vladimirovich Efimov, *Problemy istorii i etnografii Ameriki* (Problems of America's history and ethnography) (Moscow, 1979) contains a section on Russian America with contributions by M. I. Belov, R. G. Liapunova, S. G. Fedorova, G. I. Dzeniskevich, and R. V. Makarova. These articles are well-documented, illustrated, and cover Novaia Zemlia, Hieromonk Gedeon (St. German or Herman), Ivan Kuskov, the Athapaskan natives, and the liquidation of the Russian American Company.

Basil Dmytryshyn and E. A. P. Crownhart-Vaughan provide a well illustrated translation of E. E. Blomkvist's article "A Russian Scientific Expedition to California and Alaska, 1839–1849: The Drawings of I. G. Voznesenskii" (in *Oregon Historical Quarterly* 73, no. 2 [1972]: 101–70; originally in Russian "Risunki I. G. Voznesenskogo . . ." in *Sbornik Muzei antropologii i etnografii*, no. 13 [1951]: 230–303). Richard Pierce discusses "Voznesenskii, Scientist in Alaska" (in *Alaska Journal* 5, no. 1 [1975]: 11–15), and gives a short biography with explanations for many of Voznesenskii's drawings.

A. I. Alekseev points out that there are many unpublished works by Voznesenskii in his article "Puteshestviia I. G. Voznesenskogo po Dal'nemu Vostoku i Russkoi Amerike v 1839–1949 gg." (I. G. Voznesenskii's travels through the Far East and Russian America in 1839–1849) (in *Istoriia geograficheskikh znanii i istoricheskaia geografiia, etnografiia*, no. 4 [1970]: 36–39 of the *Materialy Moskovskogo filiala Geograficheskogo Obshchestva SSSR*). Alekseev himself partialy fulfills this need with a biography of *Il'ia Gavrilovich Voznesenskii* (Moscow, 1977). Based on Voznesenskii's ten-year travels through Russian America, California and parts of Siberia, this illustrated work uses archival materials, and details the rich ethnographical, geological, botanical, and zoological collections which were an important addition to the Museum of Anthropology and Ethnography in Leningrad.

The present-day inhabitants of a small group of islands at the western end of the Aleutians are described by L. M. Paseniuk in *Idu po Komandoram* (Through the Commander Islands) (Moscow, 1974).

Svetlana Fedorova surveys the formation of the Russian ethnic community in her essay "Etnicheskie protesessy v Russkoi Amerike," in a collection of essays entitled *Natsional'nye protsessy v SShA* (Nationality processes in the USA) (Moscow, 1973). This chapter was translated into English by Antoinette Shalkop as *Ethnic Processes in Russian America*, Occasional Paper, no. 1 (Anchorage, 1975), and is a supplement to Fedorova's book on the *Russian Population in Alaska and California* (see next section).

A study of the decline and near extinction of the Aleut population and culture is made by L. C. Milan's "Ethnohistory of Disease and Medical Care Among the Aleuts" (in *Anthropological Papers*, University of Alaska, 16, no. 2 [1974]: 15–40).

Several additional articles contain descriptions useful to ethnographers: F. P. Wrangell's "The Inhabitants of the Northwest Coast of America," translated, edited, and introduced by James Van Stone (in *Arctic Anthropology* 6, no. 2 [1970]: 1–20); S. G. Fedorova's "Pervoe poselenie russkikh na Unalaske i Dzh. Kuk" (The first settlement of Russians in Unalaska and James Cook) in *Novoe v izuchenii Avstralii i Okeanii* (New studies about Australia and Oceania) (Moscow, 1972), 228–36; J. B. Townsend's "Journals of 19th Century Russian Priests to the Tanaina: Cook Inlet, Alaska" (in *Arctic Anthropology* 11, no. 1 [1974]: 1–29); A. K. Konopatskii's "Legenda o dereve zhizni Aleutskogo naroda i ee istoricheskie korni (iz polevykh nabliudenii na Aleutskikh ostrovakh" (The legend about the tree of life of the Aleutian people and its historical roots [From Field Observations on the Aleutian Islands]) (in *Sovetskaia etnografiia*, no. 6 [1976]: 111–15); Lydia Black's "The Konyag (the Inhabitants of the Island of Kodiak) by Iosaf [Bolotov] (1794–1799) and by Gideon (1804–1807)" (in *Arctic Anthropology* 14, no. 2 [1977]: 79–108); and A. A. Arsev'ev's "Etnograficheskie nasledie I. E. Veniaminova" (The ethnographic heritage of I. E. Veniaminov), in *Sovetskaia etnografiia*, no. 5 [1979]: 76–89.

A new publication on population genetics and the intercontinental connections among Siberia, Asia, and America has been published as *Populiatsionnaia genetika narodov Severo-Vostochnoi Azii* (Population genetics of the peoples of Northeastern Asia) (Moscow, 1978) by V. A. Sheremet'eva and Iu. G. Rychkov. This study is based on numerous articles published over the last decade by the same authors, one of which is available in English as *Population Genetics of the Aleuts of the Commander Islands* (Miami: Field Research Projects, 1976).

Four conference papers are worth noting. At the Ninth International Congress of Anthropological and Ethnological Sciences held in Chicago in August and September 1973, Dr. S. Fedorova delivered a paper called "Novye dannye o russkikh issledovaniiakh po geografii i etnografii Aliaski (pervaia polovina XIX v.)" (New data on Russian geographic and ethnographic investigations in Alaska [first half of the nineteenth century]). In the English translation of this cursory survey, Fedorova includes maps done by the two Vasil'evs. At the same congress Leonid

Shur presented a paper, "Russkie istochniki po etnografii narodov Ameriki (XIX v.)" (Russian Sources on the Ethnography of America's Peoples). For the Fourteenth Pacific Science Congress held in Khabarovsk, USSR, in August 1979, R. G. Liapunova wrote a pamphlet called *Etnografiia narodov Tikhookeanskogo Severa Ameriki. Russkie i sovetskie issledovaniia.* (Ethnography of the peoples of America's North Pacific. Russian and Soviet investigations.) (Moscow, 1979). She mentions the major voyages, as well as collections from the Aleut, Kenai, and other native groups in Alaska, which are housed in the Leningrad Kunstkamera. S. Fedorova also contributed a paper that was read in absentia "Russkoe nasledie v sud'bakh korennogo naseleniia Aliaski" (The Russian Heritage in the Fates of Alaska's Indigenous Population).

Materials for the Study of Alaska History. Perhaps the most significant of Richard Pierce's many endeavors is his establishment of the series: *Materials for the Study of Alaska History.* The translating of major Russian language works and reprinting of basic older works long unavailable provide a wealth of source materials. The volumes are illustrated; contain prefatory remarks; are published by Limestone Press, Kingston, Ontario; and average about $10 each. The published series numbers to date are as follows:

1. R. A. Pierce, *Alaskan Shipping, 1867–1878. Arrivals and Departures at the Port of Sitka.* 1972.
2. F. W. Howay, *A List of Trading Vessels in the Maritime Fur Trade, 1785–1825.* Reprint of articles 1930–1934. 1973.
3. K. T. Khlebnikov, *Baranov*... Translation of Russian 1835 ed. 1973.
4. S. G. Fedorova, *The Russian Population in Alaska and California (Late 18th Century–1867).* Translation of Russian 1972 ed. 1973.
5. V. N. Berkh, *A Chronological History of the Discovery of the Aleutian Islands.* Translation of Russian 1823 ed. 1974.
6. R. V. Makarova, *Russians on the Pacific, 1743–1799.* Translation of Russian 1968 ed. 1975.
7. *Documents on the History of the Russian-American Company.* Translation of Russian 1957 ed. 1976.
8. R. A. Pierce, *Russia's Hawaiian Adventure, 1815–1817.* Reprint of his 1965 ed. 1976.
9. H. W. Elliott, *The Seal Islands of Alaska.* Reprint of his 1881 ed. 1976.
10. G. I. Davydov, *Two Voyages to Russian America, 1802–1807.* Translation of Russian 1810–1812 eds. 1977.

11. *The Russian Orthodox Religious Mission in America, 1794–1837.* Translation of 1894 ed. 1978.
12. E. Belcher, *H.M.S. Sulphur on the Northwest and California Coasts, 1837 and 1839.* Edited by R. A. Pierce and J. H. Winslow. 1979.
13. P. A. Tikhmenev, *Documents.* Vol. 2 of *History of the Russian American Company.* Edited by R. A. Pierce and A. S. Donnelly. 1979.
14. N. A. Ivashintsev, *Russian Voyages around the World, 1803–1849.* Translation of various Russian eds. 1980.

One of the most significant books of this group is the translation of S. Fedorova's work on *The Russian Population in Alaska and California.* Reviewed in major Western language journals and often cited, it represents Soviet scholarship at its best and is based on extensive use of archival materials. Dr. Fedorova studies the Russians who settled in Alaska from a historical, ethnographic, geographic, and social point of view and discusses their relations with the native population. The importance of Fedorova's work was noted early by Victor Fischer when he translated the statistical appendix on *The Population of Russian America (1799–1867)* (Fairbanks: Institute of Social, Economic, and Government Research, 1973; ISEGR research note, January 1973).

California. Research continues to produce more information about the Russian settlement at Fort Ross and the Russian interest in this area as a whole. The John Hussey bibliography on Fort Ross has already been mentioned. Leonid Shur, formerly with the Academy of Sciences's Institute of Ethnography in the USSR, in the course of his studies on Russians in Latin America, has published a book and several articles on Russian America, California, and Hawaii. His *K beregam Novogo Sveta, iz neopublikovannykh zapisok russkikh puteshestvennikov nachala XIX veka* (To the shores of the New World, from the unpublished notes of early nineteenth-century Russian travellers) (Moscow, 1971) provides extensive sections from the diaries of F. F. Matiushkin, F. P. Litke and F. P. Wrangell; illustrations from previously unpublished artists; and a survey with evaluation of Russian sources for this period. The author's explanatory notes provide a valuable addition to our knowledge of California's history. Shur's article "Putevye zapiski i dnevniki russkikh puteshestvennikov kak istochnik po istorii Kalifornii" (in *Amerikanskii ezhegodnik* [1971], 295–319) was translated into English by James Gibson as "Russian Travel Notes and Journals as Sources for the History of California, 1800–1850" (in *California Historical Quarterly*

52, no. 1 [1973]: 37–63). Shur's contribution before leaving the Soviet Union was "Dnevniki puteshestvii po Kalifornii K. T. Khlebnikova (1820–1831 gg.)" (K. T. Khlebnikov's diaries of travel through California, 1820–1831) (in *Izvestiia Geograficheskogo Obshchestva SSSR* 106, no. 5 [1974]: 402–7).

Other documents translated into English are James Gibson's "California in 1824 by Dmitry Zavalishin" (in *Southern California Quarterly* 55, no. 4 [1973]: 369–412); James Gibson's "Russia in California, 1833: Report of Governor Wrangel" (in *Pacific Northwest Quarterly* 60, no. 4 [1969]: 205–15); James Gibson's "A Russian Orthodox priest in a Mexican Catholic Parish: Father Ioann Veniaminov's Sojourn at Fort Ross and Visit to Missions San Rafael, San Jose, Santa Clara, and San Francisco in 1836" (in *Pacific Historian* 15, no. 2 [1971]: 57–66); Fred Stross's translation, with notes by R. F. Heizer, of *Ethnographic Observations on the Coast Miwok and Pomo by Contre-Admiral F. P. von Wrangel and P. Kostromitonov of the Russian Colony Ross, 1839* (Berkeley: University of California, Dept. of Anthropology, Archaeological Research Facility, 1974); Richard Pierce's new translation of *Rezanov Reconnoiters California, 1806* . . . (San Francisco, 1972); A. F. Doll's and R. A. Pierce's translation of Alexander Rotchev's notes on "New Eldorado in California" (in *Pacific Historian* 14, no. 1 [1970]: 33–40); and Richard Pierce and John Winslow's *H.M.S. Sulphur at California, 1837 and 1839* . . . (San Francisco, 1969).

P. M. Kozhin has written an article based largely on Western language sources entitled "Etnograficheskie nabliudeniia I. G. Voznesenskogo v Kalifornii" (Ethnographic observations of I. G. Voznesenskii in California) (in *Ocherki istorii russkoi etnografii, fol'kloristiki i antropologii*, no. 7 [1977]: 66–76, *Trudy, novaia seriia AN Institut etnografii*, vol. 104).

The American Captain Jonathan Winship and the Russian Commander Slobodchikov of the Russian American Company, in a joint fur hunting adventure, explored the treacherous "Bay of Rezanov," which is the subject of W. Heckrotte's "The Discovery of Humboldt Bay: A New Look at an Old Story" (in *Terrae Incognitae*, no. 5 [1973]: 27–41).

Reprints are available of F. F. Hatch's *The Russian Advance into California* (San Francisco, 1971) and E. T. H. Bunje, H. Penn, and F. J. Schmitz's *Russian California, 1805–1841* (San Francisco, 1970).

Fort Ross in California has evoked particular interest recently. The State of California issued a proposal for the future of the area in the booklet *Fort Ross State Historic Park, Resource Management Plan and General Development Plan* (Sacramento: State of Calif., Dept. of Parks and Recreation, 1976). Henry Schwartz provides an informative photo essay with historical background in "Fort Ross, California: Imperial Outpost on America's Western Frontier, 1812–1841" (in *Journal of the West* 18, no. 2 [1979]: 35–48). Bill Walker offers photos with short text titled "Russia in Redwood" (in *Westways* 70, no. 7 [1978]: 50–51). Two newly revised booklets published in 1978 by the Fort Ross Interpretive Association in Jenner, Calif., are *Fort Ross: The Russian Settlement in California*, edited by Stephen Watrous, and *Fort Ross: Indians, Russians, Americans*, edited by the late Bickford O'Brien. Both provide illustrations and a good review of the history of Fort Ross. A year earlier Victor Petrov had published a Russian version entitled *Fort Ross i ego kul'turnoe nasledie* (Fort Ross and its cultural heritage) (Los Angeles: Izd. Ob-va druzei Forta Ross, 1977). A brief sketch of Fort Ross's history was presented in a lecture at the Institute of History of the Academy of Sciences, USSR in 1976 by N. I. Rokitianskii "Fort Ross" (in *Voprosy istorii*, no. 7 [1977]: 213–17).

Hawaii. The Russian American Company's activities in Hawaii were short-lived. Richard Pierce's book *Russia's Hawaiian Adventure, 1815–1817* (Berkeley/Los Angeles, 1965; Kingston, 1976) chronicles Russian connections with the Islands. N. N. Bolkhovitinov has provided a closer look at "The Adventures of Doctor Schaffer in Hawaii, 1815–1819" (in *Hawaiian Journal of History*," no. 7 [1973]: 55–78; originally in Russian "Avantura Doktora Sheffera na Gavaiiakh v 1815–1819 gg." (in *Novaia i noveishaia istoriia*, no. 1 [1972]: 121–37). Richard Pierce has issued, as a separate publication, his work on *Georg Anton Schaffer, Russia's man in Hawaii, 1815–1817* (Kingston, 1976; reprint of his article in *Pacific Historical Review* 32, no. 4 [1963]). Work done by Patrick McCoy on *Archaeological Research at Fort Elizabeth, Waimea, Kauai, Hawaiian Islands: Phase I* (Honolulu: Bishop Museum, Dept. of Anthropology, 1972, Report 72-7) is a noteworthy study of one of the Russian forts built during Sheffer's stay in Hawaii.

Richard Dillon's "Tsarist Hawaii" (in *Westways*, 70, no. 4 [1978]: 45–47, 68) is an indication of popular interest.

Sitka. The wreck of the Neva (Anchorage, 1979), which took place off Mt. Edgecumbe, is translated by Antoinette Shalkop from writings of V. N. Berkh and V. M. Golovnin (illustrations, notes, a bibliography, and introduction by Shalkop and Richard Pierce make this an extremely informative booklet).

An account of the Tlingit attack on the Russian fort at Sitka taken from the Sydney, Australia *Gazette* of 1803–4 is presented by W. Wilfried Schuhmacher in his article "Aftermath of the Sitka massacre of 1802" (in *Alaska Journal* 9, no. 1 [1979]: 58–61).

Antoinette Shalkop writes about "Stepan Ushin, Citizen by Purchase" (in *Alaska Journal* 7, no. 2 [1977]: 103–8). Ushin kept a diary of life in Sitka from 1874–95. Richard Pierce details the life of "Eadweard Muybridge, Alaska's First Photographer" (in *Alaska Journal* 7, no. 4 [1977]: 202–10). Most of the photographs included in this essay are of Sitka shortly after the sale.

Bishop Gregory provides a history of the fire and reconstruction of the Orthodox church in his booklet *Sitka and St. Michael's Cathedral* (Kodiak, 1974).

Clint Potter's *Sitka Sketches* (Anchorage, 1970 [?]) is a delightful tour of this historic city through watercolor sketches, many of which portray the buildings and events from the Russian era.

The final draft of the *Sitka National Historical Park Russian Bishop's House and Old School: Interpretive Plan* (Denver: Denver Service Center, 1979) provides not only a technical examination of this landmark house, but also brief historical sketches and a bibliography of sources important to reconstruction efforts.

A reprint of the 1922 edition of C. L. Andrew's work *The Story of Sitka*, SJS no. 94 (Seattle: Shorey Book Store, 1973) is available.

Linguistics. Under G. A. Menovshchikov's editorship, E. S. Rubtsova published an *Eskimossko-russkii slovar'* (Eskimo-Russian dictionary) (Moscow, 1971) with 19,000 words; Menovshchikov himself writes on "Eskimossko-aleutskie iazyki i ikh otnoshenie k drugim iazykovym sem'iam" (The Eskimo-Aleutian languages and their relations to other language families) (in *Voprosy iazykoznaniia*, no. 1 [1974]: 46–59), detailing many similarities; in 1975 Menovshchikov's monumental *Iazyk naukanskikh eskimosov: foneticheskoe vvedenie, ocherk morfologii, teksty, slovar'* (The language of the Naukan Eskimos: A phonetic introduction, morphological essay, texts, dictionary) (Leningrad, 1975) appeared; E. E. Blomkvist provides a survey of Russian American native languages in "Istoriia izucheniia v Rossii iazykov Severoamerikanskikh indeitsev" (A History of the Study in Russia of the Languages of the North American Indians) (in *Sbornik Muzei antropologii i etnografii*, no. 31 [1975]:94–117); and Lydia Black writes about "Ivan Pan'kov—An architect of Aleut literacy" (in *Arctic Anthropology* 14, no. 1 [1977]: 94–107).

Education. Jerome Starr has drawn on his dissertation discussed previously for an account of *Education in Russian Alaska,* Alaska Historical Library Historical Monographs, no. 2 (Juneau, 1972). He describes the mission schools, secular education, religious seminaries, and provides a bibliography of primary sources, with a glossary of terms and various useful appendices.

Orthodox Church. A very good, well-documented work with illustrations by Bishop Gregory (Afonsky) is available entitled *A History of the Orthodox Church in Alaska (1794–1917)* (Kodiak, 1977). Other items that supplement this work are Sister Victoria's "The Russian Experience" (in *Orthodox Alaska,* no. 5 [1975]: 3–4, 16–25, 27–33); F. A. Wallace's *The Flame of the Candle: A Pictorial History of Russian Orthodox Churches in Alaska* (Chilliwack, B.C., 1974); a translation by R. Nichols and R. Croskey of "The Condition of the Orthodox Church in America [by Innokentii Veniaminov]" (in *Pacific Northwest Quarterly* 63, no. 2 [1972]: 41–54); R. Croskey's translation of "Russian Orthodox Church in Alaska: Innokentii Veniaminov's supplementary account (1858)" (in *Pacific· Northwest Quarterly* 66, no. 1 [1975]: 26–29); Rev. A. P. Kashevaroff's "Ivan Veniaminov, Innocent, Metropolitan of Moscow and Koloma . . ." (in *Orthodox Alaska* 6, no. 3 [1977]: 12–22); Paul Garrett's biography of *St. Innocent: Apostle to America* (Crestwood, N.Y., 1979); A. P. Okladnikov's account "Ot Angi do Unalashki: udivitel' naia sud'ba Ivana Popova" (From Anga to Unalaska: The miraculous fate of Ivan Popov) (in *Voprosy istorii,* no. 6 [1976]: 121–29); the notes of Monk Herman and ethnographic observations of Hieromonk Gedeon are translated in *The Russian Orthodox Religious Mission in America, 1794–1837* (mentioned previously); and R. L. Shalkop's catalog of religious objects entitled *Russian Orthodox Art in Alaska* (Anchorage: Anchorage Historical and Fine Arts Museum, 1973).

Fiction. I. F. Kratt has written fictionalized accounts of Russian America in his *Ostrov Baranova* (Baranof Island) (Leningrad, 1945), and *Koloniia Ross* (Ross colony) (Leningrad, 1950; Vladivostok, 1950, 1960). The first work reconstructs Baranov's efforts, after the island had been settled, to deal with the Russian government in St. Petersburg. The second portrays the romance between Rezanov and Doña Concepcion. In 1950, with numerous printings, Kratt issued the two separate works in one volume under the title *Velikii Okean* (The great ocean).

Two stories about Baranov and Russian events in Alaska are provided by Victor Petrov's *Zavershenie tsikla* (The end of a cycle) (Los Angeles:

Rodnye dali, 1975) and *Kolumby rossiiskie* (The Russian Columbuses) (Washington, D.C. 1971). Petrov makes one of the Russian American Company founders and later plenipotentiary envoy to Japan Nikolai Petrovich Rezanov the subject of his work *Kamerger dvora* (The court chamberlain) (Washington, D.C., 1973).

The historian S. N. Markov fictionalizes the travels of the well-known ethnographer Lt. Lavrentii Zagoskin in *Iukonskii voron* (The Yukon raven) (Moscow/Leningrad, 1946, with numerous printings).

Jean Montgomery's story about Alaska and Fort Ross has been translated into a volume intended for young adult readers with the title *Ishchi na dikom beregu* (Search the wild shore) (Moscow, 1979). Svetlana Fedorova has written an introduction that provides a historical perspective.

Biography. Henry Elliott's *Biographical Sketches of Authors on Russian America and Alaska* (Anchorage: Anchorage Historical and Fine Arts Museum, 1976. Occasional paper No. 2) were notes prepared for James Wickersham. It includes a bibliography of John Carnahan in which the locations of the biographical data are listed. This work would have been improved, however, if it could have been updated and corrected before publication. For instance, a long, favorable biography of Ivan Petroff could have been recast to reflect what is now known of the dubious scholarship of this roguish character.

Artists. Relatively little is known about the artists on the Russian voyages. Leonid Shur's article "Khudozhnik-puteshestvennik Mikhail Tikhanov" (In *Latinskaia Amerika*, no. 5 [1974]: 163–80), an informative biography based on archival documents with many of the artist's drawings, is a welcome presentation. Shur and Richard Pierce published an article "Artists in Russian America: Mikhail Tikhanov (1818)" (in *Alaska Journal*, 6, no. 1 [1976]: 40–49) in which many more of Tikhanov's drawings are reproduced, though regrettably in black and white. Finally, there is a detailed study of Tikhanov's portrait of Baranov, with introductory remarks by Svetlana Fedorova, authored by N. N. Goncharova—"O portretakh A. A. Baranova" (About the portraits of A. A. Baranov) (in *Letopis' Severa*, no. 9 [1979]: 263–72).

The artist on the Bellingshausen-Lazarev voyage of 1818–21 and the Staniukovich voyage of 1826–29 is presented by L. Shur and R. Pierce in "Pavel Mikhailov, artist in Russian America" (in *Alaska Journal* 8, no. 4 [1978]: 360–63) with several illustrations published for the first time.

Miscellaneous. Works on a variety of diverse topics have filled in some of the gaps in studies on Russian America. A. Doll and R. Pierce joined efforts for "Alaskan Treasure—Russian Skin Money" (in *Alaska* 35, no. 11 [1969]: 22) and "Alaska Treasure—Our Search for the Russian Plates" (in *Alaska Journal* 1, no. 1 [1971]: 2–7). An oral account of Serebrennikov's expedition of Russian traders who perished in the Copper River area is translated by Fred and Katie John as "The Killing of the Russians at Batzulnetas Village" (in *Alaska Journal* 3, no. 3 [1973]: 147–48). W. S. Hanable recounts the short-lived settlement of Russians at Yakutat in "New Russia . . ." (in *Alaska Journal* 3, no. 2 [1973]: 77–80). M. W. Grauman discusses "Women and Culture in Russian America" (in *American West* 11, no. 3 [1974]: 24–31). R. Pierce reviews the suicide of a Russian girl of noble blood in "The Ghost of Baranov Castle: Folklore or Fakelore?" (in *Alaska* 36, no. 5 [1970]: 25–26, 39). M. Kildare addresses the same incident, basing his story on Tarakanov's tale of the tragic death of a woman murdered by Indians who later haunted the Baranov Castle in Sitká in "Anna Petrovna's Ghost" (in *True West* 23, no. 2 (132) [1975]: 22–24, 38–39). Richard Pierce gives an account of "The Russian Coal Mine on the Kenai" (in *Alaska Journal* 5, no. 2 [1975]: 104–8). Svetlana Fedorova's "The Flag of the Russo-American Company" (in *Pacific Historian*, no. 14 [1970]: 25–32) is a translation from a chapter in *Ot Aliaski do ogennoi zemli* (From Alaska to the fiery land) (Moscow, 1967).

V. A. Chernykh published a letter proposing that the London emigré journal *The Bell* be printed also in Sitka in "Kolokol' v Russkoi Aliaske (Novyi dokument iz zagranichnogo arkhiv A. I. Gertsena)" ('The Bell' in Russian America [a new document from the Foreign Archive of A. I. Hertzen]) in the book *Istochnikovedenie i arkheografiia Sibiri* (Study of sources and early texts of Siberia) (Novosibirsk, 1977), 59–63.

Two articles dealing with the money used during the Russian tenure in A. F. Dolgopolov "Numizmaticheskie pamiatniki Russkoi Ameriki" (Numismatic Relics of Russian America) (in *Voenno-istoricheskii vestnik* 31 [1968]: 28–35) and I. S. Shikanova "Denezhnye znaki Rossiisko-Amerikanskoi Kompanii pervoi poloviny XIX veka" (Banknotes of the Russian-American Company of the first half of the nineteenth century) (in *Numizmaticheskii sbornik* no. 7 [1979].

An interesting collection of reports issued with no title describes aspects of Russian-Alaskan postal history (in *The Journal of the Rossica Society of Russian Philately* 68 [1965]: 11–19).

The Russians in America is a chronology and fact book, compiled and edited by Vladimir Wertsman, Ethnic Chronology Series, no. 24

(Dobbs Ferry, N.Y.: Oceana Pubs., 1977). It contains previously published materials, including a reproduction of the document for the Alaska purchase in 1867, "Russian Buildings and Places in Sitka," and "Nikolaevsk, a New Russian Village in Alaska."

Victor Petrov provides a general survey with illustrations in his *Russkaia Amerika* (Russian America) (Los Angeles: Friends of Fort Ross, 1975). Organized by the Kennan Institute for Advanced Russian Studies of The Wilson Center, the Conference on Russian America held in Sitka in August 1979 already has elicited this volume, as well as an article by S. Frederick Starr on "Why Did Russia Let Seward's Folly Go on the Cheap?" (in *Smithsonian* 10, no. 9 [1979]: 129–44).

Further Study. The period of Russian involvement on the Northwest coast of America is so fascinating that it continues to arouse scholarly interest. Several topics would benefit from further study. A needed reference work is a comprehensive one-volume bibliography on Russian America, which cites works in Russian, English, and other languages. The biographical dictionary of Henry Elliott, if expanded, could be a useful reference tool. Barbara Smith provides a list of research topics to be pursued with the Orthodox church records. John Hussey calls for further identification of Russian language materials in connection with Fort Ross. Further, an examination of Russian America within the broad context of the history and foreign policy of Siberia and the Northwest Coast is still needed. Certainly an economic history of the Russian American Company is conspicuous by its absence.

Our Soviet colleagues are in the best position to continue efforts to make materials within their country available to Western scholars. In lieu of published collections of documents, works with extensive quotations would be valuable. Even a *putevoditel'* (guide) to archives containing Russian American materials would be a great aid. A joint project can be envisioned of publishing documents and other primary materials.

The Kennan Institute's Sitka Conference of 1979 was testimony to the value of Soviet-American collaborative ventures in enriching the bibliography of this important field of study.

Archival and Bibliographic Materials on Russian America outside the USSR

Richard A. Pierce

The history of Russian America—that is, of Alaska from 1741 until 1867—is still far from complete. We know the general outlines, of course, and some fundamental works became available rather early, particularly William Coxe's compilation of accounts of explorations in the Aleutians (1780), G. I. Shelikhov's account of his establishment of a permanent settlement on Kodiak Island (1790), books by both G. A. Sarychev and Martin Sauer (1802) on the northeastern expedition of 1785–95, and the accounts of circumnavigations by Kruzenstern (2 vols., 1809–13), Lisianskii (1812), von Langsdorff (1812), von Kotzebue (1821 and 1828), Golovnin (1822), and Lutke (1835–36). A little later came Father Ivan Veniaminov's outstanding description of the inhabitants of the Unalaska district (1840), L. A. Zagoskin's lively account of explorations in the Alaska interior (1847–48), and the general histories by P. A. Tikhmenev (1861–63) and H. H. Bancroft (1885). A period of neglect then ensued, which has ended only in more recent times with a revival of scholarly activity in this field.

Thus, there are still major gaps in our knowledge. In North American terms the history of Russian America resembles what was known of French Canada and the Spanish Southwest a century and a half ago. Specialists in those fields now know the routes of expeditions, when settlements were founded, who took part, what political and economic measures were taken, and the minutiae of daily life; there is abundant source material, made accessible by bibliographic aids.

It is not so with the history of early Alaska, in which much of the basic work has yet to be done. Researchers of several countries must reconstruct and fill out the record. Points of view will inevitably differ somewhat, since for Soviet historians Russian America is part of their Russian national past, whereas for non-Soviets it is a chapter in the history of North America and the Pacific. Both, however, will need to work with the same materials, will benefit from each other's approaches, and will have the same goals of depicting events truthfully and accurately. This is a brief survey of materials outside the Soviet Union which will help in achieving those goals.

At the outset it should be noted that quantitatively the resources available to Soviet researchers in this field are superior to those available abroad. They can draw upon a number of central and local archives containing many fundamental collections, on individuals and institutions. North Americans have no comparable collection on any individual, and only two large archival collections to work with—the correspondence of the chief managers at Sitka, and the Alaska Church Collection. Foreign researchers on Russian America therefore welcome the publication of source materials in the USSR, the more so since most of the local archives are at present closed to foreigners. The relative paucity of material outside the USSR makes knowledge of bibliography very important.

In Alaska, the State Historical Library at Juneau is one of the best for the study of Russian America, with a large collection of printed works begun early in this century by Judge James Wickersham. The library of the University of Alaska at Fairbanks and the privately owned Heritage Library at Anchorage also have valuable material, and there are useful smaller collections at Kodiak and in the Clarence Andrews collection at Sheldon Jackson College in Sitka.

Farther south, at Victoria, the library of the Provincial Archives of British Columbia contains a number of Alaskan historical works and a unique Russian source, a hand-drawn, colored atlas of the North Pacific, prepared in the early 1780s by the navigator Grigorii Lovtsov, indicating all that was then known of that area.[1]

At Seattle, the Northwest Collection at the Library of the University of Washington has printed works, manuscripts of the post-1867 period, and photostatic copies of documents made by Professor Frank Golder in Russian archives in 1914. Generously given access to the principal archives in St. Petersburg and Moscow, Golder spent eight months seeking materials relating to American history. These are listed in his *Guide to Materials for American History in Russian Archives*, 2 vols. (Washington, 1917, 1937). His photostatic copies of a number of documents are now in the Library of Congress and the University of Washington. Requiring skill at Russian paleography, this collection has been neglected by American researchers, but will doubtless receive closer attention in the future. Originally made for Golder's own use, the photostats in large measure reflect his interests, which were particularly strong on the Bering voyages. An index of the Golder photostats was provided in *Documents Relative to Alaska History*, an unpublished compilation made in the 1930s by the Alaska History Research Project of the Works Progress Administration. A reorganized index, prepared in 1967 at the University of Washington by Rudy Neunherz, relates the photostats to microfilms of them now in a number of libraries (Seattle, 1967, unpublished). Stanford University, at Palo Alto, California, has Golder's papers, including copies and summaries of a few documents mentioned in his *Guide*, but they are not photographed.

The Bancroft Library at the University of California, Berkeley, is well known for its manuscripts on Russian America.[2] The collection was amassed by Bancroft during preparation of his thirty-volume history of the American West, including his *History of Alaska*, published in San Francisco in 1886. The Alaskan material includes the manuscript series "Russian America," comprising translations of Russian printed sources on Alaska made by Bancroft's assistant Ivan Petrov and transcripts of some of Petrov's interviews with individuals, an early use of oral history.

This material must be used in the light of what is now known of Petrov himself. In the later 1870s he was a U.S. Treasury agent on Kodiak Island. In 1880 he took the Alaska census and compiled his comprehensive *Report on the Population, Industries, and Resources of Alaska* (Washington, 1884), a useful work which helped to acquaint Americans with their country's new territory. He then helped Bancroft write the *History of Alaska*. Later he took the Alaska census of 1890, embodying the results in another volume, and soon after was employed to translate Russian American Company documents for the U.S. delegation negotiating with the British in the Seal Islands Controversy. But here his star set. A junior clerk, who was studying Russian, undertook to practice by comparing Petrov's translations with the originals. He reported discrepancies, and charged that Petrov had been falsifying his translations to improve the U.S. case. The heads of the delegation discharged Petrov at once, and apologized to the British. Petrov was also fired from the Census Bureau and his name was expunged from the 1890 census report.

The wretched Petrov dropped out of sight. Nothing was known of his fate for seventy years. Then the historian Morgan Sherwood, in his history of scientific exploration in Alaska,[3] showed that Petrov had exaggerated the extent of some of his travels in Alaska, and moreover, that he had deserted after serving in the Union Army at the end of the end of the Civil War.

Further information of Petrov ferreted out by the present author, along with information from other sources,[4] makes it clear that Petrov habitually lied about his origins, his military career, and his achievements in Alaska. His origins are still unclear, and he may not even have been a Russian. He had enlisted in the United States Army not once but several times, evidently to get the bounty, and each time had deserted. Later he worked on the *San Francisco Bulletin*, writing articles purportedly as a correspondent covering the Russo-Turkish War of 1878, until it came to light that he was taking his information from the *New York Times* and he was discharged. Soon afterward he took the post of treasury agent on Kodiak Island, which started his career as an authority on Alaska.

These details help build up a picture of a man who compiled a great deal of Bancroft's *History of Alaska*. Some of his many works are indeed dubious. The "diary" of the monk Iuvenalii, to which Bancroft gives several pages, is clearly a fabrication. The often cited report of the *promyshlennik* Tarakanov concerning captivity at the hands of the Spanish in California is also a fake. On the other hand, Petrov did some good work. The extent and nature of his influence will bear closer study.[5]

Outstanding among Bancroft Library holdings are copies of documents from the archives of Spanish and Mexican California. The originals were later destroyed in the San Francisco fire of 1906, so the copies provide a unique record of Russian relations with Spain and Mexico, with many references to trade, sea otter hunting, and the Russian establishment at Fort Ross.

The Bancroft Library's holdings of the diaries and papers of another Bancroft assistant, the French anthropologist and philologist Alphonse Louis Pinart, include accounts of journeys in Alaska in the 1870s and a portfolio of copies of documents made by Pinart in Russian archives on a journey financed by Bancroft. Most of the latter pertain to the adventurer Dr. Schaffer's attempt to seize the Sandwich (Hawaiian) Islands for Russia in 1815–17.[6]

A recent purchase by the Bancroft Library, the Honeyman Collection, includes sketches and watercolors made by the naturalist Georg von Langsdorff, during his voyage around the world from 1803 to 1807, the basis for the engravings which later appeared in his book.[7] Aside from this and a few other acquisitions by purchase or donation, the Bancroft Library has added little to its original fund of documents on Alaska. Nonetheless, it remains one of the main collections in the field.

The Library of Congress in Washington, D.C., has owned the large Yudin collection since 1905.[8] The printed works were merged in the general collection, and the documents, including original materials on Shelikhov and Rezanov, placed in the Manuscript Division. The papers include a personnel book kept on the *Three Saints* during Shelikhov's voyage to America, listing amounts owed by the crewmen and ship's officers, with candid appraisals of each man's character. The papers on Rezanov, evidently left among his effects when he died at Krasnoiarsk, include remarks on his difficulties with Kruzenstern and Lisianskii during the voyage from European Russia, a list of company personnel wishing to stay in America, and the log of the ship *Juno* which bore Rezanov and von Langsdorff to California in 1806.

The Manuscript Division also houses the vast Alaska Church Collection, consisting of over 900 cartons of papers from the early nineteenth to the early twentieth centuries donated to the library in 1940. This collection contains records of baptisms, marriages, and deaths of Alaska parishioners, and much information of value for ecclesiastical and social history. The journals of local missionary priests, such as Fathers Netsvetov and Salamatov, are rich in details of everyday life before and after 1867. The diary of the excommunicate, Ushin, reveals the plight of certain Russians and creoles who remained behind in Alaska after the transfer of 1867, impoverished, with no place under the new regime. Previously almost unusable because of its extent and sketchy classification, the church collection is now being catalogued. Meanwhile, in 1974 the Alaska Diocese of the Orthodox church retrieved documents and printed works from cellars and belfries in its far-flung parish system. These materials are preserved in the Archives of the Alaska Diocese in Kodiak.[9]

The U.S. National Archives, also in Washington, D.C., contain the surviving records of the Russian American Company. When Aleksandr Baranov was replaced as chief manager in 1818 and ordered back to Russia, the files of his twenty-eight year administration, including correspondence, log books, reports of explorations, census data, and maps, were sent with him. Baranov died on the way, but the files presumably ended up in the company archives in St. Petersburg, there to be kept until the entire archive was destroyed following liquidation of the company several years after 1867. Only a few documents of this early period can be found in other Soviet archival collections, such as those from the former imperial ministries of finance, foreign affairs, and the navy.

Remaining in the U.S. National Archives are the files of Baranov's successors from 1818 to 1867, which were turned over to the United States under the cession treaty. Also surviving is one document of 1802 which somehow was left behind when the other papers were shipped in 1818. The Washington, D.C., archive includes "communications received" at Novo-Arkhangel'sk (Sitka), mostly from the main office, others to various district offices in Russian America. There are about 800 communications in each category per year, or about 80,000 documents for the fifty-year period. Some are routine and repetitious, but in general they are a mine of information on economic and administrative matters and—to a lesser degree—on cultural and social matters. Use has been hindered by lack of a calendar of the documents, except for the first decade of "communications received."[10] The remaining years will be listed in the course of translations now being made under auspices of the National Endowment for the Humanities.

The Beinecke Library at Yale University in New Haven, Connecticut, has many rare printed works on Alaska as well as drawings made by Ludwig Choris during his round-the-world voyage with von Kotzebue, including portraits of Alaska natives. The New York Public Library and the Widener Library at Harvard University also have Alaskan material. The library of the Presbyterian Historical Society in Philadelphia contains the Sheldon Jackson Collection of books and papers, mostly pertaining to the post-1867 period. In Winnipeg, Manitoba, the Hudson's Bay Company archives contain records of relations with the Russian American Company, particularly of the Sitkine incident, and the subsequent accommodation and lease by the British company of part of the present "Alaska Panhandle."

The library of the University of Helsinki in Finland, until 1917 a deposit library receiving one copy of every book published in the Russian Empire, contains many printed works on Russian America that are unavailable in North America. The Bibliothèque Nationale in Paris, France, contains material on the voyage of La Perouse. In Spain, records of Spanish voyages on the Northwest Coast are available in the Archivo General de Indias in Seville and the Archivo Historico Nacional in Madrid. The Biblioteco Nacional of Mexico has materials on Spanish and Mexican relations with Russia, particularly negotiations concerning Fort Ross, in California.

Books and documents in many far-flung libraries can be difficult enough to find, or to reach, but even greater difficulty is offered by materials in private hands, usually unknown. Finding such material requires tracing rumors, genealogical research, and much correspondence and travel. The following examples are typical of what may be found in this under-researched field.

The papers of most officials of the Russian American Company, if they have survived the attrition of time and changing regimes, are most likely to be found in the USSR. However, there are exceptions. Thus, a great-great-grandson of Baron F. P. von Wrangell, the late Baron Wilhelm von Wrangell, of Bremen, West Germany, provided materials concerning his ancestor, and referred me to a relative in New York, who had several paintings made of Sitka by an unknown artist, possibly the Baroness von Wrangell.[11]

The University of Helsinki library contains a diary of the same period, kept by Reinhold Sahlberg, a young member of a Swedish family from Finland, who spent a year at Novo-Arkhangel'sk as a physician.

A few years later another Swede from Finland, Arvid Adolph Etholen (1840–45), governed Russian America. A great-grandson living in Stockholm preserves in his possession three paintings made in the early 1840s, along with letters and other papers.[12] Etholen's wife, who journeyed with him to America, kept a diary which is today in the library of the University of Turku (Abo) in Finland. Deeply religious, the diarist suffused her writings with mysticism and expressions of grief at the death in Novo-Arkhangel'sk of her infant son, Edward. His grave marker, an iron cross, may be seen in the old Russian cemetery. Probably at her insistence, she and her husband were accompanied on their voyage to America by a Lutheran pastor, Uno Cygnaeus, later prominent in the development of education in Finland; a few of his papers also exist, including a floor plan of the church he established at Sitka, in the National Archives in Helsinki.

Etholen's assistant, Lieutenant Johan Bartram, later prominent in Finland as a civil engineer, also left papers, which survive in Helsinki in the hands of a descendant. Dr. Edward Blashke, a physician in Novo-Arkhangel'sk at that time, published an account of the region, stressing medical aspects, particularly from the point of view of topography and climate, which he thought had a strong effect on health. This book is in Latin,[13] but the Alaska Historical Library in Juneau possesses two unpublished English translations.

Letters from another native of Finland, Johan Hampus Furuhjelm, governor at the colonial capital from 1859 to 1863, survived in the hands of descendants until World War II, when some were destroyed in a fire. The present author is fortunate to have obtained copies of others the originals of which have also since burned. Descendants of Dr. Alexander Franckenhaeuser, a physician at Novo-Arkhangel'sk during Furuhjelm's time, now live near Helsinki. They preserve some of his letters and have provided copies to the author. Descendants of Captain Lars Krogius, a Finnish sea captain who made several round-the-world voyages on Russian American Company vessels and later founded the well-known Finland Steamship Company, provided me with copies of two watercolors of the capital in the 1850s which are among his papers in the family archive in Helsinki. The diary of the Lutheran pastor Gabriel Plathan, in Novo-Arkhangel'sk from 1845 to 1852, is also to be found in the library of the University of Helsinki.[14]

The governor's brother, Enoch Hjalmar Furuhjelm, a mining engineer, was employed in the Ural region of Russia. Rejected by the girl he loved, he signed on with the Russian American Company to go to the most remote place he could think of, Novo-Arkhangel'sk. He was given the task of opening a coal mine at English Bay on the Kenai Peninsula. His diary, preserved by his descendants in Finland, describes at length the tedious voyage around the world and a trip to San Francisco to buy a steam engine and mining machinery. Letters summarize his years at English Bay. His papers also include several specimens of Russian American Company paper currency of a type devised especially for workers on the coal mining project, recently sold to a private collection in Helsinki.

Probably still more Russian American Company material remains to be found in Finland. Parish records now in the National Archives in

Helsinki record the names of scores of individuals who left for service in Novo-Arkhangel'sk in the 1850s and 1860s. These people must have sent home letters and souvenirs, some of which might still exist in private hands—if they could be located.

Furuhjelm was succeeded by Prince Maksutov (1863–67), the last governor of Russian America. After 1917, one son left Russia and entered the U.S. merchant marine. He had a few small items pertaining to his father—a notebook, a couple of letters, and photographs—and in turn handed these to his son, a petroleum engineer now living in New York. They provide a record of the elder Maksutov's voyages and crossings of Siberia, two marriages (his first wife lies in the Sitka cemetery), births and deaths, and bankruptcy.

Such facts are not trivial; they restore some of the flavor of former times, aid understanding of historical figures and their problems, and can sometimes be combined with other facts, like parts of a mosaic, to form a larger picture. For example, in 1906 the Emperor Nicholas II gave an ornate silver goblet to the Sitka resident George Kostromitinov in recognition of the latter's service to the Russian community and church. What had become of it? It was possible to trace the goblet to one of Kostromitinov's descendants, living in California. Moreover, she also has several pieces of furniture, a samovar, and several other items from the old residence of the Russian governors at Novo-Arkhangel'sk, popularly (and inaccurately) known as "Baranov's castle." The Beinecke Library at Yale University possesses a watercolor made about 1869 by Vincent Collyer, of the ballroom of the "castle." A postcard formerly on sale in Sitka shows a photograph of another room, perhaps the governor's study, with the ornate furnishings of the time. The Alaska Historical Library at Juneau has an inventory taken in the early 1860s enumerating the items of furniture in different rooms in the castle and in other quarters occupied by company personnel. This in turn ties in with a sketch, in the Etholen family papers, showing the layout of both floors of the castle. Contemporary accounts provide further details. These materials give an idea of the castle interior, and combined with photographs of the exterior taken before the building burned in 1894, could even permit its reconstruction.

Many private collectors have interesting material, usually given little advertisement. The late Alexander Dolgopolov, of Laguna Beach, California, from the time of his arrival in the United States in 1922 until his death in 1977, collected everything relevant to Russian America which he could find, and carried on a worldwide correspondence in search of information. The Dolgopolov collection has been donated to the Alaska Historical Library in Juneau. Another collector in Montreal possesses an imperial citation issued Lieutenant Waxell, one of Bering's officers, in the 1740s. Beautifully decorated, it contains miniature pictures of ships—including one of Bering's vessel—animals, natives of eastern Siberia and Alaska, and Russian fur hunters. And a collector in Pasadena has several specimens of the valuable Russian American Company currency, found under a false bottom in an old compass case.

A survey of archival materials on Russian history throughout the United States now being conducted by the Kennan Institute will help to locate other resources of this type. But useful information can also be conveyed by nondocumentary materials and means. Archaeological investigation of the sites of Russian settlement would yield very much, but so far only "Old Sitka" has been excavated—and rather badly—in the 1930s, leaving Slavorossiia (Yakutat), Ozerskoi Redoubt, Nuchek, the English Bay coal mining settlement, and Voskresenskaia Gavan' (Resurrection Bay), to name only a few former places of habitation, untouched except by souvenir hunters.

Museum collections on Russian America are surprisingly sparse, but should not be neglected. The various chief managers sent home priceless ethnographic collections, now to be seen in Leningrad, Helsinki, Copenhagen, and Berlin, but nothing to illustrate the Russian way of life. Native artifacts were cherished for their novelty, whereas Russian artifacts were commonplace, and hence used until they wore out and were discarded. Therefore, in the whole of Alaska there are hardly enough objects to fit out a single museum room. Only the Sitka Historical Society owns enough items of the time of the transfer or soon afterward to furnish portions of a bedroom and a living room. Otherwise, the few original items still existing are scattered far and wide. A number of cannon have been preserved, and there are two or three falconets, but probably no musket, pistol, or powder horn of the time. Samovars, most of them imported long after 1867, are often seen, cherished as symbols of a gracious way of life which scarcely existed during the Russian period except in the governor's mansion. The State Historical Museum at Juneau has copper pots and other utensils; in the Sheldon Jackson Museum at Sitka are several pieces of furniture made by Father Veniaminov. The National Historic Park at Sitka displays artifacts from "Old Sitka," including a unique "possession plate." In the museum of the University of Alaska at Fairbanks may be seen a specimen of Russian brick tea; and the Kodiak Historical Society exhibits a perhaps unique example of a torsion trap, used before the introduction of the steel trap. These items, along with an occasional coin, brick, or handful of rusty nails, are little enough to represent one hundred and twenty years.

All of the foregoing books, documents, and artifacts contribute to our knowledge of Russian America. Inevitably, there have also been losses. A newspaper article enumerating items being assembled for the Alaska-Yukon-Pacific Exposition in Seattle in 1908 mentioned paintings by Natalia Shelikhova, who with her husband spent the years 1784 to 1786 on Kodiak Island. What were these? There is nothing else to indicate that Mrs. Shelikhova could paint, but even if they were wrongly attributed and were from later in the Russian period they would still be of great interest. However, no further mention of them has been found in accounts of the exposition or of the Alaska exhibit.

The Etholen papers include a description of Sitka illustrated by several paintings of the town made by looking in various directions from the "castle." They were evidently sent to Finland, but whether they still exist is unknown.

Some of Baron von Wrangell's letters were taken to India by a female descendant, a missionary. During World War II she died there, and her effects, including the letters, vanished.

Papers of General Tidball, with the U.S. Army force which took over Alaska in 1867, including diaries about Sitka and Kodiak, sketches, and letters, were listed in the catalog of a Philadelphia dealer in 1966, priced even then at $5,000. Hoping to find the present owner and consult the papers, the present author managed to get in touch with the dealer, only to find that all of the material had been stolen soon after the catalog was issued and never recovered.

In 1906, a great deal of Alaska material went up in smoke in the San Francisco fire. Some of it was in the hands of individuals; much was in the Alaska Commercial Company building, which was among those destroyed. Some papers of the Alaska Commercial Company fortunately are still extant and can be found at the University of Alaska at Fairbanks and at Stanford University.

Buildings can be as perishable as written sources. At Sitka, fire consumed the "castle" in 1894, and the cathedral in 1966, although the latter was soon rebuilt. Decay and demolition have removed most of the other pre-1867 buildings in the one-time capital. A road was put through the cemetery, and the site of "Old Sitka" was bulldozed away during World War II. Elsewhere, tidal waves and "urban renewal" have taken their toll. At California's Fort Ross, the southern extension of Russian America, arsonists burned the chapel in 1970, though it, too, has since been rebuilt.

Much, then, has been found, and much has been lost. The perishable nature of historical material, especially that which is unorganized and in private hands, vulnerable to fire and theft, is clear and provides good reason for hastening the development of resources in this field.

What are the specific needs for advancement of the study of Russian America? Much more bibliographic research is required. A biographical dictionary is needed, one which can provide facts on the many people—native, Russian, British, French, Spanish, German, Scandinavian and American—who have figured in the period studied. A detailed chronology is needed. The last was compiled in 1870 by William Healey Dall, in his *Alaska and Its Resources* (Boston, 1870). Such a work, with close attention to dates, could provide a standard against which many conflicting accounts of events could be compared and corrected. Along this line, a list of voyages made during the Russian period would be useful. Judge F. W. Howay's *List of Trading Vessels on the Northwest Coast, 1785–1825* clarifies the comings and goings of foreign vessels, but mentions few Russian voyages.[15]

Closer attention ought to be given to paintings, sketches, and photographs which together provide the only visual record we have of the Russian period. No photographs are known to have been made in Alaska before Eadweard Muybridge's visit to Sitka in 1868, but his and later photographs are indicative of the architecture and appearance of the settlement in earlier times.

Ethnohistory, a new concept of investigation, needs to be pursued more extensively. Featuring the use of archaeology, ethnography, history, and other disciplines, it provides new information about early societies, the nature of native society at the time of contact with Europeans, and subsequent exchange of cultural traits. Oral history is a related technique which should be used to greater effect. The recollections of old-timers, coupled with other research, can help in reconstructing the society of the years following the American purchase of Alaska. Native traditions can sometime corroborate or supplement what is known from other means. In the Aleutian Islands there were until recent times traditions of early visits of Russian explorers and fur traders. The Tlingits of Yakutat have handed down for generations a vivid and consistent story of the establishment of the Russian settlement of Slavorossiia and its destruction in 1806. Around present-day Sitka, the destruction of the original Russian establishment—"Old Sitka"—in 1802 and the retreat over the mountains by the natives after the Russian reconquest in 1804 are still narrated.

Genealogical research can also be expanded. Extensive data was collected in connection with native claims. Proof of native blood was required, so genealogies were assembled which in many cases went back to the early Russian period. This information, combined with that in the records of the Russian American Company and the Alaska Church Collection, would make it possible to list most of the people who were in the Russian-occupied areas of Alaska over many generations and down to the present. Computer science would enable conclusions to be drawn as to origins, occupations, longevity, age and sex ratios, and public health.

Much more data can still be gathered on daily life in Russian America. Such data could provide a more realistic picture of the culture that was lost in 1867, or which declined thereafter. We need to know more about uniforms and everyday dress, about charcoal making, carpentry, blacksmithing, boat building, stevedoring, and architecture. We need to know about cookery, kitchen utensils, weaponry, songs, reading matter, bookkeeping, social groups, and holidays. The study of printed and manuscript sources, archaeological excavations, oral history, and the examination of analogous settlements of the same era in eastern Siberia will help to narrow this gap.

Notes

The Discovery of Russian America

1   J. Baker, *Istoriia geograficheskikh otkrytii i issledovanii* (Moscow, 1950) p. 231, a translation of *A History of Geographical Discovery and Exploration* (London, 1945).

2   On the determination of the precise date of I. U. Moskvitin's exit onto the Pacific, see *Strany i narody Vostoka*, no. 20 (Moscow, 1979), 93–96.

3   For the significance of the "large rocky bow" concept, see B. P. Polevoi, "O tochnom tekste dvukh otpisok Semena Dezhneva 1655 goda," in *Izvestiia akademii nauk SSSR: Seriia geograficheskaia* 2 (1965): 102–10. See also R. H. Fisher, "Dezhnev's Voyage of 1648 in the Light of Soviet Scholarship," *Terrae Incognitae* 5 (1973): 7–26; and R. H. Fisher, *The Voyage of Semen Dezhnev in 1648, Bering's Precursor with Selected Documents* (London: The Hakluyt Society, 1981), 220–37.

4   For example see L. S. Berg, *Otkrytie Kamchatki i ekspeditsii Beringa 1725–1742* (Moscow/Leningrad, 1946), 30.

5   Afanasii Mel'nikov's report on Alaskan Eskimos may be cited as an example: "It is a day's journey on foot from the Chukotsk rocky bow to their dwellings on the island on to the island called the 'big land,'" *Polnoe sobranie zakonov rossiiskoi imperii*, 8:100.

6   See *Izvestiia akademii nauk SSSR: Seriia geograficheskaia*, 2 (1965): 109; see also B. P. Polevoi, "Iz istorii otkrytiia severo-zapadnoi chasti Amerika (ot pervogo izvestiia sibirskikh zemleprokhodtsev ob Aliaske do pervogo plana poiska morskogo puti k Amerike," in *Ot Aliaski do Ognennoi Zemli* (Moscow, 1967), 108.

7   *Zapiski russkogo geograficheskogo obshchestva po otdeleniiu etnografii* 10, no. 1 (1882): 123.

8   The question of the possible connection between Asia and America had also previously interested several Muscovites. Even before N. G. Spafarii was sent to Siberia in early 1675, an original "account which indicated it is impossible to cross over

to the Chinese state by sea and thence to West India" was produced in the Secret Affairs Department. It contains the phrase: "Is the New Land an island or solid ground linked to America; i.e., adjoined to the New World: Many geographers have said that the New Land adjoins North America"; see *Russko-kitaiskie otnosheniia v 17-om veke; Materialy i dokumenty* (Moscow, 1969), 1: 488.

9 A. A. Titov, *Sibir' v 17-om veke: Sbornik starinnykh russkikh statei o Sibiri i prilezhashchikh k nei zemliakh* (Moscow, 1890), 53–54.

10 B. P. Polevoi, "K istorii formirovaniia geograficheskikh predstavlenii o severo-vostochnoi okonechnosti Azii v 17 v. (Izvestiia o 'kamennoi peregrade'. Vozniknovenie i dal'neishaia metamorfoza legendy o 'neobkhodymom nose')," in *Sibirskii geograficheskii sbornik*, no. 3 (Moscow/Leningrad, 1964), 224–70.

11 *Russkie morekhody v Ledovitom i Tikhom okeanakh: Sbornik dokumentov o velikikh russkikh geograficheskikh otkrytiiakh na severo-vostoke Azii v 17 veke*, comp. M. I. Belov (Leningrad/Moscow, 1952), 116.

12 *Dopolneniia k aktam istoricheskim, sobrannyia i izdannyia arkheograficheskoi kommissiiei* 6, no. 13G (St. Petersburg, 1857), II, p. 407.

13 For details see Polevoi, "K istorii formirovaniia," 227, 239.

14 Titov, *Sibir v 17-om veke*, 53–54. S. P. Krasheninnikov noted this also: "As the land is so narrow in these places, reliable reports indicate that in good weather the sea is visible on both sides from the high mountains," *Opisanie zemli Kamchatki* (Moscow, 1949), 99.

15 On data indicating that the "stone protrusion" was believed to be the Kamchatka Peninsula, see Polevoi, "K istorii formirovaniia," 227.

16 The M. E. Saltykov-Shchedrin State Public Library, Leningrad, Manuscript Division, Ermitazhnoe sobranie no. 376: 20.

17 Titov, *Sibir' v 17-om veke*, 84–85.

18 In greater detail: B. P. Polevoi, "O proiskhozhdenii nazvaniia 'Kamchatka,'" in *V. P. Kuskov Kratkii toponimicheskii slovar' Kamchatskoi oblasti* (Petropavlovsk-Kamchatskii, 1967), 96–112.

19 See L. S. Bagrow, *Sparvenfeld's Map of Siberia*, (London, 1947), 70.

20 See M. P. Alekseev, *Sibir' v izvestiiakh zapadnoevropeiskikh puteshestvennikov i pisatelei. Vvedenie, teksty i kommentarii 13–17 vv.*, 2d ed. (Irkutsk, 1941), 464.

21 In Ibid. The original is Ph. Avril, *Voyage en divers etats d'Europe et d'Asia enterpris pour découvrir un nouveau chemin a la Chine* (Paris, 1692), 211.

22 Only two copies of Witsen's map have been preserved in the USSR. The first is held in the cartography division of the M. E. Saltykov-Shchedrin State Public Library in Leningrad. In 1977 the second was found in the F. R. Osten-Saken collection in the Central State Archive of Ancient Documents in Moscow. For the best reproduction of this map, see F. G. Kramp, *Remarkable Maps of the 15th, 16th, and 17th Centuries* (Amsterdam, 1897), vol. 4.

23 B. P. Polevoi, "Piotr Pervyi, Nikolai Witsen: Problema 'sochlas li Amerika s Aziei,'" *Strany i narody Vostoka*, no. 17 (Moscow, 1975), 21.

24 Berg, *Otkrytie Kamchatki*, 44–45.

25 Polevoi, "Piotr Pervyi," 22.

26 See the journal *Priroda* 5 (1965): 94.

27 A. Kamienski-Dluzyk, *Dyaryusz wiezienia moskiewskiego, miast i miejsc spisany przez Adam Kamienskiego-Warta. Ksiazka zbiorowa ofiarowana ksiedzu Franciszkowi Bazynskiemu proboszczowi przy Kosciele sw. Wojciecha w Poznaniu na Jubileusz 50-letniego kaplanstwa w dniu 23 kwietnia 1874 r. od jego przyjaciol i wielbicieli* (Poznan, 1874), 378; B. P. Polevoi, "O prebyvanii v Rossii Adama Kamenskogo-Dluzhika, avtora pervogo pol'skogo sochineniia o Sibiri," in *Historia kantaktow Polsko-Rosyjskich w dziedzinie geologii i geografii—Monografie z dziejow nauki i techniki* (Wroclaw, 1972), 82: 276–81.

28 Five copies of the 1667 general map of Siberia are known. Three are Swedish and two are by S. U. Remezov, the first of which was included in the so-called *Khorograficheskaia chertezhnaia kniga* (S. U. Remezov, *Atlas of Siberia*, ed. L. Bagrow [The Hague, 1958], 4); the second is in the *Sluzhebnaia chertezhnaia kniga*, which is preserved in the M. E. Saltykov-Shchedrin State Public Library, Leningrad, Manuscript Division, Ermitazhnoe sobranie no. 237: 30.

29 A. V. Florovsky, *Maps of the Siberian Route of the Belgian Jesuit A. Thomas, 1690* (London, 1951) 8: 103–8.

30 Cited herein based on: M. P. Alekseev, *Sibir' v izvestiiak*, 482; and J. B. Du-Halde, *Description geographique, historique, chronologique, politique et physique de l'empire de la Chine et la Tartarie Chinoise*, ed. by P. G. Lemercier (Paris, 1735) 4: 57.

31 N. Witsen, *Noord en Oost Tartarye* (Amsterdam, 1705), 799. Russian translation: V. G. Trisman, "O russkoi etnograficheskoi karte 17 v.," in *Kratkie soobshcheniia instituta etnografii AN SSSR* 10 (1950): 56.

32 D. J. Ray, *The Eskimos of the Bering Strait, 1650–1895* (Seattle/London, 1975).

33 N. N. Ogloblin, "Dve 'skazki' Vl. Atlasova ob otkrytii Kamchatki," in *Chteniia v obshchestve istorii i drevnostei Rossiiskikh pri Moskovskom universitete* 3 (1891): 1, 12.

34 A. V. Efimov, *Iz istorii velikikh russkikh geograficheskikh otkrytii na Severnom Ledovitom i Tikhom okeanakh, 17 i pervaia polovina 18 vv.* (Moscow, 1950), 142.

35 Witsen, *Noord en Oost Tartarye*, 71.

36 Polevoi, "Piotr Pervyi," 22.

37 See: *Atlas geograficheskikh otkrytii v Sibiri i v severozapadnoi Amerike 17–18 vv.*, ed., with an introduction by A. V. Efimov (Moscow, 1964), pl. 48, 50, 54, 55, 60.

38 In Tobolsk, however, the Swedish prisoner Tabbert (Stralenberg) heard a version of a possible junction between the "New Land" and the "Big Land" across from the Chukotsk Peninsula. This notion was embodied in his 1717 map of Siberia, which later became the property of the merchant P. V. Müller. Tabbert quickly became convinced that this version was incorrect, and in his subsequent maps he portrayed the Big Land as a separate land.

39 See K. Müller, *Gottfried Wilhelm Leibnitz und Nicolaas Witsen* (Berlin, 1955), 6.

40 *Sbornik pisem i memorialov Leibnitsa, otnosiashchikhsia k Rossii i Petru Velikomu*, ed. V. Ger'e (St. Petersburg, 1873), 19.

41 V. Ger'e, *Otnoshenie Leibnitsa k Rossii i Petru Velikomu, po neizdannym bumagam Leibnitsa v gannoverskoi biblioteke* (St. Petersburg, 1871), 146–47.

42 Ibid., 187.

43 Ibid.

44 L. S. Berg, *Otkrytie Kamchatki* (Leningrad, 1935), 7–9.

45 Cf. B. P. Polevoi, "O 'Pogyche'—Pokhache," *Voprosy geografii Kamchatki* 6 (1970): 82–85.

46 A photocopy of the copy of these instructions was included by A. I. Andreev in *Izvestiia VGO* 2 (1943): 5; and by V. Y. Vize in his book *Moria sovetskoi arktiki* (Moscow, 1948), 60.

47 This concept was elaborated on at length by A. S. Sgibnev in the article "Popytki russkikh k zavedeniiu torgovykh cnoshenii s Iaponiei v 18 i nachale 19 stoletiia," *Morskoi sbornik* 1 (1969): 41; and particularly by S. I. Baskin in the article "Puteshestvie Evreinova i Luzhina v Kuril'skii arkhipelag," *Izvestiia VGO* 4 (1952): 363–79.

48 This is discussed in detail in Witsen, *Noord en Oost*, 123.

49 Ibid., 63.

50 A. I. Andreev, "Ekspeditsii na vostok do Beringa: V sviazi s kartografiei Sibiri pervoi chetverti 18 veka," *Trudy istoriko-arkhivnogo instituta* (Moscow, 1946) 2: 198.

51 *Ekspeditsiia Beringa: Sbornik dokumentov*, ed. A. Pokrovskii, Glavnoe arkhivnoe upravlenie (Moscow, 1941), 21.

52 A photocopy of this document was first published by F. A. Golder in *Bering's Voyages: An Account of the Efforts of the Russians to Learn the Relation of Asia and America* (New York, 1922), 1: 7.

53 Pokrovskii, *Ekspeditsiia Beringa*, 59.

54 B. P. Polevoi, "O karte Kamchadalii I. B. Homann 1722 G.," *Izvestiia AN SSSR, seriia geograficheskaia* 1 (1970): 99–105.

55 On interpretation of Peter I's instructions see B. P. Polevoi, "Glavnaia zadacha pervoi Kamchatskoi ekspeditsii po zamyslu Petra I," *Voprosy geografii Kamchatki* 2 (1964): 88–94.

56 See map in Polevoi, "Iz istorii otkrytiia," 112; or Polevoi, "Piotr Pervyi," 30.

57 Pokrovskii, *Ekspeditsiia Beringa*, 273.

58 Ibid., 206.

59 Polevoi, "Piotr Pervyi," 27.

60 In St. Petersburg Bering was reproached for sailing northward "even to a latitude of 67 degrees," Pokrovskii, *Eskpeditsiia Beringa*, 91.

61 These maps by Joseph Delisle have been reproduced in the literature repeatedly. See M. Zhdanko, "Raboty russkikh moriakov v Okhotskom more," *Zapiski po gidrografii* 5 (1916): 844; F. A. Golder, *Bering's Voyages*, 1:72; S. Vaksel', *Vtoraia Kamchatskaia, Vitusa Beringa*, ed. A. I. Andreev (Leningrad/Moscow, 1940), 56; *Atlas geograficheskikh otkrytii*, 78, and other publications.

62 See S. Vaksel' *Vtoraia Kamchatskaia*, 51.

63 Pokrovskii, *Ekspeditsiia Beringa*, 29–30.

64 See S. G. Fedorova, *Russkoe naselenie Aliaski i Kalifornii* (Moscow, 1971), 82, 103, 104.

65 *Polnoe sobranie zakonov Rossiiskoi imperii* 8:749 (no. 6023); 774 (no. 6042).

66 M. V. Lomonosov, *Polnoe sobranie sochinenii* (Moscow/Leningrad, 1959), 8:703.

67 P. A. Tikhmenev, *Istoricheskoe obozrenie obrazovaniia Rossiisko-amerikanskoi kompanii i deistvii ee do nastoiashchego vremeni* (St. Petersburg, 1861), 267.

68 R. V. Makarova, *Russkie na Tikhom okeane vo vtoroi polovine XVIII-ogo veka* (Moscow, 1968), 47.

69 Archive of the Geographical Society of the USSR, razriad 60, no. 3:27.

70 I. Veniaminov, *Zapiski ob ostrovakh Unalashkinskogo otdela*, pt. 2 (St. Petersburg, 1840), 2.

71 Berg, *Otkrytie Kamchatki*, 225–26. He borrowed this version from *Handbook of American Indians*, pt. 1, ed. E. Hodge (Washington, D.C., 1912), 36.

72 I. S. Vdovin, "K voprosy o proiskhozhdenii nazvaniia 'aleut,'" *Strany i narody Vostoka*, no. 6 (Moscow, 1968), 102.

73 Ibid.

74 Ibid., 103

75 Ibid., 103.

76 See R. G. Liapunova, "Novyi dokument ob rannikh plavaniiakh na Aleutskie ostrova ('Izvestiia' Fedora Afanas'evicha Kul'kova, 1764 g.)," in *Strany i narody Vostoka*, no. 20 (Moscow, 1979), 100, 104.

77 G. A. Menovshchikov, *Sovetskaia etnografiia* 1 (1980): 109–16.

78 For comprehensive information on G. A. Menovshchikov's work, see M. E. Kraus, "Eskimo-Aleut," in *Modern Trends in Linguistics*, 10:800–49, 875–76.

79 See "Otkrytie neizvestnykh ostrovov kazakom Ponamarevym," in *Arkhiv admirala P. V. Chichagova* (St. Petersburg, 1885), 1:133, 134; "O Kamchatskoi ekspeditsii 1758 goda (Rukopis' 17 v.)," in *Shchukinskii sbornik* 5 (1906): 172—73; *Russkye otkrytiia v Tikhom okeane i Severnoi Amerike v 18 i 19 vekakh*, 28, 29.

80 M. V. Lomonosov, *Polnoe sobranie sochinenii* (Moscow/Leningrad, 1952), 6:510.

81 Ibid.

82 O. M. Medushevskaia, "Kartograficheskie istochniki po istorii Russkikh geograficheskikh otkrytii na Tikhom okeane vo vtoroi polovine 17 veka," in *Trudy moskovskogo gosudarstvenogo istoriko-arkhivnogo institua* (Moscow, 1954), 7:105.

83 On his work on this map, see M. V. Lomonosov, *Polnoe sobranie sochinenii*, 6:507–14.

84 In detail: B. P. Polevoi, "O rannem variante vtoroi poliarnoi karty M. V. Lomonosova," in *Izvestiia AN SSSR, seriia geograficheskaia* 2 (1977): 122–34. A color copy of this map was published in the journal *Nauka i zhizn'* 12 (1976).

85 M. V. Lomonosov, *Polnoe sobranie sochinenii*, 6:511.

86 R. V. Makarova, *Russkie na Tikhom okeane*, 144.

87 See A. V. Efimov, *Atlas geograficheskikh otkrytii*, map 149, and also A. V. Efimov, *Iz istorii velikikh*, 166–67. Bechevin himself remained in Irkutsk.

88 B. P. Polevoi, "O rannem variante," 126.

89 R. V. Makarova, *Russkie na Tikhom okeane*, 59, 61.

90 "O Kamchatskoi ekspeditsii 1758 goda," 172–73.

91 B. P. Polevoi, "O rannem variante," 126.

92 I. V. Glushankov, *Sekretnaia ekspeditsiia Krenitsyna-Levashova*, 58.

93 S. G. Fedorova, "Issledovatel' Chukotki i Aliaski: Kazachii sotnik Ivan Kobelev," *Letopis' severa* 5 (1971): 156–72.

94 *Pamiatniki sibirskoi istorii*, no. 1 (St. Petersburg, 1883), 456–59.

95 See the chart of Chukotsk and Anadyr in *Atlas geograficheskikh otkrytii*, map 55, or in A. V. Efimov, *Iz istorii velikikh*, 156–57.

96 Ibid.

97 See *Atlas geograficheskikh otkrytii*, 1964, maps 48, 50, 55, 60. For a new dating for these maps see B. P. Polevoi, "Semen Remezov i Vladimir Atlasov," in *Izvestiia AN SSSR, seriia geograficheskogo* 2 (1970): 99–105.

98   B. P. Polevoi, "O karte Kamchadalii Y. B. Homanna 1722 g.," 99–105.

99   A. V. Efimov, *Iz istorii velikikh*, 204.

100. Ibid.

101   A. S. Sbignev, "Bol'shoi Kamchatskii nariad," in *Morskoi sbornik*, 1868, no. 12:138.

102   Shestakovs appeared on Kolyma as early as the mid-seventeenth century.

103   *Tzentral'nyi arkhiv drevnich aktov, Fond Iakutskoi prikaznoi izby*, schedule 3, 1697, no. 3.

104   Fedorov and Gvozdev's expedition is described by V. A. Divin, *K beregam Ameriki* (Moscow, 1956).

105   See the composite map of the Second Kamchatkan Expedition of 1746, in *Atlas geograficheskikh otkrytii*, map 111.

106   Pokrovskii, *Ekspeditsiia Beringa*, 207.

107   A. I. Andreev, *Russkie otkrytiia*, 106.

108   Pokrovskii, *Ekspeditsiia Beringa*, 207.

109   B. P. Polevoi, "Piotr Pervyi," 24.

110   M. V. Lomonosov, *Polnoe sobranoe sochinenii*, 6:451. Lomonosov wrote that "The well-known geodecist Gvozdev has said that there is land—an island or a continent—across from the Chukotsk cape; reports by the local inhabitants support this. All this land unquestionably is part of America, since it is known from the tales of the Chuchki and the people stranded there that this is an enormous land with a large number of people, forests and animals and great flowing rivers." (Ibid., 451).

111   For a critique of this version, see A. V. Efimov, *Iz istorii velikikh*, 209–12.

112   S. G. Fedorova, *Russkoe naselenie Aliaski i Kalifornii*, 89–95.

113   Ibid., 79–88.

114   S. G. Fedorova, *Pervoe postoiannoe poselenie Russkikh v Amerike i Dzh. Kuk; Novoe v izuchenii Avstralii i Okeanii* (Moscow, 1972), 228–36.

115   B. P. Polevoi, *Grigorii Shelikhov-Kolumb Russkii* (Magadan, 1960), 32–33.

116   Ibid.

117   S. B. Okun, *Rossiisko-amerikanskaia kompaniia* (Moscow/Leningrad, 1939), 32–33.

118   See A. V. Efimov, *Atlas geograficheskikh otkrytii*, map 184.

119   For new information on the circumstances surrounding the death of G. I. Shelikhov, see G. I. Shelikhov, *Rossiiskogo kuptsa Grigoriia Shelikhova stranstvovaniia iz Okhotska po vostochnomu okeanu k amerikanskim beregam* (Khabarovsk, 1971), 125.

120   *Russkie otkrytiia v Tikhom okeane i Severnoi Amerike v 18 veke; Sbornik dokumentov*, ed. A. I. Andreev (Moscow, 1948), 342. On August 9, 1794, G. I. Shelikhov asked A. A. Baranov to name the main Russian settlement "beyond the St Ilia Cape 'Slavorossiia' in honor of Russia's glory."

Russian Expansion in Siberia and America

This paper appeared in somewhat different form in *The Geographical Review* 70 (1980): 127–36, and appears here with the permission of Douglas McManis, the editor.

1   See George V. Lantzeff and Richard A. Pierce, *Eastward to Empire: Exploration and Conquest on the Russian Open Frontier, to 1750* (Montreal and London, 1973). Also

see John A. Harrison, *The Founding of the Russian Empire in Asia and America* (Coral Gables, 1971), and George Alexander Lensen, ed., *Russia's Eastward Expansion* (Englewood Cliffs, 1964).

2 See Raymond H. Fisher, *The Russian Fur Trade, 1550–1700* (Berkeley and Los Angeles, 1943); P. N. Pavlov, *Pushnoi promysel v Sibiri XVII v.* (Krasoiarsk, 1972); and P. N. Pavlov, *Promyslovaia kolonizatsiia Sibiri v XVII v.* (Krasnoiarsk, 1974).

3 See Donald W. Treadgold, *The Great Siberian Migration: Government and Peasant in Resettlement from Emancipation to the First World War* (Princeton, 1957); M. M. Gromyko, *Zapadnaia Sibir' v XVIII v.: Russkoe naselenie i zemledel'cheskoe osvoenie* (Novosibirsk, 1965); Francois-Xavier Coquin, *La Sibérie: Peuplement et immigration paysanne au XIXe siècle* (Paris, 1969); George Kennan, *Siberia and the Exile System*, 2 vols. (New York, 1891); and L. M. Goriushkin, ed., *Ssylka i katorga v Sibiri (XVIII-nachalo XX v.)* (Novosibirsk, 1975).

4 See James R. Gibson, "Sables to Sea Otters: Russia Enters the Pacific," *Alaska Review* 3 (1968–69): 203–17.

5 D. W. Meinig, "A Macrogeography of Western Imperialism: Some Morphologies of Moving Frontiers of Political Control," in *Settlement & Encounter: Geographical Studies Presented to Sir Grenfell Price*, ed. Fay Gale and G. H. Lawton (Melbourne, 1969), 213–40.

6 Richard A. Pierce, ed., *Documents on the History of the Russian-American Company*, trans. Marina Ramsay (Kingston, 1976), 38.

7 See James R. Gibson, "The Russian Fur Trade," in *Old Trails and New Directions: Papers of the Third North American Fur Trade Conference*, ed. Carol M. Judd and Arthur J. Ray (Toronto, 1980), 217–30.

8 See R. G. Liapunova, *Ocherki po etnografii Aleutov (konets XVIII-pervaia polovina XIX v.)* (Leningrad, 1975).

9 Archibald Campbell, *A Voyage Round the World . . .* (Honolulu, 1967), 46.

10 Margaret Lantis, "The Aleut Social System, 1750 to 1810, from Early Historical Sources," in *Ethnohistory in Southwestern Alaska and the Southern Yukon*, ed. Margaret Lantis (Lexington, 1970), 179.

11 See Clifford M. Foust, *Muscovite and Mandarin: Russia's Trade with China and Its Setting, 1727–1805* (Chapel Hill, 1969).

12 A. P. Okladnikov and V. I. Shunkov, eds., *Istoriia Sibiri* (Leningrad, 1968), 2:183.

13 See V. I. Shunkov, *Ocherki po istorii zemledeliia Sibiri (XVII vek)* (Moscow, 1956).

14 James R. Gibson, *Imperial Russia in Frontier America: The Changing Geography of Supply of Russian America, 1784–1867* (New York, 1976), 20.

15 See R. M. Kabo, *Goroda Zapadnoi Sibiri: Ocherki istoriko-ekonomicheskoi geografii (XVII-pervaia polovina XIX vv.)* (Moscow, 1949); O. N. Vilkov, ed., *Goroda Sibiri (ekonomika, upravlenie i kul'tura gorodov Sibiri v dosovetskii period)* (Novosibirsk, 1974); O. N. Vilkov, ed., *Istoriia gorodov Sibiri dosovetskogo perioda (XVII-nachalo XX v.)* (Novosibirsk, 1977); O. N. Vilkov, ed., *Goroda Sibiri (epokha feodalizma i kapitalizma)* (Novosibirsk, 1978); and O. N. Vilkov, ed., *Sibirskie goroda XVII-nachala XX veka* (Novosibirsk, 1981).

16 See James R. Gibson, "The Significance of Cook's Third Voyage to Russian Tenure in the North Pacific," *Pacific Studies* 1 (1978): 119–46.

17   See Mary E. Wheeler, "Empires in Conflict and Cooperation: The 'Bostonians' and the Russian-American Company," *Pacific Historical Review* 40 (1971): 419–41. Also see Howard I. Kushner, *Conflict on the Northwest Coast: American-Russian Rivalry in the Pacific Northwest, 1790–1867* (Westport, 1975); and James R. Gibson, "Bostonians and Muscovites on the Northwest Coast, 1788–1841," in *The Western Shore: Oregon Country Essays Honoring the American Revolution,* ed. Thomas Vaughan (Portland, 1975), 81–119.

18   See James R. Gibson, *Feeding the Russian Fur Trade: Provisionment of the Okhotsk Seaboard and the Kamchatka Peninsula, 1639–1856* (Madison, 1969).

19   See Richard A. Pierce, *Russia's Hawaiian Adventure, 1815–1817* (Berkeley and Los Angeles, 1965).

20   See N. Nozikov, *Russian Voyages Round the World,* trans. Ernst and Mira Lesser (London, n.d.); and E. F. McCartan, "The Long Voyages—Early Russian Circumnavigation," *Russian Review* 22 (1963): 30–37.

21   Gibson, *Imperial Russia,* 18; Okladnikov and Shunkov, *Istoriia Sibiri,* 2: 183.

22   Gibson, *Imperial Russia,* 18.

23   See Svetlana G. Fedorova, *The Russian Population in Alaska and California Late 18th Century–1867,* trans. Richard A. Pierce and Alton S. Donnelly (Kingston, 1973).

24   Gibson, *Imperial Russia,* 47. Also see James R. Gibson, "Smallpox on the Northwest Coast, 1835–1838," *BC Studies* 56 (1982–83): 61–81.

25   R. M. French, *The Eastern Orthodox Church* (London, 1961), 108. Also see Ernst Benz, *The Eastern Orthodox Church* (Garden City, 1963), chap. 7, especially 121–125.

26   See R. V. Makarova, *Russians on the Pacific 1743–1799,* trans. Richard A. Pierce and Alton S. Donnelly (Kingston, 1975). Also see Mary E. Wheeler, "The Origins of the Russian-American Company," *Jahrbücher für Geschichte Osteuropas* 14 (1966): 485–94.

27   See P. A. Tikhmenev, *History of the Russian-American Company,* trans. and ed. Richard A. Pierce and Alton S. Donnelly (Seattle, 1978). Also see S. B. Okun, *The Russian-American Company,* trans. Carl Ginsburg (Cambridge, 1951).

28   See Gibson, *Imperial Russia.*

29   See James R. Gibson, "Old Russia in the New World: Adversaries and Adversities in Russian America," in *European Settlement and Development in North America: Essays on Geographical Change in Honour and Memory of Andrew Hill Clark,* ed. James R. Gibson (Toronto, 1978), 46–65.

30   See James R. Gibson, "Russia on the Pacific: The Role of the Amur," *The Canadian Geographer* 12 (1968): 15–27. Also see Mark Bassin, "The Russian Geographical Society, the 'Amur Epoch,' and the Great Siberian Expedition, 1855–1863," *Annals of the Association of American Geographers* 73 (1983): 240–56; P. I. Kavanov, *Amurskii vopros* (Blagoveshchensk, 1959); R. K. I. Quested, *The Expansion of Russia in East Asia, 1857–1860* (Kuala Lumpur and Singapore, 1968); John J. Stephan, *Sakhalin: A History* (Oxford, 1971); and John J. Stephan, *The Kuril Islands: Russo-Japanese Frontier in the Pacific* (Oxford, 1974).

31   See Geoffrey Wheeler, "Russian Conquest and Colonization of Central Asia," in *Russian Imperialism from Ivan the Great to the Revolution,* ed. Taras Hunczak (New Brunswick, 1974), 264–98. Also see Richard A. Pierce, *Russian Central Asia, 1867–1971: A Study in Colonial Rule* (Berkeley and Los Angeles, 1960).

32 See James R. Gibson, "The Significance of Siberia to Tsarist Russia," *Canadian Slavonic Papers* 14 (1972): 442–53.

The Russian American Company and the Imperial Government

1 *Polnoe sobranie zakonov rossiiskoi imperii s 1649 goda, Sobranie pervoe,* 56 vols. (St. Petersburg, 1830–39), no. 1706 (October 27, 1699), 3:653–54. (Hereinafter cited as *P.S.Z.*)

2 Ibid., no. 19233, 25:923–25. Because the North Pacific was the northeastern ocean in relation to European Russia, Alaska was usually referred to as the Northeast Coast of America.

3 Semen Bentsionovich Okun, *Rossiisko-amerikanskaia kompaniia* (Moscow-Leningrad, 1939), 37, 49; Nikolai Nikolaevich Bolkhovitinov, *Stanovlenie russko-amerikanskikh otnoshenii, 1775–1815* (Moscow, 1966), 304–5; Raisa Vsevolodovna Makarova, *Russkie na Tikhom okeane vo vtoroi polovine XVIII v.* (Moscow, 1968), 159–60; Svetlana Grigor'evna Fedorova, *Russkoe naselenie Aliaski i Kalifornii, konets XVIII veka—1867 r.* (Moscow, 1971), 121–22.

4 Mary E. Wheeler, "The Origins of the Russian-American Company," *Jahrbücher für Geschichte Osteuropas* 14 (1966): 485–94.

5 Vasilii Nikolaevich Berkh, *Khronologicheskaia istoriia otkrytia aleutskikh ostrovov ili podvigi rossiiskago kupechestva s prisovokupleniem istoricheskago izvestiia o tekhovoi torgovle* (St. Petersburg, 1823), prilozhenie 1; Aleksei Vladimirovich Efimov, *Iz istorii russkikh ekspeditsii na Tikhom okeane (pervaia polovina XVIII veka)* (Moscow, 1948), 291–309; Makarova, *Russkie na Tikhom okeane,* 182–88; "Istoricheskii kalendar'," in A. I. Blinov et al., eds., *K istorii Rossisko-amerikanskoi kompanii (Sbornik documental'nikh materialov)* (Krasnoiarsk, 1957), 14–20.

6 The few sources available for the formation of this company do not mention that shares would be sold, but this conclusion has been made on the basis of a letter Shelikhov wrote in 1789, in which he said that "our shares, under the present unsettled conditions are selling for less than seven hundred rubles. If I had not raised the price myself by bringing in one hundred thousand rubles in cash, no one would pay even four hundred rubles for them; however, do not mind this, the time will come when the price of goods will not decrease." "Pis'mo Shelikhova Delarovu," in Aleksandr Ignatevich Andreev, ed., *Russkie otkrytiia v Tikhom okeane i severnoi Amerike v XVIII veke* (Moscow, 1948) 287.

7 Petr Aleksandrovich Tikhmenev, *Istoricheskoe obozrenie obrazovaniia Rossiisko-amerikanskoi kompanii i deistvii ee do nastoiashchago vremeni,* 2 vols. (St. Petersburg, 1861–63), 1, no. 7.

8 Okun, *Rossiisko-amerikanskaia kompaniia,* 31.

9 "Donoshenie G. I. Shelekhova [sic] irkutskomu general-gubernatoru I. V. Iakobi," in Aleksandr Ignatevich Andreev, ed., *Russkie otkrytiia v Tikhom okeane i severnoi Amerike v XVIII–XIX vekakh* (Moscow, 1944), 66–73.

10 Tikhmenev, *Istoricheskoe obozrenie,* 1, no. 7; MS, A. S. Polonskii, "Perechen' puteshestvii russkikh promyshlennykh v Vostochnom okeane," Arkhiv Vsesoiuznogo Geograficheskogo Obshchestva (hereinafter cited as AVGO), razriad 60, op. 1, ed. khr. 2, pp. 95–96.

11   MS, AVGO, 60:1:2:95–96.

12   Blinov, *K istorii Rossiisko-amerikanskoi kompanii*, 20.

13   Golikov accused Shelikhov of not only taking the profits of the company for himself but of "naming himself owner in my place and appropriating all my capital as his own with the assistance of my treacherous clerk, Polevoi." Aleksandr Romanovich Vorontsov to Governor-General Pil', February 22, 1792, Tsentral'nyi Gosudarst-vennyi Arkhiv Drevnikh Aktov (hereinafter cited as TsGADA), f. 1261, op. 1, ed. khr. 745; Golikov to Petr Vasil'evich Lopukhin, December 16, 1798, Tsental'nyi Gosudarstvennyi Istoricheskii Arkhiv (herinafter cited as TsGIA), f. 1374, op. 1, ed. khr. 819.

14   A search of the published documents and of the collections in TsGADA and TsGIA did not reveal any petitions by Lebedev-Lastochkin or the Kiselev brothers.

15.   The reports and petitions have been collected and published by A. I. Andreev in *Russkie otkrytiia v Tikhom okeane i severnoi Amerike v XVIII veke.*

16   June 20 and December 31, 1793, *P.S.Z.*, nos. 17135 and 17171, 23:440–41, 478.

17   Ibid., 23:478.

18   "Pis'mo Shelikhova k Delarovu," in Tikhmenev, *Istoricheskoe obozrenie*, 2:Prilozhenie:25; and "Donoshenie Shelikhova Piliu" and "Raport Pilia," in Andreev, *v XVIII veke*, 295, 303.

19   "Istoricheskii kalendar" and "Predpisanie Shelikhova Popovu," in Blinov, *K istorii Rossiisko-amerikanskoi kompanii*, 21, 53; Tikhmenev, *Istoricheskoe obozrenie*, 1:31–32, 45; *Arkhiv Gosudarstvennago soveta* (hereinafter cited as *A.G.S.*), 16 vols. in 5 (St. Petersburg, 1869–1904), 1, pt. 2, 663–64.

20   "Donoshenie Shelikhova Piliu," November 18, 1794, in Andreev, *v XVIII veke*, 353–86; "Pis'mo Shelikhovoi k Zubovu," November 22, 1795, in Tikhmenev, *Istoricheskoe obozrenie*, 2:Prilozhenie, 111.

21   Tikhmenev, *Istoricheskoe obozrenie*, 1:46–47; Kiril Timofeevich Khlebnikov, "Zhizneopisaniia dostopamiatnykh Russkikh: Grigorii Ivanovich Shelikhov," *Syn otechestva* 2 (1838): 82.

22   Makarova, *Russkie na Tikhom okeane*, 99.

23   Ibid.

24   *Senatskii arkhiv*, 15 vols. (St. Petersburg, 1888–1913), 14:444–45 (hereafter cited as *S.A.*).

25   During the reign of Elizabeth, in 1750, the Governing Senate granted the Irkutsk merchant Emel'ian Iugov the exclusive privilege of sending four ships to hunt and trade for furs. In return for this temporary monopoly Iugov was to pay the Crown one-third of all the furs collected. Unfortunately this merchant reaped no benefits from the privilege as he died during the course of his first voyage. This was the only monopoly granted in the Pacific fur trade until the formation of the Russian American Company in 1799 (*P.S.Z.*, no. 9480, 12:929–33).

26   V. A. Perevalov, *Lomonosov i Arktika: Iz istorii geograficheskoi nauki i geograficheskikh otkrytii* (Moscow, 1949), 282–83.

27   Ibid., 292–303, 435–58.

28   William Coxe, *Account of the Russian Discoveries between Asia and America. To which are added, The Conquest of Siberia, and The History of the Transactions and Commerce between Russia and China*, 4th ed. (London, 1803), 349; Martin Sauer, *An Account of a Geographical and Astronomical Expedition to the Northern Parts of Russia for Ascertaining the Degrees of Latitude and Longitude of the Mouth of the*

River Kovima; of the Whole Coast of the Tshutski, to the East Cape; and of the Islands in the Eastern Ocean, Stretching to the American Coast. Performed by Command of Her Imperial Majesty Catherine the Second, Empress of All the Russias, by Commodore Joseph Billings in the Years 1783, &c to 1794 (London, 1802), vii–ix.

29 Sauer, *An Account*, viii; *P.S.Z.*, no. 16563, 22:881–82.

30 See Sauer, *An Account*, and Gavriil Andreevich Sarychev, *Puteshestvie po severo-vostochnoi chasti Sibiri, Ledovitomu moriu i Vostochnomu okeanu*, ed. N. N. Zubov, 2 vols. in 1., 2d ed. (Moscow, 1952).

31 *P.S.Z.*, no. 16530, 22:836–37; Makarova, *Russkie na Tikhom okeane*, 152.

32 *Materialy dlia istorii russkago flota*, 17 vols. (St. Petersburg, 1865–1905), 13:197–200.

33 "Zamechaniia Imperatritsy Ekateriny II na doklad Komissii o kommertsii o plavanii i torgovle v Tikhom okeane," in Andreev, *v XVIII veke*, 281–82.

34 *Pis'ma i bumagi Imperatritsy Ekateriny II khraniashchiiasia v Imperatorskoi Publichnoi Biblioteke* (St. Petersburg, 1873), p. 65.

35 "Zamechaniia," in Andreev, *v XVIII veke*, 282.

36 Shelikhova to Catherine II, 15 October 1795, TsGADA, f. 11, ed. khr. 1117.

37 Ibid.

38 Ibid.

39 Tikhmenev, *Istoricheskoe obozrenie*, 2:Prilozhenie:108–13; Shelikhova to Nagel, 5 November 1796, TsGIA, f. 1374, op. 1, ed. khr. 236.

40 *Russkii biograficheskii slovar'*, 25 vols. incomplete (St. Petersburg, 1896–1918), Pri-Rel:539–41; Gavriil Romanovich Derzhavin, *Sochineniia*, 9 vols. (St. Petersburg, 1864–83), 5:152–53.

41 *S.A.*, 1:126, 246, 438, 561. In December of 1799 Rezanov was appointed chief procurator of the First Department of the Senate, and in 1800 Tsar Paul presented him with 3,000 *desiatiny* of land in Saratov guberniia (ibid., 569, 634–635).

42 Selifontov to Kurakin with attachments, 9 February 1797, TsGIA, f. 1374, op. 1, ed. khr. 236.

43 *P.S.Z.*, no. 16985, 23:249–51; P. O. Bartenev, ed., *Arkhiv Kniazia Vorontsova*, 40 vols. in 24 (Moscow, 1830–95), 24:188 ff.; also see [Adam Laxman], "Puteshestviia Laksmana v Iaponiiu (Zapiski)," *Russkii arkhiv* 3 (1865): 848–51; Iurii Zhukov, *Russkie i Iaponiia: Zabytye stranitsy iz istorii russkikh puteshestvii* (Moscow, 1945): and George Alexander Lensen, *The Russian Push Toward Japan: Russo-Japanese Relations, 1697–1875* (Princeton, 1959).

44 Selifontov to Kurakin with attachments, February 9, 1797, TsGIA, 1374:1:236.

45 Ibid.

46 "Primernyi opyt' uchrezhdeniia kompanii," ibid., 11. 5–11.

47 Berkh, *Khronologicheskaia istoriia*, 115–16.

48 TsGIA, 1374:1:236.

49 Nagel to Kurakin, April 24, 1797, ibid.

50 "Vsepodanneishi raport," April 24, 1797, ibid.

51 Kurakin to Emperor, August 5, 1797, ibid.

52 Nagel to Kurakin, July 22, 1797, ibid.

53 *Istoricheskoe obozrenie*, 1:61–62. The problems and the expense involved in building and provisioning ships at Okhotsk were both exceedingly great; see James R. Gibson,

Feeding the Russian Fur Trade: Provisionment of the Okhotsk Seaboard and the Kamchatka Peninsula, 1639–1856 (Madison, 1969).

54 *Rossiisko-amerikanskaia kompaniia*, 38–39.

55 *Istoricheskoe obozrenie*, 1:61–62.

56 Buldakov to Rezanov, 4 July 1800, TsGIA, f. 1374, op. 3, ed. khr. 2404. Although it usually took seven to eight weeks for letters to reach Irkutsk from St. Petersburg, it is conceivable that the news of the emperor's decision of 9 June approving Myl'nikov's company reached Shelikhova prior to 19 July.

57 TsGIA, f. 1374, op. 1, ed. khr. 236, 11. 35–50, 55; 11. 56, 41–48. These are bound documents and 11. 55 and 56 are bound out of place.

58 Ibid., 11. 23–24.

59 Ibid., 11. 25–27.

60 Ibid., 11. 25–27. Myl'nikov's proposal is not included in this fond, but from other sources it is evident that he proposed to call his company the American Commercial Company (ibid., 28–29).

61 Ibid., 11. 26–27. Okun incorrectly identified Kurakin's report as being from the Commerce College (*Rossiisko-amerikanskaia kompaniia*, pp. 39–40).

62 TsGIA, f. 1374, op. 1, ed. khr. 236, 1.28. Also see *P.S.Z.*, no. 18076, 24:670.

63 TsGIA, f. 1374, op. 1, ed. khr. 236, 1. 30.

64 Makarova, *Russkie na Tikhom okeane*, 162; also see n 3 above.

65 *A.G.S.*, 2:517.

66 Ibid.

67 *P.S.Z.*, no. 18131, 24:725.

68 "Vsepoddaneishii raport," TsGIA, 1374:1:236.

69 Ibid.

70 *A.G.S.*, 2:517. Monopolies had not existed in Russia for a number of years. Peter III began abolishing monopolies in March 1762 (*P.S.Z.*, no. 11489, 15:959–966), and Catherine II continued this policy until all monopolies had been withdrawn (*P.S.Z.*, no. 11630, 16:31–38; no. 13141, 18:695–96).

71 See Okun, *Rossiisko-amerikanskaia kompaniia*, 41–43.

72 *S.A.*, 1:316. Shelikhova was now a member of the gentry but unlike other members of this group she could engage in retail trade. For a discussion of the right of gentry to trade, see Victor Kamendrowsky and David M. Griffiths, "The Fate of the Trading Nobility Controversy in Russia: A Chapter in the Relationship Between Catherine II and the Russian Nobility," *Jahrbücher für Geschichte Osteuropas*, 26:198–221.

73 *A.G.S.*, 2:518.

74 Ibid.

75 "Akt Amerikanskoi soedinennoi kompanii," TsGADA, op. 1, d. 794; *P.S.Z.*, no. 19030, 15:704–18.

76 "Spiski aktsionerov," TsGIA, f. 994, op. 2., ed. khr. 828.

77 "Akt," TsGADA, op. 1, d. 794.

78 "Doklad kommerts-kollegii Pavlu I," TsGADA, f. 1261, op. 1, ed. khr. 797. For a discussion of the voting question, see Okun, *Rossiisko-amerikanskaia kompaniia*, 44–45.

79 *A.G.S.*, 2:523.

80 Ibid.

81 Ibid.

82 *P.S.Z.*, no. 19030 (July 8, 1799), 25:699–718.

83 Ibid., no. 19233, 25:923–25.

84 Ibid.

85 This comparison is based on the charters granted to the French West India Company, May 28, 1664, in Médéric Louis Elie Moreau de Saint-Méry, *Loix et constitutions des colonies francaises de l'Amérique sous le vent: suivies, 1°. D'un tableau raisonné des différéntes parties de l'administration actuelle de ces colonies: 2°. d'observations générales sur le climat, la population, la culture, le caractere et les moeurs des habitans de la partie francaise de Saint-Dominque: 3°. d'une description physique, politique et topographique des différénts quartiers de cette même partie; le tout terminé par l'historie de cette isle et de ses dépendances, depuis leur découverte jusqu'à nos jours,* 6 vols. (Paris, 1784–90), 1:100–14; and to the French East India Company, September 11, 1664, in Henri Grolous, *La campagnie francaise des Indes Orientales de 1664 considérée comme Société de Commerce* (Paris, 1911), 147–59. See Mary E. Wheeler, "The Origins and Formation of the Russian-American Company" (Ph.D. diss., University of North Carolina, Chapel Hill, 1965), 181–83. The first Russian company charter that appears to have been modeled on the French charters was issued to three Moscow merchants in 1757 (*P.S.Z.*, No. 10694, 15:726–33).

86 *P.S.Z.*, no. 19030, 25:708.

87 Ibid., no. 28756, 37:846–47.

88 There were Russian precedents for financial assistance to companies. In 1763, Catherine II invested 10,000 rubles (20 shares at 500 rubles each), which was 10 percent of the capital, in a company organized by four Tula merchants. The purpose of the company was to trade via the Mediterranean, and Catherine agreed to provide them with a Crown ship for one year (*P.S.Z.*, no. 11938, 16:387–89); and in 1767 she approved a five-year interest free loan of 20,000 rubles to a company of Nizhni-Novgorod merchants (ibid., no. 12904, 18:134–37).

History of the Liquidation of the Russian American Company

1 Reprinted from *Probblemy istorii i etnografii Amerikii* (Moscow, 1979).

2 A. Tikhmenev, *Istoricheskoie obozreniia Possiisko-Amerikanskoi kompanii i deistvii ee do nastoiashchego vremeni* (St. Petersburg, 1861, 1863), chaps. 1–2. V. Mirzoev, "O Tikhmeneve P.A. kak istorik," in *Istoriografiia Sibiri. Perbaia polobina XIX veka* (Kemerovo, 1965), 75–86.

3 S. B. Okun, *Rossiisko-Americanskaia kompaniia* (Moscow/Leningrad, 1939).

4 S. L. Narochnitskii, *Kolonial'naia politika kapitalistichkikh derzhav na Dal'nem Vostoke 1860–1895* (Moscow, 1956), 177–81.

5 *Mezhdunarodnye otnosheniia na Dal'nem Vostoke. Kniga pervaia. S. kontsa XVI veka do 1917 goda* (Moscow, 1973), 117–18.

6 A. I. Alekseev, *Sud'ba Russkoi Ameriki* (Magadan, 1975), 312–16.

7 P. B. Markova, *Vneshnaia politika Rossii na Dal'nem Vostoke. Vtoraia polovina XVIII v—60-e gody XIX v.* Uchebnoe posobie po spetskursu dlia studentov zaochnogo facul'teta MGIAI (Moscow, 1974), 108–12.

8 S. G. Fedorova, *Russkoe Naselenie Aliaski i Kalifornii. konets XVIII v.–1867 g.* (Moscow,

1971); Canadian edition: S. G. Fedorova, *The Russian Population in Alaska and California: Late XVIII Century–1867* (Kingston, 1973).

9   S. G. Fedorova, "Etnicheskie protsessy v Russkoi Amerike," in *Natsional'nye protsessy v SShA* (Moscow, 1973). American edition: Svetlana G. Fedorova, "Ethnic Processes in Russian America," trans. Antoinette Shalkop (Anchorage, 1975).

10 Frank A. Golder, "The Purchase of Alaska," *American Historical Review* 25 (April 1920): 411–25.

11 Archie W. Shiels, *The Purchase of Alaska* (Washington, 1967); Hector Spevigny, *Russian America The Great Alaskan Venture, 1741–1867* (New York, 1965); Ronald J. Lensen, *The Alaska Purchase and Russian-American Relations* (Seattle, 1975); "Frontier Alaska: Proceedings of the Conference on Alaskan History" (Washington, 1968); James R. Gibson, *Imperial Russia in Frontier America: The Changing Geography of Supply of Russian America. 1784–1867* (New York, 1976).

12 Victor J. Farrar. *The Annexation of Russian America to the United States* (New York, 1966).

13 V. Zbyshevskii, "Zamechaniia o kitolovnom promysle v Okhotskom more," *Morskoi sbornik* 15, no. 4 (1863): 229.

14 *Moskovskie vedemosti*, April 17, 1862; *Severnaia pchela*, February 17, 1862; *Russkoie slovo*, 1864, no. 7:66.

15 *Doklad komiteta ob ustroistve russkikh americanskikh kolonii* (St. Petersburg, 1863, 1864), 1–2.

16 Ibid., 1863, pt. 1, p. 157.

17 Ibid., 197–98, 200–201.

18 Ibid., 237.

19 Ibid., 314–15.

20 Ibid., 316.

21 Ibid., 317.

22 Ibid., pt. 2, p. 466.

23 Ibid., 345; G. A. Agranat, *Ob osvoenii russkimi Aliaski—Letopis' Severa* (Moscow, 1971), 5: 188; S. G. Fedorova, "Etnicheskie protsessy v Russkoi Amerike," in *Natsional'nye protsessy v SShA* (Moscow, 1973), chap. 5, p. 163.

24 "Doklad komiteta," pt. 2, p. 519.

25 Ibid., 545.

26 Ibid., 546.

27 *Arkhiv vneshnei politiki Rossii* (AVPR), Fund Rossiisko-Amerikanskoi Kompanii (RAK), op. 888, 1807, 1824–88, d. 181, 1. 97.

28 AVPR, F. RAK, op. 888, 1807, 1824–88, d. 181, 1. 103 ob.

29 AVPR, F. RAK, op. 888, 1807, 1824–88, d. 181, 1.104.

30 *Moskovskie vedemosti*, Aug. 8, 1865.

31 Ibid., Oct. 9, 1865.

32 AVPR, F. RAK, op. 888, 1807, 1824–88, d. 181, 11. 111—ob. 136.

33 Ibid., 11.130 ob., 136.

34 Ibid., 1. 139.

35 Ibid., 1. 139 ob.

36 Ibid., 1. 140.

37 Ibid., d. 397, 1. 4.

38 Archie W. Schiels, *The Purchase of Alaska* (Washington, 1967), chap. 2, "Early Attempts to Purchase Russian America," 6–11.

39 "K istorii russko-amerikanskikh otnoshenii vo vremya grazhdanskoi voiny v SShA," *Krasnyi arkhiv* 3, no. 94 (1939): 122, 125, 126, 146, 147.

40 *Amerikantsy v Peterburge. Druzhestvennyi soiuz Rossii i Ameriki i podrobnoe opisanie monitora "Miantonomo"* (St. Petersburg, 1864), 4; S. B. Okun, *Rossiisko-Amerikanskaia kompaniia.*, 246–47.

41 *Amerikantsy v Rossii i russkie v Amerike. Prasdnestva i rechi amerikantsev i russkikh v N'iu-Iorke, S. Peterburge, Moskve, Nizhnem-Novgorode i podrobnoe opicanie monitora "Miantonomo"* (St. Petersburg, 1866), 3–8.

42 *Moskovskie vedomosti*, August 14, 1866.

43 Okun, *Rossiisko-Amerikanskaia kompaniia*, 247.

44 AVPR, F. RAK, op. 888, 1858–68, d. 399, 1. 19; Okun, *Rossiisko-Amerikanskaia kompaniia*, 247.

45 Frank A. Golder, "The purchase of Alaska," *The American Historical Review* 25, no. 3 (April 1920): 413.

46 *Golos*, March 25 [April 6], 1867.

47 ABPR, F. RAK, op. 888, 1858–68, d. 399, 1. 10.

48 For full text of the treaty, see *Polnoe sobranie zakonov Rossiiskoi imperii*, second collection, vol. 42, sec. 1, 1867 (St. Petersburg, 1871), no. 44518, 421–24; A. I. Alekseev, *Sud'ba Russkoi Ameriki*, 312–13.

About the confirmation of this treaty in the U.S. Congress, and the arguments on the given question, see T. M. Bagueva, "Prokhozhdenie dogovora o pokupke Aliaski v kongresse SShA v 1867–1868 godakh," *Novaia i Noveishaia istoriia*, 1971, no. 4: 117–24.

49 See the leading article of the English newspaper *Morning Herald*, reprinted in "Moskovskie vedomosti," July 20, 1868.

50 Letter of Karl Marx to Ludwig Kugelman, February 17, 1868, in Karl Marx and Friedrich Engels, *Collected Works*, 2d ed. (New York: International Publishers, 1975–83), 32:542.

51 Quotation according to *Golos*, April 23 (May 5), 1867.

52 AVPR, F. RAK, op. 888, 1866–68, d, 412, 11. 364–66 ob.

53 Ibid., 1. 366 ob.

54 *Kostromskie gubernskie vedomosti*, February 3, 1868; S. G. Fedorova, "Flag Rossiisko-Amerikanskoi kompanii," in *Ot Aliaski do Ognennoi zemli* (Moscow, 1967), 126–28.

55 AVPR, F. RAK, op. 888, 1807, 1824–88, d. 181, 1. 319 ob.

56 Ibid., 1. 323.

57 Ibid., 1. 327.

58 Ibid., 1. 144.

59 Ibid., 1. 162.

60 Ibid., 1869, d.415, 11. 28–47.

61 Ibid., 1824–88, d. 181, 1. 297.

62 Ibid., 11. 347–48.

63 Ibid., 1. 293.

64 Ibid., 1. 346 ob.

65 Ibid., 1. 349.

66 *Pravitel'stvennyi vestnik,* November 8 [20], 1881.

Russian Dependence upon the Natives of Alaska

This chapter is a revised version of "European Dependence upon American Natives: The Case of Russian America," *Ethnohistory* 25 (1978): 359–85. It is republished here with the kind permission of that journal's editor, Charles Bishop.

1 For example, Robin Fisher, "Indian Control of the Maritime Fur Trade and the Northwest Coast," in *Approaches to Native History,* ed. D. A. Muise (Ottawa, 1977), 65–86; and Arthur J. Ray, "Fur Trade History as an Aspect of Native History," in *One Century Later,* ed. Ian A. L. Getty and Donald B. Smith (Vancouver, 1978), 7–18.

2 Anonymous, "Obozrenie sostianiia deistvii Rossiisko-Amerikanskoi Kompanii s 1797 po 1819 god," *Zhurnal manufaktur i torgovli* (1835), 92.

3 In 1834, for example, sea otter pelts and fur seal skins, respectively, fetched an average of 561 rubles and 32.5 rubles each at Kiakhta on the Russian-Chinese frontier (in terms of tea) and 600 rubles and 23 rubles each in St. Petersburg and Moscow (United States National Archives, File Microcopies of Records in the National Archives, no. 11, "Records of the Russian-American Company, 1802–1867: Correspondence of Governors General" [hereinafter USNA], roll 9, pp. 110v., 135v).

4 F. Vrangel', "O pushnykh tovarakh Severo-Amerikanskikh Rossiiskikh vladenii," *Teleskop* (1835): 501.

5 Otto von Kotzebue, *A New Voyage Round the World in the Years 1823, 24, 25 and 26* (London, 1830), 2:47.

6 G. H. von Langsdorff, *Voyages and Travels in Various Parts of the World . . .* (London, 1813–14), 2:41.

7 Urey Lisianskii, *A Voyage Round the World in the Years 1803, 4, 5, & 6* (London, 1814), 204.

8 A. P. Lazarev, *Zapiski o plavanii voennogo shliupa Blagonamerennogo v Beringov proliv i vokrug sveta* (Moscow, 1950), 186.

9 Veniaminov voyaged in kayaks with Aleuts for fourteen to twenty hours at a time with no more than one stop for no longer than fifteen minutes—and that break was taken at sea, not on shore (I. Veniaminov, *Zapiski ob ustrovakh Unalashkinskago otdela* [St. Petersburg, 1840], 2:12.

10 Ibid., 13–14.

11 [K. T. Khlebnikov], *Colonial Russian America,* trans. Basil Dmytryshyn and E. A. P. Crownhart-Vaughan (Portland, 1976), 35.

12 L. A. Shur, *K beregam Novogo Sveta: Iz neopublikovannykh zapisok russkikh puteshestvennikov nachala XIX veka* (Moscow, 1971), 145.

13 It took an Aleut a year or more to build a kayak, largely from driftwood and hide, so it was very expensive. See G. A. Sarychev, *Puteshestvie po severovostochnoi chasti Sibiri, Ledovitomu moriu i Vostochnomu okeanu* (Moscow, 1952), 113, 213; Martin Sauer, *Expedition to the Northern Parts of Russia* (Richmond, England, 1972), 159; Veniaminov, *Zapiski,* 2:221.

14 Veniaminov, *Zapiski,* 2:222.

15 Vrangel', "O pushnykh tovarakh," 496.

16 Captain Lisianskii had warned that "the Aleutians . . . from their skill, are sure to commit dreadful depredations wherever they go," and he was right (Urii Lisianskii, *A Voyage Round the World*, 242).

17 Sauer, *Expedition*, 179.

18 Lazarev, *Zapiski*, 186, 235, 282.

19 USNA, roll 33, p. 169v.

20 Quoted by V. M. Pasetskii, *Ferdinand Petrovich Vrangel' 1796–1870* (Moscow, 1975), 134.

21 K. Khlebnikov, "Zapiski o Koloniiakh Rossiisko-Amerikanskoi Kompanii," MS, Archive of the Geographical Society of the USSR, raz. 99, op. 1, no. 112, pp. 356v.–57.

22 James R. Gibson, trans., "Russian America in 1821," *Oregon Historical Quarterly* 77 (1976): 187; Khlebnikov, "Zapiski," p. 212; Semën Iakovlevich Unkovskii, "Zapiski russkogo moriaka nachala XIX v.," MS, Lenin Library, Manuscript Division, f. 261, car. 20, pp. 79–82.

23 Contre-Admiral von Wrangell, *Statistische und ethnographische Nachrichten uber die Russischen Besitzungen an der Nordwestküste von Amerika* (St. Petersburg, 1839), 22.

24 Richard A. Pierce, ed., *The Russian Orthodox Religious Mission in America, 1794–1837*, trans. Colin Bearne (Kingston, 1978), 55.

25 Veniaminov, *Zapiski*, 2:172.

26 For example, 165 Aleuts were killed by Tlingits in 1802 and 300 Aleuts were drowned in 1805 ([K. T. Khlebnikov], *Colonial Russian America*, 145). By 1815 there were 150 Aleuts at Novo-Arkhangel'sk, and in 1821 one-third of the town's 639 residents were Aleuts (Vladimir Romanov, ["Diary"], MS, Bancroft Library, p. [3]; Semën Iakovlevich Unkovskii, "Zapiski russkogo moriaka nachala XIX v.," MS, Lenin Library, Manuscript Division, f. 261, car. 20, p. 74).

27 Captain Pavel Golovin, who inspected Russian America in 1860–61, alleged that the Aleut population may have been halved by Russian contact between the middle and the end of the eighteenth century (Captain-Lieutenant Golovin, "Obzor russkikh kolonii v Severnoi Amerike," *Morskoi sbornik* 57 [1862]: 38); also see Sarychev, *Puteshestvie*, 21.

28 Otto von Kotzebue, *A Voyage of Discovery into the South Sea and Beering's Straits* . . . (London, 1821), 3:315n.

29 Sauer, *Expedition*, 171.

30 G. I. Davydov, *Two Voyages to Russian America, 1802–1807*, trans. Colin Bearne (Kingston, 1977), 194–95.

31 Khlebnikov, "Zapiski," 118v.; Veniaminov, *Zapiski*, 1: vi.

32. Khlebnikov, "Zapiski," 119.

33 A. Sturdza, *Pamiatnik trudov pravoslavnykh blagovestnikov russkikh s 1793 do 1853 goda* (Moscow, 1857), 222.

34 Khlebnikov, "Zapiski," 119v.–20.

35 Ibid., 137v.; Davydov, *Two Voyages*, 196.

36 Every April during the 1820s, 400 to 600 Kenais gathered at Fort St. Nikolai to trade (K. Khlebnikov, "Zapiski o Koloniiakh Rossiisko-Amerikanskoi Kompanii," MS, Archive of the Geographical Society of the USSR, raz. 99, op. 1, no. 112, p. 138).

37 Romanov, ["Diary"], 5.

38 James R. Gibson, *Imperial Russia in Frontier America: The Changing Geography of Supply of Russian America, 1784–1867* (New York, 1976).

39 Only in Russian California (Fort Ross, Port Rumiantsev, and several ranchos) did grain growing and stock raising meet with some success. Even that, however, was wrought largely by Pomo Indian laborers; they with some Aleuts did most of the farm work. In 1838 at Kostromitinov Rancho, for example, 4 Russians supervised 250 Pomo laborers (Lieutenant V. Z[avoiko], *Vpechatleniia moriaka vo vremia dvukh puteshestvii krugom sveta* [St. Petersburg, 1840], 2:97).

40 Richard A. Pierce and John H. Winslow, eds., *HMS Sulphur on the Northwest and California Coasts, 1837 and 1839* (Kingston, Canada, 1979), 105–6.

41. [Khlebnikov], *Colonial Russian America*, 78, 99.

42 Ibid., 54, 78, 99; USNA, roll 27, p. 288v. Potatoes also did fairly well in the Kodiak District, where yields averaged eightfold in the 1860s (USNA, roll 65, pt. 2, p. 66v).

43 *Doklad komiteta ob ustroistve russkikh amerikanskikh kolonii* (St. Petersburg, 1863–64), 2: supp. xi.

44 Lisianskii, *Voyage*, 237, 242.

45 Anonymous, "Obozrenie," 63.

46 Veniaminov, *Zapiski*, 3:29; Z[avoiko], *Vpechatlenii moriaka*, 2:90. According to Father Veniaminov, in 1840 the Tlingits numbered 5,000 to 5,850, the Aleuts 2,380, the Kodiaks 1,508 to 1,719, and the Kenais 1,606 to 1,628 (A. Sturdza, *Pamiatnik trudov*, 221–22, 241–42).

47 Henry Aaron Coppock, "Interactions Between Russians and Native Americans in Alaska, 1741–1840" (Ph.D. dissertation, Michigan State University, 1969).

48 Edward Sapir, "The Social Organization of the West Coast Tribes," in *Indians of the North Pacific Coast*, ed. Tom McFeat (Toronto, 1966), 28–48.

49 Von Langsdorff, *Voyages and Travels*, 2:130.

50 [Khlebnikov], *Colonial Russian America*, 101.

51 Fleet Captain Golovnin, *Puteshestvie vokrug sveta . . .* (Moscow, 1965), 141–42.

52 [V. M. Golovnin], *Sochineniia i perevody Vasiliia Mikhailovicha Golovnina* (St. Petersburg, 1864), 5:179–80.

53 According to the political radical and naval officer Dmitrii Zavalishin, at first up to six sea otter pelts fetched one ordinary musket, which the Indians "quickly learned to use well" (Dmitrii Zavalishin, "Zapiski o Russkoi Amerike" MS, Central State Archive of the October Revolution and Socialist Construction, f. 48, op 1, no. 48, p. 277v).

54 Lisianskii, *Voyage*, 236. Similarly, in 1815 another Russian observer contended that if the Russian American Company had competed with the Americans by offering the Tlingits "realistic" prices "without deception," it would have been able to get another 8,000 to 10,000 sea otter skins yearly (Unkovskii, "Zapiski," p. 74). The Americans paid (in goods) from two to three times as much as the Russians for Tlingit furs, as did the British in the early 1830s (Unkovskii, "Zapiski," 74; USNA, roll 8, p. 330v). In 1837 Midshipman Francis Simpkinson of HMS *Sulphur* noted that although the Russian American Company theoretically monopolized the fur trade of Russian America, "they [the Tlingits] are glad however at any time to get an opportunity of smuggling them [furs] for barter as they in general make a great deal more by the foreign vessels than by the Russians who only give them a certain price for their furs" (Richard A. Pierce and John H. Winslow, eds., *H.M.S. Sulphur*, 96).

55 Ibid., 231, 238–39.

56 On arms see Richard A. Pierce and Alton S. Donnelly, eds., *A History of the Russian-American Company*, trans. Dmitri Krenov (Kingston, 1979), 2:156. In addition to guns and ammunition, incidentally, American skippers dealt in blankets, tobacco, rum, rice, and molasses, which the Tlingits then traded to interior Indians at a profit of 200 to 300 percent (S. W. Jackman, ed., *The Journal of William Sturgis* [Victoria, 1978], 44).

57 Von Kotzebue, *New Voyage*, 2:54.

58 V. Rimskii-Korsakov, ed., "Iz putevykh pisem P. N. Golovina" *Morskoi sbornik* 6 (1863): 181.

59 *Doklad komiteta ob ustroistve russkikh amerikanskikh kolonii* (St. Petersburg, 1863–64), 2:158.

60 Von Kotzebue, *New Voyage*, 2:38.

61 When Novo-Arkhangel'sk was refounded in 1804 at least 100 totems (each topped with a box of human ashes) were destroyed by the Russians (Lisianskii, *Voyage*, 240–41).

62 Ibid., 219; P. A. Tikhmenev, *A History of the Russian-American Company*, trans. Richard A. Pierce and Alton S. Donnelly (Seattle, 1978), 65.

63 A. I. Andreyev, ed., *Russian Discoveries in the Pacific and in North America in the Eighteenth and Nineteenth Centuries*, trans. Carl Ginsburg (Ann Arbor, 1952), 174.

64 The American fur trader William Sturgis reported in 1799, when Sitka was originally founded, that "vessels that have been the first on the Coast have purchased in this [Norfolk] Sound upwards of Eight hundred Skins in four days"; he added that "upwards of a thousand skins have been got there in a season, and I do not know but what I may say twelve hundred, and seven and eight hundred have been bought by one vessel on her first visit" (Jackman, *Journal*, 34, 88).

65 Tikhmenev, *History*, 99.

66 Ibid., 353; [Russian-American Company, Head Office], *Otchet Rossiisko-Amerikanskoi Kompanii Glavnago Pravleniia az odin god* [hereinafter ORAK] (St. Petersburg, 1843–65), 1854–55, 33–36. Another source states that seven company employees were killed and sixteen wounded (USNA, roll 60, pp. 78v.–79).

67 *Doklad*, 1:130; D. I. Nedel'kovich, "Vospominaniia o puteshestvii sukhim putem iz Kronshtadta v Novo-Arkhangel'sk . . ." MS, State Historical Museum, Division of Written Sources, f. 92, no. 99445/4650, p. 28; USNA, roll 51, p. 427.

68 Captain-Lieutenant Golovnin, "Obzor russkikh kolonii," 51; [Khlebnikov], *Colonial Russian America*, 102; Pierce and Winslow, *H.M.S. Sulphur*, 20; Z[avoiko] *Vpechatleniia*, 2:90.

69 USNA, roll 57, p. 331.

70 On the assemblies see Golovin, "Obzor russkikh kolonii," 51; [Khlebnikov], *Colonial Russian America*, 102; Andrei Lazarev, *Plavanie vokrug sveta na shliupe Ladoge v 1822, 1823 i 1824 godakh* (St. Petersburg, 1832), 161. Occasionally, too, several Tlingit groups gathered at Sitka for talks, as in mid-March of 1831, when up to 2,000 congregated at the colonial capital (USNA, roll 33, p. 137).

71 *Doklad*, 1:114, 2:23–26.

72 Ibid., 310–11; Golovin, "Obzor," 47–48.

73 Golovin, "Obzor russkikh kolonii," 48.

74 Lisianskii, *Voyage*, 237–38.

75 Von Langsdorff, *Voyages and Travels*, 2:111, 131.

76 Lazarev, *Zapiski*, 283.

77 Baron F. and Baronin E. von Wrangell, "Briefe aus Sibirien und den Russischen Niederlassungen in Amerika," *Dorpater Jahrbücher für Literatur, Statistik und Kunst, besonders Russlands*, 2 (1834): 361.

78 [K. T. Khlebnikov], "Zapiski o Koloniiakh v Amerike Rossiisko-Amerikanskoi Kompanii. Chast' 1," MS, Archive of the Geographical Society of the USSR, raz. 99, op. 1, no. 111, pp. 107–07v., 108v., 112v.–13.

79 Sir George Simpson, *Narrative of a Journey Round the World, During the Years 1841 and 1842* (London, 1847), 2:2.

80 Henry N. Michael, ed., *Lieutenant Zagoskin's Travels in Russian America, 1842–1844* (Toronto, 1967), 73.

81 Alexander Rowand, *Notes of a Journey in Russian America and Siberia, During the Years 1841 and 1842* (Edinburgh, n.d.), p. 7.

82 No sooner had American fur trading vessels disappeared from Russian-American waters than they were replaced by American whaling ships. Already by 1842 up to 200 Yankee whalers were plying the far North Pacific (USNA, roll 46, p. 363).

83 USNA, roll 38, p. 103v.

84 Sturdza, *Pamiatnik*, 215; Veniaminov, *Zapiski*, 3:128–30.

85 Golovin, "Obzor," 48, 50.

86 Rimskii-Korsakov, "Iz putevykh pisem," 48, 50. Also see Pierce and Winslow, *H.M.S. Sulphur*, p. 20.

87 [Khlebnikov], *Colonial Russian America*, 101; Von Kotzebue, *New Voyage*, 2:43–44.

88 At the end of 1841 a company agronomist, Egor Chernykh, reported from Sitka that the Tlingits had "recently" begun to cultivate potatoes and now grew them in "large numbers"; he added that in the fall of 1841 the company steamer *Nikolai I* bought up to 100 barrels of potatoes from the Tlingits while trading in the straits (E. Chernykh, "Izvestiia iz Novoarkhangel'ska," *Zhurnal selskago khoziaistva i ovtsevodstva* [1843]: 93). Right up to the sale of Russian America in 1867 the company was still sending a ship into the straits once or twice every fall to buy potatoes (and black-tailed deer and, from 1862, turnips as well) at 5 rubles per barrel (see, for example, USNA, roll 63, pt. 1, p. 164v. and pt. 2, pp. 154–54v.); in October of 1861, for instance, the steamer purchased 260 barrels (USNA, roll 64, pt. 1, p. 56v.).

89 This fair commonly lasted two days in the middle of April. In 1851 up to 2,000 Tlingits, plus slaves (paddlers), attended (USNA, roll 57, p. 245v.).

90 USNA, roll 50, p. 344, roll 51, pp. 166v., 187v.

91 Ibid., roll 50, p. 359v.

92 Kodiak hunting was limited largely to sea birds and ground squirrels, whose skins were sewn by the women into parkas for the company's Aleuts. During the middle 1820s in the Kodiak District 20,000 to 25,000 ground squirrels were bagged annually— enough for 200 to 250 parkas (Khlebnikov, "Zapiski," 128v.); probably from two to three times as many sea birds were killed.

93 Davydov, *Two Voyages*, 213.

94 Ibid.

95 Lisianskii, *Voyage*, 238; Von Kotzebue, *New Voyage*, 2:45; Von Langsdorff, *Voyages and Travels*, 2:75.

96 [Khlebnikov], *Colonial Russian America*, 99; Dmitrii Zavalishin, "Krugosvetnoe

plavanie fregata 'Kreiser' v 1822–1825 gg. po komandoiu Mikhaila Petrovicha Lazareva," *Drevniaia i novaia Rossiia* (1877): 153.

97 *Doklad*, 2:95, supp. xvii.

98 Similarly, George Simpson of the Hudson's Bay Company found in 1841 that the British Fort Taku (Durham) just south of Novo-Arkhangel'sk was maintained chiefly on venison (Sir George Simpson, *Narrative of a Journey Round the World, During the Years 1841 and 1842* [London, 1847], 1:214.

99 *Doklad*, 1:118, 2:95–96.

100 Lazarev, *Zapiski*, 284.

101 Zavalishin, "Krugosvetnoe plavanie," 150.

102 USNA, roll 33, pp. 3–3v., 114v.

103 Golovnin, *Puteschestvie*, 134.

104 [Khlebnikov], *Colonial Russian America*, 54.

105 Tikhmenev, *History*, 84.

106 ORAK, 1860, p. 44, 1861, p. 17, 1862, p. 28; USNA, roll 62, pt. 2, pp. 71v.–72; roll 63, pt. 1, p. 76v., pt. 2, pp. 39v–40; roll 64, pt. 1, p. 59v., pt. 2, pp. 41v.–42.

107 USNA, roll 42, p. 306v.; roll 43, p. 220v.; roll 45, p. 274; roll 46, p. 266v.; roll 47, p. 426v.; roll 48, p. 332v.; roll 50, p. 204v.; roll 51, p. 188; roll 52, p. 326v.; roll 54, p. 209v.

108 Ibid., roll 51, pp. 187–88v.

109 ORAK, 1844, p. 31.

110 Nedel'kovich, "Vospominaniia," 28v.

111 Rimskii-Korsakov, "Iz putevykh pisem," 181–82.

112 *Doklad*, 2:70.

113 Ibid., 66.

114 USNA, roll 65, pt. 2, p. 8.

115 Ibid., roll 60, p. 51.

116 USNA, roll 62, pt. 3, p. 38.

117 *Doklad*, 2:supp. xxi.

118 USNA, roll 30, p. 25v.

119 In 1806 Count Nikolai Rezanov, who was making a tour of inspection of the colony, recommended to the minister of commerce that anyone who wanted to go to Russian America be allowed to do so and that 150 to 200 exiles be sent there (P. A. Tikhmenev, *A History of the Russian-American Company*, trans. Richard A. Pierce and Alton S. Donnelly [Seattle, 1978], 95). In 1808, however, the State Council announced that it had rejected the minister's suggestion that "free persons" be permitted to settle in Russian America for fear that the state would lose taxpayers and conscripts (Union of Soviet Socialist Republics, Ministerstvo Inostrannykh del, *Vneshniaia politika Rossii XIX i nachala XX veka: dokumenty Rossiiskogo Ministerstva Inostrannykh del*, first ser. (Moscow, 1965), 4:617–18, n. 168).

120 V. Kashkarov, ed., "Zapiski Semëna Ivanovicha Ianovskago," *Izvestiia Kaluzhskoi uchënoi arkhivnoy komissii 1898 god* 1 (1899): 137; Rimskii-Korsakov, "Iz putevykh pisem," 309.

121 [Golovnin], *Sochineniia i perevody*, 5:182n.

122 USNA, roll 40, p. 246.

123 ORAK, 1843, p. 25.

124 USNA, roll 6, p. 47v.; roll 7, pp. 124–24v.; roll 8, p. 317; roll 10, pp. 450v., 493v.–94; roll 11, p. 161; roll 30, p. 37; roll 31, p. 56; roll 32, p. 108; roll 42, p. 462.

125 Ibid., roll 51, p. 426.

126 Ibid., roll 55, p. 136v.

127 Ibid., roll 57, p. 331v.

128 ORAK, 1859, p. 106.

129 USNA, roll 65, pt. 3, pp. 5v.–6.

130 Lazarev, *Zapiski*, 234–35.

131 Ivan Barsukov, *Innokentii Mitropolit Moskovskii i Kolomenskii po ego sochineniiam, pis'em i razskazam sovremennikov* (Moscow, 1883), 10.

132 So was the accident rate. In 1799, for instance, 115 Aleut hunters died of mussel poisoning and up to 90 Russians were drowned in the sinking of the *Phoenix* (Gibson, *Imperial Russia*, 13–14).

133 USNA, roll 31, p. 389v.

134 Pierce and Winslow, *H.M.S. Sulphur*, 22.

135 Rowand, *Notes*, 3; Simpson, *Narrative*, 2:190.

136 ORAK, 1860, p. 94.

137 Ibid., 73.

138 Pierce and Donnelly, *History*, 2:160, 167, 170, 172.

139 *Materialy dlia istorii russkikh zaselenii po beregam vostochnago okeana*, pt. 1 (St. Petersburg, 1861), 8.

140 Simpson, *Narrative*, 2:207.

141 Rowand, *Notes*, 51.

142 USNA, roll 51, p. 426.

143 Golovin, "Obzor," 30.

144 Rimskii-Korsakov, "Iz putevykh pisem," 299.

145 Nedel'kovich, "Vospominaniia," 31v.

146 S. F. Fedorova, *Russkoe naselenie Aliaski i Kalifornii konets XVIII veka-1867 g.* (Moscow, 1971), 190.

147 Golovin, "Obzor," 30.

148 USNA, roll 20, p. 21; roll 34, p. 141v.

149 Golovin, "Obzor," pp. 32–33.

150 The company also had an ulterior motive for hiring Tlingits. In 1847 twenty Tlingit day laborers were hired for 1 ruble per day "for the sole purpose of greater rapprochement with us," according to Governor Teben'kov (USNA, roll 53, p. 97).

151 ORAK, 1843, p. 40.

152 Winston Lee Sarafian, "Russian-American Company Employee Policies and Practices, 1799–1867" (Ph.D. dissertation, University of California at Los Angeles, 1970), 209–10.

153 Sturdza, *Pamiatnik*, 213.

154 USNA, roll 61, pt. 1, pp. 102–2v.

155 Gibson, *Imperial Russia*, 18; Golovin, "Obzor," 34; [Khlebnikov], "Zapiski," 110v.; Tikhmenev, *History*, 161; Wrangell, "Briefe," 326.

156 During the middle 1820s at Novo-Arkhangel'sk the Tlingit concubines (mostly girls and slaves) tended to impoverish the *promyshlenniki* (whose gifts went to the owners

of the concubines) and to spread venereal disease, but they also prevented what one colonial official called "the sinful unnatural [homosexual] acts which . . . would otherwise result from the shortage of women" ([Khlebnikov], *Colonial Russian America*, 71). Both Aleut and Kodiak chiefs sometimes kept homosexual boys (*schopans*) as concubines, and the Russians apparently risked doing likewise.

157 Golovin, "Obzor," 35; Michael, *Lieutenant Zagoskin's Travels*, 68.
158 Richard A. Pierce, ed., *Documents on the History of the Russian-American Company*, trans. Marina Ramsay (Kingston, 1976), 41.
159 Kashkarov, "Zapiski," pt. 2:3.
160 Golovin, "Obzor," 35.
161 Ibid.
162 Sarafian, "Employee Policies and Practices," 140.
163 Anonymous, "Obozrenie," 66, 79; Golovnin, *Puteshestvie*, table A.
164 Von Wrangell, "Briefe," 22.
165 Golovin, "Obzor," 34–35; ORAK, 1843, p. 30.
166 Lazarev, *Zapiski*, 234.
167 Tikhmenev, *History*, 236, 240.
168 USNA, roll 14, pp. 110v.–11.
169 In 1820–21 only 352 (one-sixth) of the company's colonial labor force of 5,475 were Russians, the rest being natives and creoles, and only one-third of Novo-Arkhangel'sk's 639 residents were Russians (Romanov, ["Diary"], [3], [9], [14], [16–18]). In 1860 Russian America's "pacified" population consisted of 2,428 Aleuts, 2,217 Kodiaks, 937 Kenais, 456 Chugaches, and only 595 Russians (Golovin, "Obzor," 34, 44–45).

Relations with the Natives of Russian America

1 S. B. Okun, *Rossiiski-Amerikanskaia Kompania* (Moscow/Leningrad, 1939).
2 V. F. Shirokii, "Iz istorii khoziaistvennoi deiatel'nosti Rossiisko-Amerikanskoi Kompanii," *Istoricheskie zapiski*, vol. 12 (Moscow, 1942).
3 G. A. Agranat, "Ob osvoennii Russkimi Aliaski," *Letopis' Severa*, vol. 5 (Moscow, 1971).
4 N. N. Bolkhovitinov, *Stanovlenie Russko-amerikanskikh otnoshenii, 1775–1815* (Moscow, 1966); *Russko-Amerikanskie otnosheniia, 1815–1832* (Moscow, 1975).
5 S. G. Fedorova, *Russkoe naselenie Aliaski i kalifornii konetz XVIII–1867 g.* (Moscow, 1971); "Etnicheskie protsessi v Russkoi Amerike," *Natsional'nye protsessy v SShA* (Moscow, 1973).
6 U. P. Averkieva, *Rabstvo u indeitsev Severnoi Ameriki* (Moscow, 1941): "K istorii obshchestvennogo stroia u indeitsev severo-zapadnogo poberezh'ia Severnoi Ameriki," *Amerikanskii etnograficheskii sbornik* 1 (1960); "Rozlozhenie rodovoi obshchiny i formirovanie ranneklassovykh otnoshenii v obshchestve indeitsev severo-zapadnogo poberezh'ia Severnoi Ameriki," *Trudy Institua Etnografii AN SSSR*, new ser., vol. 20 (Moscow, 1961); "Rod i obshchina algonkinov i atapaskov amerikanskogo severa," *Rozlozhenie rodovogo stroia i formirovanie klassovogo obshchestva* (Moscow, 1968); L. A. Fainberg, "K voprosu o rodovom stroe aleutov," *Kratkie soobshcheniia IE AN SSSR* 20 (1955) and *Obshchestvennyi stroi eskimosov i aleutov* (Moscow, 1964); R. G. Liapunova, *Ocherki po etnografii aleutov* (Leningrad, 1975); G. I. Dzheniskevich, *Traditsionnaia kul'tura Atapaskov Aliaski* (konetz XVIII-XIV vv) (dissertation for Candidate of Sciences, Leningrad State University, 1978).

7 V. N. Berkh, *Khronologicheskaia istoriia otkrytiia aleutskikh ostrovov ili podvigi rossiiskogo kupechestva* (St. Petersburg, 1823); R. V. Makarova, *Russkie na Tikhom Okeane vo vtoroi polovine XVIIIv.* (Moscow, 1968).

8 A. I. Andreev, "Russkie otkrytiia v Tikhom Okeane v XVIIIv (obzor istochnikov i literatury)," *Russkie otkrytiia v Tikhom okeane i Severnoi Amerike v XVIIIv* (Moscow, 1948); L. S. Berg, *Otkrytie Kamchatki i ekspeditsii Beringa, 1725–1742 gg.* (Moscow, Leningrad, 1946); A. V. Efimov, *Iz istorii velikikh Russkikh geograficheskikh otkrytii* (Moscow, 1949); V. A. Divin, *Russkie moreplavaniia na Tikhom okeane v XVIIIv*, and the works cited above.

9 Makarova, *Russkie na Tikhom Okeane* 43–44.

10 Ibid.

11 Archive of the VGO, r. 60, op. 1, d. 2; A. S. Polonskii, *Perechen' puteshestvii russkikh promyshlennykh v vostochnom okeane s 1743 po 1800 god.*

12 Berkh, *Khronologic eskaia istoriia*, 8–9.

13 Archive of the VGO, r. 60, op. 1, d. 3; A. S. Polonskii, *Promyshlenniki na aleutskikh ostrovakh (1743–1800)*, 48.

14 Ibid., 49–50.

15 Ibid., 51–52.

16 Ibid., 54–56.

17 *Russian Discoveries*, 113–20; R. G. Liapunova, "Novyi dokument o rannikh plavaniiakh na aleutskie ostrova" (*Izvestiia*, F. A. Kul'kova, 1764), *Strany i narody Vostoka*, ser. 20, no. 4 (Moscow, 1979).

18 *Russian Discoveries*, 117.

19 Archive of the VGO; Polonskii, *Promyshlenniki*, 59.

20 Makarova, *Russkie otkrytiia v Tikhom okeane i Severnoi Amerike v XVIII-XIX vekakh* (Moscow, 1944), 25.

21 I. Veniaminov, *Zapiski ob ostrovakh Unalashkinskogo otdela*, pt. 2 (St. Petersburg, 1840), 186–94; *Russkaia Amerika v neopublikovannykh zapiskakh K. T. Khlebnikova* (Leningrad, 1979), 86–94, 144–45; Berg, *Otkrytie Kamchatki*, 285–92.

22 LO of the Archives of the Academy of Sciences of the USSR, r. 2, op. 1, d. 275, 1. 26–27 ob.

23 TsGADA, f. 199, no. 528, ch. 2, d. 10, 1. 10.

24 TsGAVMF, f. 179, op. 1, d. 131.

25. Archives of the VGO; Polonskii, *Perechen' puteschestvii*, 79.

26 *Russkaia Amerika*, 133–36.

27 *Russkaia Amerika*, 136.

28 *P.S.Z.*, collection 1, vol. 22, no. 16563, 881–82.

29 G. A. Sarychev, *Puteshestvie po severo-vostochnoi chasti Sibiri, Ledovitomy moriu i Vostochnomu okeanu* (Moscow, 1952), 288–89.

30 TsGAVMF, f. 214, op. 1, d. 29, 1. 101.

31 Sarychev, *Puteshestvie*, 144.

32 TsGAVMF, f. 172, op. 1, d. 408, ch. 1, 1. 173.

33 Ibid., 430.

34 TsGAVMF, f. 214, d. 29, 1. 90.

35 *Etnograficheskie materialy severo-vostochnoi geograficheskoi ekspeditsii* (Magadan, 1978), 68.

36 Okun, *Rossiiski-Amerikanskaia Kompania,* 183.
37 Veniaminov, *Zapiski,* 184–86.
38 On the activities of G. I. Shelikhov, see the republication of his work: *G. I. Shelikhov,* edited and with an introduction, afterword, and notations by B. P. Polevoi (Khabarovsk, 1971).
39 *G. I. Shelikhov,* 42.
40 Ibid., 44–45.
41 Ibid., 48.
42 Ibid.
43 Central State Historical Archives, f. 1147, op. 1, d. 103.
44 *Polnyi svod zakonov rossiiskoi imperii,* collection 1, vol. 22, no. 16709, pp. 1105–7.
45 *Russkie otkrytiia,* 288.
46 *G. I. Shelikhov,* 49.
47 Ibid., 50.
48 *Russkie otkrytiia,* 187.
49 Central State Historical Archives, f. 13, op. 1, d. 103.
50 Ibid., 13–29.
51 See Okun's cited work, as well as those of Bolkhovitnikov and Fedorova.
52 Veniaminov, *Zapiski,* chap. 2, 13–14.
53 Berkh, *Khronologicheskaia istoriia,* 152.
54 Veniaminov, *Zapiski,* 152–53.
55 Central State Historical Archives, f. 796, op. 85, d. 564, for 1804, pp. 1–6; *Valaamskie missionery w Amerike (v kontse XVIII stoletiia)* (St. Petersburg, 1900), 238.
56 R. G. Liapunova, "Zapiski ieromonakha Gedeona (1803–1807); odin iz istochnikov po istorii i etnografii Ameriki Russkoi," *Problemy istorii i etnografii Ameriki* (Moscow, 1979).
57 *Valaamskie missionery,* 247.
58 G. I. Davydov, *Dvykratnoe puteshestvie v Ameriku morskikh ofitserov Khvostova i Davydova* pts. 1 and 2 (St. Petersburg, 1810, 1812); pt. 2, 127.
59 Ibid., 74–75.
60 Iu. F. Lisianskii, *Puteshestvie vokrug sveta na korable "Neva" v 1803–1806 godakh* (Moscow, 1947), 191.
61 Ibid.
62 I. F. Kruzenstern, Puteshestvie vokrug sveta w 1803, 4, 5 and 1806 godakh ... pt. 1 (St. Petersburg, 1810), 118–28.
63 Central State Historical Archives, f. 13, op. 2, d. 1243.
64 Ibid., f. 155, op. 1, for 1821, d. 989.
65 Ibid., f. 18, op. 2, for 1815, d. 222, 1. 217–21.
66 *Materialy po istorii russkikh zaselenii po beregam Vostochnogo okeana,* addendum to *Morskoi Sbornik,* nos. 1, 2, 3, 4 (1861); (editions 1–4; see 1st ed., 49–50.
67 Ibid., 1st ed., 100.
68 Ibid., 4th ed., 105–6.
69 Ibid., 1st ed., 126.
70 Tikhmenev, *Istoricheskoe,* pt. 1, addendum, 55–59.
71 Ibid., pt. 2, 56–63.
72 Veniaminov, *Zapiski.*
73 I. Veniaminov, *Opyt grammatiki aleutsko-lis'evskogo iazyka* (St. Petersburg, 1846).

74   GAPO, f. 445, d. 161, 1. 19 ob.

75   Ibid., 1. 17 ob.

76   Ibid., 1. 21.

77   *Materialy dlia istorii russkikh zaselenii . . .* 3d ed.; *Russkaia Amerika v neopublikovan-nykh zapiskakh K. T. Khlebnikova* (Leningrad, 1979).

78   *Russkaia Amerika*, 60.

79   L. A. Zagoskin, *Puteshestviia i issledovaniia leitenanta Lavrentiia Zagoskina v Russkoi Amerike v 1842–1844 gg.* (Moscow, 1956); F. P. Wrangell, *Statistische und ethnog-raphische Nachrichten uber die Russischen Besitzungen an der Nordwestküste von Amerika* (St. Petersburg, 1839); F. P. Wrangell, *O torgovykh snosheniiakh narodov Severo-zapadnoi Ameriki s Chukchami, Teleskop* (1835), pt. 26, and also by him: "Obitateli severo-zapadnykh beregov Ameriki," *Syn otechestva* 7 (1839).

80   See the above mentioned works by S. G. Fedorova.

The Early Architecture and Settlements of Russian America

1   Research and travel funds for this study were provided by the Graduate School and the Division of Arts and Humanities at the University of Maryland at College Park. The fine research assistance in Washington, D.C., of B. Lynn Davis is gratefully acknowledged.

2   Such temporary shelters were described by Captain James Cook, whose party anchored for repairs in Samgunudkha Harbor on Unalaska Island in October 1778. See *The Voyage of the "Resolution" and "Discovery," 1776–1780*, ed. James C. Beag-lehole, vol. 3 of *The Journals of Captain James Cook on his Voyages of Discovery* (Cambridge, 1967), 450. Hereinafter referred to as *Cook Journals 1776–1780*.

3   In *Russkie otkrytiia v Tikhom Okeane i Severnoi Ameriki v XVIII veke*, ed. Aleksandr I. Andreev (Moscow, 1948), 132.

4   A persuasive case for regarding Illiuliuk and not, as had long been supposed, Three Saints Harbor as the first permanent Russian settlement in northwest America is made by Svetlana G. Fedorova in *Russkoe naselenie Aliaski i Kalifornii* (Moscow, 1971), 106–9. Federova's argument is based on the abundant new evidence supplied by the publication for the first time of diaries kept by several members of Captain James Cook's third voyage round the world, which stopped off at Unalaska Island in 1778 (see n. 5 below). These same diaries also do much to enhance our knowledge both of early (pre-Russian) Aleut dwellings and of their adaptation by the first Russian settlers in the Aleut chain (see n. 2 above).

5   Members of Cook's party whose diaries were published in the definitive 1967 edition are Captain Charles Clerke, Lieutenant (later Captain) James King, Navigator Thomas Edgar, and Surgeon's Mate David Samwell.

6   Cook referred to the settlement as Eguchshak, *Cook Journals, 1776–1780*, 449. The name *Soglasie* [Harmony] was first given to the settlement in 1805 by Nikolai P. Rezanov to commemorate the exceptional amity he found prevalent among the inhabitants; see Petr A. Tikhmenev, *Istoricheskoe obozrenie obrazovaniia Rossiisko-Amerikanskoi kompanii i deistvie ee do nastoiashchago vremeni*, 2 vols. (St. Petersburg, 1861), 1:134. Louis Choris, in his *Voyage pittoresque autour du Monde* (Paris, 1822), 3, noted that the Russians had named the settlement *Dobroe soglasie* [Good Harmony] and indicated that it was commonly known as Illiuliuk.

7   See I. V. Glushankov, "Aleutskaia ekspeditsiia Krenitsyna i Levasheva," *Priroda* 12 (1969): 84–92.

8   Thomas Edgar's journal, in *Cook Journals, 1776–1780*, 1354.

9   Ibid., 1355.

10 James King's journal, in *Cook Journals, 1776–1780*, 1452.

11 Choris, *Voyage*, pl. 11. Choris, a Russian artist, took part in the voyage of 1815–18 undertaken by Otto von Kotzebue, a German navigator in the Russian service; the Kotzebue expedition stopped over in Illiuliuk in June 1817.

12 Cook's journal, in *Cook Journals, 1776–1780*, 460. Cook provides one of the most vivid known descriptions of the Aleut dwelling.

13 Ibid. See also Edgar, *Cook Journals, 1776–1780*, 1353–54; and King, ibid., 1443. For a scholarly treatment of Aleut settlements and dwellings, see Roza G. Liapunova, *Ocherki po etnografii Aleutov (konets XVIII–pervaia polovina XIX v.)* (Leningrad, 1975), chap. 4.

14 King, *Cook Journals, 1776–1780*, 1443.

15 Ibid.

16 David Samwell's journal, in *Cook Journals, 1776–1780*, 1144.

17 King, ibid., 1443

18 George H. von Langsdorff, *Voyages and Travels in Various Parts of the World during the Years 1803–1807*, 2 vols. (London, 1813–14), 2:32.

19 Cook, *Cook Journals, 1776–1780*, 460.

20 King, ibid., 1443.

21 Clerke, ibid., 1334.

22 Precisely when the Russians began using mica panes at Illiuliuk is not known. Edgar noted as early as 1778 that the Russians had a window on the east side "made of tulc," or talc (mica), that "gives a tolerable good light" (Edgar, *Cook Journals, 1776–1780*, 1354). Choris observed in 1817 that "The windows of the houses of the Russians [at Illiuliuk] have panes of mica instead of glass" (Choris, ibid., 3). The other glazing material employed was sea animal intestines, which were dried and oiled to the point of becoming translucent.

23 Edgar, ibid., 1354–55.

24 Lavrentii A. Zagoskin, *Puteshestviia i issledovaniia leitenenta Lavrentiia Zagoskina v Russkoi Amerike v 1842–1844 gg.* (Moscow, 1956), 183–84.

25 For historical treatment of pertinent traditions in Russian wooden architecture see, inter alia, S. Zabello, V. Ivanov, and P. Maksimov, *Russkoe dereviannoe zodchestvo* (Moscow, 1942); I. V. Makovetskii, *Pamiatniki narodnogo zodchestva russkogo severa* (Moscow, 1955); I. V. Makovetskii, *Arkhitektura russkogo narodnogo zhilishcha* (Moscow, 1962); and P. N. Maksimov and N. N. Voronin, "Dereviannoe zodchestvo XIII–XVI vekov," in *Istoriia russkogo iskusstva*, ed. Igor E. Grabar', et al., 2d ed. (Moscow, 1959), 4:91–120.

26 Adam Olearius, *Offt begehrte Beschreibung der newen orientalischen Reise* (Schleswig, 1647–96), 2d ed., *Moskowischen und persische Reise*, ed. Eberhard Meissner (Berlin, 1959); and Jacob von der Sandrart, *Kurtze beschreibung von Moscovien oder Reussland . . .* ([n.p.], 1711). Significantly, the view of Tobolsk rendered by Sandrart is identical in layout, composition, and detail to that sketched out earlier by Semen E. Remezov in his *Chertezhnaia kniga Sibiri*, which was prepared in 1701 with the

intention of printing it in Holland; see *The Atlas of Siberia by Semyon U. Remezov*, facsimile ed. with introd. by Leo Bagrow (The Hague, 1958), 164.

27 For historical treatment of Siberian wooden architecture see, inter alia, E. A. Ashchepkov, *Russkoe narodnoe zodchestvo v zapadnoi Sibiri* (Moscow, 1950); E. A. Ashchepkov, *Russkoe narodnoe zodchestvo v vostochnoi Sibiri* (Moscow, 1953); I. V. Makovetskii, "Dereviannoe zodchestvo srednego priangaria (XVII–XX vv.)," in *Byt i iskusstvo russkogo naseleniia Vostochnoi Sibiri*, 2 vols. (Novosibirsk, 1971), 1:106–43; I. V. Makovetskii, "Arkitektura russkogo narodnogo zhilishcha zabaikala," in ibid., 2:33–47; I. V. Vlasova, "Poselenie zabaikala," in ibid., 2:21–32; A. N. Kopylov, *Ocherki kul'turnoi zhizni Sibiri XVII-nachala XIX v.* (Novosibirsk, 1974) 112–61; and N. V. Sultanov, "Ostatki Iakutskogo ostroga i nekotorykh drugikh pamiatnikov dereviannogo zodchestva v Sibiri," in *Izvestiia Imp. Arkheologicheskoi komissii* (St. Petersburg, 1907) 24:1–154, with pl. 1–18.

28 *Kratkaia Sibir'skaia letopis' (kungurskaia) so 154 risunkami* (St. Petersburg, 1880). Cf. Semen U. Remezov, *Chertezhnaia kniga Sibiri, sostavlennaia Tobol'skim synom boyarskim Semenom Remezovym v 1701 godu* (St. Petersburg, 1882); see n. 26 above for facsimile ed. with introd. by Leo Bagrow. See also Bagrow's "Semyon Remezov, A Siberian Cartographer," *Imago Mundi* 11 (1954): 111–25; and L. A. Goldenberg, "The Atlases of Siberia by S. U. Remezov as a Source for Old Russian Urban History," *Imago Mundi* 25 (1971): 39–46. Remezov's work after 1695 in planning various building projects in Tobolsk has been assayed by V. V. Kirillov in "Proekty 'obraztsovykh domov' razrabotannye S. U. Remezovym dlia Tobol'ska," *Arkhitekturnoe nasledstvo* 12 (1960): 155–66; and his "Postroiki Semena Remezova v Tobol'ske (Prikaznaia palata i Dmitrievskie vorota Tobol'skogo kremlia)," *Arkhitekturnoe nasledstvo* 14 (1962): 109–24.

29 See Aleksandr I. Alekseev, *Okhotsk—kolybel' russkogo Tikhookeanskogo flota* (Khabarovsk, 1958) and Fedor G. Safronov, *Russkie na severo-vostoke Azii v XVII–seredine XIX v.* (Moscow, 1978), 185–94. For settlement patterns in Eastern Siberia, see Raisa V. Makarova, *Russkie na Tikhom Okeane vo vtoroi polovine XVIII v.* (Moscow, 1968); see also James R. Gibson, *Feeding the Russian Fur Trade: Provisionment of the Okhotsk Seaboard and the Kamchatka Peninsula, 1639–1856* (Madison, 1969).

30 Published in Safronov, *Russkie na severo-vostoke Azii*, 191.

31 Martin Sauer, *An Account of a Geographical and Astronomical Expedition to the Northern Parts of Russia Performed by Commodore Joseph Billings in the Years 1785, etc. to 1794* (London, 1802), 40.

32 Ivan F. Kruzenshtern [Kruzenstern], *Voyage Round the World in the Years 1803, 1804, 1805, and 1806 by Order of His Imperial Majesty Alexander the First On Board the Ships "Nadezhda" and "Neva" under the Command of Captain A. J. von Krusenstern*, trans. Richard B. Hoppner (London, 1813), 217. For historical material on the founding and growth of Petropavlovsk, see Safronov, *Russkie na severo-vostoke Azii*, 195–98.

33 Archibald Campbell, *A Voyage Round the World, 1806–1812* (Edinburgh, 1816), 23.

34 Ibid.

35 Kruzenstern, *Voyage*, 235–36.

36 In *Russkie otkrytiia v Tikhom Okeane i Severnoi Amerike v XVIII veke*, ed. Aleksandr I. Andreev (Moscow, 1948), 208.

37 Sauer, *Account*, 182.

38   Ibid., 173. The "Delareff" to whom Sauer refers was Evstrat I. Delarov, who had been sent to Kodiak Island by Shelikhov to manage the company's ventures and explore the American coast. He was replaced in July 1791 by Alexander Baranov.

39   Hubert H. Bancroft, *History of Alaska, 1730–1885* reprint of 1886 ed. (New York, 1960), 362, 365.

40   Yuri F. Lisiansky [Iurii Lisianskii], *A Voyage Round the World in the Years 1803, 4, 5, & 6 Performed by Order of His Imperial Majesty Alexander the First, Emperor of Russia, in the Ship Neva* (London, 1814), 183.

41   Bancroft, *History of Alaska*, 324n.

42   In *Russkie otkrytiia v Tikhom Okeane*, 52–53.

43   James R. Gibson, *Imperial Russia in Frontier America* (New York, 1976), 93–95, 99, 105, 109.

44   Published in *Russkie otkrytiia v Tikhom Okeane*, 256.

45   Ibid., 262.

46   Ibid., 263.

47   Ibid., 262.

48   There appears to be a signature just below and to the right of the cartouche at the bottom center of the plan's border. Unfortunately, it cannot be made out in the published version.

49   Illustrations of the Iakutsk *ostrog* are contained in the excellent study by N. V. Sultanov cited above, n. 27.

50   Shelikhov's letter to Baranov, dated August 9, 1794, quoted in Semen B. Okun, *Rossiisko-Amerikanskaia kompaniia* (Moscow-Leningrad, 1939), 33.

51   Reference has already been made to Gibson's having established Shelikhov's intentions to create a broad-based agricultural enterprise in Russian-America; see above, n. 43.

52   In *Russkie otkrytiia v Tikhom Okeane*, 337.

53   Ibid., 339.

54   Quoted in Fedorova, *Russkoe naselenie Aliaski*, p. 196.

55   In *Russkie otkrytiia v Tikhom Okeane . . .*, p. 342.

56   Fedorova, *Russkoe naselenie Aliaski*, 197. These eastern Siberian "connected houses" are discussed in L. M. Saburova, *Kul'tura i byt russkogo naseleniia Priangar'ia* (Leningrad, 1967), 104–23.

57   In *Russkie otkrytiia v Tikhom Okeane*, 340.

58   Ibid., 342.

59   Ibid.

60   Ibid., 339–40.

61   Ibid., 342.

62   See Viktor I. Kochedamov, "Anton Losev—Irkutskii arkhitektor kontsa XVIII–nachala XIX vv.," *Arkhitekturnoe nasledstvo* 19 (1972): 102–06.

63   In *Russkie otkrytiia v Tikhom Okeane*, 342.

64   Ibid.

65   See, inter alia, A. N. Petrov, S. A. Zombe, and T. M. Sytina, "Gradostroitel'stvo," *Istoriia russkogo iskusstva*, ed. I. E. Grabar' et al. (Moscow, 1961), 6:236–77; and T. M. Sytina, "Arkhitektura russkoi provintsii," in ibid. (Moscow, 1963), 8: 243–45.

66   In *Russkie otkrytiia v Tikhom Okeane*, 337.

67 Father Gedeon, "Iz rukopisi sobornago iermonakha Aleksandro-Nevskoi lavry o. Gedeona," in *Ocherk iz istorii Amerikanskoi Pravoslavnoi Dukhovnoi Missii (Kad'iakskoi Missii 1794–1837 gg.)* (St. Petersburg, 1894), 197.

68 Lisiansky, *Voyage*, 215.

69 Archibald Campbell, who visited the hospital, writes that it was "called the Chief District College of Counsellor and Chevalier Baranoff"; Campbell, *Voyage*, 190.

70 Father Gedeon, "Iz rukopisi," 197–98.

71 Campbell, *Voyage*, 74.

72 Ibid.

73 George H. von Langsdorff, *Voyage and Travels in Various Parts of the World During the Years 1803–06*, 2 vols. (London, 1814), 2:229.

74 Ibid., 79.

75 Published in Fedorova, *Russkoe naselenie Aliaski*, pl. 8. In this connection, it is significant to recall Father Gedeon's above-quoted observation that eight of the houses extended from the library "in the form of an elongated rectangle," which also suggests the use of lot lines and geometrical alignment to regulate building layout.

76 For Trezzini's schemes, see, inter alia, Yuri A. Egorov, *The Architectural Planning of St. Petersburg*, trans. Eric Dluhosch (Athens, Ohio, 1969), chap. 1. For a discussion of the planning programs undertaken by Catherine II and Alexander I, see V. I. Piliavskii, "Gradostroitel'nye meropriiatiia i obraztsovye proekty v Rossii v nachale XIX veka," *Nauchnye trudy Leningradskogo inzhenerno-tekhnicheskogo instituta* (Leningrad, 1958), 21:75–112. See also E. Beletskaia, N. Krashenninikova, L. Chernozubova, and I. Ern, *"Obraztsovye" proekty v zhiloi zastroike russkikh gorodov XVIII and XIX vv.* (Moscow, 1961).

77 This view is published in E. E. Blomkvist, "Risunki I. G. Voznesenskogo (Ekspeditsiia 1839–1849 gg.)," *Sbornik muzeia antropologii i etnografii* 13 (1951): 250, dwg. 11; English trans. by Basil Dmytryshyn and E. A. P. Crownhart-Vaughn: "A Russian Scientific Expedition to California and Alaska, 1839–1849: The Drawings of I. G. Voznesenskii," *Oregon Historical Quarterly* 73 (June 1972): 101–70. The drawing in question is reproduced on p. 117.

78 A descriptive but brief account of New Russia is contained in Tikhmenev, *Istoricheskoe*, 1:54 ff. For an account incorporating native sources, see William S. Hanable, "New Russia," *Alaska Journal* 3 (Spring 1973): 77–80. The site is now entered in the National Register of Historic Places as the "New Russia Archaeological Site."

79 Tikhmenev, ibid., 54.

80 Ibid.

81 Ibid., 150–52.

82 Baranov's letter to Medvednikov of 19 April 1800, describing the elements and methods of the fort's construction, is reproduced in *K istorii Rossiisko-Amerikanskoi kompanii: Sbornik dokumental'nykh materialov*, ed. P. N. Pavlov (Krasnoiarsk, 1957), 95–106.

83 Baranov's letter to Larionov of July 24, 1800, written from Kodiak Island, reprod. in Tikhmenev, *Istoricheskoe*, 2:144.

84 Lisiansky, *Voyages*, 218.

85 Ibid., 163.

86 Von Langsdorff, *Voyage and Travels*, 2:87.

87 In *Russkie otkrytiia v Tikhom Okeane i Severnoi Amerike v XVIII–XIX vekakh*, ed. A. I. Andreev (Moscow/Leningrad, 1944), 188. Korobitsyn continued his description by adding a list of buildings erected below the fort along the shore.

88 The juxtaposition of Korobitsyn's and Rezanov's descriptions of the same site provides a fairly detailed profile of the site for the period 1804–05.

89 Rezanov's letter to the directorate of the Russian American Company, dated November 6, 1805, and written from Novo-Arkhangel'sk, reprod. in Tikhmenev, *Istoricheskoe*, 2:198.

90 Peter C. Corney, *Voyages to the North Pacific: The Narrative of Several Trading Voyages from 1813–18, between the Northwest Coast, the Hawaiian Islands and China, with a Description of the Russian Settlements and California* (Honolulu, 1896; reprint of 1821 ed.), 30.

91 Ibid., 31.

92 Ibid.

93 The military settlements are discussed in *Graf Arakcheev i voennye poseleniia* (St. Petersburg, 1871). See also Allen McConnell, *Tsar Alexander I: Paternalistic Reformer* (New York, 1970), chap. 8.

94 For brief references to the planning of these military settlements see T. M. Sytina, "Arkhitektura russkoi provintsii," *Istoriia*, 8:244.

95 Eugene Duflot de Mofras, *Exploration de Territoire de l'Oregon, des Californies et de la mer Vermeille exécutée pendant les années 1840, 1841, et 1842* (Paris, 1844), pl. 21.

96 Fedor P. Lutke [Litke], *Voyage autour le Monde fait par ordre de sa majesté l'Empereur Nicolas 1er, sur la Corvette le Seniavine, dans les années 1826, 1827, 1828 et 1829*. The accompanying volume, containing the lithographs in question and accompanying commentary, is *Partie Historique Atlas: Lithographié d'après les dessins originaux d'Alexandre Postels, Professeur Adjoint de l'Université Imperiale de St. Petersbourg, et du Baron Kittlitz* (Paris, 1835).

97 Ibid., 4.

98 According to Bancroft, *History of Alaska*, 700, "an ecclesiastic named Sokolof arrived [in 1817], and a temporary [church] building was at once erected, the altar being built of timbers cast ashore after the wreck of the *Neva*." Rev. A. P. Kashevarov, in his later history, *St. Michael's Cathedral, Sitka, Alaska* (Juneau, [1938]), [1], suggests that the structure, originally built as a chapel, was already standing when Father Alexis Sokoloff [Aleksei Sokolov], the first ordained priest sent to Novo-Arkhangel'sk, arrived in October 1816. "Immediately [upon his arrival]," Kashevarov writes, "the chapel then in use was converted into a church." His passing reference does not make clear whether this "conversion" was accompanied by any significant remodeling or enlargement of the building itself. It notes only that "the iconostasis . . . was assembled from remnants of a rich collection of church materials which had been shipped from the Mother Country in the ship *Neva* in 1813, only to be wrecked on Cape Edgecumbe." Bishop Gregory (Afonsky), in his *History of the Orthodox Church in Alaska (1794–1917)* (Kodiak, 1977), 42, 52, states that regular church services were performed in the Church of St. Michael from 1808 until 1816, but sheds no further light on the building itself.

99   Edward Belcher, *Narrative of a Voyage Round the World*, 2 vols. (London, 1843), 1: 298.
100   See above, n. 87, for Korobitsyn's description and inventory.
101   Kiril T. Khlebnikov, *Zhizneopisanie Aleksandra Andreevicha Baranova, Glavnago pravitelia Rossiiskikh vladenii v Amerike* (St. Petersburg, 1835), 117.
102   M. I. Vavilov, "Poslednie dni v russkoi Amerike. Iz zapisok ochevidtsa," *Russkaia starina*, pt. 1, 49 (March 1886): 551.
103   Clarence L. Andrews, *The Story of Alaska* (Caldwell, Ohio, 1938), 88.

The Russian Orthodox Church in Alaska

1   Unless otherwise noted, all the data on the church in Alaska come from the Alaska Russian Church Archives, a collection of documents donated to the Library of Congress in 1927 and 1941 by the Russian Orthodox church in New York. Since the collection is not yet fully organized, it is not possible to provide more specific references.

2   The background material for this article has been drawn from a number of sources, some of which are nineteenth-century history books on the Russian Orthodox church in Russia, Siberia and the colonies, Russian America, and, after 1867, Alaska. One should mention the *Izvlechenie iz Otcheta Ober-Prokurora*, annual reports of the Over-Procurator of the Holy Synod; N. Olshevskii's *Sviateishii Pravitel'stvuiushchii Sinod pri Petre Velikom* (Kiev, 1894); Fedor V. Blagovidov's *Ober-Prokurory Sviateishago Sinoda v XVIII i v pervoi polovine XIX stoletia, Razvitie Ober-Prokurorskoi vlasti v Sinodalnom Vedomstve* (Kazan, 1899); a number of Russian Orthodox publications in the second half of the nineteenth century, like *Tserkovnye Vedomosti and Pravoslavnyi Amerikanskii Vestnik*, established in the United States in 1896; and the standard reference work, *Spiski Arkhiereev Ierarkhii Vserossiiskoi* (St. Petersburg, 1896). Among modern texts, George Vernadsky's works on the history of Russia have been used; the comprehensive history of the Russian church by Igor Smolitsch is *Geschichte der Russischen Kirche, 1700–1917* (Leiden, 1964).

3   P. Tikhmenev, *Istoricheskoe obozrenie obrazovaniia Rossiisko-Amerikanskoi Kompanii...*, 2 vols. (St. Petersburg, 1861–63), 1:228.

4   The value of the confessional records should not be underestimated, even those of the early twentieth century, for they were a required document and often contain more complete information on given individuals than the vital statistics do; for one thing, the vital statistics give only a report of the events for one particular year and do not reflect the number of the entire population. The confessional records include different kinds of information; occasionally there is an appendix giving a list of new converts; sometimes the new converts are listed directly in the confessional register. It is through the confessional lists that we learn about the number of inhabitants of Fort Ross in California in 1837. This record prepared by Veniaminov on April 29, 1838, includes the inhabitants of Novo-Arkhangel'sk, Kodiak, Fort Dionisius, Fort Ross and the Orthodox population at the Kostromitinov settlement not far from Fort Ross.

5   Beginning in 1841 the annual salaries for the clergy in Novo-Arkhangel'sk were:

	Paper Rubles	or	Silver Rubles
Headpriest	5,040		1,440
Priest	3,430		980
Deacon	1,995		570
2 Deacon Helpers	840 each		240 each
2 Church Assistants or Sextons	420 each		120 each
Prosfirnia (bread baker)	189		54

For comparison with secular salaries, the governor received 35,000 and a simple laborer 410 paper rubles a year.

6 The Nushagak parish was alternately under the control of Kenai and Kodiak; the Kenai priest was also responsible for missionary developments in the Prince William Sound area among the Chugach people.

7 The decree described in detail all the steps to be taken and the new salaries of the hierarchy involved. A later *ukaz* also issued by Tolstoi, dated May 8, 1859, gave details concerning the new communal school, its curriculum and staff.

8 Bishop Petr, whose name was Fedor Ekaterinovskii, was born in 1820 and received his education in the Moscow Academy; he was in charge of the Irkutsk seminary from 1844 to 1857; then from 1857 to 1859 he headed the school in Novo-Arkhangel'sk. He served as vicar general there from March 29, 1859, to 1866, at which time he was moved to Iakutsk, where he was vicar general until 1867. From 1867 through 1869 he served as a member of the Moscow Synod Office. He died on May 27, 1889, in Moscow.

9 Bishop Pavel or Petr Popov, born in 1813, was educated at the Irkutsk seminary and served as Bishop of Iakutsk from 1860 to 1866. He served in Novo-Arkhangel'sk, or Sitka as it was already called at that time, until 1870. He died in 1877 in Blagoveshchensk.

10 According to article III of the treaty, the population of the Russian colonies was divided into three categories: (1) The inhabitants of the ceded territory, according to their choice, reserving their natural allegiance, may return to Russia within three years; (2) but if they should prefer to remain in the ceded territory, they with the exception of uncivilized native tribes, shall be admitted to the enjoyment of all the rights, advantages and immunities of citizens of the United States, and shall be maintained and protected in the free enjoyment of their liberty, property and religion; (3) the uncivilized tribes will be subject to such laws and regulations as the United States may, from time to time, adopt in regard to aboriginal tribes of that country.

11 After the sale of Alaska most papers show two dates; the Julian and Gregorian calendars were twelve days apart.

12 One of Bishop Vladimir's documents, dated December 16, 1887, is a speech delivered to the Holy Synod upon his appointment to America as Bishop of the Aleutian Islands and Alaska. These five legal-size pages represent views held all too often by the clergymen of the period; by that time the impact of three major reactionary Russian educators, Protassov, Tolstoi, and Pobedonostsev was being felt in the world outlook of representatives of the church. Sokolovskii thought that his primary duty as a missionary was to fight Protestant pastors and Polish Catholic priests.

Just before his assignment to America, while serving in Poland, then occupied by Russia, he became well acquainted, in his words, with the "inconceivable guiles of Catholic propaganda." In his opinion, the Polish Roman Catholic churches served as dens of the enemies of Orthodoxy and the Russian people. His speech concluded by stating that now he was going off to fight heretics and to teach people who were "politically" friendly towards Russia. He listed among these the Tlingits, Aleuts, other Indians, creoles, and "the great Anglo-Saxon tribe." He remarked with apprehension, however, that because Americans were bored with their comfort and their many religions, they were joining the Masons and other liberal organizations.

13 Bishop Nikolai's narrations appeared in several issues of the *Tserkovnye Vedomosti* as well as in the *American Orthodox Messenger*, better known by its Russian name, *Pravoslavnyi Amerikanskii Vestnik*, which even included selected essays by over-procurator, Konstantin Pobedonostsev, on the subject of Orthodoxy and Russian nationality (*narodnost'*). This publication was partially bilingual and contained a number of articles with intolerant views and paradoxical ideas; as a principle it proclaimed the undisputed superiority of the Russian Orthodox religion, was concerned with the influence other denominations had over what the Russian church felt was its flock, and advanced admonitions and warnings to those who were spreading heterodox views (issue of September 15, 1896). Such articles as "How Is All This to Be Reconciled with the Principles of the American Constitution" (February 13, 1897, p. 196) put the American ideals to test in the discussion of petty misunderstandings over territorial missionary rights. One of the problems was that the priests who came from Russia confused the right given to them by the Treaty of 1867 to use the land on which their churches stood, and territorial rights for preaching Russian Orthodoxy. They bitterly resented competition; several Protestant denominations and the Catholic church went to work very energetically in the interior of Alaska trying, in their way, to help the native people of Alaska. This impelled the Russian Orthodox church to seek new converts among the native people of Alaska.

14 During the Russian period, financial collections were compulsory; they varied in purpose and the amount raised. Some were arranged to pay for the adornment of the local church, and a large number of embellishments and ritual vessels were purchased by donations from the creole and native parishoners; the most interesting documents of this nature come from the Aleutian Islands, with long lists of inhabitants and their signatures.

15 Vladimir Donskoi from Sitka, the priest in charge of Alaskan parishes from 1886 to 1893, could not leave for Russia because he used his travel funds to pay off a debt of eight hundred dollars to Petr Ionovich Kostromitinov, a local merchant; Vladimir Vechtomov, another Russian member of the hierarchy, had a difficult time making ends meet in San Francisco; so did Nikolai Mitropolskii and many others.

16 A large part of Netsvetov's journals has been translated by Lydia Black, *The Journals of Iakov Netsvetov, the Atkha Years 1828–1844* (Kingston, 1980).

17 In 1896, Ioann Bortnovskii, a priest from Kenai, mentioned in his travel journal that he saw in Tyonek, on the eastern wall of the St. Nicholas chapel, about twelve small icons painted locally.

18 People died of boils, ulcers (*vereda*), of colic pains (*kolotia*); with changes of weather, priests mentioned infections (*povetrie*) and other obscure ailments.

19 Deacon Vasilii Orlov, a creole, served in the Nushagak and Kuskokwim areas; he spoke the local dialect, understood several others and was a conscientious worker who lived in very restricted circumstances. On February 15, 1894, Orlov recorded in his church service journal an example of the reverse effect of Christianity: "One of the newly baptized Kuskokwim men came to me [he wrote] and told me that in his settlement an orphan girl gave birth to a baby and died during childbirth, but the infant remained alive. His comrades took the dead girl, put her into a walrus skin with her child, tied her up with leather straps, took her outside and threw her into a hole; but the child kept screaming and crying. He was suffocating." As the Kuskokwim man expressed pity for the child, Deacon Orlov asked him why he did not take it. The man replied that he had no wife, but primarily because his "comrades would not have thrown out the infant if the mother and the child had been baptized; they said that an unbaptized man is worse than a dog and that is why they threw them out like dogs." More than a decade later, Vasilii Kashevarov, another creole, wrote at length about the influence of the shamans among the people around Togiak River. Like Orlov, he served in the Nushagak area; in his church service record of March 21, 1907, and again two years later on March 8, 1909, he complained, "the inhabitants of the river Togiak are fierce pagans. There is a shaman in every village who exercises a tremendous influence on the inhabitants." The natives refused to have their children baptized and hid them when the priest came to their village; this, according to Kashevarov, was because the shamans told the people that the ritual of cutting the hair of the infant at baptism endangered his life. These people did not cut their hair until the age of twenty. Vasilii Kashevarov also described some of their dwellings and customs that persisted into the twentieth century.

20 One of his enemies was Zubov, who had an obscure past himself and in some documents is called Count Zubov, a descendant of Platon Aleksandrovich Zubov, a favorite of Catherine II. He was also accused of being a nihilist. Zubov, who himself endured persecutions from the Russian government, was strongly antisemitic and wrote some political accusations against the poor monk. Iosif Florovich Zubov always listed himself as an American citizen and did not get along with the other Russians; he was married to Anna Maksimova Vakhrameeva, daughter of the former manager of St. Michael Redoubt and Olimpiada Malakhova, a creole woman, and had a peaceful relationship with the local Indians.

21 The biographic information on Iakov Netsvetov has been taken from his dossier in the Alaska Russian Church Archives at the Library of Congress.

22 *Ukaz* no. 2172, dated April 8, 1852, addressed to Veniaminov concerning the development of other mission centers in the interior, gives the opinion of the imperial government on this subject after the initial experiment set up in 1845. The Russian American Company was not disposed at that time to spend any more money on such missions in the interior because "the hostility of the independent natives of the Yukon area evidently is increasing toward the Russians."

23 Anna Gavrilovna Netsvetov's fate was not any better; she also died young, in June of 1879, and left her children orphans. Until 1883, the girl Evgenia was kept by her grandmother Natal'ia Kashevarov, but after her death the Sitka priest, Nikolai Mitropol'skii, could not find any shelter for the ten-year-old child and stated that the

girl should be sent to Victoria to a Catholic monastery to save her from becoming a prostitute like other homeless young girls in Sitka. Since the Russian church could not help this daughter of a priest, she was placed in an orphanage, the Boys and Girls Aid Society of San Francisco. Several years later we learn from the correspondence of Ioann Sobolev, who served as deacon in San Francisco, that he tried to collect money for her keep since she had moved in with him and his wife Olga. Eventually Evgenia Netsvetov married a young priest, Aleksandr Iaroshevich.

24 The biographic information on Vasilii Shishkin has also been taken from the Alaska Russian Church Archives. He has a substantial dossier. The 1839 records of the Unalaska church give Shishkin's age as twenty-seven, and that of his wife, Paraskeva, as seventeen. He died when he was seventy-four years old.

25 In December of 1868, Alaska was still part of the Kamchatka diocese, but by 1870 this term had become obsolete; the new diocese was called Aleutian Islands and Alaska diocese. This changed the situation and Alaska priests were not "natives of the Kamchatka diocese" any longer and therefore were not entitled to receive any benefits.

26 The so-called citizen class was created by the decree of April 2, 1835, and included Russian old men and invalids who chose to remain in Russian America permanently; several of them stayed in Alaska with their families.

Science and Education in Russian America

1 S. G. Fedorova, *Russkoe naselenie Aliaski i Kalifornii* (Moscow, 1971), chaps. 1 and 2.

2 L. I. Sternberg, "Tikhii Okean: Russkie nauchnye issledovaniia," *Etnografiia* (Leningrad, 1926), 148.

3 G. W. Steller, *Beschreibung von dem Land Kamschatka, desen Einwohner, deren Sitten, Wahmen Lebensart und verschiedenen Gewohnheiten, herausgegeben von L.B.S.* (Frankfurt and Leipzig, 1774).

4 Sternberg, *Tikhii Okean*, 151.

5 Archives of the Academy of Sciences of the USSR (AAS), file 3, op. 1, d. 800, pp. 224–46.

6 AAS, fund 3, op. 1, d. 812, pp. 218–19.

7 Ibid., 5, op. 1–3, d. 36, 26 pages in length.

8 Ibid., 1, op. 13, d. 39:

9 Ibid., 4, op. 1, d. 151.

10 AAS, Protokoly konferentsii 2, pp. 133–35; AAN, file 3, op. 1, d. 813, pp. 28, 29, 31, 32.

11 P. S. Pallas, *O Rossiiskikh otkrytiiakh na moriakh mezhdu Aziei i Amerikoi*; works selected from monthly journals (1790), vol. 4.

12 *Sravnitel'ny slovar' vsekh iazikov i narechii po azbuchnomu poriadku raspolozhennii* (St. Petersburg, 1780), vol. 1.

13 *Russkie otkrytiia v ikhom okeane i severnoi Amerike XVIII v.* (Moscow, 1948), 316.

14 Ibid., 244–49.

15 Ibid., 221.

16 Ibid., 194.

17 Ibid., 195.

18 Ibid., 224.

19 Ibid., 229.

20 Ibid., 324.

21 Ibid., 323.

22 Ibid., 328.

23 *Kratkii slovar' dvenadtsati narechii raznykh narodov, obitaiushchikh v severnoi chasti Sibiri i na Aleutskikh ostrovakh, in Puteshestvie kapitana Billingsa i plavanie kapitana, izvlecheno iz raznykh zhurnalov Gavrilom Sarychevym* (St. Petersburg, 1811), 91–129.

24 *Etnograficheskie materialy severo-vostochnoi geograficheskoi ekspeditsii 1785–1795 gg.* (Magadan, 1978).

25 Central State Archive, Army/Navy Collections (TsGAVMF), file 214, op. 1, d. 26, 34.

26 R. G. Liapunova, "Kollektsiia severo-vostochnoi geograficheskoi ekspeditsii Billingsa-Sarycheva (1785–1794)," unpublished MS.

27 G. H. von Langsdorff, *Bermerkungen auf einer Reise um die Welt in Jahren 1803 bis 1807* (Frankfurt, 1812), 1:2.

28 A. P. Lazarev, *Zapiski plavanii voennogo shliupa "Blagonamerennogo" v Beringov proliv i vokrug sveta dlia otkrytii v 1819, 1820, 1821, 1822, vedennye gvardeiskogo ekipazha leitenantom A. P. Lazarevym* (Moscow, 1950).

29 *Puteshestvie vokrug sveta, sovershennoe na voennom shliupe Kamchatka v 1817, 1818, 1819, flota kapitanom Golovninym* (Moscow, 1965).

30 *Dvukratnoe puteshestvie v Ameriku morskikh ofitserov Khvostova i Davydova, pisannoe sim slednim* (St. Petersburg, 1810–12), vols. 1 and 2.

31 Ibid., pt. 2, 150–59.

32 Ibid., pt. 2, 7.

33 Ibid., 99, 1113.

34 Ibid., 100.

35 Ibid., 99.

36 K. T. Khlebnikov, *Russkaia Amerika v neopublikovannykh zapiskakh K. T. Khlebnikova* (Leningrad, 1979), 22–23.

37 Ibid., 24, 35.

38 Ibid., 49, 52, 56, 70, 77, 96, 114.

39 *Tvoreniia Innokentiia, mitropolita Moskovskogo*, ed. Ivan Barsukov (Moscow, 1888), 81.

40 Ibid., 271–315.

41 Ibid., 485.

42 Ibid., 573.

43 I. E. Veniaminov, "Mifologicheskie predaniia i sueveriia Koloshei, obitaiushchikh na severo-zapadnom beregu Ameriki," *Syn otechestva*, 9 (1839): 40–82.

44 Central State Historical Archive, Leningrad (TsGIAL), 1841, drawer 2, d. 903, p. 1.

45 TsGIAL, F. E. L. von Fisher, "O poseve i posadke lesa na o. Unalashke," in TsGIAL, 1841, drawer 2, d. 903, p. 2.

46 TsGIAL, "Vypiska iz pis'ma G. E. Chernykh iz byvshei kolonii Ross v Novoi Kalifornii ot 19 sent. 1840 g. k chlenu obshchestva P.L. Kh.," in TsGIAL, file 91, 1841, drawer 2, d. 903, p. 6.

47 A. A. Shtraukh, *Zoologicheskii muzei Imperatorskoi akademii nauk; piatidesiatiletie ego sushchestvovaniia* (St. Petersburg, 1889), 46.

48 P. M. Kozhin, "Etnograficheskie nabliudeniia I.G. Voznesenskogo v Kalifornii," *Trudy Instituta Etnografii*, new ser. 7 (1977): 104.

49 Ibid., 67.

50 Ibid., 71–76.

51 A. I Alekseev, *Il'ia Gavrilovich Voznesenskii* (Moscow, 1977), 55.

52 *Puteshestviia i issledovaniia leitenanta Lavrentiia Zagoskina v Russkoi Amerike v 1842–1844 gg.* (Moscow, 1956).

53 P. Tikhmenev, *Istoricheskoe obozrenie obrazovaniia Rossiisko-Amerikanskoi Kompanii* (St. Petersburg, 1863), 197.

54 F. Litke *Puteshestvie vokrug sveta, sovershennoe . . . na voennom shliupe "Seniavin" v 1826–29 gg flota kapitanom Fedorom Litke,* otdelenie istoricheskoe (St. Petersburg, 1834), 1:1.

55 Ibid., 9–12, 15–16.

56 Ibid., 21.

57 Ibid., 20.

58 Ibid., 21.

59 Ibid., 24.

60 Ibid., 223.

61 Ibid., 155–62.

62 Ibid., 161.

63 Ibid., 153.

64 Ibid., 150.

65 Ibid., 152.

66 Ibid., 158.

67 Ibid., 166.

68 Ibid., 146.

69 N. P. Golovnin, *Obzor russkikh kolonii v Severnoi Amerike kapitan-leitenanta Golovnina* (St. Petersburg, 1862), 11–12.

70 Ibid., 11–12.

71 K. T. Khlebnikov, *Materialy dlia istorii russkikh zaselenii po beregam Vostochnogo okeana (Zapiski K. T. Khlebnikova ob Amerike)* (St. Petersburg, 1861), 3:120.

72 Ibid., 121.

73 *Puteshestviia . . . Zagoskina,* 372.

74 R. Fisher, *Records of the Russian-American Company 1802, 1817–67* (Washington, D.C., 1971) 115.

75 Tikhmenev, *Istoricheskoe,* 250.

76 TsGIAL, file 37 for 1865, drawer 53, d. 179, p. 1.

77 Ibid., p. 2.

78 Ibid., p. 5.

79 Fedorova, *Russkoe,* 218–22; R. G. Liapunova, "Zapiski ieromonakha Gedeona (1803–1807) odin iz istochnikov po istorii i etnografii Russkoi Ameriki," *Problemy istorii i etnografii Ameriki* (Moscow, 1969), 215–29.

80 Fedorova, *Russkoe,* 220.

81 *Russkie otkrytiia na Tikhom okeane i v Severnoi Amerike* (Moscow, 1948), 188.

82 Ibid., 332.

83 Ibid., 300.

84 *Vstrecha Vankuvera i ego sputnikov s promyshlennymi russkimi arteliami v Kenaiskom i Chugatskom zalivakh.* (St. Petersburg, 1861) 4:12, 29.

85 TsGIAL, file 13, drawer 1 for 1802, d. 41, p. 1.

86 *Valaamskie missioneri* (St. Petersburg, 1900), 99.

87 Khlebnikov, *Russkaia Amerika*, 246.

88 Ibid., 246.

89 P. N. Golovnin has written in detail about the all-colonial academy as well as the girls' school founded in 1839 along with others in "A Review of Russian Colonies in North America" (St. Petersburg, 1862), 64–70.

90 TsGIAL, fund. 796 for 1867, op. 148, d. 1592, p. 1.

91 TsGIAL, fund 796, drawer 139 for 1858, d. 1851, pp. 1–2.

92 TsGIAL, fund 796, drawer 319 for 1858, drawer 947.

93 Tikhmenev, *Istoricheskoe*, 274.

94 Fedorova, *Russkoe*, 222.

95 TsGIAL, fund 796 for 1804, op. 85, drawer 564, p. 1.

96 Kratkie ob'iasneniia, sdelannie sootvetstvenno zapiske, prislannoi ot Sviateishego pravitel'stvennogo sinoda ob amerikanskom ostrove Kad'iake severo'vostochnoi amerikanskoi dykhovnoi missii nachal'stvuiushchim Kad'iakskim arkhimandritom Iosafom (LOII, file 115, drawer 117, p. 15).

97 *Russkaia Amerika v neopublikovannykh zapiskakh K. T. Khlebnikova ob Amerike* (Leningrad, 1979), 243.

98 Ibid., 246.

99 L. D. Starr, "Education in Russian Alaska," *Alaska State Library Historical Monographs*, no. 2 (London, 1972), 7.

100 *Valaamskie missioneri* (St. Petersburg, 1900), 99.

101 Ibid., 100.

102 R. G. Liapunova, "Zapiski ieromonakha Gedeona (1803–1804)—odin iz istochnikov po istorii i etnografii Russkoi Ameriki," *Problemy istorii i etnografii Ameriki* (Moscow, 1979), 215–29.

103 Ibid., 227.

104 I. Barsukov, ed., *Tvoreniia Innokentiia*; R. G. Liapunova, *Ocherki po etnografii aleutov* (Leningrad, 1975); A. P. Okladnikov, "Ot Angido Unalashkii Udivitel'naia sud'ba Iv. Popova," *Voprosi istorii* 6, no. 6 (1976): 80–88; A. A. Arsen'ev "Etnograficheskoe nasledie I. E. Veniaminova," *Sovetskaia etnografiia* 5 (1979).

105 *Otchet Rossiisko-Amerikanskoi kompanii po 1 jan. 1847 g.* (St. Petersburg, 1847), 36.

106 Tikhmenev, *Istoricheskoe*, 271.

107 *Polnoe sobranie zakonov Rossiiskoi imperii*, 14, directive no. 124, 34.

108 TsGIAL, fund 796, op. 126 for 1845, d. 295.

109 Ibid., fund 796 for 1860, op. 141, d. 2284, p. 26.

110 Ibid., p. 32.

111 TsGIAL, fund 796 for 1866, d. 147, 2133, pp. 453–54.

112 Ibid., p. 493.

113 L. D. Starr, *Education in Russian Alaska* (London, 1972), n. 2.

114 TsGIAL, p. 2, file 796 (1843–44), drawer 125, d. 59, p. 77 ob.

115 Ibid., p. 67 ob.

116 Ibid., p. 70.

117 Ibid., p. 77 ob.

118 "Mnenie shtab-lekaria Aleksandra Romanovskogo o prepodavanii meditsinskikh nauk v Novo-Archangel'skom dukhovnom uchilishche," TsGIAL, file 796 for 1843–44, op. 125, d. 59, pp. 78–79 ob.

119 Ibid., p. 78.

120 Ibid.

121 Ibid., p. 79–79 ob.

122 Ibid., p. 78.

123 TsGIAL, file 796 for 1852, op. 133, d. 596, p. 2.

124 Ibid., and file 796 for 1851.

125 TsGIAL, file 796 for 1844, op. 125, d. 59.

126 Ibid., file 796 for 1846, op. 127, d. 33.

127 Ibid., file 796 for 1847, op. 188, d. 57.

128 Ibid., pp. 13, 14.

129 Ibid.

130 Ibid., p. 1.

131 Ibid., pp. 20–28.

132 TsGIAL, file 796 for 1843, op. 124, d. 1288, p. 95.

133 TsGIAL, file 796 for 1853, op. 134, d. 1861.

134 Ibid., file 796 for 1845, op. 126, d. 353, p. 2.

135 Ibid., file 796 for 1846, op. 127, d. 1514, f. 796 for 1858–59, op. 139, d. 2315.

136 "Materialy dlia istorii Russkikh zaselenii po beregam Vostochnogo okeana: Zapiski K. T. Khlebnikova ob Amerike," *Morskoi sbornik* 3 (1861): 162.

Russian America and International Relations

1 A. V. Efimov, *Iz istorii velikikh russkikh geograficheskikh otkrytii*, 2d ed. (Moscow, 1971), 288.

2 On this subject see also B. P. Polevoi, "Petr Pervyi, Nikolai Vitsen i problema soshlasia li Amerika s Aziei," *Strany i narody Vostoka*, no. 17 (Moscow, 1976), 19–40; R. H. Fisher, *Bering's Voyages: Whither and Why* (Seattle, 1977), 162–79.

3 *Polnoe sobranie zakonov Rossiiskoi imperii*, 1649 godo (*PSZRI*) (St. Petersburg, 1830), 7, no. 4649: 413.

4 R. V. Makarova, *Russkie na Tikhom okeane vo vtoroi polovine XVIII v*, (Moscow, 1968), 182–97.

5 *Ekspeditsiia Beringa; Sbornik documentov*, comp. A. Pokrovskii (Moscow, 1941), 29–30.

6 V. Berkh, *Khronologicheskaia istoriia otkrytiia Aleutskikh ostrovov* (St. Petersburg, 1823), p. 46; Makarova, *Russkie na tikhom*, 185; E. M. Dvoichenko-Markova, *Shturman Gerasim Izmailov, ix Morskie zapiski*, (New York, 1955), 13, no. 4: 14–27.

7 See J. Ledyard, *A Journal of Captain Cook's Last Voyage to the Pacific Ocean* (Chicago, 1963), 98–100.

8 Ia. M. Svet and S. G. Fedorova, "Captain Cook and the Russians," *Pacific Studies* 2, no. 1 (Fall 1978): 1–2.

9 *Tret'e plavanie kapitana Dzhemsa Kuka: Plavanie Tikhom okeane v 1776–1780 gg.*, trans. from the English, with introduction and comments by Ia. M. Svet (Moscow,

1971), 389–96. Full English original is *The Voyage of the Resolution and Discovery, 1776–1780*, ed. J. C. Beaglehole, vol. 3 of *The Journals of Captain James Cook on His Voyages of Discovery* (Cambridge, 1967).

10 Ibid., 395–96.

11 S. F. Fedorova, "Pervoe poselenie russkikh na Unalashke i Dzh. Kuk," in *Novoe v izuchenii Avstralii i Okeanii* (Moscow, 1972), 228–36. It is not accidental that Unalaska was chosen by G. I. Shelikhov as an "assembly place" where he spent about ten days— from July 13 to 22, 1784 (Old Style). "Having repaired all the necessary things on Unalaska Island and taking with us two interpreters and ten Aleutians who voluntarily agreed to do service," Shelikhov then sailed to Kodiak Island, leaving appropriate instructions for his third galiot *Sv. Mikhail* (St. Michael). See Shelikhov, *Rossiiskogo kuptsa Grigoria Shelikhova stranstvovania*, ed. B. P. Polevoi, (Khabaraovsk, 1971), 36–37.

12 *Tret'e plavanie kapitana Dzhemsa Kuka*, 396–97, 562–64.

13 For more details see E. Vila Vilar, *Los rusos en America* (Sevilla, 1966), 19–45; E. Volkl, *Russland und Lateinamerika, 1741–1841*, (Wiesbaden, 1968), 49–76. In his notes, K. T. Khlebnikov quotes A. Humboldt's testimony that the vice-royal archive in Mexico contained a thick volume under the heading "Reconocimiento de los quatro Establecimiento Rusos al Norte de la California hecho en 1783 [*sic*, 1788]." See *Russkaia Amerika v neopublikovannykh zapiskakh K. T. Khlebnikova*, ed. R. G. Liapunova and S. G. Fedorova (Leningrad, 1979), 93–94.

14 The end of the dispatch setting forth changes in the diplomatic corps has been omitted.

15 Arkhiv vnesnei politiki Rossii (AVPR), f. Souskeniia Rossii s Ispaniei (Relations of Russia with Spain), d. 465, 11. 57–58; original in Russian. Supplement: ibid., 11. 59–60; copy in French.

16 See, in particular, "Obozrenie sostoianiia i deistvii Rossisko-amerikanskoi kompanii, 1797 do 1819g" and P. I. Poletika's letter to J. K. Adams of March 21 [April 2], 1822, AIPR, f. Russian-American Company (RAC), d. 288, 11. 7–93; ASPFR, vol. 4, p. 363.

17 Ia. I. Svet and S. G. Fedorova, *Istoria piatnadtsati—"Brigantina"*, (Moscow, 1971), 64; Volkl, *Russland und Lateinamerika, 1741–1841.* p. 60.

18 *John Ledyard's Journey through Russia and Siberia, 1787–1788: The Journal and Selected Letters*, ed. with introduction by S. D. Watrous (Madison, 1966), 46.

19 For more details see N. N. Bolkhovitinov, *Stanovlenie russko-amerikanskikh otnoshenii 1773-1815* (Moscow, 1966) 287–95; Bolkhovitinov, *The Beginnings of Russian-American Relations, 1775–1815* trans. E. Levin, (Cambridge/London, 1975), 156–62, 425–26; and Bolkhovitinov, *Rossia i voina SShA za nezavisimost', 1775–1783* (Moscow, 1976), 176–92.

20 *The United States and Russia: The Beginning of Relations, 1765–1815.* (Washington, D.C., 1980), 244.

21 F. W. Howay, *A List of Trading Vessels in the Maritime Fur Trade, 1783–1825* (Kingston, 1973), 3–24.

22 See also E. Gunther, *Indian Life on the Northwest Coast of North America*, (Chicago, 1972); *Early Visitors to Southeastern Alaska*, ed. E. N. de Armond (Anchorage, 1978); *Voyages of Enlightenment: Malaspina on the Northwest Coast 1791–1792*, ed. Th. Vaughan, E. A. P. Crownhart-Vaughan, and M. P. de Inglesias (Portland, 1977).

23   The texts of Paul I's decree of July 8 [19], 1799, "rules" and "privileges" are to be found in *PSZRI* (St. Petersburg, 1830), 25:699–704. The archival original is preserved in the Central State Historical Archive of the USSR (TsYIA SSSR), f. 1329, op. 1, d. 217.

24   G. Vancouver, *A Voyage of Discovery to the North Pacific Ocean, and Round the World . . . Performed in the Years 1790–1795 in the "Discovery", Sloop of War . . .*, 3 vols. (London, 1789).

25   Records of the Russian American Company, 1802–61, vol. 1, RG 261, National Archives, Washington, D.C.

26   The full text of N. P. Rezanov's 17-point "testament" is in the Library of Congress, Manuscript Division, G. V. Yudin Collection, Box 1, Folder 11. An excerpt from the "testament" (point 7) is published in the collection, *The United States and Russia: The Beginning of Relations, 1765–1815* (Washington, D.C., 1980), p. 455–57.

27   See also "The List of Persons Wishing to Stay in America," enumerating the full names of thirty-four people, mainly from among urban middle classes and peasants, "who have married American women and have children," Library of Congress, Manuscript Division, G. V. Yudin Collection, box 1.

28   Ibid.

29   N. P. Rumiantsev to Alexander I, November 12 [24], 1809 (TsGIA-SSSR), f. 13, op. I, d. 287, 11. 78–84. The full text of the report is published in *The United States and Russia*, 618–21.

30   F. P. Palen to N. P. Rumiantsev, July 9 [21], 1810, *The United States and Russia*, 677.

31   F. W. Howey, *A List*. W. Z. Cook, *Flood Tide of Empire: Spain and the Pacific Northwest, 1543–1819* (New Haven 1973), app. 3, p. 551.

32   J. R. Gibson, *Bostonians and Muscovites on the Northwest Coast, 1788–1841—The Eastern Shore*, ed. Thomas Vaughan (Portland, 1975), 97–99.

33   John D'Wolf, *A Voyage to the North Pacific and a Journey through Siberia More Than Half a Century Ago* (Cambridge, 1861), 22.

34   For the full text of the contract between A. A. Baranov and G. W. Ayres, see *The United States and Russia*, 511–16.

35   See V. M. Golovnin, *Puteshestvie na shliupe "Diana" iz Kronstadta v Kamchatku, sovershennoe pod nachalstvom flota leitenanta Golovnina v 1807–1811 godakh* (Moscow, 1961), 324–27.

36   A. G. Mazour, "The Russian-American and Anglo-Russian Conventions, 1824–1825," *Pacific Historical Review* 14, no. 3 (1945): 304; H. Chevigny, *Russian America* (New York, 1965), 181; M. E. Wheeler, "Empires in Conflict and Cooperation," *Pacific Historical Review* 40, no. 4 (1971): 434; H. I. Kushner, *Conflict on the Northwest Coast: American-Russian Rivalry in the Pacific Northwest, 1790–1867* (Westport, 1975), 32.

37   N. N. Bolkhovitinov, *Russko-amerikanskie otnoshenia, 1815–1832* (Moscow, 1975), 162–82.

38   See S. B. Okun, *Rossiisko-amerikanskaia kompania* (Moscow/Leningrad, 1939), 26–50, 90–94, 145, 257–58. Traces of this conception are observed also in many other works on Russian America, not excluding A. I. Alekseev's new book *Sud'ba russkoi Ameriki* (Magadan, 1975), 176.

39   A. A. Guber, ed., *Politika evropeiskikh derzhav v Iugovostochnoi Azii (60-e gody XVIII v.—60-e gody XIX v.) Dokumenty i materialy* (Moscow, 1962), 10.

40   See Ia. O. Lambert's note of January 2 [14], 1817, and M. A. Saltykov's comments on
     P. Dobell's proposals (1816–1817), in ibid., 477—90; AVPR, f. Chancellery, d. 13378,
     11. 165–73; K. V. Nesselrode to Alexander I, May ... 1819," AVPR, Glavnyi arkiv, 1–10,
     d. 1, 11. 131–35; N. N. Bolkhovitinov, "Vydvizhenie i proval proektov P. Dobella
     (1812–1832)," in *Amerikanskii ezhegodnik* (Moscow, 1976), 264–82.

41   The main directorate of the Russian American Company to E. F. Kankrin, May 14
     [26], 1824, AVPR, Russian American Company, d. 314, 11. 19–21; minutes of the
     company's   directorate   of   "June ... 1824"   with   K.   F.   Ryleev's autograph,
     Gosydarstvennyi arkhiv Permskoi oblosti, f. 445, op. 1, d. 78, 1. 1, and especially the
     materials submitted to Nikolai I together with K. V. Nesselrode's report of October
     27 [November 8], 1826, AVPR, f. Chancellery, 1826, op. 468, d. 2995, 11. 5–191.

42   E. F. Kanfrin's note of March 4 [16], 1825, AVPR, f. Russian-American Company, d.
     258, 1. 13.

43   K. V. Nesselrode to Nikolai I, October 27 [November 8], 1826, AVPR, f. Chancellery,
     1826, op. 468, d. 2995, 11. 179–80. Also see "Memoire D.B. [Dmitrii Bludov]," ibid.,
     11. 192–99.

44   Along with the above-mentioned monograph, see also H. I. Kushner's articles "The
     Oregon Question Is ... a Massachusetts Question," *Oregon Historical Quarterly* 75,
     no. 4 (1974): 317–35; "The Russian-American Diplomatic Contest for the Pacific Basin
     and the Monroe Doctrine," *Journal of the West* 15, no. 2 (1975): 65–80.

45   Howard I. Kushner, *Conflict on the Northwest Coast: American-Russian Rivalry in
     the Pacific Northwest, 1790–1867* (Westport, Conn., 1975), xi–xii, 158.

46   Ibid. For more details see N. N. Bolkhovitinov, *Zorubezhnye issledovaniia o Russkoi
     Amerike—SShA—ekonomika, politika, ideologiia* (Moscow, 1985), 87–95.

47   N. N. Bolkhovitinov, *Doktrina Monro (proiskhozhdenie i kharakter)* (Moscow, 1959),
     pp. 186–209. Noting that I confirm W. A. Williams's conclusion when I point out
     the anti-English edge of the Monroe Doctrine, Professor Kushner does not take into
     account the fact that my main works on the question appeared in the second half
     of the 1950s, that is, prior to and independently of W. A. Williams's book *The
     Contours of American History* (Chicago, 1961); H. E. Kushner, *Conflict on the North-
     west Coast*, 57, 173.

48   Bolkhovitinov, *Stanovlenie russko-amerikanskikh otnoshenii*, 325, 331.

49   Wheeler, "Empires in Conflict and Cooperation," 419–41.

50   N. K. Krabbe to A. M. Gorchakov, 7 [19] December 1866, N26-AVPR, f. RAC, d. 399, 1.
     11; d. 410, 11. 8–9; Opinions of Grand Duke Konstantin, Reitern, and Stoeckl [12 [24]
     December 1866], AVPR, f. Glavnyi orkhiv 1–9, 1857–68, 11. 66–67; D. H. Miller *The
     Alaska Treaty* (Kingston, 1981), 61–62.

51   N. N. Bolkhovitinov, *SShA: problemy istorii i sovremennaia istoriografiia* (Moscow,
     1980).

The Sale of Russian America to the United States

An abbreviated and undocumented version of this paper was published as "Why the
Russians Sold Alaska," *Wilson Quarterly* 3 (1979): 179–88. The complete, documented
version initially appeared in *Acta Slavica Iaponica* 1 (1983): 15–37 and is republished
here with the permission of its editorial board.

1   George E. Baker, ed., *The Works of William H. Seward* (New York, 1972), 5:601–2.
2   See Victor J. Farrar, *The Annexation of Russian America to the United States* (New York, 1966), and Archie W. Shiels, *The Purchase of Alaska* (Fairbanks, 1967).
3   *Charles Sumner: His Complete Works* (New York, 1969), 15:38, 41, 43, 48.
4   "Papers Relating to the Cession of Alaska, 1856–67," annex no. 21, Microcopy no. T-495, U.S. National Archives, Washington, D.C.
5   See David E. Shi, "Seward's Attempt to Annex British Columbia, 1865–1869," *Pacific Historical Review* 47 (1978): 217–38. In 1846 Seward declared that "our population is destined to roll its restless waves to the icy barriers of the north, and to encounter oriental civilization on the shores of the Pacific," and in 1860 he predicted that Russian America and western Canada would "yet become the outposts of the United States" (Baker, *Works of William H. Seward* 3:409, 4:333).In a speech at Salem, Oregon in 1869 Seward stated that two of his guiding and steadfast political convictions had been "that if a nation desires to be independent and prosperous, and enjoy peace at home and abroad, it must expand itself commensurately with its resources and advantages" and "that the permanent continuance of European or monarchial government in the American hemisphere would be injurious and dangerous to the United States" (Baker, *Works of William H. Seward,* 5:572). Seward subsequently rated the Alaska Treaty his foremost achievement. Many of the official American and Russian papers concerning the acquisition/disposal of Alaska have been published in David Hunter Miller, *The Alaska Treaty* (Kingston, 1981).
6   See Howard I. Kushner, *Conflict on the Northwest Coast: American-Russian Rivalry in the Pacific Northwest, 1790–1867* (Westport, 1975), and "'Seward's Folly'?: American Commerce in Russian America and the Alaska Purchase," *California History* 54 (1975): 4–26.
7   See, for example, Kushner, "'Seward's Folly'?," 17.
8   *Charles Sumner,* 15:20–21.
9   "Papers," annex no. 43, U.S. National Archives. For an English translation of this document, see Ernest Gruening, ed., *An Alaskan Reader, 1867–1967* (New York, 1966), 41–48.
10 Actually, American editorial (if not public) opinion largely favored—or at least did not oppose—the purchase. See Richard E. Welch, Jr., "American Public Opinion and the Purchase of Russian America," *American Slavic and East European Review* 17 (1958): 481–94.
11 *Doklad komiteta ob ustroistve russkikh amerikanskikh kolonii* (St. Petersburg, 1863–64) 2:563; Frank A. Golder, "The Purchase of Alaska," *American Historical Review* 25 (1920): 417; [Russian American Company, Head Office], *Otchet Rossiisko-Amerikanskoi Kompanii Glavnago Pravleniia za odin god . . .* (St. Petersburg, 1843–65), 1842, p. 10; [Dmitrii Zavalishin], *Rossiisko-Amerikanskaia kompaniia* (Moscow, 1865), 3.
12 S. B. Okun, "K istorii prodazhi russkikh kolonii v Amerike," *Istoricheskie zapiski* 2 (1938): 233.
13 Ibid., p. 47.
14 In fact, in 1864 London banking circles offered a loan to the Russian American Company on the condition that its monopoly be continued, but this the Russian government refused to guarantee.
15 Quoted by Okun, "K istorii," 225.

16 "Papers," annex no. 1, U.S. National Archives.

17 The tenor of the Kostlivtsov-Golovin findings is indicated by the following remark by Golovin, who, enroute to Sitka from San Francisco aboard the *Tsaritsa* in late 1860, blamed a sailor's death on the lack of a doctor on the company's ship: "The poor seaman, for want of help, passed from this world to the next, *where he will undoubedly be better off than in the service of the Russian-American Company*" [Golovin's italics] (V. Rimskii-Korsakov, ed., "Iz putevykh pisem P. N. Golovina," *Morskoi sbornik* 6 [1863]: 176). These letters have been published in translation as *Civil and Savage Encounters: The Worldly Travel Letters of an Imperial Russian Navy Officer, 1860–1861*, trans. Basil Dmytryshyn and E. A. P. Crownhart-Vaughan [Portland, 1983]. Golovin's official report has appeared in translation as *The End of Russian America: Captain P. N. Golovin's Last Report 1862*, trans. Basil Dmytryshyn and E. A. P. Crownhart-Vaughan [Portland, 1979].) By 1860 the company seems to have fallen into considerable official and public disfavor in the motherland, apparently largely because its exploitation of the natives was out of keeping with the mood in favor of emancipation of the serfs. During the polemics that began in 1862 upon the expiration of its franchise, the company was criticized mainly for enserfing the natives, neglecting its employees, monopolizing trade, keeping the colony underdeveloped, and making business transactions that were disadvantageous to the state ([Zavalishin], *Rossiisko-Amerikanskaia kompaniia*, 4–5).

18 *Doklad*, 2 vols. In addition, the Naval Ministry issued a special supplement to its literary organ, *Morskoi sbornik*, that was critical of the Russian American Company's operations; see *Materialy dlia istorii russkikh zaselenii po beregam vostochnago okeana* (St. Petersburg, 1861).

19 P. Tikhmen'ev, *Istoricheskoe obozrenie obrazovaniia Rossiisko-Amerikanskoi kompanii i deistvii eia do nastoiashchago vremeni*, 2 vols. in 1 (St. Petersburg, 1861–63). This work has been published in an English translation as P. A. Tikhmenev, *A History of the Russian-American Company*, trans. and ed. Richard A. Pierce and Alton S. Donnelly (Seattle and Kingston, 1978–79), 2 vols.

20 Konstantin to Gorchakov, March 22 [April 3], 1857, "Documents Relating to the Cession of Alaska," Library of Congress, Manuscript Division.

21 See Svetlana G. Fedorova, *The Russian Population in Alaska and California Late 18th Century–1867*, trans. Richard A. Pierce and Alton S. Donnelly (Kingston, 1973), 277–78.

22 Tikhmenev, *History*, 393–94. Also see the Russian American Company's annual *Otchet* (St. Petersburg, 1843–65), 21 vols.

23 Hallie M. McPherson, ed. and trans., "The Projected Purchase of Alaska, 1859–60," *Pacific Historical Review* 3 (1934): 82.

24 *Doklad*, 1:400–403. Moreover, as the onetime Decembrist Dmitrii Zavalishin pointed out, Russia's territory on the less remote Asiatic side of the Pacific (the Kamchatka Peninsula and Okhotsk seaboard) was no better off than that on the American side ([Zavalishin], *Rossiisko-Amerikanskaia kompaniia*, 4).

25 Ibid., 99; S. B. Okun, *The Russian-American Company*, trans. Carl Ginsburg (Cambridge, 1951), 232.

26 *Doklad*, 1:133, 203; Tikhmenev, *History*, 366.

27 *Doklad*, 1:134–35.

28 Tikhmenev, *History*, 201.

29 Ibid., 163.

30 Ibid., 153, 207, 360. In fact, the Russian American Company was nearly bankrupted in the first half of the 1820s by mismanagement on the part of the directors Benedict Kramer and Andrei Severin.

31 Ibid., 238, 392.

32 Okun, *Russian-American Company*, 225.

33 Dmitrii Nedel'kovich, a naval officer in the employ of the Russian American Company, expressed the prevailing air of uncertainty over the future of the Company and its territory when he exclaimed in late 1860 that "God knows what awaits the Company!" (D. I. Nedel'kovich, "Vospominaniia o puteshestvii sukhim putem iz Kronshtadta v Novo-Arkhangel'sk . . . ," State Historical Museum, Division of Written Sources, f. 92, no. 99445/4650, p. 35).

34 "Papers," annex no. 1.

35 Ibid., annex no. 3.

36 The value of the company's shares did not fall until after Kostlivtsov and Golovin had left St. Petersburg for Sitka in 1860 to inspect the colony (Rimskii-Korsakov, "Iz putevykh pisem," 288). And they fell, according to Zavalishin, because of "talk of a shake-up of the Company" after the expiration of its charter at the end of 1861 ([Zavalishin], *Rossiisko-Amerikanskaia kompaniia*, 3). Other factors included the lower profits on tea from 1862 (following the government's abolition of the company's monopoly on the importation of Chinese tea by sea) and the government's termination in 1862 of the company's sharing in revenue from tariffs on imports into Russia of foreign beaver and fur seal skins (*Doklad*, 1:391).

37 Konstantin to Gorchakov, March 22 [April 3], 1857, "Documents."

38 "Papers," annex no. 2, U.S. National Archives.

39 Oleh W. Gerus, "The Russian Withdrawal from Alaska: The Decision to Sell," *Revista de Historia de America*, 75–76 (1972–1973): 173; Okun, "K istorii," 235; Okun, *Russian-American Company*, 266.

40 Hunter Miller, ed., "Russian Opinion on the Cession of Alaska," *American Historical Review* 48 (1943): 525; "Papers," annex no. 15, U.S. National Archives.

41 Oleh Gerus has contended that Russian America might well have become even more viable economically if the Russian government had taken a more positive and more imaginative approach to the colony's potential; see "Russian Withdrawal," 157–78.

42 See James R. Gibson, *Imperial Russia in Frontier America: The Changing Geography of Supply of Russian America, 1784–1867* (New York, 1976).

43 In 1853 British outnumbered Russian warships by more than two to one (Ronald J. Jensen, *The Alaska Purchase and Russian-American Relations* [Seattle, 1975], 4).

44 Quoted by Okun, "K istorii," 216.

45 "Papers," annex no. 12, U.S. National Archives.

46 A. I. Martynov, "Relations between the Tsarist Government and the Russian-American Company in 1857–1867" [in Russian], Kennan Institute for Advanced Russian Studies, Occasional Paper No. 74 (1979): 11n.

47 Konstantin to Gorchakov, March 22 [April 3], 1857, "Documents."

48 Quoted by Martynov, "Relations," 22.

49 *Doklad*, 1:171.

50 Ibid., 1:116, 2:185; "Records of the Russian-American Company, 1802–1867: Correspondence of Governors General," roll 47, p. 384, roll 53, p. 66, File Microcopies of Records in the U.S. National Archives: no. 11.

51 "Papers," annex no. 12, U.S. National Archives.

52 Frank A. Golder, "The Attitude of the Russian Government toward Alaska," in *The Pacific Ocean in History*, ed. H. Morse Stephens and Herbert E. Bolton (New York, 1917), 269.

53 McPherson, "Projected Purchase," 82.

54 *Doklad*, 2:545.

55 Ibid., 1:174–75.

56 "Papers," annex no. 15, U.S. National Archives.

57 Probably either Petr Kostromitinov, Russian commercial agent in San Francisco in the 1850s, or Rear Admiral Andrei Popov, commander of Russia's Pacific fleet and, like his commander-in-chief Konstantin, an advocate of the sale of Alaska.

58 Ibid., annex no. 9, U.S. National Archives.

59 Ivan Barsukov, *Graf Nikolai Nikolaievich Murav'ev-Amurskii*...(Moscow, 1891), 1:322–23.

60 Konstantin to Gorchakov, March 22 [April 3], 1857, "Documents."

61 "Papers," annex no. 2, U.S. National Archives.

62 Konstantin to Gorchakov, December 7 [19], 1857, "Documents," Konstantin also believed that trading firms like the Russian American and Hudson's Bay Companies were "not fit" to both administer and exploit territories and peoples. He opined that "the role of merchant and administrator, combined in one person, is not feasible, and such a combination is very harmful to the company's subject peoples, who suffer greatly from second-rate agents, and from London or St. Petersburg the directors of the company cannot see what is happening" (Konstantin to Gorchakov, December 7 [19], 1857, "Documents").

63 "Papers," annex no. 4, U.S. National Archives.

64 Ibid., annex no. 43; Miller, "Russian Opinion," 529–30.

65 Miller, "Russian Opinion," 529; "Papers," annex no. 43, U.S. National Archives. Rather than remaining diplomatically aloof, de Stoeckl immersed himself in American life. He married a Yankee, and he became a friend of some prominent American expansionists, including California's Senator William Gwin. Captain Golovin met the so-called baron in Washington, D.C., in 1860 and remarked: "Stoeckl, who has lived here many years [since 1841], has almost become an American" (Rimskii-Korsakov, "Iz putevykh pisem," 151). In the process of becoming Americanized de Stoeckl uncritically accepted American expansionist ideology, and he exaggerated the political ramifications of the clash between Russian and American commercial interests on the Northwest Coast (see Gerus, "Russian Withdrawal," 163–64, 173–74).

66 V. I. Lenin, *Collected Works*, trans. Dora Cox (Moscow, 1963), 17:121.

67 See James R. Gibson, "Russia on the Pacific: The Role of the Amur," *Canadian Geographer* 12 (1968): 15–27. Also see Mark Bassin, "The Russian Geographical Society, the 'Amur Epoch,' and the Great Siberian Expedition, 1855–1863," *Annals of the Association of American Geographers* 73 (1983): 240–56.

68 Tikhmenev, *History*, 273–74.

69 McPherson, "Projected Purchase," 82–83.
70 When Alaska was sold in 1867, the Russian government tried to settle as many of the repatriated Russians and creoles as possible in Amuria.
71 Miller, "Russian Opinion," 530; "Papers," annex no. 43, U.S. National Archives.
72 "Papers," annex no. 12, U.S. National Archives.
73 Konstantin to Gorchakov, December 7 [19], 1857, "Documents."
74 Barsukov, *Graf,* 1:389–90.
75 Ibid., 2:104–5.
76 Ibid., 1:305.
77. Ibid., 309.
78 Ibid., 527.
79 In early 1865 the Russian American Company offered to either lease or sell the "Stikine Territory" (*lisière*) to the Hudson's Bay Company, which chose to rent (Provincial Archives of Manitoba, Hudson's Bay Company Archives, f. 29/2, pp. 224–25). The Honorable Company's interest in the panhandle had declined as the value of its fur trade had fallen; see C. Ian Jackson, "The Stikine Territory Lease and Its Relevance to the Alaska Purchase," *Pacific Historical Review,* 36 (1967): 289–306.
80 Quoted by Okun, "K istorii," 232.
81 Quoted by Clarence C. Hulley, *Alaska, 1741–1953* (Portland, 1953), 199.
82 Quoted by Okun, "K istorii," 233.
83 McPherson, "Projected Purchase," 83.
84 Quoted by Okun, "K istorii,: 232. Similarly, Konstantin and the other pro-cession officials who counseled the tsar to sell pointed to the "exceptional advantages" to Russia of a "close alliance with the North American [United] States" and referred to the "necessity of removing everything that could give rise to disagreement between the two great powers [Russia and the United States]" (N. N. Bolkhovitinov, "Zarubezhnye issledovaniia o Russkoi Amerike," *SShA: ekonomika, politika, ideologiia,* 4 [1985]: 95, n. 50, quoting AVPR, f. RAK, d. 399, 1:11).
85 Karl Marx, *Letters to Dr. Kugelmann,* trans. Jane Tabrisky (Moscow/Leningrad, 1934), 100.
86 McPherson, "Projected Purchase," 83.
87 "Papers," annex no. 13, U.S. National Archives. As Frederick Starr has generalized, "Russian imperial policy . . . was planned and executed with an eye first to its impact on the other imperial powers" ("Tsarist Government: The Imperial Dimension," in *Soviet Nationality Policies and Practices,* ed. Jeremy R. Azrael [New York, 1978], 31).
88 Ibid., annex no. 8; Golder, "Purchase," 412.
89 Okun, "K istorii," 216.
90 Ibid., 216, 228–29.
91 Quoted by ibid., 229.
92 Quoted by ibid., 230.
93 Quoted by ibid. In fact, Russia feared both Great Britain and the United States, especially the former because it was the stronger of the two powers (particularly in the wake of the enervating American Civil War). So it was in Russia's best interest to play one off against the other.
94 The Russian American Company had for some time been receiving various indirect and direct subsidies from the government, e.g., exemption from the customs duties

on tea imports and 25 percent of the tariff charges on imports of fur seal and beaver pelts.

95   *Doklad,* 1:173, 181.

96   The tsar rewarded de Stoeckl with his "special thanks" and 25,000 rubles ("Papers," annex nos. 32–33, U.S. National Archives). The Russian American Company, on the other hand, lost more than 4 million rubles because the treaty failed to protect fully its interests and property in Alaska (R. V. Makarova, "K istorii likvidatsii Rossiisko-Amerikanskoi kompanii," in *Problemy istorii i etnografii Ameriki,* ed. Iu. V. Bromlei [Moscow, 1979], 272). The company was liquidated in 1881.

97   In 1860 Captain Golovin had complained that *"in point of fact our American company does not have regular communication with its colony. This is outrageous but true"* [Golovin's italics] (Rimskii-Korsakov, "Iz putevykh pisem," 173). Communication by ship from St. Petersburg to Novo-Arkhangel'sk took from seven to eight months (*Doklad,* 1:186).

The Significance of the Alaska Purchase to American Expansion

If a source exists in both U.S. and Soviet archives, I have cited the U.S. holding. Whenever possible I have cited the English language edition of a text. I wish to thank several scholars who have made helpful suggestions on this essay, including Frederick Drake, Ross Dunn, Haggai Erlich, Martin Luster, Richard Ruetten, Arthur W. Schatz, Stephen Scheinberg, and Richard Steele.

1   See for instance, Frank A. Golder, "The Purchase of Alaska," *American Historical Review* 25 (April 1920): 411–25; Thomas A. Bailey, "Why the United States Purchased Alaska," *Pacific Historical Review* 3 (March 1934): 34–49; Victor J. Farrar, *Purchase of Alaska* (Washington, 1935), 19; A. G. Mazour, "The Prelude to Russia's Departure from America," *Pacific Historical Review* 10 (September 1941): 316.

2   Thomas A. Bailey, *A Diplomatic History of the American People* (New York, 1969), 365. More recently, James R. Gibson has concluded that the inability to supply food "was a major feature of the overall plight that disposed the Russian Government to part with Russian-America." These problems of supply when added to "the monopolistic character of the company, and the traditional backwardness of the colonizers, helps to explain why Alaska did not remain a Russian colony." Gibson presents a strong case that the company virtually had collapsed from an economic point of view by the 1850s. Nevertheless, it is one thing to demonstrate that the *company* was not profitable and quite another to conclude that the Russian government sold the *colony* to the United States for that reason. Moreover, such an analysis does not explain why the United States would buy Russian America. See James R. Gibson, *Imperial Russia in Frontier America: The Changing Geography of Supply of Russian America, 1784–1867* (New York, 1976).

3   The most recent presentation of this view appears in Ronald J. Jensen, *The Alaska Purchase and Russian-American Relations* (Seattle, 1975), 63–67. While Jensen produces much evidence of a long-term conflict between Russia and the United States in the Pacific Northwest, he ignores it when reaching his conclusions. Perhaps the reason that Jensen's thesis is so similar to Golder's and Bailey's is that he is con-

strained by the questions he poses: Why did Russia want to sell and why did Seward wish to buy?

4   William A. Williams, *American-Russian Relations, 1781–1947* (New York, 1952), 20–22.

5   S. B. Okun, *The Russian-American Company*, trans. by Carl Ginsburg (Cambridge, 1951), 248–49.

6   Ibid., 257–58.

7   A. V. Efimov, *Ocherki istorii SShA: Ot otkrytii Ameriki do okonchaniia grazhdanskoi voiny* 2d ed. (Moscow, 1958), 1:382–402, 503–75, 670–90; and "Diplomatiia SShA v 40-60-kh godakh 19 v. i v period grazhdanskoi voiny," *Istoriia diplomatii*, 2d ed. (Moscow, 1959), 1:670–90.

8   T. M. Batueva, *Amerikanskaia ekspansiia v russkikh Vladeniakh na severe Tikhogo okeana v seredine 19 v. i pokupka Aliaski SShA v 1867* (Moscow, 1953); also see her "Prokhozhdenie dogovora o pukupka Aliaski v kongresse SShA v 1867–1868," *Novaia i noveishaia istoriia* 4 (1971): 117–24.

9   A. L. Narochnitskii, *Kolonial'nai politika kapitalisticheskikh derzhav na Dal'nem Vostoke, 1860–1895* (Moscow, 1956), 167–87.

10 M. Belov, "O prodazha Aliaski," *Nauka i zhizn'* 1 (1967): 69–73; Belov's article was translated into English and published as "Sale of Alaska," *Alaska Review* (Spring/Summer, 1967): 8–19.

11 See R. V. Makarova, "K istorii likvidatsii rossiisko-amerikanskaya kompanii," in *Problemy istorii i etnografii Ameriki*, ed. I. V. Bromlei et al. (Moscow, 1979), 264–74; Nikolai V. Sivachev and Nikolai N. Yakovlev, *Russia and the United States*, trans. by Olga A. Titlebaum (Chicago, 1979), 12–13; Alexander I. Martynov, "Relations between the Tsarist Government and the Russian-American Company in 1857–1867" [in Russian], Kennan Institute for Advanced Russian Studies, Occasional Paper No. 74 (1979).

12 This evolution is particularly graphic in Bolkhovitinov's studies of the Monroe Doctrine. Compare his *Doktrina Monro: Proishozhdenie i kharaktr* (Moscow, 1959) with his later "Russia and the Declaration of the Non-Colonization Principle: New Archival Evidence," *Oregon Historical Quarterly*, 72 (June 1971): 101–27. Also see his *Stanovlenie russko-amerikanskikh otnoshenii, 1775–1815*, (Moscow, 1966), published in English as *The Beginnings of Russian-American Relations, 1775–1815*, trans. Elana Levin (Cambridge, Mass., 1975); and *Russko-amerikanskie otneshenia, 1815–1832* (Moscow, 1975).

13 For instance, see Henry R. Huttenbach's reply to Belov's essay in the *Alaska Review* (Spring/Summer 1970): 33–45. Huttenbach concludes that "the Russian government, freely, without pressure from the United States, disengaged itself from Alaska."

14 See John Lewis Gaddis, *Russia, The Soviet Union, and the United States: An Interpretive History* (New York, 1978), 1–26.

15 Howard I. Kushner, *Conflict on the Northwest Coast: American-Russian Rivalry in the Pacific Northwest, 1790–1867* (Westport/London, 1975); Peter Buzanski, "Alaska and Nineteenth Century Diplomacy," *Journal of the West*, 6 (July 1967): 451–67.

16 Kushner, *Conflict on the Northwest Coast*, xi.

17 N. N. Bolkhovitinov, "Russia and the Declaration of the Non-Colonization Principle," 101–2.

18 Bolkhovitinov, *Beginnings of Russian-American Relations* 357–59. See also V. N. Ponomarev, *Voprosy istorii* 9 (September 1978): 185–87.

19 Thomas A. Bailey, *America Faces Russia: Russian-American Relations from Early Times to Our Day* (Ithaca, 1950), 47, 50; see especially chap. 5, "The Calm of Despotism," 45–56.

20 Richard A. Pierce, "Review," *Slavic Review* 35 (December 1976): 734.

21 Basil Dmytryshyn, "Review," *Russian Review* (April 1976): 192.

22 C. Bickford O'Brien, "Review," *California Historical Quarterly* 55 (Spring 1976): 88–89.

23 Nikolai P. Rezanov to Nikolai P. Rumiantsev, June 17 [19], 1806, *The United States and Russia: The Beginning of Relations, 1765–1815*, ed. N. N. Bashkina et al. (Washington, D.C. and Moscow, 1980), 446–52; K. T. Khlebnikov, *Baranov, Chief Manager of the Russian Colonies in America*, trans. C. Bearne, ed. R. A. Pierce (Kingston, 1973), 41–42.

24 Nikolai Petrovich Rezanov, *The Rezanov Voyage to Neuva California in 1806* (San Francisco, 1926), 69–72.

25 Ibid., 56–58, 72–73; Adele Ogden, *The California Sea Otter Trade* (Berkeley, 1941), 47; and Ogden, "Russian Sea-Otter and Seal Hunting on the California Coast, 1803–1841," *California Historical Quarterly* 12 (September 1933): 226–27.

26 Rumiantsev to Harris, May 17, 1808, *American State Papers, Foreign Relations* (hereinafter, *ASP:FR*), 5:349.

27 Dashkov to Smith, January 4, April 24, 1810, *ASP:FR*, 5:438–39, 441; Smith to Dashkov, May 5, 1810, ibid., 441–42; Smith to Adams, May 5, 1810, NA RG59, "Diplomatic Instructions, Russia"; Adams to Smith, October 5 and 30, 1810, *ASP:FR*, 5:442–43.

28 Adams to Smith, October 12, 1810, *ASP:FR*, 5:443.

29 Rumiantsev to Alexander I, November 12 [24], 1809, *United States and Russia to 1815*, 618–22; "Memorandum of the Governing Board to the Tsar," December 18, 1811, in Okun, *Russian-American Company*, 75; *Guide to Materials for American History in Russian Archives*, ed. Frank A. Golder, 2 vols. (Washington, 1917, 1937), 1:139.

30 Report from the main directorate of the Russian American Company to Rumiantsev, May 16 [28], 1811, *United States and Russia to 1815*, 751–54; Mikhail M. Buldakov to Rumiantsev, October 19 [31], 1811, ibid., 799–800. See also Gibson, *Imperial Russia in Frontier America*, 73–89.

31 *Annals of Congress*, 16 Cong., 2 sess., January, 1821, 946–59 (see 955–56 on Russia).

32 Poletica to Nesselrode, January 21 [February 2], 1821, in Okun, *Russian-American Company*, 78–80; *Guide to Russian Archives*, 1:37.

33 Vasilli Golovnin, "Letters of Captain Golovnin on the Condition of Russian-America in the Year 1818," MSS, Bancroft Library, University of California, Berkeley; *Ukaz* of September 4 [16], 1821, *ASP:FR*, 4:857–67; *Proceedings of the Alaska Boundary Tribunal*, 2 vols. (Washington, D.C., 1904), 2: appendix, 26–28.

34 Nesselrode to Poletica, October 7, 1821, "Correspondence of the Russian Ministers in Washington, 1818–1825," *American Historical Review* 18 (January 1913): 329–31; Nesselrode to Lieven, October 7, 1821, *Alaska Tribunal*, 2: appendix, 99–100.

35 Kushner, *Conflict on the Northwest Coast*, 35–39.

36 William Sturgis, "Examinations of the Russian Claims to the Pacific Northwest Coast of America," *North American Review* 15 (October 1822): 370–401. Also see *Boston Daily Advertiser*, January 28 and 31, February 6 and 20, 1822; Adams to Middleton, July 22, 1823, *ASP:FR*, 5:436–37; Ivanov to Nesselrode, November, 1822, January, 1823, *Guide to Russian Archives*, 1:77. For instance, see *Niles Weekly Register*,

December 29, 1821, 278–79; July 17, 1822, 239; November 9, 1822, 157; *National Intelligencer,* December 22, 1821, February 12 and 13, 1822; *Newburyport Herald,* quoted in *Niles Weekly Register,* June 8, 1822, 226–27; *Baltimore Chronicle,* quoted in ibid., May 10, 1823, 146.

37 For instance, see Howard I. Kushner, "The Russian-American Diplomatic Contest for the Pacific Basin and the Monroe Doctrine," *Journal of the West* 15 (April 1976): 73–78.

38 Middleton to Adams, August 8 [21], 1822, *Alaska Tribunal,* 2: appendix, 42–45, which includes "inclosure #1"; Middleton to Nesselrode, July 24 [August 5], 1822, "note verbale" (prepared, but not delivered), ibid., 44–45.

39 On August 12, 1822, the Russian government secretly instructed the Russian American Company that new negotiations were in progress and that the *Ukaz* was suspended pending further instructions. See Guriev to chief manager of the Russian American Company, July 18 [30], 1822, "secret," *Alaska Tribunal,* 2: appendix, 40–41; Board of administration of Russian American Company to chief manager, July 31 [August 12], 1822, ibid.

40 Adams to Lloyd, January 15, 1823, Adams Papers, Massachusetts Historical Society, Boston, letterbook 22, 240–42; John Quincy Adams, *Memoirs,* July 17, 1823, ed. C. F. Adams, 12 vols. (Philadelphia, 1874–77), 6:163.

41 Adams, *Memoirs,* 6:194, 200–203, 208; Adams to Tuyll, November 27, 1823, NA, "Notes to Russian Legation."

42 Kushner, *Conflict on the Northwest Coast,* 59–62.

43 Nesselrode to Mordvinov, 1824, in Okun, *Russian-American Company,* 89.

44 Middleton to Adams, April 7 [19], 1824, *ASP:FR,* 5:457–62; Adams to Rush, July 22, 1823, ibid., 5:447.

45 Ryleyev to Kankrin, March 1824, in Okun, *Russian-American Company,* 90–91.

46 Ibid., pp. 91–92.

47 P. A. Tikhmenev, *The Historical Review of the Russian-American Company,* (St. Petersburg, 1861–63), trans. by D. Krenov (Seattle, 1968), 1:398–99.

48 "Correspondence with Russia, 1835–1838," House Executive Document, 2:25, U.S. Cong., 3rd sess., p. 53; Wilkins to Forsyth, November 23, 1835, ibid., p. 61; Wilkins to Nesselrode, November 1 [13], 1835, ibid., pp. 63–65.

49 Wilkins to Forsyth, December 11, 1835, ibid., pp. 66–70.

50 Forsyth to Dallas, April 19, 1837, ibid., p. 54.

51 Forsyth to Dallas, November 3, 1837, ibid., pp. 58–59.

52 Dallas to Nesselrode, March 5 [17], 1838, ibid., pp. 82–83.

53 Nesselrode to Kankrin, January 4, 1839, *Alaska Tribunal,* 2: appendix, 312.

54 Bodisco to Nesselrode, August 10 [22], 1829, May 1840, *Guide to Russian Archives,* 1:65–66. For terms of the lease, see Tikhmenev, *Russian-American Company,* 1:411–12, appendix, 323–25; see also Gibson, *Imperial Russia in Frontier America,* 202–8.

55 Tikhmenev, *Russian-American Company,* 2:152; also see Howard I. Kushner, "'Hellships': Yankee Whaling Along the Coasts of Russian-America, 1835–1852," *New England Quarterly* 45 (March 1972): 81–95.

56 Tikhmenev, *Russian-American Company,* 2:153–57, 164; see also Gibson, *Imperial Russia in Frontier America,* 72.

57 For instance, see Kushner, *Conflict on the Northwest Coast,* 122–24.

58 Hallie M. McPherson, "The Interest of William McKendree Gwin in the Purchase of Alaska," *Pacific Historical Review* 3 (March 1934): 29–30.

59 Howard I. Kushner, "The Oregon Question Is . . . a Massachusetts Question," *Oregon Historical Quarterly* 75 (December 1974): 316–35.

60 Howard I. Kushner, "'Seward's Folly?': American Commerce in Russian-America and the Alaska Purchase," *California Historical Quarterly* 54 (Spring 1975): 5–26.

61 William H. Seward, *Works*, ed. G. E. Baker (Boston, 1884–85), 4:422.

62 See Wrangell to tsar, April 9, 1857, NA RG59, "Cession of Alaska," annex 2; Memorandum of the tsar, April 29, 1857, ibid., annex 3; Tikhmenev, *Russian-American Company*, 2:195.

63 Kushner, "'Seward's Folly'," 5–26.

64 De Stoeckl to Gorchakov, July 12 [24], 1867, "Cession of Alaska," annex 43. Upon reading this memorandum Gorchakov wrote "très remarquable" on the top and sent it on to Tsar Alexander, who wrote under Gorchakov's comment, "Yes, and we must make an extract and publish it."

65 This was especially true during the Crimean War. See Tikhmenev, *Russian-American Company*, 2:195; Wrangell to tsar, April 9, 1857, "Cession of Alaska," annex 2; Memorandum of the tsar, April 29, 1857, ibid., annex 3.

66 Popov, "Memorandum," February 7, 1860, "Cession of Alaska," annex 9.

67 Pierce, "Review," 734; Jensen, *The Alaska Purchase*, 39–61; Gibson, *Imperial Russia in Frontier America*, 28–29.

68 The most persuasive presentation of this view appears in Gibson, *Imperial Russia in Frontier America*, 28–29.

69 Mary E. Wheeler, "Review," *Western Historical Quarterly* 7 (July 1976): 313.

70 Jensen, *The Alaska Purchase*, 34; O'Brien, "Review," 88–89.

71 Jensen, *The Alaska Purchase*, 58, 69, 72–73.

72 However, it is one thing to demonstrate that the monopolistic Russian American Company failed to sustain high profits and quite another to conclude that Russian America was of little economic value to Russia—either actually or potentially. Also, as Gibson admits, by the mid-1850s Russian America's food supply was no longer a problem since abundant provisions were available from California. Gibson, *Imperial Russia in Frontier America*, 196–97.

73 McPherson, "Interest of Gwin in Alaska," 29–30.

74 Kushner, *Conflict on the Northwest Coast*, 134.

75 De Stoeckl, quoted in F. A. Golder, "The Purchase of Alaska," 412.

76 Konstantin to Gorchakov, December 7, 1857 (o.s.), Manuscript Division, Library of Congress.

77 Wrangell, "Concerning the Cession of the American Colonies to the Government of the United States," April 9, 1857, "Cession of Alaska," annex 2.

78 "Memorandum Concerning Cession to the U.S. of Our Possessions in North America," April 1857 (see tsar's notation of April 29, 1857), ibid., annex 3.

79 *Doklad komiteta ob ustroistve russkikh amerikanskikh kolony*, 2 vols. (St. Petersburg, 1863), 1:233–37, MSS (translation in English), Bancroft Library, University of California, Berkeley.

80 Kushner, "'Seward's Folly'," 5–17.

81 Gorchakov to Tsar, December 12, 1866 (o.s.) "Cession of Alaska," annex 12.

82 Osten-Saken to Gorchakov, December 16, 1866, (o.s.), ibid., annex 15.

83 Gorchakov to Alexander II, December 1866, ibid., annex 12; also see item 5.

84 American commercial activity in Russian Asia began in Kamchatka in the mid-1830s with the trading company of William H. Boardman of Boston. This commerce continued and expanded to Okhotsk in the 1840s and to the Amur region in the 1850s. Increasing complaints about the behavior of Yankee traders in Russian Asia were lodged with the Russian officials. See Tikhmenev, *Russian-American Company*, 1:408; Todd to Webster, April 20 [May 2], 1843; Todd to Upshur, August 7 [19], 1843, NA RG59, "Despatches, Russia"; Cass to de Stoeckl, December 8, 1860, ibid., "Notes to Russian Legation."

85 Nesselrode to Kankrin, January 4, 1839, *Alaska Tribunal* 2: appendix, 312.

86 Osten-Saken to Gorchakov, December 16, 1866 (o.s.), "Cession of Alaska," annex 15.

87 See Frank A. Golder, "The Russian Fleet and the American Civil War," *American Historical Review* 20 (July, 1915): 801–12; Bailey, *America Faces Russia*, 81–94. For a critical review of the historiography surrounding the fleet visit, see Howard I. Kushner, "The Russian Fleet and the American Civil War: Another View," *The Historian*, 34 (August 1972): esp. 633–35. Also see I. Ia. Levitas, "Russkie eskadry v Amerike," *Istoriia SSSR* 12 (September/October 1958): 135–41.

88 Kushner, "Russian Fleet and Civil War," 633–49.

89 Of course, politicians like Seward and Charles Sumner were not above using the fleet visit as one argument among many to persuade some congressmen and the press to support the cession treaty. See Charles Sumner, *Complete Works* (Boston, 1900), 11:228–30.

90 De Stoeckl to Gorchakov, March 22 [April 3], 1867, "Cession of Alaska," annex 26.

91 Kushner, *Conflict on the Northwest Coast*, 143–44, 146–47, 149, 152.

92 Sumner, *Works*, 11:181–349.

93 Jensen, *The Alaska Purchase*, 108, 113–20.

94 See Ernest Paolino, *The Foundations of American Empire: William H. Seward and U.S. Foreign Policy* (Ithaca, 1973), esp. 105–44.

95 De Stoeckl to Gorchakov, July 12 [24], 1867, "Cession of Alaska," annex 43.

96 A full discussion of this appears in an unpublished paper by Frederick C. Drake, "Southern Expansionism Reconsidered" (Presented at the Fourteenth Annual Meeting of the Canadian Association of American Studies, Montreal, Quebec, October 28, 1978); also see Charles Vevier, "American Continentalism, An Idea of Expansion, 1845–1910," *American Historical Review* 65 (January 1960): 329–30.

97 See Peter Dobkin Hall, "Marital Selection and Business in Massachusetts Merchant Families, 1700–1900," in Michael Gordon, ed., *The American Family in Social-Historical Perspective*, 2d ed. (New York, 1978), 101–14; Kushner, "Hellships," 86–90.

98 For a discussion of this in relation to the ice trade and other enterprises, see Richard D. Brown, *Modernization: The Transformation of American Life, 1600–1865* (New York, 1976), 132–38.

Archival and Bibliographic Materials on Russian America outside the USSR

1   Atlas Shturmana Lovtsova, MS, Cartographic Division, Provincial Archives of British Columbia.

2 See Dale L. Morgan and George Hammon, *A Guide to the Manuscript Collections of the Bancroft Library* (Berkeley, 1963).

3 Morgan Sherwood, *Exploration of Alaska, 1865–1900* (New Haven, 1965).

4 See H. H. Bancroft, *Literary Industries*, vol. 39 of *Works* (San Francisco, 1890).

5 See R. A. Pierce, "New Light on Ivan Petroff, Historian of Alaska," *Pacific Northwest Quarterly*, 59, no. 1 (1968): 1–10.

6 R. A. Pierce, *Russia's Hawaiian Adventure, 1815–1817* (Berkeley/Los Angeles, 1965).

7 Georg von Langsdorff, *Bemerkungen auf einer Reise um die Welt, in den Jahren 1803–1807*, 2 vols. (Frankfurt am Main, 1812).

8 See Alexis V. Babine,*The Yudin Library, Krasnoiarsk (Eastern Siberia)* (Washington, D.C., 1905).

9 See Barbara S. Smith, "A Preliminary Survey of New Archival Material of the Alaska Diocese, Orthodox Church in America," in Robert A. Fredericak and Patricia A. Jelle, *A Guide to Research*, vol. 1 of *Writing Alaska's History* (Anchorage: Alaska Historical Commission, 1974), 112–14.

10 Raymond H. Fisher, *Records of the Russian-American Company, 1802, 1817–1867* (Washington, D.C.: National Archives and Records Service, General Services Administration, 1917).

11 See R. A. Pierce, "Alaska's Russian Governors," *Alaska Journal* (Anchorage), 1, no. 2 (Spring 1971) through 3, no. 1 (Winter 1973).

12 Ibid.

13 Edward L. Blashke, *Topographia Medica Portus Novi-Archangelscensis* (St. Petersburg, 1842).

14 See note 11 above.

15 F. W. Howay, *List of Trading Vessels on the Northwest Coast, 1785–1825* (Kingston, 1973).

Index of Names
and Places

Contributors

S. FREDERICK STARR was educated at Yale University, King's College, Cambridge, and Princeton. Among his publications bearing on the theme of Russian America are *Decentralization in Self Government in Russia, 1830–1870* (1972), and a chapter in *The Zemstvos: Russia's Democratic Experiment* (1982) and *Soviet Nationality Policies and Practices* (1978). He served as founding secretary of the Kennan Institute for Advanced Russian Studies and in that capacity organized the conference in Sitka, Alaska, upon which the present volume is based.

NIKOLAI N. BOLKHOVITINOV is a fellow of the Institute of General History of the Academy of Sciences of the USSR and a leader among Soviet specialists on American history. His first research resulted in a 1959 monograph on the Monroe Doctrine. He published *Establishment of Russian-American Relations, 1775–1815,* in Moscow in 1966; an English edition was issued by Harvard in 1975. A further study, *Russia and the American Revolution,* was also translated (1976). He has written widely on Russian foreign policy and contemporary American affairs, with articles appearing in the *Journal of American Studies* and other scholarly publications in the United States.

JAMES R. GIBSON is Professor of Geography at York University, Toronto, Canada. A native of British Columbia, Dr. Gibson obtained his Ph.D. at the University of Wisconsin-Madison. His major works include *Feeding the Russian Fur Trade: Provisionment of the Okhotsk Seaboard and the Kamchatka Peninsula, 1639–1856* (1969), *Imperial Russia in Frontier America: The Changing Geography of Supply of Russian America, 1784–1867* (1976), and *Farming the Frontier: The Agricultural Opening of the Oregon Country, 1786–1846* (1985). Dr. Gibson, an associate editor of *Soviet Geography* and a former Guggenheim Memorial Fellow, holds a Killam Fellowship for the compilation of two collections of documents on Russian California and on the Hudson's Bay Company and the coast trade. His book on the maritime fur trade of the Northwest Coast, *Otter Skins, Boston Ships, and China Goods,* is in press.

HOWARD I. KUSHNER is Professor of History at San Diego State University. He received his Ph.D. in 1970 from Cornell University. His publications on American-Russian relations include *Conflict on the Northwest Coast: American-Russian Rivalry In the Pacific Northwest, 1790–1867* (1975). Kushner also has written extensively on the relationship between history and psychoanalysis and presently is preparing a study on the history of suicide in the United States.

ROZA G. LIAPUNOVA is a senior fellow at the Institute of Ethnography in Leningrad. An alumna of the Department of Ethnography in the History Faculty at Leningrad State University, she is the author of a series of major works dealing with Russian America and Alaska, including *Ocherki po etnografii aleutov (Essays on the History of the Aleuts)* (1975); "Rukopis' K. T. Khlebnikova 'Zapiski o koloniiakh v Amerike' kak istochnik po istorii i etnografii Aliaski" (K. T. Khlebnikova's Manuscript, "Notes on the Colonies in America," as a Source on the History and Ethnography of Alaska) in *Ot Aliaski do Ognennoi Zenli* (1967); and "Etnograficheskoe zanchenie ekspeditsii k Aleutskim ostrovam kapitanov P. K. Krenitsyna i M. D. Levashova, 1764–1769 gg." (The Ethnographic Meaning of the Expedition to the Aleutian Islands Undertaken by Captains P. K. Krenitsyn and M. D. Levashov, 1764–1769), *Sovetskaia etnografiia* (1971). Her other studies treat such diverse issues as the I. G. Voznesenskii collections and the Aleut materials in the Museum of Anthropology and Ethnography in Leningrad.

RAISA VSEVOLODOVNA MAKAROVA is associated with the Historical-Archival Institute in Moscow. Her 1968 work *Russians on the Pacific, 1743–1799*, has been translated into English (1975) and has become a standard work of reference. She is also the author of an important article, "On the History of the Liquidation of the Russian-American Company," which appeared in *Problems in the History and Ethnography of America (Problemy istorii i etnografii Ameriki)* (1979).

ELENA ALEKSEEVNA OKLADNIKOVA is associated with the Institute of Ethnography, the USSR Academy of Sciences, Leningrad. She has written widely on the ethnography of Eastern Siberia and the related zones of North America and has published articles in *Questions of Ethnography*. Her major books include *Ancient Drawings of Kyzyl-Khelkila* (1985), *The Petroglyphs of Middle Katuna* (1984), and *The Problematic Lichiny of Asia and America* (1979). She is the daughter of the noted Siberian archeologist A. P. Okladnikov, with whom she has collaborated on several projects.

RICHARD A. PIERCE received his B.A. and Ph.D. degrees from the University of California. He has held both Fulbright and Guggenheim Fellowships, and since 1972 has edited the Alaska History Series. His major publications include *Russian Central Asia, 1867–1917: A Study in Colonial Rule* (1960), *Russia's Hawaiian Adventure, 1815–1817* (1965), with G. V. Lantzeff, *Eastward to Empire: Exploration and Conquest on the Russian Open Frontier, to 1750* (1973), and, with A. S. Donnelly, a translation of P. A. Tikhmenev, *History of the Russian-American Company* (1978). He is Professor of History Emeritus at Queen's University, Ontario.

PATRICIA POLANSKY obtained a B.A. in Russian language, a Master's in Library Science, and a certificate from the Institute on Slavic Librarianship (Urbana, 1970). She has worked at the University of Hawaii's Hamilton Library since 1970 as Russian bibliographer.

In 1977 she received an IREX young faculty grant to work on an annotated bibliography of Russians in the Pacific. She has received other awards and grants from the Council on Library Resources, Title IIC Project at Berkeley, the University of Hawaii Research Institute for Advanced Russian Studies of The Wilson Center.

Ms. Polansky has twice been an invited guest in the USSR, once to attend a conference on problems in the Pacific basin and once as a guest of the Institute of Oriental Studies.

She has presented papers and attended conferences in the Philippines, Germany, England, and France, and at the Slavic Research Center in Sapporo, Japan. Her articles include surveys of publishing of Russian materials on Asia, Siberia, and the Pacific.

BORIS P. POLEVOI is Professor at the Institute of Ethnography of the USSR Academy of Sciences in Moscow. He is the author of *Grigorii Shelikhov—The Russian Columbus* (1960). His numerous articles on Russian expeditions of discovery, on the cartographic history of Eastern Siberia and Alaska, and on the explorers of those regions have appeared in the series *News of the Academy of Sciences of the USSR* (*Izvestiia AN SSSR*, Geographical Series), *Lands and Peoples of the East* (*Strany i narody Vostoka*), and the *Siberian Geographical Collection* (*Sibirskii geograficheskii sbornik*). Among his best-known studies are articles on the relationship between Peter I and Nikolai Witsen, on Semen Remezov and Vladimir Atlasov, and on the writing of Semen Dezhnev.

ANATOLE SENKEVITCH, JR., is Associate Professor in the College of Architecture and Urban Planning at the University of Michigan, where he heads the graduate historic preservation program. He previously taught at the New Jersey Institute of Technology, Cornell University and the University of Maryland. Professor Senkevitch received a B.S. in Architectural Studies from the University of Texas at Austin, a Master's in Architectural History from the University of Virginia, and a Ph.D. from Cornell University. His fields of specialization include the history of Russian, American, and modern architecture, as well as preservation planning.

In 1965 Professor Senkevitch spent six months in the Soviet Union on the staff of the "Architecture-USA" Exhibit, sponsored by the United States Information Agency. In 1974 he was a member of the U.S. Historic Preservation Team (of the U.S.-USSR Joint Working Group on the Enhancement of the Urban Environment) that traveled for a month in the Soviet Union to inspect historic sites and preservation projects and to meet with Soviet preservation specialists and officials. In 1975 he served as Cochairman of the Conference on Architecture and Historic Preservation in Central and Eastern Europe that was sponsored by the Society of Architectural Historians (U.S.). In 1977 he spent five months in the Soviet Union as a senior exchange scholar on IREX and Fulbright fellowships. He is the author of numerous articles and books, including *Soviet Architecture, 1917–1962: A Bibliographic Guide to Source Material* (1974), the translation of and introductory essay for Moisei Ginzburg's *Style and Epoch* (1983), and "Aspects of Spatial Form and Perceptual Psychology in the Doctrine of the Rationalist Movement in Soviet Architecture in the 1920s," *VIA* (1983).

ANTOINETTE SHALKOP was born in Paris, France, and holds degrees in French, Russian, and Library Science. She has published numerous articles on Russian America in *Orthodox Alaska, Pacific Northwest Quarterly, The Alaska Journal*, and *Orthodox Missionary*. In addition, she has translated and annotated *The Wreck of the "Neva"* (1979) and is the author of a detailed guide to the Alaskan Russian Church Archives in the Library of Congress. She resides in Anchorage, Alaska.

MARY ELIZABETH WHEELER received a B.A. in history from Norfolk College of William and Mary in 1959, and the M.A. and Ph.D. in Russian history from the University of North Carolina, Chapel Hill, in 1962 and 1965. She has served as instructor at Old Dominion College and is currently Professor of Russian History and head of the Department of History at North Carolina State University. Her research has been supported by IREX and Fulbright-Hayes Awards for research in the USSR. She has contributed articles to the *Jahrbücher für Geschichte Osteuropas* and the *Pacific Historical Review*.